KT-467-688

IRISH LITERATURE
THE NINETEENTH CENTURY

VOLUME I

A NEW ANNOTATED ANTHOLOGY OF EIGHTEENTH AND NINETEENTH CENTURY IRISH LITERATURE

Major new book series which demonstrates the growth, variety and achievement of Irish writing in the eighteenth and nineteenth centuries. Covering prose, poetry and drama, the volumes not only contain work by major authors but also include less obvious material gleaned from sources such as letters, diaries, court reports, newspapers and journals.

Irish Literature The Eighteenth Century
An Annotated Anthology
Edited and Introduced by
A. Norman Jeffares and
Peter van de Kamp

Irish Literature in the Eighteenth Century illustrates not only the impressive achievement of the great writers—Swift, Berkeley, Burke, Goldsmith and Sheridan—but also shows the varied accomplishment of others, providing unexpected, entertaining examples from the pens of the less well known. Here are examples of the witty comic dramas so successfully written by Susannah Centlivre, Congreve, Steele, Farquhar and Macklin. There are serious and humorous essayists represented, including Steele, Lord Orrery, Thomas Sheridan and Richard Lovell Edgeworth. Beginning with Gulliver's Travels, fiction includes John Amory's strange imaginings, Sterne's stream of consciousness, Frances Sheridan's insights, Henry Brooke's sentimentalities and Goldsmith's charm. Poetry ranges from the classical to the innovative. Graceful lyrics, anonymous jeux d'esprit, descriptive pieces, savage satires and personal poems are written by very different poets, among them learned witty women, clergymen and drunken ne'er-do-wells. Politicians, notably Grattan and Curran, produced eloquent speeches; effective essays and pamphlets accompanied political activity. Personal letters and diaries—such as the exuberant Dorothea Herbert's Recollections—convey the changing ethos of this century's literature, based on the classics and moving to an increasing interest in the translation of Irish literature. This book conveys its fascinating liveliness and rich variety.

Irish Literature
The Nineteenth Century
Volume I
An Annotated Anthology
Edited and Introduced by
A. Norman Jeffares and
Peter van de Kamp

'This anthology is a superlative achievement and for at least a generation is sure to be the outstanding work in its field. Jeffares and van de Kamp bring to their task a fine blend of scholarship, good judgment and innovation. And they have produced a fascinating collection of Irish writing which scholars, students and general readers will find both inviting and accessible.'

James H. Murphy, President of The Society for the
Study of
Nineteenth-Century Ireland

This, the first of three volumes, spans the first third of the nineteenth century. It documents Ireland's significant literary contribution to an age of invention, with Thomas Moore's romantic Melodies, Maria Edgeworth's regional fiction, and Charles Maturin's voyeuristic Gothic stories. It witnesses the rise of a quest for authenticity—mapping and transmuting the Gaelic past (in Hardiman's *Irish Minstrelsy*, Petrie's essay on the round towers, and O'Curry's research into Irish manuscripts) and faithfully depicting the real Ireland (in the first-hand accounts of Mary Leadbeater, William Hamilton Maxwell, Asenath Nicholson, the peasant fiction of William Carleton and the Catholic fiction of the Banim brothers). In Jonah Barrington's Sketches it records the demise of the rollicking squirearchy, while in the stories of Lover it portrays the rise of the stage Irishman. But it also offers a selection from political documents and speeches, and from popular writings which were imprinted on the Irish consciousness. These are contextualised by historical documents, and by Irish forays into European Romanticism.

A NEW ANNOTATED ANTHOLOGY OF EIGHTEENTH
AND NINETEENTH CENTURY IRISH LITERATURE

Irish Literature
The Nineteenth Century
Volume II

An Annotated Anthology
Edited and Introduced by
A. Norman Jeffares and
Peter van de Kamp

The second of the three volumes, roughly spans the middle decades of the nineteenth century, a period dominated by the enormity of the Great Famine. Its terror is recorded in first-hand accounts and in the powerless yet forceful reactions which this cataclysmic event engendered in such writers as John Mitchel (who in his *Jail Journal* pits the self against the state). This volume documents the rise of cultural nationalism, in the work of the contributors to *The Nation* (Davis, Mangan, Lady Wilde), and the response of Unionist intelligentsia in the *Dublin University Magazine*. It juxtaposes the authentic Gaelic voice in translation (Ferguson and Walsh) against the haunting intensity of Mangan and the non-conformism of his fellow inauthenticator 'Father Prout'. It witnesses the stage Irishman in Lever's fiction being placed on Boucicault's popular podium, in his reworking of Gerald Griffin's account of *The Colleen Bawn*. It records the rise of Fenianism (in such writers as Charles Kickham), and it sees Ireland taking stock (in the work of W.E.H. Lecky). It notes the emergence of a new literary confidence in the works of Sigerson and Todhunter. It extends well beyond examinations of Irish identity, not only in encapsulating popular writing, but also by incorporating writers of Irish descent who investigated different cultures.

Irish Literature
The Nineteenth Century
Volume III
An Annotated Anthology
Edited and Introduced by
A. Norman Jeffares and
Peter van de Kamp

The last of the three volumes, roughly spans the last thirty years of the nineteenth century, a period which saw the emergence of the Land League, the dynamiting campaign of the Fenians, and the rise and fall of Charles Stewart Parnell. It witnessed changes in all literary genres. Standish James O'Grady conveyed a sense of heroic excitement in his affirmation of Gaelic Ireland's literary heritage. Douglas Hyde promoted Irish language and culture through his foundation of the Gaelic League. Writers affiliated with the Irish Literary Society tried to re-energise Young Ireland's ideals of cultural nationalism. Under the aegis of Ireland's literary renaissance a new interest in Celticism became manifest. The year after the publication of Allingham's *Collected Poems* W.B. Yeats's *The Wanderings of Oisin* marked the emergence of Irish mythology and legend in an elegant, sensuous and highly influential manner. With Wilde, Shaw, Martyn and George Moore he expanded Ireland's aesthetic horizons; as Yeats introduced French *Symbolisme* in *The Secret Rose* and *The Wind Among the Reeds*, Oscar Wilde preached the paradoxes of decadence, Shaw uncovered society's hypocrisies, while Martyn embraced Ibsen's social realism, and Moore combined Zola's naturalism with the synaesthesia of Totalkunst. Major writers combined to form Ireland's National Theatre. Pioneers such as Lafcadio Hearn were exploring different cultures, which were to influence European literature and drama. The last decades of the nineteenth century were a powerfully creative period, rich in its literary collaborations, and profoundly impressive in its vitality.

IRISH LITERATURE
THE NINETEENTH CENTURY

VOLUME I

Irish Literature
The Nineteenth Century
Volume I

Editors

A. NORMAN JEFFARES
AND
PETER VAN DE KAMP

RISHTOWN
LIBRARY

IRISH ACADEMIC PRESS
DUBLIN • PORTLAND, OR

First published in 2006 by
IRISH ACADEMIC PRESS
44 Northumberland Road, Dublin 4, Ireland

and in the United States of America by
IRISH ACADEMIC PRESS
c/o ISBS, Suite 300
920 NE 58th Avenue
Portland, Oregon 97213-3786

Website: www.iap.ie

© 2005 A. Norman Jeffares and Peter van de Kamp

1080858

BISHOPSTOWN
LIBRARY

British Library Cataloguing in Publication Data
An entry can be found on request

ISBN 0-7165-2800 2 (cloth)
ISBN 0-7165-2805-3 (paper)

Library of Congress Cataloging-in-Publication Data
An entry can be found on request

*All rights reserved. Without limiting the rights under copyright reserved
alone, no part of this publication may be reproduced, stored in or
introduced into a retrieval system, or transmitted, in any form or by any
means (electronic, mechanical, photocopying, recording or otherwise),
without the prior written permission of both the copyright owner and the
above publisher of this book.*

Printed by MPG Books Ltd, Bodmin Cornwall

Contents

Contents

NOTE ON THE TEXT
Where possible, original spellings, syntax and punctuation have been
retained. The editors have, however, made a small number of necessary textual corrections, which do not impair the authenticity of the
original text.

xv

Alexander Norman (Derry) Jeffares (11 August 1920 – 1 June 2005)

On the morning of 1 June, Derry passed away peacefully in his sleep. The night before he had sent an ambulance home, and had gone to bed. He died in harness: on 30 May we had finished correcting the proofs of the nineteenth-century anthology, Vol. One; not long before he had submitted his final contribution to our joint venture, the introduction to the last volume. His part of our mammoth task was completed (as always he was ahead of me in getting things done). And Derry was going to allow himself to take off that coat of armour: intending our anthologies to be the last of his 'academic' publications, he had started writing his memoirs, which, in style, he called his 'anecdotes'. Derry's final full stop marked the end of an incredibly distinguished academic career, which had been set in motion when as a schoolboy editor of sixteen he had called on W.B. Yeats, a former pupil of the Erasmus Smith High School in Dublin, asking him for a poem for *The Erasmian*, the school magazine (Yeats sent him home, but a week later he submitted 'What Then'). That schoolboy would become renowned for his extensive work on Yeats, and on eighteenth-century Irish literature, for which he shared Yeats's love, but his many publications were to extend beyond the field of Irish studies, to include English, Commonwealth and American literature (he championed Walt Whitman). I asked Derry years ago how many books he had published; he replied, under his breath, 'Well, over two hundred.' He was the general editor of various series of texts, including *A Review of English Literature*, the influential *Writers and Critics* series of monographs, and of the *York Notes*. He edited the refreshing journals *AREL* and *ARIEL*. His enterprising spirit took him to three continents; first to Groningen in post-War Holland—when he left there to take up a lectureship at Edinburgh University he had to assure the Dutch Queen that he could support his wife Jeanne (an assurance he kept all his life, aided by mutual reliance: she vetted anything he wrote, and he couldn't understand scholars who baulked at that criterion). He was to hold chairs in Adelaide, Leeds, where he was known as the king-maker, transforming the university to a remarkable centre of excellence, and Stirling, taking a very active part in Scottish arts as chairman of PEN Scotland, of Book Trust Scotland, and vice chairman of the Scottish Arts Council. He was also a member of the Arts Council of Great Britain, Fellow of the Royal Society of Literature, of the Royal Society of Edinburgh and the Australian Academy of the Humanities, Honorary Fellow of Trinity College, Dublin, and honorary Doctor of the Universities of Stirling and Lille.

Derry *had* become a legend in his lifetime. He took considerable pleasure from my relaying to him the question asked by several people what it was like to work with his grandson. Collaborating with him, daily, for years, was always great fun, and deserves hyperbole, for his generosity was unparagoned in academe, his energy unequalled, his sense of humour, his bonhomie, infectious. He was really looking forward to the launch of these books; seeing them into publication without him is a lonely enterprise.

Peter van de Kamp, Tralee, July 2005

Foreword

The study of Irish writing in English, often in the context of Irish Studies courses, has burgeoned internationally since the 1980s. This intensification of interest in the culture of the island of Ireland and of its diaspora, has not, unhappily, been accompanied by any systematic effort by publishers to make available as individual texts the many works by writers other than Joyce, Yeats, Beckett, upon which such academic enterprises must depend. Certainly, publishers from time to time will re-issue works by lesser-known writers, but often in small print runs that are not thereafter reprinted. So the harassed teacher compiling a reading list in Irish Studies must depend on the vagaries of the book trade in a way that reflects a key fact about the history of Irish literature in English itself. For such publishers are often English, as Irish writers have so often had to depend on publishers in their neighbouring island to bring their work before the world (a fact made evident in the careers of many of the writers anthologised in this volume). In the field of literary production itself that dependency has often involved complex issues of reading communities with different expectations in England and Ireland, raising in modern criticism and cultural commentary the shibboleths of caricature, misrepresentation and exploitation (matters which have been seen as relevant to such writers as Thomas Moore, William Carleton and Samuel Lover, represented in this volume). In the area of academic study this dependency has sometimes meant courses have had to concentrate on the major figures while representing their cultural hinterland by such works by lesser figures as may only from time to time and temporarily have been in print.

In this context the anthology has been recognised as a necessity. In 1991 *The Field Day Anthology of Irish Writing* appeared, seeking to represent by judicious choice the entire field of Irish writing in English. More recently David Pierce has edited his *Irish Writing in the Twentieth Century: A Reader* (2001). Poetry in English in the sixteenth, seventeenth and eighteenth centuries has been well served by two admirable anthologies edited by Andrew Carpenter, and the present editors have complemented their work with an accessible anthology which covers the eighteenth century. To date the nineteenth century, increasingly a focus of critical interest, has not had its anthology. Pierce, it is true, included some extracts from the 1890s in his volume, and Field Day's venture encompassed a valuable selection from nineteenth century authors; its responsibilities however were to many centuries, not to one. Accordingly, the opportunity existed to aid academics and gratify interested readers everywhere by supplying a sound, extensive anthology, dedicated to nineteenth century Irish texts, which, very usefully, the editors of this three-volume work have now done. That this signal contribution to the field of Irish Studies should have been the last task brought to pre-publication completion the day before his death, by the renowned scholar A.N. ('Derry') Jeffares, makes the work itself an appropriate testament to a man who gave so much over sixty years to the development of the field of Irish literary studies. And I know his fellow editor in this work, Peter van de Kamp, will understand my singling out Derry Jeffares in this way in this foreword, since creative, generous collaboration was so much a part of what made Derry the remarkable, wonderfully life-enhancing man he was.

The body of work which Volume One of this enterprise anthologises allows the student and reader to consider aspects of Irish cultural dependence on England (adverted to above). It also permits reflection on how in the period from the Act of Union (1800) until the catastrophic Great Famine of the 1840s, Irish literature in English, with roots in both the Irish language and popular English-language culture, began to make itself felt as a distinctive phenomenon in a subtle process of production and interpretation. As can be derived from the work gathered here, together with a reading of the thoughtful historical Introduction provided by the two editors, this creative dynamic in Irish culture in a period of profound economic difficulties and political agitation was affected by developments which transcended the Irish/English duality: Romanticism, cultural nationalism, the concept of national character expressed in song and poem, the cult of the primitive, the turn to anthropological investigation. All of these find expression in the texts selected below, which will allow the student to set the fraught matter of British/Irish relations and the import of the Union and its aftermath (the substance of key fictional texts from Edgeworth's *Castle Rackrent* onwards) in a broadly European historical framework. In this respect Thomas Woolf's poem 'The Burial of Sir John Moore', with its modern Iberian peninsular setting, might be set against Thomas Moore's nostalgia for specifically Irish glories in the days of old.

However, the editors in their selection—and this is to be welcomed—do not restrict their choices to those which illustrate a theme. As they put it: 'our criteria for selection have been generous; we have included texts which are beyond the domain of Ireland's nineteenth century history outlined in [our] introduction'. One senses in this statement of editorial principle that they know that literature is one of the dimensions of human activity where individual eccentricity most frequently threatens to make nonsense of grand narratives. In this volume the work of such writers as George Darley and William Maginn might be adduced as evidence that a literary tradition has its genetic sports, those writers who encourage us to savour particularity, the unique, the idiosyncratic, those whose work cannot easily be reduced to explanatory critique about it. They encourage us too to read an anthology such as this is with the awareness that how we construct the past is itself historically conditioned, is itself only partially explanatory of that past, and that any set of choices about what to include in an anthology is itself an act of arrangement and interpretation, which must generate further critical debate.

TERENCE BROWN
University of Dublin, Trinity College
July 2005

Acknowledgements

These volumes grew out of a suggestion made by Prof. Augustine Martin in 1983 to produce a series of Irish Readers. We should like to acknowledge our indebtedness to Prof. Terence Brown (Trinity College, Dublin), Peter Costello (Dublin), Prof. Jacques Chuto (University of Paris XII), Prof. Anne Crookshank (Trinity College, Dublin), Prof. Adèle Crowder (Queen's University, Kingston), Prof. Christopher Crowder (Queen's University, Kingston), Prof. Warwick Gould (University of London), Prof. John Kelly (University of Oxford), Prof. Brendan Kennelly (Trinity College, Dublin), Dr Peter Liebregts (University of Leiden), Sarah Mahaffy, Daphne Maxwell, Dr James H. Murphy (de Paul University, Chicago), Dr Neil Murphy (Nanyang University, Singapore), Prof. Ellen Shannon-Mangan (Astoria, Oregon), Prof. Colin Smythe, Dr Bruce Stewart (University of Ulster), Dr Wim Tigges (University of Leiden), Prof. Loreto Todd (University of Ulster) and Deirdre Toomey.

The librarians of the Athenaeum, the National Library of Ireland, Trinity College, Dublin, Trinity College, Cambridge, University College, Dublin, the University of St. Andrews, the University of Stirling, and of the Institute of Technology, Tralee were indispensable in making material available to us. We should particularly like to thank Siobhan O'Callaghan for her unstinting efforts to get us more than just the books and journals we wanted, and Joanne Ball for her help in tracing and proffering images for our covers.

Introduction

The following introduction provides a summary historical context for our three volumes of selections from nineteenth-century Irish writing. References to actual authors are only intended to illustrate the historical perspective. The parameters of Irish writing are an ongoing matter for debate: our criteria for selection have been generous; we have included texts which are beyond the domain of Ireland's nineteenth-century history outlined in this introduction.

I

Published just after the Act of Union, Maria Edgeworth's *Castle Rackrent* is set before 1782, the year that the Irish Parliament gained its legislative independence. The novel describes the rise of a new, pragmatic Catholic middle class and the fall of the old order. Thady Quirk is the unreliable chronicler of the demise of the Rackrents, erstwhile Catholic gentry converted to the Established religion to claim the title to their land; he is their self-proclaimed 'faithful servant', but he is also the father of Jason, educated as a lawyer, to whom Sir Connolly, the last in a line of reckless landlords, signs away the estate – Thady's complicity in the Rise and Fall remains obscure. *Castle Rackrent* is not a plea for Protestant landlords to put their house in order: it presents a *fait accompli*; as such it bears witness to the social shifts that came to a climax in the last two decades of the eighteenth century, which replaced the certainties of the *ancien régime* with a heterogeneous interplay of social class, nationalism and religion. The demise of the 'moral economy', which was based on an unwritten code of respect in the relations between landlords and their tenants (with long leases and low rents), was accompanied by the emergence of a commercial middle class. The Penal laws had contributed to Catholics directing their energy to trade. A series of Relief Acts (in 1778, 1782, 1792 and 1793) exemplified a growing spirit of religious tolerance. In 1775 around one third of wholesale merchants in Dublin were Catholics and one quarter in Cork. The most prosperous

1

undertook momentous building programmes (such as Arthur's Quay), but by and large they shared Thady Quirk's reticence about his son's business exploits; yet their prosperity was evident – they were a class to be reckoned with.

Their Protestant counterparts were more outspoken: the term 'protestant ascendancy' was coined by Sir Boyle Roche, renowned for his malapropisms, in 1782, in the debate about the Catholic Relief Bill; by 1787 it had come to imply their claim on a monopoly of trade and commerce. Well over a century later, W. B. Yeats used it to show the superiority of the class who shaped Ireland's culture. Outnumbered by over four to one, Irish Protestants of divergent status had a common sense of superiority – an Irish gentleman being a Protestant, it was assumed that an Irish Protestant was a gentleman. They could muster considerable military strength. Among them emerged a sense of patriotism, fuelled by their grievances against the economic constraints which England had placed on their economic development (Jonathan Swift, in a similar fashion, had earlier argued to 'burn everything English but their coal'). Their case for an independent Ireland under the British Crown was argued in the 1770s by Flood and Grattan in the Irish Commons, and by Charlemont in the Lords (it had originally been proposed by Molyneux and Swift). Their cause was aided by the American War of Independence, which broke out in 1775; as the regular troops were moved to combat and the British government lacked funds to revive the militia, independent companies were formed, recruiting members mainly from the Protestant urban and rural middle classes, and officers from the gentry and aristocracy. The threat of an invasion from France forced government to authorize the Volunteers. By May 1782 their numbers estimated 60,000. They had become an oppositional political movement in military uniform, banking on support from the British Whigs. They played a leading part, under Grattan and Charlemont, in the 1779 campaign for free trade, and in the drive for legislative independence.

On 16 April 1782, Henry Grattan carried Repeal of the Declaratory Statute, George I, the Perpetual Mutiny Bill, and abolition of the Privy Council's unconstitutional powers. Ireland was still headed by a Viceroy, appointed by the British government, but only the King could now suppress Irish Bills. For the next eighteen years, Ireland's parliament was independent. It came to be known as Grattan's Parliament. Grattan's Declaration of Independence contains echoes of Molyneux and Swift:

I am now to address a free people: ages have passed away, and this is the first moment in which you could be distinguished by that appellation.... I found Ireland on her knees. I watched over her with a paternal solicitude; I have traced her progress from injuries to arms, and from arms to liberty.... Ireland is now a nation; in that new character I hail her, and bowing to her august presence, I say, *Esto perpetua*.

Grattan's Parliament roughly coincided with a period of considerable prosperity, with the development of textile manufactures and brewing, the spread of tillage, and the general expansion of trade; absentee landlords returned; the population grew, from some three million in 1750 to about five million in 1800. Dublin, now an independent capital, flourished. The Bank of Ireland, the Royal Irish Academy (with Charlemont as its first president) and the Royal College of Surgeons were established. The centre of Dublin still retains its Georgian appeal, in the civilized symmetry of Fitzwilliam, Mountjoy and Merrion Squares, and, majestically, in James Gandon's classicist Custom House and the Four Courts.

However, the 'free people' that Grattan addressed in the Irish Parliament were exclusively of the Established Church. He realized the need for Catholic emancipation, as did Burke in England, but his liberal views were not shared by his colleagues. Concessions were made – piecemeal: Catholics got a limited right to vote in 1793, and in 1795 St Patrick's College of Maynooth was founded, and partially endowed, for the education of the clergy (taking the sting out of the education of priests in revolutionary Europe).

Nor did all classes in Ireland share in the economic prosperity. With the rise in rents and the general cost of living, the divide between rich and poor widened, manifestly in rural areas. Agrarian protest was rife, particularly in Munster and south Leinster, where the Rightboys revived Whiteboy activity. In Ulster, agrarian unrest was coupled with sectarianism. In north Armagh, Protestant weavers who felt threatened by the Catholic expansion in the linen industry and on the land formed the Peep of Day boys. Catholics formed the Defenders in response. In September 1795, in the wake of a Defender attack, Protestants organized themselves into the Orange Order (after William of Orange, Protestant Stadtholder of the Dutch Republic, who after a successful incursion into Ireland in 1690 had driven his Catholic father-in-law off the British throne, which he shared with his wife Mary). They were to become a major force in upholding the status quo in Ireland, against a radical movement which, enthused by the French Revolution, had formed the Society of United Irishmen in 1791, in Dublin and Belfast. The Belfast Society, made up of drapers, tanners and merchants, was largely Presbyterian; their Dublin counterpart consisted of members of the Protestant and Catholic middle class, with a smattering of gentry and aristocracy. Theobald Wolfe Tone was a co-founder of both the Belfast and the Dublin society. The following year he took the place of Richard, the son of Edmund Burke, as secretary of the radicalized Catholic Committee. The United Irishmen forged ties with the Catholic Committee, with Defenders, and, after their suppression in 1794, with southern Whiteboys and Rightboys. Wolfe Tone, who had been charged with sedition, prepared an invasion from France, with *liberté, égalité*, and the *fraternité* of a united Ireland, free from sectarian divisions, in his idealistic banner. When eventually a rising did take place, in 1798, any figure-heads, such as the gallant Lord Edward Fitzgerald (a cousin of the Whig leader, Charles James Fox), had been eliminated, thanks to a well-informed secret service, and the hopes of mass support were quenched by insoluble divisions in society. '98 was the first in a list of ill-disciplined insurrections which, hopelessly disorganized, served an ideological purpose after they were quenched. Of them it had most chances of success – if the French forces had materialized; if the Government had not frustrated the preparations – and it has lived on most tenaciously in lore and literature (early histories blamed the fiasco on a variety of sources, including Catholic treachery, government repression, and landlord *naïveté*; with the rise of cultural nationalism, the Rising was transformed into a heroic struggle). The rebellion affected eighteen counties, seven of them seriously. A force of 4,000 Presbyterians was checked at Antrim town. 7,000 United Irishmen were captured at Ballynahinch. The most persistent fighting was in the north-east and Co. Wexford, where rebels captured and plundered Enniscorthy and Wexford Town but were eventually defeated at Vinegar Hill. Co. Wexford had a high incidence of Protestants, with economic rivalry between communities which escalated into sectarian atrocities – the Protestant Yeomen massacred Catholics; the rebels massacred Protestants (at Scullabogue and Wexford Bridge), and the militia continued the massacre. The small French force that did land fought gallantly under General Humbert, but surrendered at Ballinamuck. Wolfe Tone was captured off the coast of Donegal and committed suicide in gaol, under sentence of hanging. Five years later, Robert Emmet led a brief, and even more ramshackle, rising in

Dublin, which had its roots in the United Irishmen – it too was distinguished by its failure.

As a consequence of '98 the government pressed for the Act of Union, which it achieved through the machinations of Lord Castlereagh in 1800. The ailing Grattan, an anachronism in his Volunteer uniform, held a passionate plea for maintaining independence, but the time for oratory had passed. The Irish Parliament voted itself out of existence.

Among the opposing MPs was Sir Jonah Barrington. In his *Historic anecdotes and secret memoirs of the legislative union* (2 vols., 1809–30) and *The Rise and Fall of the Irish Nation* (1833), he gave accounts of the financial and positional bribery that secured the passage of the Union. He was also the author of *Personal Sketches of his Own Times* (2 vols. 1827; 3rd vol., 1833), which describes the entertaining exploits of the hard-riding, hard-drinking, duelling squirearchy to whom Maria Edgeworth's Rackrents belonged. They became a welcome stereotype looming large in Charles Lever's early novels; in reality, by 1800 they had ceased to exist.

II.

In Maria Edgeworth's novel *The Absentee* (1812), Sir James Brooke acquaints the young Lord Colambre with the changes the Union initially brought about in Dublin:

> From the removal of both houses of parliament, most of the nobility, and many of the principal families among the Irish commoners, either hurried in high hopes to London, or retired disgusted and in despair to their houses in the country. Immediately, in Dublin, commerce rose into the vacated seats of rank; wealth rose into the place of birth. New faces and new equipages appeared: people, who had never been heard of before, started into notice, pushed themselves forward, not scrupling to elbow their way even at the castle.... the decorum, elegance, polish, and charm of society was gone....

Dublin breathed absence. Maturin, in *Women; or Pour et Contre* (1818) observed that 'the magnificent architecture of its public buildings seem [ed] like the skeleton of some gigantic frame, which the inhabiting spirit has deserted'. 105 MPs took their seats in the

Commons in Westminster, 32 peers joined the Lords; Parliament house was sold to the Bank of Ireland. The Act of Union brought martial law and coercive legislation (it is not surprising that the first people Lord Colambre meets in Ireland are soldiers). A colonial officialism emerged – in describing it, in her novel *Florence Macarthy* (1818) Lady Morgan imported the phrase 'bureaucracy' ('Mr Commissioner ... represented the *Bureaucratie*, or office tyranny by which Ireland has been so long governed'). With the transfer of the legislature to London, absenteeism increased, and with the withdrawal of capital from the country, the economy weakened. Ireland had to bear two seventeenths of the UK's total expenditure, and between 1801 and 1817 the Irish debt rose by 250 per cent. The end of the Napoleonic Wars brought a recession, the population increased, tenants' plots of land were subdivided, and agricultural hardship grew, with a string of minor famines (such as the partial failure of the potato crop in 1817); the woollen industry collapsed – and the government scrutinized, filling Blue Books with statistics. Terror was rife – Whiteboys used it as a form of protection against evictions, while in the cities Ribbonmen (a secret society that sprang out of the Defenders) were associated with crime and disaffection. In growing contrast, Belfast's linen industry prospered with the introduction of the wet-spinning process in the 1820s.

One Irish political man of letters who operated in the courts of the conqueror was Thomas Moore. He had come to England in 1799, aged 20, fearing that he might be arrested for his association with Robert Emmet and his revolutionary friends. Some two years before when Moore had played an Irish air ('Let Erin Remember') on the piano in his home at Aungier Street, Emmet had exclaimed 'Oh, that I were at the head of twenty thousand men and marching to that tune!' Now, with considerable acumen, enjoying, indirectly, the patronage of the Prince of Wales, in London, in one year he mourned the death of Lord and Lady Moira, and indirectly of Fox and the Constitution in heroic couplets and that of Emmet in an Irish melody. When Moore went to London he discovered that Burns's songs and Scott's *Minstrelsy of the Scottish Border* were in fashion. Moore appealed to the vogue for folk music in his *Irish Melodies*, which proved immensely popular, appearing in ten volumes between 1808 and 1834. Their music (arranged by John Stevenson) was heard throughout Europe – France adopted the word 'mélodie' for 'chanson'. Some of Moore's tunes were from an oral source (he may have picked up the air of 'Let Erin Remember' from his Cork friend,

Edward Hudson), but most were based on Edward Bunting's *A General Collection of the Ancient Irish Music* (1796), comprising 66 – inaccurate – transcriptions of the airs he heard from nine harpists at the Belfast Harpers' Festival (1792).

For Moore, music was 'the source of my poetic talent, since it was merely the effort to translate into words the different feelings and passions which melody seemed to me to express.' Those 'feelings and passions' were the universals of loss, and Moore, in politics an eighteenth-century Whig, presents himself as the archetype of Romanticism: 'I was *but* as the wind,' to the sleeping harp, and 'all the wild sweetness I wak'd was thy own.' That which was lost extends beyond the personal to a shimmering Celtic past. The interest in that past had been awakened by an ancient Celtic manuscript forged by a Scotsman. James Macpherson's *The Poems of Ossian* sent reverberations through Europe. Goethe translated parts, and used it to illustrate the heightened *Sturm und Drang* sensitivity of the self-destructive Young Werther; Napoleon, who commissioned Ingres to paint 'The Dream of Ossian', took a copy of Macpherson's book with him on his Russian campaign. Ireland claimed Ossian rightly as its own; Charlotte Brooke incorporated six Ossianic poems in her *Reliques of Irish Poetry* (1789), claiming in her Preface that Irish poetry is 'the elder sister' to the British. The past offered a national identity: antiquarianism was associated with a national cause – the Harpers' Festival was organized by a society which had prominent support among the Belfast United Irishmen; it concluded on Bastille Day. The United Irishmen's seal showed a harp with a liberty cap on a pike, and the words 'It is new strung and shall be heard'. The growing interest in Turlough Carolan (1670-1738) as 'the last Irish harper' betrays not merely a nostalgia for a lost tradition, or a romantic interest in the lone bard (after Thomas Gray's poem, 'The Bard') – it is of symbolic importance.

In Moore's *Melodies* the harp 'that once through Tara's halls / the soul of music shed' is a symbol of Ireland's past glory, struggling 'against muteness and cultural amnesia'. The *Melodies* are the first successful manifestation of cultural nationalism: the turbulent present shimmers obliquely through the glorious past, which lights up a putative future. There are echoes of Brennan's 'Dawning of the day': in its present misery, Erin must remember 'the days of old', 'the glories of Brian the brave', the bravery of the Red Branch Knights, to 'light us to victory yet' as 'avenging and bright falls the swift sword of Erin'. His was not an 'appeal to the passions of an ignorant and angry multitude'; he performed in the drawing rooms of 'the rich and educated who can afford to have their national zeal a little stimulated without exciting much dread of the excesses into which it may hurry them'. But the refrain about the return of a Celtic age would be taken up by generations of belligerent nationalist poets. Moore's balancing act is exemplified in 'An Irish Peasant to his Mistress', a poem supposedly about 'the ancient Church of Ireland' which presents images of martyrdom (the crown of thorns, the catacombs) in the context of the struggle for Catholic Emancipation, concluding:

> They slander thee sorely, who say thy vows are frail —
> Hadst thou been a false one, thy cheek had looked less pale!
> They say, too, so long hast thou worn those lingering chains,
> That deep in thy heart they have printed their servile stains:
> Oh, foul is the slander! – no chain could that soul subdue –
> Where shineth thy spirit, there Liberty shineth too!

Emancipation had been a *sub rosa* proviso of the Act of Union, which therefore had received Catholic support. It met conscientious opposition from the King, and, the government being divided, Pitt failed to press it through in 1801. Catholics relied on supportive MPs such as Henry Grattan to represent their cause, but the issue was too politically sensitive – and the increasingly less powerful Ascendancy too guarded – for it to be resolved, even by the short-lived governments of James Fox (1806) and George Canning (1827), who both supported Emancipation. It required a populist of the stature of Daniel O'Connell to turn the petitioning of Catholic boards into the demands of a Catholic people. Those boards, and even the Vatican, had offered concessions, granting the government the right to veto episcopal appointments, but these were denounced by O'Connell. With Richard Lalor Sheil he founded the Catholic Association in May 1823, opening its associate membership to the public at one penny a month. Within a year this 'Catholic Rent', as it was labelled by its detractors, brought in £1,000; over five years it raised £15,000. More important than its financial success, the Catholic Association mobilized a 'degraded caste', spurred on by 'The Counsellor's' fearless language, into confidently supporting a 'national' cause, which was greater than just voting Catholics into parliament. In 1825 the Catholic Association was suppressed, but O'Connell continued it under a different name. A pro-Emancipation candidate was elected at Waterford in 1826, and O'Connell was returned for Clare in 1828. A

Catholic, he was not able to take his seat. The crisis was resolved by the government of Wellington and Peel; on threat of Civil War, a Catholic Relief Bill was passed by both houses of Parliament. O'Connell was seen to score a victory which in the popular mind elevated him into the legendary 'Liberator'. He had also delivered a deadly blow to the Protestant Ascendancy.

Thomas Moore, who shunned O'Connell's confrontational style, expressed amazement: 'I little thought I should ever live to see the end of my politics.' That O'Connell could mobilize mass public opinion attests to the spread of education and the homogenization of the Catholic population. The middleman, typically a figure from the ranks of the Protestant sub-gentry, became an anachronism in the early nineteenth century (almost half a million Protestants emigrated from Ireland); and as estate administration became more professional, the role of the Catholic tenant farmers was strengthened (it was the landlord and not the erstwhile intermediary who bore the brunt of agrarian dissatisfaction). Rents rose little after 1815. Landlords, realising their duties, made determined efforts to prevent rundale, and to make improvements in housing, and in schooling.

Hedge–schools had played an important role in the education of the lower orders. They were non-denominational, independent of the authorities of church and state, monitored *ad hoc* by parents, and run by teachers from the peasantry who had no formal training, and who established their authority in contests with another hedge schoolmaster (often adjudicated by the parish priest). William Carleton, who has provided a comprehensive description of his first-hand experience of the hedge school, describes them 'as superior in literary knowledge and acquirements to the class of men who are now engaged in the general education of the people, as they were beneath them in moral and religious character'. But the early nineteenth century witnessed a mass extension of schools under education societies. The most effective of these was the Society for the Education of the Poor of Ireland, founded in 1811; offering education uninfluenced by religious creed, it was initially supported by O'Connell and approved by the Catholic clergy. By 1831, the Kildare Place Society, as it was popularly known, counted 1,634 schools and was educating 140,000 pupils. But it had been taken over by Evangelicals.

The rise of zealous evangelism was observed by Charles Robert Maturin; in his novel *Women; or, Pour et Contre* he makes a significant attack on fanatical Calvinism. Evangelism had been spreading through educational societies, to which the Roman Catholics had responded with the foundation of the Christian Brothers by Edmund Rice, but it was not until 1822, when William Magee, the archbishop of Dublin, called for a 'Second Reformation' that proselytism had 'officially' come to the fore. That this led to public polemics with such Catholic luminaries as the formidably eloquent, but moderate, James Warren Doyle ('J. K. L.') was indicative of the changing status of an increasingly assertive Catholic clergy. The creation in 1831 of a non-denominational system of elementary schooling was seen by many Protestant churchmen as a snub to those who maintained the prerogative of the Established Church. There was a victim in the introduction of one of the most advanced systems of education in Europe, and in Catholic Emancipation – the Irish language. O'Connell did not think it a good medium for communication with the British, and the British did not think it a good medium for the education of the Irish.

III.

Maria Edgeworth's Lord Colambre was not the only young gentleman to come from abroad, go back to his roots beyond the Pale, and make reparations. In Lady Morgan's *The Wild Irish Girl* (1806) young Horatio is sent by his father, the Earl of M—, into Irish exile to recuperate from dissipation. Both Colambre and Horatio end up married to 'a girl from the country', and in both novels this union signifies a synthesis of the indigenous (the racy, good-natured, precipitate Irish) and the exogenous (the estranged ascendancy). Both books influenced Walter Scott, who acknowledged his indebtedness to Edgeworth in a postscript to *Waverley*, while his plots, characters, scenery and theme are reminiscent of Lady Morgan's *The Wild Irish Girl*. But there are differences: Edgeworth's novel is a product of dutiful enlightenment; Colambre's Gracey Nugent is a foster-child in search of her identity (which Colambre traces for her). Lady Morgan's is a Romantic extravaganza: Horatio's Glorvina is the lofty harp-playing daughter of the Gaelic Prince of Inismore who holds court in his ruined Connaught Castle. In Edgeworth's plot, Colambre's liaison with Gracey Nugent creates a line of suspense (the intensity of Colambre's efforts to solve Gracey's illegitimacy has led to various far-fetched conjectures), but it is subservient to his dutifully setting his father's affairs in order; in Lady Morgan's the marriage of Horatio and Glorvina is the central and symbolic resolution, as 'national marriages' would be in her novels *O'Donnel* (1814) and *Florence Macarthy* (1818).

The journey towards greater consciousness was a universal Romantic device which in 'the West' of Ireland could be given a local habitation and a name. The Romantic quest for the past gave meaning to the present, through etymological investigation and historical linguistics, architectural research, and the collection of ancient literature and folklore. In Ireland, that past was omnipresent: not only was the country littered with 'shards of a lost tradition', that tradition was still alive in and among the Irish-speaking peasantry. Philologists such as Charlotte Brooke, Joseph Cooper Walker and Charles Vallancey found Gaelic Catholic scholars at their disposal. Vallancey, author of *Essay on the Antiquity of the Irish Language* (1772) and *A Grammar of the Iberno-Celtic or Irish Language* (1773) traced those shards to the Middle East: he saw the Irish Round Towers as Phoenician fire temples (Mangan would later quip that for Vallancey 'every Irishman is an Arab'). It was not until George Petrie published his prize-winning essay on the 'Origin and Uses of the Round Towers of Ireland' (1832) that their Christian medieval provenance was established.

Poets were collecting Gaelic verse and rendering it into English. J. J. Callanan, whose verse translations include 'The Convict of Clonmel', 'The Dirge of O'Sullivan Bear' and 'The Outlaw of Loch Lene', travelled the south-west gathering folklore for a collection of Munster poetry. James Hardiman collected the literary remains of Carolan and drew on oral poetry and ancient manuscripts to produce transliterations which were rendered into verse by such poets as John D'Alton, William Drummond and Thomas Furlong, published as *Irish Minstrelsy, or Bardic Remains of Ireland* (2 vols., 1831).

The Act of Union gave rise to a growing English interest in the other part of the Kingdom of Britain and Ireland. Mobility was enhanced by steamships, and Ireland became an attractive destination. Its appeal is reflected in a host of depictions of Irish life and customs, collections of folklore, and travellogues. Anna Maria Hall was the most popular travel writer, with *Sketches of Irish Character* (1829), *Lights and Shadows of Irish Life* (1838), *Stories of Irish Peasantry* (1840) and *Hall's Ireland* (3 vols., 1841–43). Among first-hand accounts are Mary Leadbeater's *Collection of Lives of the Irish Peasantry* (1822), Michael James Whitty's *Tales of Irish Life* (1824), Thomas Crofton Croker's *Researches in the South of Ireland* (1824), Caesar Otway's *Sketches in Ireland* (1827), Mrs Samuel Carter's *Sketches of Irish Character* (1829), W. H. Maxwell's entertaining *Wild Sports of the West of Ireland* (1832), and Isaac Butt's *Irish Life: In the Castle, the Courts, and the Country* (3 vols., 1840). Croker's *Fairy*

Legends and Traditions of the South of Ireland (1825) is regarded as the first significant collection of folk tales, and was translated into German by the Grimm brothers (it is marred by plagiarism and by giving the English reader the instant picture that he desired).

Authenticity was the commodity; writers vied with each other in giving the most faithful rendering. This sense of authenticity pervaded Irish fiction – which was written for a British market. Michael and John Banim, sons of a prosperous Catholic farmer-merchant, coupled unflinching accounts of the violence in Ireland's recent history, of Whiteboy aggression and the '98 rising, with an unsentimental picture of contemporary rural hardship. Gerald Griffin, noted in his time for *Holland Tide; or Munster Popular Tales and Tales of the Munster Festivals* (1827), a collection of adaptations of oral stories, wrote a fictionalized account of the true tragedy of Eily O'Connor, who fell victim to the divided loyalty of the squireen Hardress Cregan. But the champion of authenticity was William Carleton. In the Preface to the first edition of his *Traits and Stories* (1830), he assures the reader that 'what he offers is, both in manufacture and material genuine Irish' because it is 'drawn by one born amidst the scenes he describes – reared as one of the people whose characters and situations he sketches – and who can cut and dress a shillaly as well as any man in his Majesty's dominion; ay, and use it too: so let the critics take care of themselves'. He was born on a small farm in Co. Tyrone; his mother spoke only Irish. Carleton was bilingual, and this enabled him, he claimed, to capture the flavour of peasant speech. Some allege that he wrote exclusively for an Irish audience, choosing to express Ireland rather than exploit it. But to call him a 'social historian' would be an overstatement. He wrote from – a tainted – memory, and his descriptions of hedge schools, faction fights, Irish weddings and wakes, rural aggression, evictions and famine display in their double perspective of detached running commentary and involved narrative the ambivalence of a writer who moved from a Catholic vocation through allegiance to Caesar Otway's proselytizing Protestantism to a modicum of disinterested urban respectability.

After Catholic Emancipation, a new figure emerged in Irish fiction (or rather an old one, wrenched from the stage onto a rural setting). It has been suggested that, faced with the realities of a burgeoning Irish Catholic class, and shirking the horrors of Irish poverty, the stage Irishman offered the British reader a welcome escape into caricature. The character emerges with Samuel Lover's move from the folk tales and songs of *Legends and Stories of Ireland* (2 vols., 1831 and 1834) to the wider expanse of the novel in *Rory O'More* (1837) and *Handy Andy* (1842) (the novels are really tales loosely stitched together around a capering character). *Handy Andy* was very popular; it presents a series of side-splitting misadventures set in a context of drunken squires, a contested election, duels, hedge schools and poteen distillers. Rural squalor is a source of fun; Andy's mother and cousin Oonah wear tattered clothes, subsist on potatoes, and share their thatched hovel with the ever-present pig. Andy Rooney has an inveterate tendency to blunder because he aspires to actions that are beyond his grasp – when told to put several bottles of champagne on ice, he opens the bottles and empties them into a tub of cracked ice. In a telling dramatic twist, the novel ends with the discovery that Andy is the long-lost son of an eccentric aristocrat; he is whisked away to England, and prepared for polite society.

Equally popular was Charles Lever's first novel, *The Confessions of Harry Lorrequer*, which was serialized in the *Dublin University Magazine* in 1837. Lever was amazed: 'If this sort of thing amuses them, thought I, I can go on forever.' He continued his light-hearted merriment in *Charles O'Malley* (1841), and raised the ire (and envy) of William Carleton, who charged Lever with 'pandering to the selfish interests of those who have no sympathy in common with Irishmen'. The accusation was unfair, but it stuck: Daniel O'Connell, at the height of his popularity attacked Lever in Dublin; and such champions of the literary revival as W. B. Yeats and Lady Gregory dismissed Lever from the Irish tradition, probably without ever having read his later *engagé* portrayals of Irish political and social issues. The distorting mirror of the fool that the stage Irishman held up seemed insensitive in an era of hardship and privation – and it did not offer the 'authentic' self-image that the Irish wished to see.

Two authors spurned authenticity with intense idiosyncracy. James Clarence Mangan opens his sketch of Charles Maturin with a rhyme by John Anster, the Irish translator of Goethe's *Faust*: 'Maturin! Maturin! What an odd hat you're in!' Mangan explains that 'Maturin, morally to speak, *was* always in "an odd hat". He was one of those three-corned men whom society insists upon infixing into circular cavities.' So was Mangan, whose conical hat must have also surprised many a passer-by. Mangan recalls 'every second person staring' at Maturin 'and the extraordinary double-belted and treble-caped rug of an old garment, neither coat nor cloak, which enveloped his person' – just as they stared at his own bulging coat and two umbrellas. 'Charles Robert Maturin', Mangan continues, 'lived unappreciated – and died unsympathised with, uncared for, unenquired after – and only *not* forgotten, because he had never been thought about'. Mangan can boast the title of being Ireland's *poète maudit* – he is the most frequently forgotten Irish poet, and died of cholera or starvation in the Meath Hospital after being picked up off the street.

Attempts have been made to fit both writers into the Irish tradition – the interest in the Gothic was to have emanated from Anglo-Irish guilt (in the case of Maturin) and from Catholic victimization (in the case of Mangan) – but fit they will not. Mangan has been claimed, body and soul, for the cause of Irish nationalism – to which, indeed, he publicly subscribed later in life. Parallels have been drawn between his tragic life and his country's; it has even been suggested, hyperbolically, that he was an indirect victim of the Famine and of English *laissez faire*. The interest of both in the supernatural can be seen in the light of the spread of evangelicalism. Maturin, a clergyman of the Established Church, details the cruelty of religious fanaticism in *Women; or, Pour et Contre*, and, with voyeuristic prurience, in *Melmoth the Wanderer* (1820). Mangan in his Sketch quotes the last sentence of the former, which 'at once characterises the author and the hero', and which equally applies to himself: 'When great talent is combined with calamity, their union forms the "tenth wave" of human misery: grief becomes immortal from the inexhaustible fertility of genius; and the serpents that devour us are generated out of our own vitals.' For Maturin's Gothic masterpiece, written in the style of Godwin (whom Mangan admired, just as he admired Maturin) he has no overt praise; 'Melmoth himself', Mangan writes, 'is a bore of the first magnitude, who is always talking grandiloquent fustian, and folding his cloak about him' – and this from the person who styled himself 'the man in the cloak', and whose story of that name is an adaptation of Balzac's 'Melmoth reconcilié'!

Mangan is the greatest Irish inauthenticator ever, attributing his own verse to others, and the verse of others to himself (his translations of Hafiz are only 'half his'). He is a polyglot who seems to have never travelled beyond Co. Meath. His *Anthologia Germanica* and *Literae Orientales* show him attuned to the literary fashions of his era. His own translations from the Irish (based on transliterations, for Mangan's Irish was scant) are unsurpassed in the intensity of emotion and rhythmic energy (they have been criticized by some Gaelic scholars for being divergent from their originals).

Paradoxically, Mangan was employed for some time by Petrie to work on the most regimented enterprise of philological authentication undertaken in Ireland in the nineteenth century. The Ordnance Survey was a comprehensive investigation into Irish place names and their history. It brought together such scholars as John O'Donovan and Eugene O'Curry, who made available the Ossianic cycle and the Red Branch tales, and it garnered the optimistic support of a poet called Samuel Ferguson.

For Ferguson, a Tory Protestant, authenticity was synonymous with loyalty, inauthenticity with dissent. In 1834 he had taken Hardiman to task for his attack on British policy in his rehabilitation of the native Irish in *Irish Minstrelsy*. Had not the Protestant gentry granted their misguided Catholic brethren Emancipation? Hardiman had been disloyal to the ruling Ascendancy; he had sown dissent. And the translations in *Minstrelsy* were unfaithful to the spirit of the original. Ferguson presents his argument with rhetorical vehemence:

> We will leave the idiotic brawler, the bankrupt and fraudulent demagogue, the crawling incendiary, the scheming, jesuitical, ambitious priest – that perverse rabble on whom the mire in which they have wallowed for the last quarter of a century, has caked into a crust like the armour of the Egyptian beast, till they are case hardened invulnerably in the filth of habitual impudence, ingratitude, hipocrisy, envy and malice ... and sing the songs of men who might well rise from honourable graves, and affright the midnight echoes of Aughrim or Benburb with their lamentations, if they could know that their descendants were fools enough to be led by such a directory of knaves and cowards.

Ferguson argues that the versions in Hardiman's anthology, imitative of Thomas Moore, do not do justice to the 'savage sincerity' of the originals. And he demonstrates this, first by his own literal prose translations, and, conclusively, in vibrant poetry which in its very unconventionality of prosody and diction manages to express the Gaelic world through the English medium. Ferguson's translations are indeed an act of union.

Like Mangan and Ferguson, George Darley experimented daringly with prosody, but unlike them he did not did not express political allegiances in or through his poetry. He moved to London in 1820, when he was twenty-five. He coupled mathematical genius with shyness, and an embarrassing stammer. But, more than any of his contemporaries, he gave vent to a Keatsian adoration of beauty. His long poem *Nepenthe* roams over the globe, soars to heaven in elation and thuds down to earth in desolation. He is proof that the history of Irish literature extends beyond the context of its politics.

IV.

Having gained Catholic Emancipation, Daniel O'Connell launched a campaign which, it seemed, would consolidate his popular appeal at home, and increase his power of intimidation in Westminster. Indeed, for the next fifteen years Repeal of the Union was a carrot he dangled in Ireland, the answer to any national grievance, and a stick he could wave in Parliament in order to expedite reforms (Mangan quipped 'The Tories are friends of Peel; the Irish Rads. are friends of *re*-peal'). It was also an anachronism. Returning Ireland to the state it was in 'when I was born' (in 1775 – seven years prior to the period of Ireland's legislative independence which he is referring to) was a facile slogan. No Catholics could be returned to Grattan's autocratic Parliament. The Post-Union Kingdom of Britain and Ireland had, with O'Connell's help, moved toward the first intimations of democracy. With his call for Repeal, he was offering a re-match without the pieces he had taken; nor was he playing the same opponent. In the 1780s and 1790s England had had to contend with revolt in Europe, America and Ireland; in 1830 the revolution was an industrial one, which was transforming the country into an Empire – which the legion of Irish in the British forces would help to expand.

O'Connell's agenda was a liberal one; an abolitionist and supporter of civil rights, he favoured universal suffrage, and endorsed the struggle for independence in Belgium and South America. He was a constitutional politician, who balanced his call for repeal with continual expressions of loyalty to Queen Victoria. To pressurize the government he founded a series of societies, which were quickly suppressed. A Proclamation of 13 January 1831 forbade any Association under any name ('I'll make myself an Association!' O'Connell exclaimed). In 1833 he turned down the offer of the attorney-generalship ('I should be their servant – that is, their slave'). However, he co-operated with the Whigs to effect practical reforms – of the magistry, church establishment, and of tithes.

Discontentment with a tax levied on land to support the Established Church led to the Tithe War, a campaign of non-payment which started in Co. Kilkenny, in October 1830, and spread through Leinster and Munster. Established clergymen, such as the father of the novelist Joseph Sheridan Le Fanu, were financially disadvantaged. Government responded by sending in the police and the military. In 1831, twelve demonstrators were killed in one incident; eleven police and soldiers fell victim in another a few months later. The campaign of disobedience was supported by Archbishop MacHale and Bishop Doyle, and by many of O'Connell's followers, even though O'Connell publicly dissociated himself from it. It was resolved in the Tithe Rentcharge Act of 1838, which transferred tithe payment from occupiers to landlords.

O'Connell allied himself with Whig and Radical politicians in the Wichfield House Pact (1835), which engineered the resignation of Peel's Tory ministry, and saw the appointment of the Earl of Mulgrave as Lord Lieutenant, Viscount Morpeth as Chief Secretary and Thomas Drummond as Under-Secretary. The latter was particularly instrumental in reforming law enforcement, reorganizing the police, and suppressing the Orange Order. Effectively, between 1835 and 1840, Dublin Castle was regarded as an ally of Irish liberals and Catholics, a substantial number of whom were appointed to Crown offices. Yet O'Connell grew increasingly dissatisfied: the Poor Law of 1838 had extended the English relief system to Ireland, dividing the country into poor-law districts, each with a workhouse under the control of a board of guardians – he had urged instead for state aid and public works; the Municipal Corporations Act of 1840 had restricted municipal franchise to £10 householders and offered only limited powers of corporation. Drummond died in 1840; the following year the Tories returned to power, and O'Connell, who was voted lord mayor of Dublin, reverted to his call for Repeal. Developments in transport and the printing press facilitated a mass campaign, in which he was aided by such Catholic luminaries as Archbishop MacHale, but also by a group of young journalists who used the press to manipulate public opinion through nationalist propaganda. In October 1842, three graduates of Trinity College, Dublin, Thomas Davis, a Protestant barrister from Co. Cork, and two Catholics, John Blake Dillon and Charles Gavan Duffy, founded *The Nation*, a weekly newspaper, which was the mouthpiece for a movement of cultural nationalism that came to be known as Young Ireland. Inspired by Mazzini and influenced by Thomas Carlyle, Davis bolstered the spirit of nationality through a respect for Ireland's history, and through stirring ballads; his was an (idealized) self-reliant Ireland, its economy based on local industry. 'Racy of the soil', *The Nation* was intended for all Irishmen regardless of creed:

It must contain and represent all the races of Ireland. It must not be Celtic; it must not be Saxon; it must be Irish. The Brehon law, and the maxims of Westminster – the cloudy and lightning genius of the Gael, the placid strength of the Sacsanach, the marshalling insight of the Norman – a literature which shall exhibit in combination the passions and idioms of all, and which shall equally express our mind, in its romantic, its religious, its forensic, and its practical tendencies – finally, a native government, which shall know and rule by the might and right of all, yet yield to the arrogance of none – these are the components of such a nationality.

Initially appearing in a print-run of 12,000, the weekly could boast a readership of perhaps 250,000 at the height of its popularity.

For the Repeal Movement of 1842–43 O'Connell revived the techniques of the campaign for Catholic Emancipation, including nationwide fund-raising (through 'the repeal rent'), but he enhanced them by following the precepts of Theobald Mathew's temperance movement, which, in May 1841, claimed to count 4.3 million members (and effected a serious slump in the sale of whiskey). Between 1840 and 1843, Father Mathew conducted 350 major temperance missions, attracting crowds in excess of 10,000. O'Connell harnessed support from the Temperance movement for his monster meetings.

In the autumn of 1842 he declared 1843 the Repeal Year. Three million people enrolled in the National Repeal Association, which had been founded in 1840, and between the spring of 1843 and the autumn of 1845, fifty monster meetings were held, notably at historical sites across the three southern provinces, attracting, according to some estimates, a quarter of the population. At the meeting at Tara Hill in August 1843, some reports counted a crowd of 800,000. They were one-day or two-day collective spectacles with ritual pomp and symbolic circumstance. A great procession of bands, floats, tradesmen and fraternities carrying banners and wearing sashes would pass through triumphal arches; O'Connell's speech would be followed by an evening banquet for the Liberator and paying guests. 'The peaceable demeanour of the assembled multitudes is one of the most alarming symptoms' wrote Sir Edward Sugden, the Irish Lord Chancellor, to Sir Robert Peel.

Emancipation had been granted on the vague threat of Civil War; now Peel refused to be intimidated. Government found an excuse to proscribe a monster meeting planned for Clontarf in the autumn of 1843; O'Connell, who never publicly advocated unconstitutionality, cancelled the proceedings. Following his call for arbitration courts to replace the courts of justice, he was convicted of conspiracy and imprisoned in May 1844; 'by a miracle', the Lords quashed the sentence, and in September O'Connell emerged from Richmond gaol, triumphantly waving a green cap; a cheering crowd returned him in grand procession to his house (from which he had sneaked back to the prison earlier that day, after he had been silently released the day before). However, his indomitable spirit had been affected, and as he grew more cautious and conciliatory, a rift emerged between the chieftain of Old Ireland and the middle-class intelligentsia of Young Ireland. It had been tested by O'Connell's short fling with Federalism; it was widened by the University Question. In 1845 Peel issued charters for three non-denominational colleges, in Belfast, Cork and Galway. The 'godless colleges' were opposed by O'Connell and MacHale (as well as by papal prescripts and the 1850 synod at Thurles), but they were supported by Young Ireland, who advocated national cultural unity. In September 1845 Thomas Davis died of scarlet fever, and John Mitchel emerged as the new, and more radical, leader of the Young Ireland movement. Their rupture with O'Connell was determined by the latter's call, in 1846, for 'peace resolutions' and total renunciation of any use of force. The Young Irelanders felt that this would mean total surrender to the new Whig government. Mediation between the two parties by William Smith O'Brien failed; during a debate, with O'Connell's son John officiating, Thomas Francis Meagher delivered his famous sword speech, which dealt a blow to any collaboration of Old and Young Ireland:

> I do not disclaim the use of arms as immoral nor do I believe it is the truth to say that the God of Heaven withholds His sanction from the use of arms.... Be it for the defence, or be it for the assertion of a nation's liberty, I look upon the sword as a sacred weapon.

In January 1847 O'Brien and the Young Irelanders founded the Irish Confederation; with its disavowal of physical force and its hearkening back to 1782 its programme seemed a copy of O'Connell's Repeal. Within eighteen months the Confederation counted 45,000 members in 224 Confederate Clubs throughout the country.

V.

O'Connell had used Repeal as a panacea for Irish grievances, but cataclysmic events made the movement an irrelevant middle-class luxury. Ireland in 1845 was the most densely populated country in Europe, with over eight million inhabitants, over six million of whom lived on the land. Over half of the population subsisted on the potato; when the crop failed, as it did, wholly or partially, sixteen times between 1826 and 1842, starvation followed. The Great Famine eclipsed earlier disasters; it brought about the greatest transformation of Ireland ever. People died of starvation or of famine-related diseases, such as typhus and famine fever. Estimates of the death toll range from 500,000 to 1.5 million; more than one eighth of the population emigrated before the end of the decade; and within twenty years the population of Ireland was halved. There is some difference of opinion about the time span of the Famine, but its onset was the failure of the potato crop in 1845. *The Nation* reported on 25 October of that year that 'fully one half of the crop on which millions of our countrymen are half-starved every year is, this season, totally destroyed or in progress to destruction.' Peel averted a catastrophe by importing £100,000 worth of Indian corn from the United States, which was sold on to nearly 700 relief committees, preventing profiteering and keeping down the price of grain. Local committees were organised to oversee the distribution of food and the raising of funds, and relief works were instituted through the Board of Works.

When the crop failed completely the following year Peel had been superseded by Lord John Russell. Charles Trevelyan, assistant secretary to the treasury, remained in office, but he subscribed to the *laissez faire* doctrine of the Whig government, which looked askance on state interference. 'It must be thoroughly understood,' said Lord Russell, 'that we cannot feed the people'. The cost of Irish poverty fell on Irish property: five million pounds was to be raised from taxes on landlords. O'Connell urged the government to do its duty, and pressed for a radical emendation of the law of property, making it illegal for a landlord to evict a tenant without financial compensation. But many estates were heavily burdened, and with the loss of income from rents, bankruptcy threatened. Some landlords assisted in the emigration of their tenants; 106,000 boarded coffin ships in 1846, by 1851 the figure had risen to a quarter of a million – one out of nine who left from Cork died before reaching America. Charitable organizations raised funds for soup-kitchens; the Quaker Central Relief

Committee, the Irish Relief Committee, the General Relief Committee, the Mansion House Committee and the British Relief Committee (supported by Queen Victoria) raised nearly half a million pounds in charity. Donations came from abroad, as did charity workers such as Asenath Nicholson, who has left harrowing accounts of the utter deprivation in the country. Foreign journalists flocked to the famine-stricken country, their reports contributing to the relief of towns like Schull and Skibbereen. At first, British public reaction was sympathetic, but sympathy gave way to suspicion in 1846 and 1847, and to revulsion at agrarian revolts and the Rising of 1848.

Eye-witness accounts of the famine are littered with the phrase 'a living skeleton'. Asenath Nicholson writes that in her childhood she 'had been frightened with the stories of ghosts, and had seen actual skeletons, but imagination had come short of the sight of this ... walking skeleton'. The gothic horror in the fiction of Maturin and Sheridan Le Fanu was turned into reality. Nicholson leaves it to her reader's imagination to conjecture why the dogs on Arranmore 'look so fat and shining ... where there is no food for the people'. Carleton was to refer to peasants as 'Frankensteins', and called ruthless agents 'vampyres' (over sixty years before Bram Stoker published *Dracula*); in *Red Hall or the Baronet's Daughter* (1852), he describes scenes of cannibalism:

> all the impulses of nature and affection were not merely banished from the heart, but superseded by the most frightful peals of insane mirth, cruelty, and the horrible appetite of the ghoul and vampire. Some were found tearing the flesh from the bodies of the carcasses that were stretched beside them ... [F]athers have been known to make a wolfish meal upon the dead bodies of their offspring.[1]

Trevelyan was not alone in believing that the Famine was divine providence. Isaac Butt, erstwhile editor of the *Dublin University Magazine* and political economist, called it 'the fearful blight with which it has pleased an all-wise God to visit the food of her people'; it was a sentiment echoed in the famine poetry of Mangan, Richard D'Alton Williams, Thomas D'Arcy McGee, and Jane Francesca Elgee, all contributors to *The Nation*.

John Mitchel claimed that 'The Almighty, indeed, sent the potato blight' but that 'the English created the famine'. O'Connell had

---

1 Melissa Fegan, *Literature and the Irish Famine, 1815–1919* (Oxford University Press, 2002) p. 158.

claimed in the Commons in 1846 that more wheat, barley and meal had been exported from Ireland to Britain in 1845 than in any other of the three previous years. To Mitchel, the exportation of food during the famine to the value of £15,000 was tantamount to genocide on the part of the British government. In actual fact, the imports of grain considerably exceeded the exports, which had dwindled from nearly half a million tons just before the famine to 146,000 in 1847.

O'Connell made his last appearance in the House of Commons in March 1847; Disraeli described him as 'a feeble old man muttering from a table.' He delivered his final plea:

> Ireland is in your hands. If you do not save her, she cannot save herself. I solemnly call on you to recollect that I predict with the sincerest conviction that one-fourth of her population will perish unless you come to her relief.

By August, three million people were fed at public expense. The burden was placed on the poor law system; apart from the workhouses, which were seriously over-populated, outdoor relief was allowed. O'Connell had died on his way to Rome, on 15 May 1847. Where 1847 had yielded a blightless, albeit small, harvest, 1848 saw another disastrous failure; yet again the treasury had to support the Irish poor law unions. In 1848 and 1849 Encumbered Estates Acts were introduced in an attempt to transfer bankrupt estates to more 'responsible' landlords who were awarded indefeasible titles by the court. They did not provide the intended influx of British capital.

O'Connell's instinctive plea for the free sale and fixity of tenure formed the basis of the political ideology of James Fintan Lalor, the son of an O'Connellite MP, who realized that Repeal was 'an impracticable absurdity'. In a series of letters to *The Nation* he preached 'moral insurrection' (*pace* O'Connell's 'moral force'), rent strike and social revolution, thus establishing the link between nationality and the law of the land which became the crucial issue in Irish politics through the Land League of 1879–82 right down to James Connolly, who would claim him as his ideological forebear. Smith O'Brien rejected Lalor's doctrine, fearing a 'war of property', but it enticed Mitchel to incite a peasant-led revolution. He broke with *The Nation* and the Confederation, and in February 1847 he founded the *United Irishman*, in which he advocated insurrection: 'I hold it is a more hideous national calamity for ten men to be cast out to die of hunger, like dogs in ditches, than for ten thousand to be hewn to pieces, fighting like men and Christians in defence of their rights.' In May 1848 he was convicted of treason-felony and transported to Tasmania.

What did spur the Young Irelanders to take up arms were the nationalist revolution in Italy in 1847, and the bloodless popular revolution in Paris in early 1848. Duffy would recall, much later, that 'the men who a few weeks before had fearlessly resisted anarchy now as fearlessly embraced revolution'. He issued a call for a 'National Guard', following the example of the French Revolutionaries (and the Volunteers of 1782). Meagher returned from Paris with an Irish version of the tricolor (an orange, white and green flag surmounted by an Irish pike). The immediate cause for the insurrection was Lord Russell's suspension of *Habeas Corpus* in Ireland. With the *United Irishman* suppressed, John Martin founded the *Irish Felon*, named in honour of Mitchel, the 'state prisoner', Lalor contributing incendiary articles before he was arrested.

The Young Irelanders decided to strike; they met in Tipperary, and toured other counties to muster support from the peasantry, who were discouraged by the clergy. Hampered by a distinct lack of discipline and organization, and the honourable but prevaricating public behaviour of Smith O'Brien, the 'rebellion' (or rather, the 'escapade', as O'Brien later dubbed it) which occurred almost by accident in Co. Tipperary culminated in the siege of a house in Ballingarry which has entered the history books as the Battle for the Widow McCormack's cabbage patch. The 'escapists' were rounded up; O'Brien was sentenced to death, but was transported, with Meagher and Martin, to Tasmania. James Stephens, an apprentice railway engineer, who had stood beside O'Brien in Ballingarry, escaped to Paris.

Mitchel failed to appreciate that a starved peasantry had, literally, no stomach for armed revolt. Central to his *Jail Journal* is a dialogue between 'Ego' and 'Doppelganger'. Ego poses the question 'Which is the more hideous evil – three seasons of famine-slaughter in the midst of heaven's abundance, at the point of foreign bayonets, with all its train of debasing diseases and more debasing vices, or a thirty years' war to scourge the stranger from your soil, though it leave that soil a smoking wilderness?' He concludes: 'Because they would not fight, they have been made to rot off the face of the earth, that so they might learn at last how deadly a sin is patience and perseverance under a stranger's yoke.' But the Irish people, Doppelganger retorts, have not yet learned their lesson: 'They are becoming, apparently, more moral and constitutional than ever; and O'Connell's son points to "Young Ireland," hunted, chained, condemned, transported, and says: "Behold the fate of those who would have made us depart from the legal and peaceful doctrines of the Liberator!'"

The Famine utterly transformed Ireland's writers.[1] Samuel Ferguson, the staunch Unionist, became a Protestant Repealer; Aubrey De Vere, the Wordsworthian dreamer, became a man of action; Thomas D'Arcy McGee turned from antiquarianism to politics, Dennis Florence MacCarthy and Richard D'Alton Williams from levity to lamentation; the genteel Lady Wilde became the seditious Speranza; and Mangan found in it a correlative for his personal nightmares. Mangan died in 1849, the year in which the harvest was good, and Queen Victoria visited Dublin and Belfast, drawing a symbolic (but not an actual) end to the famine. Its enormity, captured by Cecil Woodham Smith in *The Great Hunger* (1962), would continue to inform prose through Annie Keary's *Castle Daly* (1875) and Margaret Brew's *The Chronicles of Castle Cloyne* (1886), through Liam O'Flaherty's *Famine* (1937) right up to Joseph O'Connor's *The Star of the Sea* (2003).

VI.

The Encumbered Estates Acts, which allowed creditors to purchase land, did not yield British investment, but it did help to bring about a change in land ownership. The famine had led to a decline in the value of land. By 1859 over £21 million of estates had been sold to nearly 7,500 purchasers. The vast majority of these were Irish entrepreneurs and landed gentry. The encumbered estates courts did not offer any compensation to the tenants, and many of the new owners improved their estates by evicting tenants and increasing rents. The number of farmers increased as the number of agrarian labourers declined. In the South, tenant protection societies sprung up, often under the guidance of the clergy, using passive resistance as their weapon to bargain for fair rents. In Ulster, tenants were claiming their rights to sell their tenancy to the highest bidder. William Sharman Crawford, a Co. Down landowner and radical MP, and James McKnight of Belfast founded the Ulster Tenant Right Association, which received support from the Presbyterian general assembly. In 1850 they combined with Gavan Duffy, John Gray (of the *Freeman's Journal*) and Frederick Lucas (of *The Tablet*) in the Irish Tenant

---

1 Fegan, *Literature and the Irish Famine*, p.168.

League, which lobbied for land reform. They liaised with Whigs, radicals and Peelites to topple the Government of Lord Derby in December 1852. Their position was weakened by political ineptitude and by what 'Father Prout' dubbed the 'Cullenisation of Ireland'. The ultramontane Archbishop Cullen, with a long and – in terms of Irish clerical appointments – influential career in the Vatican behind him, advocated supreme Papal authority. He deprived the non-sectarian League of clerical grass-root support. As the decade wore on, the League lost its force. A. M. Sullivan, proprietor of *The Nation*, remarked that 'all was silence' in Ireland.

The clamour was building up outside in the New World to which the dispossessed and the insurgents had fled. In Paris, a hotbed of political exiles, James Stephens and John O'Mahony talked of founding a secret revolutionary society. O'Mahony emigrated to New York, where he encountered strong nationalist and anti-British sentiments among the Irish Americans. In 1858 he founded the Fenian Brotherhood; at the same time Stephens established a counterpart society in Dublin, which came to be known as the Irish Republican Brotherhood. The Brotherhood had none of the operatic gallantry of earlier revolutionary movements; it had the hierarchical cell structure of a terrorist organization. Its intent was simply to rid Ireland of British power as soon as possible. Gustave Cluseret, who would later, in 1871, become the military commander of the Paris Commune, summed up its programme as 'first, complete independence of Ireland from English power; second, a free church and a free state; third, the republican form of government'.

The IRB used the funeral of the Young Irelander Terence Bellew MacManus in 1861 as an occasion for revolutionary propaganda (American Fenians accompanied the remains from the States to Ireland). It needed a regular medium, and in 1863 the secret society went public through a Dublin weekly, the *Irish People*, which was edited by John O'Leary, Charles Kickham and Thomas Clarke Luby. Cullen, who claimed that the Fenians were socialist agnostics, declared that, as members of a secret society, the Fenians were excommunicated. Kickham, a devout Catholic, retorted that 'if the people were submissive to the clergy in politics ... Ireland would be allowed to perish without a hand being raised to help her'. Cullen lent his weight to the National Association, founded in 1864 to foster ties between Irish Catholics and British radicals; it promoted land reform, disestablishment and denominational education, but it got bogged down in a lengthy dispute about its rules.

With the end of the American Civil War the time seemed right for an armed insurrection. It released a host of battle-hardened Irish-American soldiers for service in Ireland. In 1865, the Fenians could rely on 50,000 men and 6,000 firearms; they could even rely on some support from British forces which they had infiltrated. Stephens planned an insurrection before the end of the year, but the government intervened: in September, the *Irish People*, which served as the IRB's headquarters, was raided. Cullen applauded the government for suppressing a weekly which spread 'the most pernicious and poisonous maxims'. Luby, O'Leary, Kickham and Jeremiah O'Donovan Rossa were arrested, tried for treason-felony, and gaoled. Stephens once again managed to escape. The following year *Habeas Corpus* was suspended, and the Brotherhood was dismantled by widespread arrests. The American Fenians were fragmented by internal power struggles, purportedly brought about by failed attempts to invade Canada. Reaching New York, Stephens found himself replaced by Colonel Thomas J. Kelly, who led an insurrection in March 1867, which failed within a day.

It attested to the power of the Fenians' structure, their resolve, and their widespread support among Irish Americans, and the Irish in Britain, that, unlike earlier insurrectionist movements, the Brotherhood survived these fiascos. In fact, in their attempts to root out the rebels, the British government contributed to their popularity. The impending execution of a Fenian in May 1867 led to widespread protests – the sentence was transmuted. In September some thirty armed Fenians tried to rescue Col. Kelly and another prisoner from a police van in Manchester, killing an unarmed policeman. In November five men, thought to be innocent of the murder, were sentenced to death; three were executed. The government had given the Brotherhood its 'Manchester Martyrs'. One of the accused had cried 'God save Ireland' from the dock; it was used as the refrain in a ballad by T. D. Sullivan – set to the tune of the American Civil War Song 'Tramp, tramp, tramp, the boys are marching' – it became the Irish nationalist anthem (up to recently it was taught in Irish primary schools).

The leaders of 'the bold Fenian men', and the radical nationalists associated with them, were respectable middle-class individuals, many of them journalists and school-teachers, who refused to be enslaved by the British system – but were not averse to enslaving others. Mitchel, their forebear, who refused the post of chief executive of the Fenian Brotherhood, held strong anti-abolitionist views, which he published in the American *Southern Citizen* and the *Daily*

News, for which he was sentenced to five months in prison. They were not averse to passing orders for the assassination of their opponents – A. M. Sullivan survived his death sentence, but his fellow Young Irelander Thomas D'Arcy McGee was liquidated for denouncing the Fenian raid on Ottawa. They, in turn, had to suffer brutalities in English prisons (recorded in O'Donovan Rossa's *Irish Rebels in English Prisons* [1874]). Yet these men had popular appeal with their heroic, if not autocratic, gestures of defiance – Kickham, who at a young age had lost his hearing in a gunpowder accident, refusing to plead since the court had ruled evidence by Luby inadmissible; O'Leary, 'all that aristocratic dream nourished amid little shops and little farms', shaking 'his noble head', denying the right of an English court to sentence him in his eloquent speech from the dock. John Keegan Casey's funeral in Dublin was said to have been attended by 50,000 people. O'Donovan Rossa's was the occasion for a famous oration by Patrick Pearse. In the heyday of their lives, and with the Fenians and Land Leaguers marginalized by Parnell, they were seen to represent a lofty idealism which had been sacrificed to Mammon. Canon Sheehan pits this idealism against 'the sty of materialism … in the present age' in *The Graves of Kilmorna* (1915). This idealism they passed on to the Gaelic Association for the Preservation and Cultivation of National Pastimes (Gaelic Athletic Association), which was founded by Michael Cusack (model for the Citizen in Joyce's *Ulysses*) and Maurice Davin in the billiard room of Miss Hayes' Commercial Hotel, Thurles, on 1 November 1884.

Political idealism informs Kickham's idyllic picture in his vastly popular novel, *Knocknagow* (1873, 1879) of a rural setting, which is destroyed by the oppressive system of land tenure. Malcolm Brown, in *The Politics of Irish Literature from Thomas Davis to W. B. Yeats*, calls it 'the most important single literary work ever written by a leading Irish revolutionist'. But the chief literary merit of O'Leary, John Boyle O'Reilly and, to a lesser extent of Kickham too, lay in their patronage of writers who would play a role in Ireland's literary Renaissance. Rose Kavanagh, who nursed Kickham in his final years, became one of the promising young Renaissance women poets, with verse full of passionate energy, her career cut short by her untimely death. O'Leary passed on his passion for belles-lettres and his autocratic set of values to W. B. Yeats, and encouraged the lesser talent of Katharine Tynan. O'Reilly offered the up-and-coming Renaissance writers a paid podium in his *Boston Pilot*.

Dramatically, Fenianism made its first popular appearance in Dion Boucicault's *The Shaughraun*, a play with a stage-Irish hero and a nationalist message. When it opened in London in 1875 Boucicault wrote an open letter to Disraeli, demanding the release of Fenian prisoners.

The Land War formed a popular subject of Irish novels in the 1880s and 1890s.[1] The British novelist Anthony Trollope contributed *The Landleaguers* (1883); Rosa Mulholland, sister-in-law of Lord Russell of Killowen, wrote *Marcella Grace* (1886), which offers the creation of a Catholic gentry as the solution of the Land Question; and Emily Lawless's *Hurrish* (1886) won the praise of Gladstone. The land war forms the haunting backdrop to George Moore's *A Drama in Muslin* (1886). Moore, a Catholic landlord from Co. Mayo, studied art in Paris, where he came under the spell of Zola's naturalism. He returned to Ireland, where, with his cousin Edward Martyn, W. B. Yeats and Lady Gregory he set out to establish a National Theatre.

VII.

That William Ewart Gladstone, the Liberal Party leader, when elected Prime Minister in 1867, declared his mission was 'to pacify Ireland' bears out the impact of Fenian violence on public opinion. He tried to effect what Cullen and the National Association had failed to do – curb Irish popular support for Fenianism by curing discontent; in Irish Catholics he found his '*corps d'armée*'. He addressed their grievances in a way which far outdid earlier reforms (nearly approximating to Cluseret's reading of the Fenian programme). In 1869 he disestablished the Church of Ireland; in 1870 he sponsored an Irish Land Bill; in 1886 he introduced the first Home Rule for Ireland Bill. Disestablishment by and large disowned Ireland's minority 'state religion' (it guaranteed the extant clergy their income for life, but most chose to take a capital sum). Gladstone's first Land Act made the customary Ulster tenant right into law, allowed for compensation of tenants evicted for other reasons than non-payment of rent, and of departing tenants who had made improvements to the land. It was hampered in its execution by the complicated procedures of the courts.

Both measures alarmed Protestant conservatives, who came to believe that it was in the interest of both Britain and Ireland that the latter should manage its own affairs. Appeasement of the Fenians was

---

1 James H. Murphy, *Ireland, A Social, Cultural and Literary History, 1791–1891* (Dublin: Four Courts Press, 2003) pp.162–3.

part of their policy. The Amnesty Association successfully campaigned for the release of Fenian prisoners. Its president, Isaac Butt, founded the Home Government Association in 1870, with the intent to garner support for an Irish parliament. The Home Government Association was dissolved in 1873, following the defeat of Gladstone's Bill for University reform, and the Home Rule League was established in its place, embracing the popular causes of land reform and denominational education with political alacrity. That same year the Supreme Council of the IRB announced a cessation of violence. Some Fenians flirted with the League's mainstream politics, and were condemned by the Supreme Council. In the election of 1874, the Home Rulers won fifty-nine seats.

The Fenians were not restraining themselves into any straitjacket of constitutionality. Among the Fenian prisoners released in 1871 was John Devoy. He united the American factions in Clan-na-Gael, the 'Irish nation in the United States', which, from 1875, acted in concert with the IRB in Ireland, assisting it with money, war material and men. In the 1880s Clan-na-Gael initiated a war of terror in English cities, and Jeremiah O'Donovan Rossa, a grocer from Skibbereen who had founded the Phoenix National and Literary Society in 1856, directed a 'dynamite war'. In 1884, London was in terror of Fenian threats to bomb the city. The House of Commons and Scotland Yard were targeted, as were railway stations and London Bridge. The campaign was denounced by the IRB, O'Leary saying there were things a man must not do, even for his country.

What did make the Fenians exploit constitutionality was the agrarian unrest, caused by the agricultural depression, and the rise of a young Protestant landlord and Home Ruler called Charles Stewart Parnell. In the House of Commons he had followed the policies of obstruction initiated by Joseph Gillis Biggar (a Belfast man, and member of the IRB's Supreme Council), preventing parliament from getting on with its business by means of interminable speeches. Butt and the majority of the Home Rulers disapproved, the Irish people did not – nor did the Fenians. In the autumn of 1878 Devoy devised a plan for agrarian unrest which hearkened back to Fintan Lalor, and which would involve constitutional agitation by the Home Rule movement. He called it the 'New Departure'. Butt died in 1879; during the spring and summer negotiations took place between Devoy, Parnell, who was heading the obstructionist Home Rule parliamentary faction, and a Fenian called Michael Davitt, whose family had been evicted during the Famine when he was four years old.

Davitt, who had been imprisoned for seven years, maintained that Fenian violence 'had nothing to offer to the mass of the Irish people except the experiences of penal servitude and the records of the abortive rising of 1867'. He was expelled by Kickham and O'Leary, the conservative leaders of the IRB. In August 1879 he founded the Land League in Co. Mayo; the Irish National Land League was established on 21 October, with Parnell as president. Its objects were: 'first to bring about a reduction of rackrents; second to facilitate the obtaining of the ownership of the soil by the occupiers of the soil'. In November Parnell described the condition of Ireland as a great 'strike' against the payment of unjust rents: fair rents should be paid for thirty years, after which the land should become the property of the occupant. Under the banner of the political objective to gain 'the three F's (fair rent, free sale, fixity of tenure) the Land League launched 'a kind of guerilla social welfare' against landlords, not ostensibly by using physical force but by placing victims in a 'moral coventry'. The first victim of such social ostracism was a Captain Hugh Boycott, the English-born agent of Lord Erne's estates in Co. Mayo, and 'boycotting' was named after him. He responded by bringing in Ulster Protestants (Orangemen) to harvest the land, but they had to be protected by 1,000 troops. The League spread through the Southern provinces, and was generously supported by American funds, making the country, Davitt claimed, 'absolutely ungovernable'. It launched its weekly, *United Ireland* in 1881. The Land War was not completely peaceful: there was a sharp rise in agrarian crime, including the assassination of landlords and agents. It convinced the historian William Edward Hartpole Lecky of Trinity College, Dublin, 'how radically and profoundly unfit Ireland was for self-government'. Anna Parnell would claim that the Land League became 'a government *de facto*'.

In 1881 *Habeas Corpus* was suspended, and Gladstone conceded the League's demands in his second Land Act, which granted the three F's, and instituted a Land Commission to oversee its execution. The main objectives of the Land League had been achieved in the second Land Act, but Parnell objected that it did not extend to leaseholders and that it did not protect tenants whose rents were in arrears. Later that year the leaders of the League were put in Kilmainham Jail. Within a few days the Land League issued its 'No Rent manifesto', urging tenants to withhold payment. To complement – and indeed continue – the League's activities, a Ladies Land League was instituted under the leadership of Parnell's sister, Anna (Davitt later claimed that they were 'honester and more sincere than the men' – that honesty informs Anna's *The Tale of a Great Sham* (MS version 1907; 1986) which describes the League's duality in placating the more powerful landlords). After the arrests, agrarian crime intensified. Gladstone and Parnell reached an agreement in the Kilmainham Treaty of 1882: the Land Act was to be amended, the League's leaders were released, and Parnell would use his influence to pacify the country.

The new alliance was tested by two gruesome murders in the Phoenix Park. W. E. 'Buckshot' Forster had resigned as Chief Secretary over the release of Parnell. His successor, Lord Frederick Cavendish was a week in the job when he and the Under-Secretary, Thomas Burke, a Catholic Irishman, were butchered outside the Vice-Regal Lodge with surgical knives by the Invincibles, a break-away group of Fenians. Parnell felt his work was being undone; he seriously considered resigning as leader of the Irish Parliamentary party but was dissuaded by Gladstone (whose wife was related to Cavendish). Gladstone was forced to maintain coercion, which Parnell was compelled to condemn, but, if anything, the Phoenix Park murders strengthened Parnell's position as party leader. He side-lined Davitt, and replaced the Land League with the Irish National League, under Tim Harrington, Tim Healy and William O'Brien.

The League was a well-organized constituency organization for the Parliamentary Party; it organised county conventions for elections of parliamentary candidates and collected financial support. Its aims were: '(1) national self-government; (2) land law reform; (3) local self-government; (4) extension of the parliamentary and municipal franchise; (5) development and encouragement of the labour and industrial resources of Ireland.' It garnered support from the Catholic clergy. In the election of 1885 the League won 85 of the 103 Irish seats (including a majority of one in Ulster), and Parnell, who had urged his supporters to vote for the Conservatives, held the balance of power. Home Rule became an unavoidable parliamentary issue. The Conservatives had made advances to Parnell through the new Viceroy, Lord Carnarvon, but he lost influence, and his party found a patriotic cause in resisting Irish self-government. Their administration was short-lived. When Gladstone returned to power in February 1886, he had become convinced that Home Rule was inevitable; in April he presented the first Home Rule Bill. It offered limited self-government, with restricted legislative functions of the Irish assembly, and circumscribed fiscal independence (Ireland would not control customs and excise), leaving ultimate authority with Westminster.

Parnell accepted the Bill as a first incontrovertible step. Tory Britain and Protestant Ulster, for whom the southern provinces were a rural backwater, combined to defeat the Bill in June, and the Conservatives returned to power.

The issue of tenancy continued to dominate Irish politics. A depression in prices for cattle and dairy left many tenants in arrears; it prompted the Irish National League to issue, in October, 'The Plan of Campaign': if the landlords did not accept a reduced rent all the tenants on an estate would pay no rent at all, transferring the money into a fund for evicted tenants. The strategy of non-payment was engineered by Healy, Harrington, O'Brien and John Dillon; it affected 203 estates and involved some 20,000 tenants. It was supported by Archbishop William Walsh and Archbishop Thomas William Croke; Parnell initially remained aloof, and Lord Salisbury's government denounced it as 'an unlawful and criminal conspiracy'. Salisbury appointed his nephew, Arthur 'Bloody' Balfour, to crush it. Balfour introduced a Perpetual Coercion Act in 1887; Dillon and O'Brien were arrested; Croke issued a 'No Tax Manifesto'. On 9 September, the day that O'Brien was ordered to appear before magistrates, a crowd of tenants gathered in Mitchelstown; the police opened fire, killing three people. General unrest and boycotting followed throughout the south. The government courted the Vatican, which issued a Papal Rescript in 1888, condemning the Plan, and in 1889 it tried to muster combined resistance by landlords. To this O'Brien responded by founding the Tenants' Defence Association, which was supported by Parnell. When Dillon and O'Brien jumped bail in October and escaped via France to America, Parnell empowered them to raise money.

In 1887 Richard Pigott made an attempt to implicate Parnell in the Phoenix Park murders by a series of forged letters which were published in *The Times*. A Special Commission was set up, and Parnell's counsel, Sir Charles Russell, unmasked Pigott by asking him to write down a number of words; he misspelled 'hesitancy', as he had done in one of the letters. Parnell's position as the 'uncrowned King of Ireland' and his alliance with Gladstone seemed unassailable. The conservative and liberal majority of 188 had shrunk by 1890 to 70. Home Rule beckoned. Before the year was out, Gladstone severed the compact, and Parnell was dethroned. Parnell had been cited as co-respondent in an action for divorce filed by Captain William O'Shea, erstwhile Home Rule MP for Clare, and the husband of Katharine Wood. The public scandal destroyed Parnell's reputation in England; the English nonconformist liberals denounced him, the Catholic clergy followed suit, and Gladstone had no choice but to repudiate his alliance with the Irish Parliamentary Party as long as it was headed by Parnell. On 1 December the Irish Party met under Parnell's chairmanship in Committee Room 15. In the heated debate, one of Parnell's supporters remarked that Gladstone seemed to be the master of the party. Tim Healy retorted, 'Who is to be the mistress of the party?' Parnell refused to resign, and the party split into several factions.

The by-elections of 1891 were fought with bitter recriminations from Parnellites and anti-Parnellites. The former condemned the role of the Catholic Church in 'the Chief's' downfall; the latter homed in on his reckless arrogance and immorality. Parnell campaigned ceaselessly; in Ennis lime was thrown in his eyes; on 27 September he spoke in Galway, his eye bandaged and his arm in a sling. He died at home in Brighton on 6 October, with Katharine, now his wife, by his side. Arthur Griffith would later remark that 'the era of constitutional possibilities for Irish nationality ended on the day Charles Stewart Parnell died'.

In January 1893 Gladstone introduced his second Home Rule Bill, again offering restricted self-government. It was eventually forced through the Commons, but was rejected by the Lords. The following year Gladstone retired, devoting himself to bible studies; his successor, Lord Roseberry, did not share his mission of bringing justice to Ireland through Home Rule.

VIII.

W. B. Yeats claimed that the Irish Literary Renaissance sprang from the lull after the death of Parnell. In actual fact, it grew from the intellectual optimism which had been fostered by the Land League. Under its rays a proliferation of societies sprouted, all sharing the belief that a cultural awareness would benefit the Irish at home and abroad, and have a beneficial socio-economic effect. In London, in February 1883, the Southwark Irish Literary Club was founded by Francis Fahy, a civil servant of the Board of Works, who had settled in London in 1873, and had become involved in the Southwark Branch of the Land and Labour League.

The Southwark Club grew out of the Southwark Junior Irish Literary Club, which had been established in 1881 to counteract the 'sad but well-known fact that the children of Irish fathers and mothers in London are growing up with no knowledge of the land of their fathers, or knowing it only by the music-hall ditty, or the sneer of the daily paper where prejudice holds it up to scorn'. Meetings of this club were held every Sunday, and children were admitted for one penny, for which they were given an Irish book from John Denvir's Irish Penny Library – which, together with Edmund Downey's Irish Library was probably the most successful Irish popularist publishing venture in the late nineteenth century. A central committee had been established in London to administer the several branches that had sprung up throughout England. It actively participated in Irish relief work, raising money through concerts for 'the destitute poor of Loughrea'. And it gave financial and educational support to the Gaelic Union, the precursor of the Gaelic League.

Literature for the sake of literature was as unthinkable to the founding members of the Southwark Literary Society as it had been to the leaders of the Young Ireland movement, upon which the club was grafted. More than being just a gathering of 'ladies and gentlemen' with an active or passive interest in Irish letters, the club offered the opportunity for 'active propagandism', of 'becoming acquainted with the true facts of the history' of Ireland, and of counteracting the English 'charges made against the Irish people'. Among its literary papers and lectures, which championed Mangan, Kickham and the poets of *The Nation*, can be found such titles as 'The Cost of Provincialism', 'The Everyday Life of an Irish Labourer', and 'Labour Representation in Ireland'.

In 1886 Fahy gained the support of W. P. Ryan, whose novel *The Heart of Tipperary* (1893) depicts the attempts by leaders of the Land League to free the Irish lower classes from the shackles of violently repressive forces. The club gained rapid support from Home Rule politicians, such as Justin McCarthy and Richard Barry O'Brien, who lectured in November 1883 on 'Political Evolution in Ireland', and from such litterateurs as D. J. O'Donoghue, who devoted his maiden speech on 30 October 1886 to condemning English critics of the densest ignorance, unfairness and prejudice with regard to Irish writers. Its number of active members more than doubled, and included the Irish Irelander D. P. Moran, who would later describe W. B. Yeats's involvement in the Renaissance as 'one of the most glaring frauds that the credulous Irish people have ever swallowed'. Its President was T. D. Sullivan, Lord Mayor and MP, editor of *The Nation*, leader of the Plan of Campaign, and, as 'T. D. S.', author of propaganda verse.

For Yeats, who paid his first visit to the Club on 21 March 1888, the Club espoused all the values that he, under O'Leary's guidance, was renouncing. As journalists, men like Fahy, Moran and Ryan did not shun rhetoric to spread the word and to establish a popularist movement with an appeal similar to that held by the Young Irelanders. In 1891, with the help of T. W. Rolleston and Standish O'Grady, Yeats set out to transform the Club into the Irish Literary Society. At the age of 21 he had expressed a wish for revival literature to reach 'the great concourse of the people', but once the Irish Literary Society and its Dublin counterpart were established he began to challenge their social and political aspirations. Rather than aiming to reach the masses, he was 'anxious to … make the upper classes read'. He lay 'to the door of rhetoric that fault of the Irish character, which made it possible for a certain type of Irishman to be perfectly sincere on the other side tomorrow'. He argued against the Gaelicisation of Ireland. He preferred mythical histories to the chronologies of Ireland's colonized plight, which were deemed essential reading by most original revivalists.

When in 'To Ireland in the Coming Times' Yeats claimed 'Nor may I less be counted one / With Davis, Mangan, Ferguson' he was responding to the criticism that he, and his friends from the higher echelons of society – O'Leary, O'Grady, Sigerson, Rolleston, Todhunter – had refined the spirit of Young Ireland from the heated air of the popular platform to the luminous ether of the literary salon. On 23 April 1899, he unfolded his plans for a Irish National Theatre in what he must have considered a stirring address to the Society. The reactions were less than enthusiastic. Clement Shorter pointed out in the ensuing discussion that 'mere attempts to appeal to a limited audience was the way in which Mr. Yeats could render the largest and most thorough service to the country he loved so well'.

Polarisation between the Yeatsian literary ideas and the political and social intentions of Ryan, Moran and Fahy was inevitable. Ryan set up the colportage of Gavan Duffy's New Irish Library Scheme, selling 3,000 copies of Davis's *The Patriot Parliament* in less than four weeks. Eventually, disgruntled with Duffy's dictatorial management, despondent about the elitism of the Irish Society, disappointed with its noncommittal stance, he, together with D. P. Moran, became one of the society's most forthright critics, specifically in Father Thomas Finlay's *New Ireland Review*, which in the 1890s offered the Irish Irelanders' alternative to the Celtic Twilight.

Fahy became the London President of the Gaelic League, which had been founded by Eoin MacNeill and Douglas Hyde in an effort to deanglicize Ireland and to revive the Irish language. As the League slowly but gradually increased its middle-class membership, counting 600 branches by 1908, the Irish Literary Society withdrew further into its elitist shell. The contemporary press time and again criticized its alienated position. Of Rolleston, one of its original foremen, it was pointed out that 'suavity and sympathy carried him a long way', but that 'a sensitive shrinking from anything extreme or revolutionary, an inability now and then to note an honest heart under anything rude and crude in form, a half belief in Carlylean dogmatism, a dash of stoicism, all kept him too remote from the people, and out of accord with them'. O'Leary is seen as a harmless old fuddy-duddy, Todhunter and Standish O'Grady are considered to be out of touch with their time and with Irish ideals. The nature of the 'coterie' is summed up by an early portrait of Yeats in the *Evening Telegraph* of January 14, 1888:

> Augustus Fitzgibbon, considered by himself and his friends to be a poet of Titanic power, who may accomplish great things, and who may not, but whose boyish head is in the meantime being turned in the most delightful and deplorable fashion by the circle which is fortunate enough to revolve round this elsewhere unappreciated star. His friends will gravely tell you that Ireland has not produced such a poet hitherto; that some of his unpublished songs are equal to Shakespeare, that in music he ranks with Shelley, in colouring with Keats; and that Coleridge himself was not more saturated with deep and transcendental philosophy. They will tell you that he is too exquisite and ethereal to be understood or appreciated by the common British reviewer, and hence his obscurity. All this, of course, Fitzgibbon fondly believes, and invites you to believe by the ingratiating sweetness with which he takes his spoiling. In his circle all are equally sincere in giving and returning flattery.

Yeats had, however, turned the tide of organized Irish cultural life from well-meaning and committed dilettantism to a genuine, specialized interest in literature. However aesthetically right his orchestrations may have been, they tore the heart – made up of popular support – out of the movement.

Terms like 'Revival' and 'Renaissance' are normally applied after the Rebirth, but the Irish Revival was born before it was conceived. For years, 'Erin renascent be our sacred charge' lay at the basis of the Literary Societies, and for years it manifested itself in the intentions of individual writers. Between 1887 and 1899 it made its presence felt in Yeats's prose; for a considerably longer period it infused the work of AE, and it culminated in their combined effort to prepare Ireland through Orphic rituals for an impending rebirth. But it also shone through the more practically deliberative lectures delivered to Irish Literary Societies by Gavan Duffy, Hyde, Sigerson and Todhunter. For this generation, the appellation 'Revivalist' is paradoxical, because their desire to effect a Revival was based on their observation of the want of one, not among the intellectuals who performed their literary or scholarly part in the societies but among the general population whom they were trying to target. Speaking to Irish Societies, lecturers constantly noted the unwanted internationalization of the Celt, with the preponderance of foreign rags in Irish households. Hyde, who called the Irish of his time 'the Japanese of Western Europe', remarked in 'The Necessity for De-Anglicising Ireland' (1892):

> What have we now left...? Scarcely a trace. Many ... read news-papers indeed, but who reads, much less recites, an epic poem, or chants an elegiac or even a hymn?... We must set our face sternly against penny dreadfuls, shilling shockers, and still more, the garbage of vulgar English weeklies like *Bow Bells* and the *Police Intelligence*.

That the Revival was considered to *have* a birthright was based on inherently conservative characteristics of the Celt, constantly harped on in reviews. Its ingredients were Celtic love of learning, contact with the soil, loyal comradeship, chivalric courtesy, great-minded heroism – in short, all those traits which set the Irish apart from the English, and which contrasted most distinctively with all that was West-Briton – a Celtic spirit which was essentially rural and conser-vative – dependent on maintaining the social status quo; D. P. Moran pointed this out in 'Is the Irish Nation Dying?':

> Improve the conditions of the peasant and you wipe out the tra-ditions and the language; advance the more intelligent of the working men, as a consequence of material prosperity, into a higher class, and you weaken the prop even of 'nationality', and add to the already large contingent of the vulgar-genteel.

Edmund Downey, the Irish publisher of literature from the Renaissance, wrote in 1896:

I am now convinced all the talk ... about the 'Irish Literary Revival' simply prevented any such literary revival. People got disgusted with the lies written & spoken. It was much easier to sell Irish books before any of the books began to be talked, & everything pointed to a real revival in the literature concerning Ireland – but the Book-Mongers spoiled it all. Christ save us from any more of them! The Scotch don't talk of literary revivals. Bad as their present literature is, at any rate they support it literally without screaming over it & lying about it.

Yet it was Yeats who, with Lady Gregory and Edward Martyn gave the Revival its most visible podium; in 1897 they conceived the idea of founding a national theatre. In May 1899 the Irish Literary Theatre featured a double bill in the Antient Concert Rooms, Yeats's *The Countess Cathleen* and Martyn's *The Heather Field*, which offered the two polarities between which the National Theatre would oscillate – poetic and suggestive drama and Ibsenite social realism. Yeats had written the play for his beau-ideal, Maud Gonne, an active radical nationalist. She chaired the Irish Transvaal Committee in October 1899, supporting Major John MacBride's 'Irish Brigade', which had joined the Boers in their fight against the English. However, popular support for the Boers was limited. Irish soldiers had contributed significantly to the expansion and protection of the British Empire. The papers, who followed the heroic exploits of the British General Charles (Chinese) Gordon, published occasional letters from the Empire's frontiers – the following letter from a Westmeath soldier appeared in the *Cork Daily Herald*, 3 April 1879:

Lower Tugella Drift, Fort Tenedos,
Zululand, 16th Feb. 1897.

Dear Father and Mother,
... We had a fight with the Zulus on the 22nd of Jan. last and defeated them with great slaughter; we are expected to be attacked here every minute of the day, but we are quite ready at any moment to fight them.... If anything happens me I have now a few pounds which you will get by writing to the Captain of the Regiment.... We will have to fight a terrible mob before long, but we are determined to do them. British pluck can do anything, and they will be beaten.

The Irish parliamentary party condemned the Boer War. Tim Healy vituperated: 'You want the two races in South Africa to mingle hand in hand waving the Union Jack and singing "Rule Britannia," and you would put in ascendency over the Dutch such men as have made their ascendency in Ireland hateful, and who call your own Irish soldiers "rebels." What wonder, then, if there is disaffection!' Yet when Queen Victoria visited Ireland in April 1900 she was 'frantically cheered'. J. R. Scott wrote an encomium of dubious literary merit for the occasion:

> Come back to Erin, Victoria Regina,
> Come back to Erin, our dear Empress-Queen;
> Come in the springtime, Victoria *mavourneen*,
> Come when our meadows with shamrocks are green.
>
> Come back to Erin, Victoria Regina,
> Come back to Erin, the land we adore;
> Come back and cheer us, Victoria the Noble,
> Come! for we love thee, Victoria *asthore*.

IX.

This crowded century, symbolically opening with the Act of Union and closing with Queen Victoria's visit to Ireland in 1900 began with reverberations of 1798 continuing in Emmet's abortive rising of 1803. It experienced vast changes, politically, economically, socially, the mid-century Famine a watershed. So it included Catholic Emancipation, the setting up of national elementary education, the abolition of Tithes, the Temperance movement, attempts to repeal the Union, various fruitless risings (in 1848 and 1867), the Fenian Brotherhood founded in USA, the Disestablishment of the Church of Ireland, the foundation of the Home Rule Movement, Gladstone's Land Acts, the National Land League established and outlawed, the Gaelic Athletic Association founded in 1884, the Home Rule Bill defeated, the Gaelic League founded, Parnell's divorce splitting the Irish parliamentary party, the Irish Agricultural Organisation set up in 1894, and the first production of the Irish Literary Theatre.

Writing in Ireland was often intimately involved in all these developments in a complex, changing society. To attempt any overview of its variety is not easy, particularly in comparison with the previous century. When he got round to reading eighteenth-century authors in his late middle age, Yeats seized upon four major, original figures as his literary ancestors, perhaps not realizing or having the time to read more widely in the large number of other authors in the period, middling as well as minor but nonetheless impressively creative as they catered for the taste of their readers. To move from the writers of the eighteenth century into a comparative contemplation of the nineteenth-century achievement is but the first step in pursuing a panoptic view of a very large literary landscape indeed.

What emerges at first sight is the increasingly influential role played by fiction. Maria Edgeworth was a pioneer in exploring the nature of Irish country life in the first regional novel which portrayed the decay of an Anglo-Irish ascendancy family and the rise of a peasant's family. Other elements soon appeared in the romantic approaches of Lady Morgan and Charles Robert Maturin, the latter adding in the Gothic frisson which was to flourish later in the writings of Sheridan Le Fanu and reach its apogee in Bram Stoker's *Dracula*.

Maria Edgeworth's explorations and methods established a strain that Somerville and Ross pursued in their portrayal of snobbishness and ambition in *The Real Charlotte*, their humour in the *Irish R.M.* harking back to the lively Irish use of English by Thady Quirk. Charles Lever, generally known for the comic energy of his earlier rollicking novels, went on to provide a sombre indictment of the Anglo-Irish establishment in his later novels, whereas the Banim brothers, Griffin and Kickham, and, especially, Carleton conveyed the pulsing vitality, the violence of life in an often impoverished countryside, while Emily Lawless in *Hurrish* foresaw a dark future.

All these writers, and the dramatists as well, were in part mediating between an oral culture and a written one. The quality of talk mattered in Ireland (witness Sir John Mahaffy's *The Principles of the Art of Conversation* [1887]), and many of the century's writers captured its nuances, its vigour and inventiveness most skilfully. Fiction was, however, to be driven by experimentalism every bit as unexpected as had been Sterne's in the previous century. George Moore moved from the naturalism of *Esther Waters* into exploration of the potentiality of the melodic line in, say, *The Lake* (1905) (he foreshadowed James Joyce in this shift from realism into an impressionistic, often poetic, prose). So the novel was written from varying points of view, those of the Anglo-Irish gentry, middle-class intellectuals and peasantry.

Lively writing with a sense of style is found not only in memoirs, in private letters and in some journalism – Mitchel's *Jail Journal*, Davitt's *Leaves from a Prison Diary*, and the Leadbeater papers come to mind – but in such contributions to history as the writings of William Hartpole Lecky and Standish James O'Grady's *History of Ireland: Heroic Period*. Shaw was beginning his devastatingly clever polemical pieces, not to mention the topographical contributions of Sir William Wilde and his wife's account of ancient Irish legends and charms.

Poetry moved up a gear with Moore's *Irish Melodies* of 1807, which created an extensive audience for Irish subject matter in England and America. The influence of Irish airs on Moore was significant; many minor poets (they included the De Veres, Edward Lysaght and George Darley) were largely influenced by English romantic poets; there were others who owed much to Gaelic (they included George Ogle, John Philpot Curran and Thomas Furlong), and yet others who translated Irish verse (among them Jeremiah Joseph Callanan). There were, however, two poets of much greater significance in James Clarence Mangan and Sir Samuel Ferguson, who turned to Irish poetry most effectively, the former capturing the dragging cadences of the Irish as well as its potent rhetoric; the latter, himself, like Mangan, a lively experimenter and innovator, giving expression to its vigour, directness and toughness.

Yet another category was idiosyncratic in the extremely ironic nature of its burlesque (and this kind of poetry was written with gusto by Milliken and 'Father Prout'). For a long time William Allingham seemed to be a Victorian regional poet who exhibited a feeling for the West of Ireland, while the violent realism of his *Laurence Bloomfield in Ireland* is now appreciated for its inherent sense of intensely dramatic events. But Allingham's *Collected Poems* (1888) marks the end of an era.

Change in all literary genres was occurring in the latter part of the century. This is the period when Standish O'Grady's influence was strong, and conveyed often in a verbose manner a sense of excitement at his discovery of Gaelic Ireland's literary and cultural heritage. Like Ferguson he was attempting a re-energizing of Irish mythology, while Douglas Hyde was trying to promote Irish language and culture through his foundation of the Gaelic League (parallel to a certain extent to the aims of the founders of the Gaelic Athletic Association). The year after the publication of Allingham's *Collected Poems* Yeats's *The Wanderings of Oisin* marked the emergence of Irish mythology and legend in a new, elegant, sensuous and highly influential manner.

Not all of Irish writing engaged in a dialectic with history and politics. Sir Richard Burton and Lafcadio Hearn widened the horizons through their personal experiences of the Middle East and Japan, introducing cultures which would play a prominent role in Yeats's mature poetry and in the arcane philosophy of his *A Vision*.

Apart from an Irish theatre moving in a far different direction to that which the melodramas of Dion Boucicault had pursued so successfully in English and American theatres, Oscar Wilde and Shaw were to please those audiences continuing the traditions of the comedy of manners to which many earlier Irish dramatists had contributed so memorably (think of Thomas Southerne, William Congreve, George Farquhar, Susannah Centlivre, Richard Steele, Charles Macklin, and after them Oliver Goldsmith and Richard Brinsley Sheridan). But Irish writers were now beginning consciously to write for Irish audiences in Ireland.

The effect of journals such as *The Nation* and the *United Irishman* did much to appeal to the Irish public and to create a powerful sense of patriotic pride, while the *Dublin University Magazine* provided a forum for heavy-weight intellectual discussion of Ireland's past, present and future. In these journals, as well as in the new writing which sought to recreate a sense of national culture, we can sense the creative tensions which gave nineteenth-century Irish writing its particular strength, an ethos which continued on into the twentieth century, with Yeats, Shaw, Samuel Beckett and Seamus Heaney winners of the Nobel Prize for Literature, with the Abbey establishing itself as a national theatre, with O'Casey giving dramatic vitality to the speech of Dublin, and Joyce profoundly influencing the course of fiction. Some of these writers spanned two centuries – the nineteenth century which has underpinned them all was a powerfully creative period, rich in its variety, profoundly impressive in its vitality.

Further Reading

Donald H. Akenson, *Small Differences: Irish Catholics and Irish Protestants, 1815–1921: An International Perspective* (Dublin: Gill & Macmillan, 1990)

Matthew Arnold, *On the Study of Celtic Literature* (London: Dent, 1910 [1867])

J. C. Beckett, *The Making of Modern Ireland. 1603–1923* (London: Faber & Faber, 1966)

J. C. Beckett, *The Anglo-Irish Tradition* (Dublin: Blackstaff, 1976)

Paul Bew, *Land and the National Question in Ireland. 1858–1882* (Dublin: Gill & Macmillan, 1978)

Angela Bourke, Siobhán Kilfeather, Maria Luddy, Margaret MacCurtain, Gerardine Meaney, Máirin Ní Dhonnchadha, Mary O'Dowd and Clair Wills (eds), *The Field Day Anthology of Irish Writing* (Cork: Cork University Press, 2002)

Ernest Boyd, *Ireland's Literary Renaissance* (Dublin: Allen Figgis, 1968 [1916])

Birgit Bramsbäck and Martin Croghan, *Anglo-Irish and Irish Literature: Aspects of Language and Culture*, 2 Vols (Uppsala: Almqvist and Wiksell, 1988)

Malcolm Brown, *The Politics of Irish Literature. From Thomas Davis to W. B. Yeats* (Seattle: University of Washington Press, 1973)

Terence Brown, *Ireland's Literature. Selected Essays* (Mullingar: The Lilliput Press; Totowa, NJ: Barnes & Noble, 1988)

James M. Cahalan, *Great Hatred, Little Room: The Irish Historical Novel* (Dublin: Gill & Macmillan, 1983)

David Cairns and Shaun Richards, *Writing Ireland: Colonialism, Nationalism and Culture* (Manchester: Manchester University Press, 1988)

Andrew Carpenter (ed.), *Place, Personality and the Irish Writer* (Gerrards Cross: Colin Smythe, 1977)

Andrew Carpenter, *Anglo-Irish Literature: A Cultural History. Literature of the Ascendancy to 1830* (Dublin: University Press of Ireland, 1986)

Malcolm Chapman, *The Celts: The Construction of a Myth* (Basingstoke: Macmillan, 1992)

S. Clark and James S. Donnelly, Jr. (eds), *Irish Peasants: Violence and Political Unrest. 1780–1914* (Dublin: Gill & Macmillan, 1983)

Tom Clyde (ed.), *Irish Literary Magazines. An Outline History and Descriptive Bibliography* (Dublin, Portland, OR: Irish Academic Press, 2003)

Anne Ulry Colman, *A Dictionary of Nineteenth-Century Irish Women Poets* (Galway: Kenny's Bookshop, 1996)

Peter Connolly (ed.), *Literature and the Changing Ireland* (Gerrards Cross: Colin Smythe; Totowa, NJ: Barnes & Noble Books, 1982)

Sean Connolly, *Religion and Society in Nineteenth-Century Ireland* (Dundalk: Dun Dealgan Press, 1985)

S. J. Connolly (ed.), *The Oxford Companion to Irish History* (Oxford: Oxford University Press, 1998)

Peter Costello, *The Heart Grown Brutal: The Irish Revolution in Literature from Parnell to the Death of Yeats. 1891–1939* (Dublin: Gill & Macmillan, 1977)

Peter Costello, *The Irish 100. A Ranking of the Most Influential Irish Men and Women of All Time* (London: Simon & Schuster, 2001)

Carol Coulter, *The Hidden Tradition: Feminism, Women and Nationalism in Ireland* (Cork: Cork University Press, 1993)

Patricia Craig, (ed.), *The Oxford Book of Ireland* (Oxford: Oxford University Press, 1998)

John Cronin, *The Anglo-Irish Novel. Volume One. The Nineteenth Century* (Totowa, NJ: Barnes & Noble, 1980)

Michael Cronin, *Translating Ireland: Translations, Languages, Cultures* (Cork: Cork University Press, 1996)

Sean Cronin, *Irish Nationalism. A History of its Roots and Ideology* (Dublin: The Academy Press, 1980)

Anne Crookshank, *Irish Art from 1600 to the Present Day* (Dublin: Foreign Affairs, 1979)

Anne Crookshank and the Knight of Glin, *The Painters of Ireland c. 1660–1920* (London: Barrie and Jenkins, 1978; 1979)

Anne Crookshank and the Knight of Glin, *The Watercolours of Ireland. Works on paper in pencil, pastel and paint. c. 1600–1914* (London: Barrie and Jenkins, 1994)

Anne Crookshank and the Knight of Glin, *Ireland's Painters. 1600–1940* (New Haven & London: Yale University Press, 2002)

Fintan Cullen, *Visual Politics: The Representation of Ireland, 1750–1930* (Cork: Cork University Press, 1997)

L. M. Cullen, *The Emergence of Modern Ireland. 1600–1900* (London: Batsford Academic and Educational Ltd., 1981)

Mary Cullen and Maria Luddy (eds), *Women, Power and Consciousness in Nineteenth-Century Ireland* (Dublin: Attic Press, 1995)

Graham Davis, *The Irish in Great Britain. 1815–1914* (Dublin: Gill & Macmillan, 1991)

Richard Davis, *The Young Ireland Movement* (Dublin: Gill & Macmillan, 1987)

Seamus Deane, *A Short History of Irish Literature* (London, Melbourne, Sydney, Auckland, Johannesburg, Notre Dame, IN: University of Notre Dame Press, 1986)

Seamus Deane, *Celtic Revivals: Essays in Modern Irish Literature. 1880–1980* (London: Faber & Faber, 1987)

Seamus Deane (ed.), *The Field Day Anthology of Irish Writing* (Derry: Field Day Publications, 1991)

James S. Donnelly, Jr. and Kerby A. Miller (eds), *Irish Popular Culture. 1650–1850* (Dublin, Portland, OR: Irish Academic Press, 1998)

Katie Donovan, A. Norman Jeffares & Brendan Kennelly (eds), *Ireland's Women. Writings Past and Present* (London: Kyle Cathie Limited; Dublin: Gill & Macmillan, 1994)

D. N. Doyle, *Ireland, Irishmen and Revolutionary America. 1769–1820* (Dublin: Mercier, 1981)

Seán Dunne (ed.), *The Ireland Anthology* (Dublin: Gill & Macmillan, 1999 [1997])

Richard Fallis, *The Irish Renaissance* (Dublin: Gill & Macmillan, 1978)

Brian Fallon, *Irish Art. 1830–1900* (Belfast: Appletree Press, 1994)

Melissa Fegan *Literature and the Irish Famine* (Oxford: Oxford University Press, 2002)

Richard Finneran (ed.), *Anglo-Irish Literature. A Review of Research* (New York: MLA, 1976)

Thomas Flanagan, *The Irish Novelists. 1800–1850*, (New York: Columbia University Press, 1959)

John Wilson Foster, *Fictions of the Irish Literary Revival. A Changeling Art* (Syracuse: Syracuse University Press, Gill & Macmillan, 1987)

R. F. Foster, *Modern Ireland. 1600–1972* (London: Penguin Books, 1988)

Laurence M. Geary, *The Plan of Campaign. 1886–1891* (Cork: Cork University Press, 1986)

Jacqueline Genet and Richard Allen Cave (eds), *Perspectives of Irish Drama and Theatre* (Gerrards Cross: Colin Smythe, 1991)

Hugh Gough and David Dickson (eds), *Ireland and the French Revolution* (Dublin: Irish Academic Press, 1990)

Maurice Harmon, *Modern Irish Literature, 1800–1967. A Reader's Guide* (Dublin: Dolmen Press, 1968)

Barabara Hayley and Enda McKay (eds), *Three Hundred Years of Irish Periodicals* (Dublin: Association of Irish Learned Journals, 1987)

D. J. Hickey and J. E. Doherty, *A Dictionary of Irish History. 1800–1980* (Dublin: Gill & Macmillan, 1980)

Kathleen Hoagland (ed.), *1000 Years of Irish Poetry* (New York: Konecky & Konecky, 1975 [1947])

Robert Hogan (ed.), *Dictionary of Irish Literature* (Dublin: Gill & Macmillan, 1979)

A. Norman Jeffares, *Anglo-Irish Literature* (Dublin: Gill & Macmillan, 1982)

A. Norman Jeffares, *Parameters of Irish Writing in English* (Gerrards Cross: Colin Smythe, 1986)

A. Norman Jeffares and Antony Kamm (eds), *Irish Childhoods. An Anthology* (Dublin: Gill & Macmillan, 1992)

A. Norman Jeffares, *A Pocket History of Irish Literature* (Dublin: The O'Brien Press, 1997)

A. Norman Jeffares, (ed.), *Irish Love Poems* (Dublin: The O'Brien Press; Boulder, CO: Irish American Book Company, 1997)

A. Norman Jeffares, *The Irish Literary Movement* (London: National Portrait Gallery, 1998)

A. Norman Jeffares, (ed.), *Ireland's Love Poems* (London: Kyle Cathie, 2000)

Robert Kee, *The Green Flag. Volume I. The Most Distressful Country* (London, Melbourne, New York: Quartet Books, 1972)

Robert Kee, *The Green Flag. Volume II. The Bold Fenian Men* (London, Melbourne, New York: Quartet Books, 1976)

Margaret Kelleher and James H. Murphy (eds), *Gender Perspectives in 19th Century Ireland: Public and Private Spheres* (Dublin: Irish Academic Press, 1997)

Brendan Kennelly, *The Penguin Book of Irish Verse* (Harmondsworth: Penguin, 1970)

Declan Kiberd, *Inventing Ireland. The Literature of the Modern Nation* (Reading: Vintage, 1996)

Declan Kiberd, *Irish Classics* (London: Granta Books, 2000)

Thomas Kinsella, *Davis, Mangan, Ferguson? Tradition and the Irish Writer* (Dublin: Dolmen, 1970)

Lynn Hollen Lees, *Exiles of Erin. Irish Migrants in Victorian London*, (Ithaca: Cornell University Press, 1979)

Melosina Lenox-Conyngham (ed.), *Diaries of Ireland. An Anthology. 1590–1987* (Dublin: The Lilliput Press, 1998)

Peter Liebregts and Peter van de Kamp (eds), *Tumult of Images. Essays on W .B. Yeats and Politics* (Amsterdam; Atlanta: Rodopi, 1995)

Maria Luddy, *Women in Ireland. 1800–1918. A Documentary History* (Cork: Cork University Press, 1995)

James Lydon, *The Making of Ireland. From Ancient Times to the Present* (London and New York: Routledge, 1998)

F. S. L. Lyons, *Culture and Anarchy in Ireland. 1890–1939* (Oxford: Clarendon Press, 1979)

Michael McAteer, *Standish O'Grady, Æ and Yeats. History, Politics, Culture* (Dublin, Portland, OR: Irish Academic Press, 2002)

Lawrence MacBride (ed.), *Images, Icons and Irish Nationalist Imagination. 1870–1925* (Dublin: Four Courts Press, 1999)

Justin McCarthy et al (eds), *Irish Literature*, 10 Vols (New York: Bigelow, Smith & Co., 1904)

Donal MacCartney, *The Dawning of Democracy in Ireland, 1800–1870* (Dublin: The Lilliput Press, 1994)

W. J. McCormack, *Ascendancy and Tradition in Anglo-Irish Literary History from 1789 to 1939* (Oxford: Oxford University Press, 1985)

W. J. McCormack, *From Burke to Beckett. Ascendancy, Tradition and Betrayal in Literary History* (Cork: Cork University Press, 1994)

W. J. McCormack (ed.), *Ferocious Humanism. An Anthology of Irish Poetry from before Swift to Yeats and after* (London: J.M. Dent, 2000)

Oliver MacDonagh, *Ireland: The Union and Its Aftermath* (London: Allen & Unwin, 1977)

Thomas McDonagh, *Literature in Ireland*, (Dublin: Talbot Press, 1916)

Sean McMahon and Jo O'Donoghue (eds), *The Mercier Companion to Irish Literature* (Cork: Mercier Press, 1998)

Janet Madden Simpson, *Woman's Part. An Anthology of Short Fiction by and about Irishwomen. 1890–1960* (Dublin: Arlen House; London & New York: Marion Boyars, 1984)

W. F. Mandle, *The Gaelic Athletic Association and Irish Nationalist Politics. 1884–1924* (Dublin: Gill & Macmillan, 1987)

Augustine Martin, *Anglo-Irish Literature* (Department of Foreign Affairs, 1980)

Augustine Martin (ed.), *The Genius of Irish Prose* (Cork: The Mercier Press, 1985)

D. E. S. Maxwell, *A Critical History of Modern Irish Drama. 1891–1980* (Cambridge: Cambridge University Press, 1984)

Arthur Mitchell and Pádraig Ó Snodaigh, *Irish Political Documents. 1869–1916* (Dublin: Irish Academic Press, 1989)

Chris Morash (ed.), *The Hungry Voice: The Poetry of the Irish Famine* (Dublin: Irish Academic Press, 1989)

Chris Morash, *Writing the Irish Famine* (Oxford: Oxford University Press, 1995)

Chris Morash and Richard Hayes (eds), *'Fearful Realities': New Perspectives on the Famine* (Dublin: Irish Academic Press, 1996)

James H. Murphy, *Abject Loyalty: Nationalism and Monarchy in Ireland during the Reign of Queen Victoria* (Washington, DC: Catholic University of America Press; Cork: Cork University Press, 2001)

James H. Murphy, *Catholic Fiction and Social Reality in Ireland 1873–1922* (Westport, CT: Greenwood, 1997)

James H. Murphy, *Ireland: A Social, Cultural and Literary History 1791–1891* (Dublin: Four Courts Press, 2003)

Damien Murray, *Romanticism, Nationalism and Irish Antiquarian Societies. 1840–1880* (Maynooth: NUI Department of Old and Middle Irish, 2000)

W. S. Neidhart, *Fenianism in North America* (Pennsylvania: Pennsylvania State University Press, 1975)

Alan O'Day and D. George Boyce, *Irish Nationalism, 1798 to the Present* (London: Routledge, 1998)

Ruán O'Donnell, *The Rebellion in Wicklow, 1798* (Dublin: Irish Academic Press, 1998)

Ruán O'Donnell, *Robert Emmet and the Rebellion of 1798* (Dublin: Irish Academic Press, 2003)

Ruán O'Donnell, *Robert Emmet and the Rising of 1803* (Dublin: Irish Academic Press, 2003)

Padraic O'Farrell, *The '98 Reader. An Anthology of Song, Prose and Poetry* (Dublin: The Lilliput Press, 1998)

Patrick O'Farrell, *Ireland's English Question: Anglo-Irish Relations, 1534–1970* (London: Batsford, 1971)

Fergus O'Ferrall, *Catholic Emancipation: Daniel O'Connell and the Birth of Irish Democracy, 1820–1830* (Dublin: Gill & Macmillan, 1985)

Cormac Ó Gráda, *Ireland Before and After the Famine* (Manchester: Manchester University Press, 1988)

John O'Kane Murray (ed.), *The Prose and Poetry of Ireland* (New York: Collier, 1877)

Patrick O'Sullivan, *The Meaning of the Famine* (London and Washington DC: Leicester University Press, 1997)

Seán Ó Tuama & Thomas Kinsella (eds), *An Duanaire. 1600–1900: Poems of the Dispossessed* (Dublin: The Dolmen Press, 1981)

Cathal Póirtéir (ed.), *The Great Irish Famine* (Dublin: Mercier, 1995)

Patrick Rafroidi, *Irish Literature in English: The Romantic Period (1789–1850)*, 2 Vols (Gerrards Cross: Colin Smythe, 1980)

Otte Rauchbauer (ed.), *Ancestral Voices: The Big House in Anglo-Irish Literature* (Dublin: The Lilliput Press, 1992)

C. A. Read and Katharine Tynan Hinkson (eds), *The Cabinet of Irish Literature*, 3 Vols (London: Gresham, 1902)

Russell Rees, *Nationalism and Unionism in 19th Century Ireland* (Newtonards: Colourpoint Books, 2001)

Stephen Regan (ed.), *Irish Writing. An Anthology of Irish Literature in English. 1789–1939* (Oxford: Oxford University Press, 2004)

Gerard Reid (ed.), *Great Irish Voices. Over 400 Years of Irish Oratory* (Dublin: Irish Academic Press, 1999)

Ernest Renan, *The Poetry of the Celtic Races & Other Studies* (New York: Kessinger Publishing, 2003 [1896])

William Patrick Ryan, *The Irish Literary Revival. Its History, Pioneers and Possibilities* (New York: Lemma, 1970 [1894])

E. A. Sharp and J. Matthay (eds), *Lyra Celtica. An Anthology of Representative Celtic Poetry* (Edinburgh: John Grant 1932 [1896])

Barry Sloan, *Writers and Protestantism in the North of Ireland. Heirs to a Damnation?* (Dublin: Irish Academic Press, 2000)

A. T. Q. Stewart, *Deeper Silence: The Hidden Roots of the United Irish Movement* (London: Faber & Faber, 1993)

Bruce Stewart, *That Other World: Supernatural and the Fantastic in Irish Literature and Its Contexts*, 2 Vols (Gerrards Cross: Colin Smythe, 1998)

Mark Storey (ed.), *Poetry and Ireland Since 1800: A Source Book* (London and New York: Routledge, 1988)

Betsey Taylor FitzSimon and James H. Murphy (eds), *The Irish Revival Reappraised* (Dublin: Four Courts Press, 2004)

Mary Helen Thuente, *The Harp Restrung. The United Irishmen and the Rise of Literary Nationalism* (New York: Syracuse University Press, 1994)

Norman Vance, *Irish Literature. A Social History* (Oxford: Basil Blackwell, 1990)

Patrick Ward, *Exile, Emigration and Irish Writing* (Dublin: Irish Academic Press, 2002)

Robert Welch, *Irish Poetry from Moore to Yeats* (Gerrards Cross: Colin Smythe, 1980)

Robert Welch, *A History of Verse Translations from the Irish. 1789–1897* (Gerrards Cross: Colin Smythe, 1988)

Robert Welch (ed.), *Irish Writers and Religion* (Gerrards Cross: Colin Smythe, 1992)

Robert Welch (ed.), *The Oxford Companion to Irish Literature* (Oxford: Clarendon Press, 1996)

Robert Welch, *The Abbey Theatre 1899–1999. Form and Pressure* (Oxford: Oxford University Press, 1999)

T. D. Williams (ed.), *Secret Societies in Ireland* (Dublin: Gill & Macmillan, 1973)

Cecil Woodham-Smith, *The Great Hunger* (London: Hamish Hamilton, 1962)

Katharine Worth, *The Irish Drama of Europe from Yeats to Beckett* (London: The Athlone Press of the University of London, 1978)

William Butler Yeats, *Representative Irish Tales* (Gerrards Cross: Colin Smythe, 1979 [1891

ANONYMOUS

The Curragh of Kildare[1]

The winter it is past,
And the summer's come at last,
    And the blackbirds sing on every tree;
The hearts of these are glad,
But mine is very sad,
    Since my true love is absent from me.

The rose upon the brier,
By the water running clear,
    Gives joy to the linnet and the bee;
Their little hearts are blest,
But mine is not at rest,
    While my true love is absent from me.

A livery I'll wear,
And I'll comb down my hair,
    And in velvet so green I'll appear;
And straight I will repair
To the Curragh of Kildare,
    For it's there I'll find tidings of my dear.

I'll wear a cap of black,
With a frill around my neck;
    Gold rings on my fingers I'll wear;
It is this I'll undertake
For my true lover's sake;
    He resides at the Curragh of Kildare.

I would not think it strange
Thus the world for to range,
    If I only got tidings of my dear;
But here in Cupid's chain,
If I'm bound to remain,
    I would spend my whole life in despair.

---

1 This lyric was first collected in 1780.

My love is like the sun,
That in the firmament does run,
    And always proves constant and true;
But his is like the moon,
That wanders up and down,
    And every month it is new.

All you that are in love,
And cannot it remove,
    I pity the pains you endure;
For experience lets me know
That your hearts are full of woe,
    And a woe that no mortal can cure.

The Palatine's Daughter
ínghean an phailitinígh.

As I roved out of an evening through
    the groves of Ballyseedy[1]
Whom should I meet on a cool retreat
    but an Irish Palatine's daughter?[2]
She asked my name and station O!
    or where was my dwelling arbour?
Or would I come along with her
    to see her own dear father?
I said I was a rakish lad,
    in Currans[3] I was in sarvice

'If you forsake the Mass and sacraments
    you'll get me and my portion,
As I have done in person and
    my forefathers before me.
You'll get gold and silver O!
    and land without tax or charges,
And a letter from Mister Oliver
    my father's unfit for sarvice,
And a pretty lass to wed with you,
    if you choose a Palatine's daughter.'

1 *Ballyseedy*: an area south of Tralee.
2The Palatines were Protestant refugees from Rheinland Pfalz who settled in Limerick and Kerry in the early eighteenth century.
3 *Currans*: a local family.

I courteously saluted her
    and twice I kissed my darling:
'And if I go home along with you
    shall I get you as my partner?'
She said, 'A thousand welcomes O!
    and be not the least alarmed,
You'll have my mother's blessing and
    best wishes of my father,
You'll get stock and property,
    and we'll be happy ever after.'

And now my song is ended and
    my pen is out of order,
She brought this handsome young man
    in presence of her father.
They agreed and soon got married O!
    and then he became master,
He got his landed property,
    his haggard and his barn,
And then he made a Catholic
    Of the Irish Palatine's daughter

I Know Where I'm Going

I know where I'm going, she said,
    And I know who's going with me;
I know who I love –
    But the dear knows who I'll marry.

Feather beds are soft,
    And painted rooms are bonny,
But I'll forsake them all
    To go with my love Johny;

Leave my dresses of silk,
    My shoes of bright green leather,
Combs to buckle my hair,
    And rings for every finger.

O some say he's black,
    But I say he's bonny –

The fairest of them all,
    My winsome handsome Johny.
I know where I'm going, she said,
    And I know who's going with me;
I know who I love –
    But the dear knows who I'll marry.

KATE KEARNEY

O, did you not hear of Kate Kearney?
She lives on the banks of Killarney,
From the glance of her eye shun danger and fly,
For fatal's the glance of Kate Kearney!
For that eye is so modestly beaming,
You'd never think of mischief she's dreaming,
Yet oh, I can tell how fatal's the spell
That lurks in the eye of Kate Kearney!

O, should you e'er meet this Kate Kearney,
Who lives on the banks of Killarney,
Beware of her smile, for many a wile
Lies hid in the smile of Kate Kearney.
Though she looks so bewitchingly simple,
There's mischief in every dimple;
Who dares inhale her mouth's spicy gale
Must die by the breath of Kate Kearney.

ANSWER

O, yes, I have seen Kate Kearney,
Who lives near the lake of Killarney
From her love beaming eye what mortal can fly,
Unsubdued by the glance of Kate Kearney;
For that eye so betwitchingly beaming,
Assures me of mischief she's dreaming,
And feel 'tis in vain to fly from the chain,
That binds me to lovely Kate Kearney.

At eve when I've met this Kate Kearney
On the flower mantled banks of Killarney
Her smile would impart thrilling joy to my heart,

As I gaz'd on the charming Kate Kearney;
On the banks of Killarney reclining,
My bosom to rapture resigning
I've felt the keen smart of love's fatal dart,
And inhal'd the warm sigh of Kate Kearney.

Castle Hyde

As I roved out on a summer's morning
    Down by the banks of Blackwater side,
To view the groves and the meadows charming,
    The pleasant gardens of Castle Hyde;
'Tis there I heard the thrushes warbling,
    The dove and partridge I now describe;
The lambkins sporting on ev'ry morning,
    All to adorn sweet Castle Hyde.

The richest groves throughout this nation
    And fine plantations you will see there;
The rose, the tulip, the rich carnation,
    All vying with the lily fair.
The buck, the doe, the fox, the eagle,
    They skip and play by the river side;
The trout and salmon are always sporting
    In the clear streams of sweet Castle Hyde.

There are fine walks in these pleasant gardens,
    And seats most charming in shady bowers.
The gladiators both bold and darling
    Each night and morning do watch the flowers.
There's a church for service in this fine arbour
    Where nobles often in coaches ride
To view the groves and the meadow charming,
    The pleasant gardens of Castle Hyde.

There are fine horses and stall-fed oxes,
    And dens for foxes to play and hide;
Fine mares for breeding and foreign sheep there
    With snowy fleeces in Castle Hyde.
The grand improvements they would amuse you,
    The trees are drooping with fruit of all kind;

The bees perfuming the fields with music,
    Which yields more beauty to Castle Hyde.

If noble princes from foreign nations
    Should chance to sail to this Irish shore,
'Tis in this valley they would be feasted
    As often heroes have been before.
The wholesome air of this habitation
    Would recreate your heart with pride.
There is no valley throughout this nation
    In beauty equal to Castle Hyde.

I rose from Blarney to Castlebarnet,
    To Thomastown, and sweet Doneraile,
To Kilshannick that joins Rathcormack,
    Besides Killarney and Abbeyfeale;
The flowing Nore and the rapid Boyne,
    The river Shannon and pleasant Clyde;
In all my ranging and serenading
    I met no equal to Castle Hyde.

The Rakes Of Mallow

Beauing, belling, dancing, drinking,
Breaking windows, damning, sinking,
Ever raking, never thinking,
    Live the rakes of Mallow.

Spending faster than it comes,
Beating waiters, bailiffs, duns,
Bacchus' true-begotten sons,
    Live the rakes of Mallow.

One time naught but claret drinking,
Then like politicians thinking
To raise the sinking-funds when sinking,
    Live the rakes of Mallow.

When at home with dada dying
Still for Mallow water crying;

But where there's good claret plying,
    Live the rakes of Mallow.

Living short but merry lives;
Going where the devil drives;
Having sweethearts but no wives,
    Live the rakes of Mallow.

Racking tenants, stewards teasing,
Swiftly spending, slowly raising,
Wishing to spend all their lives in
    Raking as in Mallow.

Then to end this raking life,
They get sober, take a wife,
Ever after live in strife,
    And wish again for Mallow.

If I Was A Blackbird

If I was a blackbird, I'd whistle and sing
And I'd follow the ship that my true love sails in,
And on the top riggings I'd there build my nest.
And I'd pillow my head on his lily-white breast.

I am a young maiden and my story is sad
For once I was courted by a brave sailor lad.
He courted me strongly by night and by day,
But now my dear sailor is gone far away.

He promised to take me to Donnybrook fair
To buy me red ribbons to bind up my hair.
And when he'd return from the ocean so wide,
He'd take me and make me his own loving bride.

His parents they slight me and will not agree
That I and my sailor boy married should be.
But when he comes home I will greet him with joy
And I'll take to my bosom my dear sailor boy.

Finnegan's Wake

Tim Finnegan lived in Walkin Street,
    A gentleman Irish mighty odd,
He had a tongue both rich and sweet,
    An' to rise in the world he carried a hod.[1]
Now Tim had a son of a tipplin' way,
    With the love of the liquor he was born,
An' to help him on with his work each day,
    He'd a drop of the craythur ev'ry morn.

Whack fol the dah, dance to your partner,
    Welt the flure, yer trotters shake,
Wasn't it the truth I told you,
    Lots of fun at Finnegan's Wake.

One morning Tim was rather full,
    His head felt heavy which make him shake,
He fell from the ladder and broke his skull,
    So they carried him home his corpse to wake,
They rolled him up in a nice clean sheet,
    And laid him out upon the bed,
With a gallon of whiskey at his feet,
    And a barrel of porter at his head.

His friends assembled at the wake,
    And Mrs. Finnegan called for lunch,
First they brought in tay and cake,
    Then pipes, tobacco, and whiskey punch.
Miss Biddy O'Brien began to cry,
    'Such a neat clean corpse, did you ever see,
Arrah, Tim avourneen,[2] why did you die?'
    'Ah, hould your gab,' said Paddy McGee.

Then Biddy O'Connor took up the job,
    'Biddy,' says she, 'you're wrong, I'm sure,'
But Biddy gave her a belt in the gob,
    And left her sprawling on the floor;
Oh, then the war did soon enrage;

---

1 *hod*: open box, attached to a pole, for carrying mortar and bricks.
2 *avourneen*: 'darling'.

'Twas woman to woman and man to man,
Shillelagh law did all engage,
    And a row and a ruction soon began.

Then Micky Maloney raised his head,
    When a noggin of whiskey flew at him,
It missed and falling on the bed,
    The liquor scattered over Tim;
Bedad he revives, see how he rises,
    And Timothy rising from the bed,
Says, 'Whirl your liquor round like blazes,
    Thanam o'n dhoul,[1] do ye think I'm dead!'

The Croppy Boy

It was early, early in the spring
The birds did whistle and sweetly sing,
Changing their notes from tree to tree
And the song they sang was 'Old Ireland Free'.

It was early early in the night,
The yeoman cavalry gave me a fright;
The yeoman cavalry was my downfall
And I was taken by Lord Cornwall.[2]

'Twas in the guard-house where I was laid,
And in a parlour where I was tried;
My sentence passed and my courage low
When to Duncannon I was forced to go.

As I was passing my father's door
My brother William stood at the door;
My aged father stood at the door
And my tender mother her hair she tore.

As I was going up Wexford Street
My own first cousin I chanced to meet;
My own first cousin did me betray

---

1 Thanam o'n dhoul: 'My soul to the devil'.
2. Charles, 1st Marquis Cornwallis (1738–1805) was joint commander-in-chief and Lord Lieutenant during the '98 Rising.

And for one bare guinea swore my life away.
As I was walking up Wexford Hill
Who could blame me to cry my fill?
I looked behind, and I looked before
But my aged mother I shall see no more.

And as I mounted the platform high
My aged father was standing by;
My aged father did me deny
And the name he gave me was the Croppy Boy.[1]

It was in Duncannon this young man died
And in Duncannon his body lies.
And you good people that do pass by
Oh shed a tear for the Croppy Boy.

The Shan Van Vocht

Oh! the French are on the say,
   Says the Shan Van Vocht;[2]
The French are on the say,
   Says the Shan Van Vocht;
Oh ! the French are in the Bay,
They'll be here without delay,
And the Orange will decay,
   Says the Shan Van Vocht.
Oh! the French are in the Bay,
They'll be here by break of day,
And the Orange will decay,
   Says the Shan Van Vocht.

And where will they have their camp?
   Says the Shan Van Vocht;
Where will they have their camp?
   Says the Shan Van Vocht;
On the Curragh of Kildare,
The boys they will be there,
With their pikes in good repair,

---

1 The Irish rebels of 1798 wore their hair cropped short as a mark of sympathy with the French revolutionaries.
2 *The Shan Van Vocht*: The poor old woman (a symbol for Ireland).

Anonymous

Says the Shan Van Vocht.
To the Curragh of Kildare
The boys they will repair,
And Lord Edward[1] will be there,
   Says the Shan Van Vocht.

Then what will the yeomen do?
   Says the Shan Van Vocht;
What will the yeomen do?
   Says the Shan Van Vocht
What should the yeomen do,
But throw off the Red and Blue,
And swear that they'll be true
   To the Shan Van Vocht?
What should the yeomen do,
But throw off the red and blue,
And swear that they'll be true
   To the Shan Van Vocht?

And what colour will they wear?
   Says the Shan Van Vocht;
What colour will they wear?
   Says the Shan Van Vocht;
What colour should be seen
Where their fathers' homes have been,
But their own immortal Green?
   Says the Shan Van Vocht.
What colour should be seen
Where their fathers' homes have been,
But their own immortal Green?
   Says the Shan Van Vocht.

And will Ireland then be free?
   Says the Shan Van Vocht;
Will Ireland then be free?
   Says the Shan Van Vocht;
Yes! Ireland shall be free,
From the centre to the sea;

---

1 *Lord Edward*: Lord Edward Fitgerald (1763–1798), a gallant leader of the United Irishmen.
He was mortally wounded during his arrest by Major Sirr on 19 May, and died on 4 June.

Then hurrah for Liberty!
  Says the Shan Van Vocht.
Yes! Ireland shall be free,
From the centre to the sea;
Then hurrah for Liberty!
  Says the Shan Van Vocht.

The Wearing of the Green

O Paddy dear, and did you hear the news that's going round?
The shamrock is forbid by law to grow on Irish ground;
St. Patrick's Day no more we'll keep, his colours can't be seen,
For there's a bloody law against the wearing of the green.
I met with Napper Tandy[1] and he took me by the hand,
And he said, 'How's poor old Ireland, and how does she stand?'
She's the most distressful counterie that ever yet was seen,
And they're hanging men and women for the wearing of the green.

Then since the colour we must wear is England's cruel red,
Sure Ireland's sons will ne'er forget the blood that they have shed.
You may take a shamrock from your hat and cast it on the sod,
It will take root and flourish there though underfoot it's trod.
When law can stop the blades of grass from growing as they grow,
And when the leaves in summer-time their verdure dare not show,
Then will I change the colour that I wear in my caubeen[2]
But till that day, please God, I'll stick to wearing of the green.

But if at last our colour should be torn from Ireland's heart,
Our sons with shame and sorrow from this dear old isle will part;
I've heard a whisper of a land that lies beyond the sea
Where rich and poor stand equal in the light of freedom's day.
O Erin, must we leave you driven by a tyrant's hand?
Must we ask a mother's blessing from a strange and distant land?
Where the cruel cross of England shall nevermore be seen,
And where, please God, we'll live and die still wearing of the green!

---

1 *James Napper Tandy* (17–1803), very popular in attacking municipal corruption, was one of the founders of the United Irishmen. He went from America to Paris, and, with the rank of brigadier general, was the second in command of a French invasion force which landed in Donegal in September 1798. After handing out green cockades and reading out a proclamation, he was carried back to the ship drunk. Captured in Hamburg, he escaped death as the arrest contravened international law. He was liberated on Napoleon's intercession in 1802. A folklore hero, he is the subject of popular ballads.
2 caubeen: 'hat.'

MARY LEADBEATER (1758-1826)

She was born at Ballitore, Co. Kildare, the daughter of Richard Shackleton, a small farmer, and granddaughter of Abraham Shackleton, who had founded a Quaker school, attended by Edmund Burke*, of which his son became headmaster. She was thoroughly educated by her father, who took her to London in 1784, where she was introduced to Burke and met Sir Joshua Reynolds and George Crabbe. She also visited Beaconsfield, and wrote a poem in praise of the place and its owner, which was rewarded with a eulogistic letter from Burke, with whom she maintained a life-long correspondence. In 1791 she married William Leadbeater, a former pupil of her father; the couple spent the rest of their lives in Ballitore, where Mary became the post-mistress (as her mother had been). She wrote poetry from an early age; her *Poems* (1808) were mostly on local and domestic subjects, but also included a metrical version of her husband's prose translation of Maffæus Vegio's 'Thirteenth Book of the Æneid'. Her second collection, *Poems* (1818), contained a verse encomium to Sir Walter Scott. Her work is informed by a desire to instruct, from the anonymously published *Extracts and Original Anecdotes for the Improvement of Youth* (1794), through *Cottage Dialogues among the Irish Peasantry* (with a preface by her friend, Maria Edgeworth*, 1811) and *Tales for Cottagers* (1814), which contains a morality play entitled 'Honesty is the Best Policy', to *Cottage Biography, being a Collection of Lives of the Irish Peasantry* (1822). She also published a memoir of her parents, and a book on the Quakers in Ireland. Her poignant journals of daily life in Ballitore were collected by her niece, and published in 1862 as *The Leadbeater Papers. Annals of Ballitore* (2 vols).

From *Annals of Ballitore*
(1862)

[1775]

The summer of 1775 was remarkably fine, and amidst the variety which marked it was the appearance of a Jew, the first of that nation who had ever entered our village. He called himself Emanuel Jacob, and carried about as a show, enclosed in a glass cage, that plant of ancient memory, the mandrake. It appeared to combine the animal and vegetable in its formation, and this was really the case; for my father's housekeeper, when she had the showman safely occupied with his breakfast, impelled by curiosity, opened the case, and found the wondrous plant to be composed of the skeleton of a frog and fibres of the root of a plant. However, as it was not her wish to deprive the man of his livelihood, she carefully closed the case, and permitted Emanuel to proceed on his way.

Robert Baxter, from Monaghan, was a parlour-boarder at my father's at this time. He was but sixteen, yet he was six feet high, and lusty in proportion. His understanding seemed mature also; it was improved by classical learning, by refined society, and by the conversation of an excellent mother. He was affectionate, artless, and unassuming, and we soon loved him. He delighted in visiting my aunt Carleton, and they entertained one another with tales of former times, hers drawn from her own experience, his from tradition. One of his anecdotes was concerning the imprisonment of Lady Cathcart by her husband[1] (afterwards wrought by the able pen of Maria Edgeworth into her tale of 'Castle Rack-rent'). He said that it was stipulated by that lady on her marriage, that she should never be required to leave England as a residence; but, by pretending that he was only taking her out in a pleasure-boat for a trip, her husband conveyed her to Ireland and confined her in his castle, where he seldom visited her except to force her property from her by cruel and unmanly treatment. She managed, however, to conceal jewels to the amount of several thousand pounds, which her brutal tyrant could not obtain. She entrusted this treasure to her attendant, Kitty Armstrong, to carry to a person of the name of Johnson. The death of her husband at length emancipated her, after years of barbarous usage, during which she was almost starved, and clothed in filthy tattered rags. She rewarded her faithful friends by a gift to Johnson of £2000, and 500 guineas to her trusty Kate, and left Ireland for ever. Poor Kitty, it would appear, was not so careful of her own property as that of her lady; for, after Lady Cathcart's death, she became a dependant in the house of Robert Baxter's father; and her character, dress, and deportment made a great impression on the little boy, especially as she used to chastise him freely. Kitty wore a scarlet riding dress, a man's hat and wig, and had a cat which used to catch snipes for her...

[1789]

The oldest man at this time in our village was Finlay McClane, a native of the Highlands of Scotland, who, to those who understood his native Gaelic, could relate the account of many a battle in which he had been engaged, including disastrous Fontenoy. He told us, and

---

1. *her huband*: Charles, 8th Baron Cathcart married Elizabeth Malyn in 1739. He died in December 1740.

we all believed he told the truth, that he was born in the year 1689. He was an out-pensioner of the Royal Hospital. His wife Mary was a very industrious body. One dark evening their chimney was perceived to be on fire. The neighbours ran thither affrighted, and Hannah Haughton put the jar of gunpowder, which she kept for sale, out of the house. Mary McClane, a little, blunt, consequential woman, stood with her arms akimbo, and thus addressed the affrighted crowd: 'Have you any thing to do at home? If you have, I advise you to go home and do it; for if I had fifteen chimneys, I would clean them in no other way.' Fortunately the house was slated, so the danger was the less. The old man at one time lay very ill in consequence of a fall which injured his hip and occasioned incurable lameness. 'There he lies,' said his sympathizing helpmate, 'and off that bed he will never rise.' The poor man looked sorrowful at this denunciation, and turned his eyes wistfully, in silence, upon us; we blamed Mary for her apprehensions, at least for expressing them in this uncomfortable manner; and we encouraged Finlay, and soon had the pleasure of witnessing his recovery to health, though not to activity. He survived his matter-of-fact spouse, and his great age had not deprived him of his sensibility, for he mourned her with many tears as he attended her to her last home. In his hundred-and-tenth year, 1798, the old Highlander once more heard the sound of war, and saw the weapon of destruction aimed at his breast by a soldier; another soldier arrested the stroke, telling his comrade that he would never serve the king as long as that old man had done.

[1798]

The attack on Willowbrook alarmed Robert Bayley, who fled from Ballitore with his handsome wife in a fright, declaring that every man, woman and child in the village were 'United Irishmen.' Now and then a person was missed, and this misfortune was unfeelingly accounted for by saying that 'Brownie had eaten them.' These mysterious disappearances were horrible, and no certainty of the fate of those victims of party rage was ever obtained. A time had come when nothing but what was honest, and fair, and 'above board' could stand the test. Amongst other precautions, the names of the inhabitants were posted on the doors of each house, and the authorities had liberty to enter at any hour, night or day, to see whether they were within or not. This appeared a necessary precaution, yet it exposed the quiet families to be sadly broken in upon.

Houses were now searched for fire-arms, proving the wisdom of our friends in banishing all such weapons from theirs. Notices were put up demanding the arms taken by the 'United men' to be restored, on pain of allowing the military to live at free quarters; for many nightly incursions had been made by these robbers to plunder houses of whatever arms they contained. A detachment of the King's County militia was at this time sent here from Athy, where Sandford Palmer, an old Ballitore boy, was stationed as their captain. The men were very well liked; perhaps it was for that reason they were so soon removed, the villagers escorting them on their way with tears and lamentations; and when my husband, from his fields, saw them departing, he sent his workmen to join the procession....

...To the Tyrone militia were now added the Suffolk fencibles; and the Ancient Britons, dressed in blue with much silver lace – a very pretty dress – came from Athy, seized the smiths' tools, to prevent them from making pikes, and made prisoners of the smiths themselves. I could not see without emotion poor Owen Finn and his brother, hand-cuffed and weeping, as they walked after the car containing those implements of industry which had enabled them to provide comfort-ably for the family. Several of these were whipped publicly to extort confessions about the pikes. The torture was excessive, and the vic-tims were long in recovering; and in almost every case it was applied fruitlessly. Guards were placed at every entrance into the village, to prevent people from entering or leaving it. The village once so peace-ful exhibited a scene of tumult and dismay, and the air rang with the shrieks of the sufferers and the lamentations of those who beheld them suffer. These violent measures caused a great many pikes to be brought in: the street was lined with those who came to deliver up the instruments of death.

A party of military from Naas entered Ballitore, and took prison-ers twelve of our neighbours, whom they removed to Naas gaol. Most of the villagers stood outside their doors to see them depart. They looked composed for the most part, though followed by their weep-ing wives and children. One child; with his cries of, 'O father, father!' excited great compassion. Six yeomen were taken prisoners to Dunlavin. I was walking in our garden when they passed on a car, with their coats turned inside out, and one of their guards, a mere boy, cried out to me in a tone of insulting jocularity. We, who did not understand this case, were only qualified to see one side, and, though we forbore audibly expressing our disapprobation, our looks betrayed the depression of our minds. This excited jealousy of us: how ill-founded! For who could expect us to rejoice at the misery and degradation of our fellow-creatures and neighbours, or even to behold them unmoved! These unfortunate yeomen were shot! There was too much exultation in the military; they were not aware, perhaps, how deeply an insult is felt and resented, and that an injury is sometimes more easily pardoned.

The morning of the 24th of the Fifth month (May) orders came for the soldiers quartered here to march to Naas. A report was circulated that Naas gaol had been broken open, – that Dublin was in arms, and so forth. All was uncertainty, except that something serious had happened, as the mail-coach had been stopped. The insurrection was to begin in Dublin, and the mail-coach not being suffered to leave the city was the signal for the general revolt. This purpose being defeated by the vigilance of the government; the mail-coach had got to Naas before it was stopped, yet its detention there persuaded the people that the day was their own. They threw off the appearance of loyalty, and rose in avowed rebellion. In the morning the Suffolk fencibles first marched out, nine men remaining to guard their baggage at the Mill, which was their barrack. The Tyrone militia followed, taking their baggage with them. All was hurry and confusion in the village. Several who had kept out of sight now appeared dressed in green, that colour so dear to United Irishmen, and proportionately abhorred by the loyal. The Suffolks went by the high road, the Tyrones through Narraghmore. As they marched out, a young woman privately and with tears told their lieutenant her apprehensions that their enemies lay in ambush in Narraghmore wood. He was therefore prepared to meet them, and sad havoc ensued; many on both sides fell, particularly among the undisciplined multitude. The court-house at Narraghmore was attacked, and many met their death there. We heard the reports of firearms, and every hour the alarm increased.

Dr. Johnson had been sent for to Narraghmnore to dress wounds; the rabble despoiled him of his horse and case of instruments, and sent him back jaded and worn out. About three o'clock in the afternoon John Dunne and many others came as far as the bridge with pikes, and Dr. Johnson turned them back; but not long after two or three hundred men armed with pikes, knives, and pitchforks, and bearing sticks with green rags fluttering from them, came in at the western side, headed by Malachi Delany on a white horse, and took possession of the town; Dr. Johnson, as representative of the yeomanry-guard, having capitulated on condition of persons and property being safe. I saw from an upper window a crowd coming towards our kitchen-door; I went down and found many armed men, who desired to have refreshments, especially drink. I brought them milk, and was cutting a loaf of bread when a little elderly man, called 'the Canny,' took it kindly out of my hand and divided it himself, saying, 'Be decent, boys, be decent.' Encouraged by having found a friend, I ventured to tell them that so many armed men in the room frightened me. The warriors condescended to my fears. 'We'll be out in a shot,' they replied, and in a minute the kitchen was empty.

Daniel Horan, a young farmer from the Long Avenue, was standing in our yard – a fine-looking fellow, I had observed a dark cloud upon his countenance when, a few days before, he was requesting a protection from the officers; that cloud was now gone, and joy and animation played on every feature, unaccompanied by any expression of malignity. A party of insurgents, as they went to the mill, met some of the wives of the soldiers stationed there, whom they sent back to tell their husbands that if they surrendered they should not be injured. But the women, instead of delivering the message, ran shrieking to announce the approach of the rebels, and the soldiers prepared to stand on the defensive; but, when they saw such a multitude, fled. In the pursuit over Max's-hill a soldier turned, fired, and shot Paddy Dempsey dead. They were soon overpowered, and their lives spared only on condition that he who had killed the insurgent should be pointed out; with this hard alternative his comrades reluctantly complied, and the soldier soon lay dead beside his victim. Another of the soldiers was killed by a shot from the Mill-field, which reached him about the middle of the avenue, and his remains are buried in the ditch just by the spot where he fell. Most of the others were wounded, but I believe none mortally.

Malachi Delany exerted himself to prevent bloodshed, and showed as much humanity as courage. He had thrown off no mask, for he never wore one, and he proved himself to be a generous enemy. A great number of strange faces surrounded us, and a message was brought to me to request any thing of a green colour. I told them we could not join any party. 'What! not the strongest?' enquired one of the strangers. 'None at all' – and though our parlour tables were covered with green cloth, they urged their request no further.

Richard Yeates, son to Squire Yeates of Moone, was brought in a prisoner, his yeomanry coat turned. A private of the yeomanry corps to which he belonged was also brought into our parlour, where my husband and I sat at tea. He was an old man; we made him sit down to tea, and invited also his captors, but they declined; one of them went to the table and helped himself to bread and butter, looked at himself in the mirror, and remarked it was 'war time.' The prisoner, with tears trickling down his cheeks, spoke sadly of his seven children; his guards strove to console him by telling him that 'he was an honest Roman, and should not be hurt.' Presently we heard a shot, and those strangers immediately said they 'supposed Richard Yeates was shot.' This was really the case. He was taken into a house, and in despite of his own entreaties, the endeavours of many others to save him, and even the efforts of Priest Cullen, who begged the life of the young man on his knees, – he was murdered, being piked and shot! That day his father had been requested, I suppose by one who knew what was intended, not to let his son leave the house; but he could not prevent him – he would join the corps. His brother-in-law, Norcott D'Esterre, narrowly escaped being taken a prisoner at the same time.

The insurgents at length left, first placing cars on the bridge as a barricade against the army. They took two of our horses. We saw several houses on fire northwards, and, while standing gazing at them outside our door, bullets whizzed by our ears, and warned us to go in for safety. There had been an engagement on the Bog-road between the army and the insurgents; the latter were worsted, and Malachi Delany, finding his efforts to rally them were in vain, fled along with them. The soldiers retreating to Athy had fired at random those shots which we had heard, and almost felt, and by which a poor woman was killed and her daughter's arm broken. They had also set the houses on fire; and one serjeant, one might think impelled by his fate, came into the village with a baggage car. It was thought he must have been in liquor, for had he his reason he could not have exposed himself to his enemies in the height of their rage. He had just gone to bed in his lodgings when those enemies rushed in, and quickly put an end to his life.

The insurgents now returned from the Bog-road, and, having increased to an immense multitude, went to Castledermot late in the evening. We laid our beds on the floor lest bullets should enter our windows to our destruction, and got some disturbed sleep. All became quiet, and in the morning messages came to us from our neighbours to tell us they were living. This was indeed good news, for we dreaded that many would never have seen the light of morning. The party who attacked Castledermot were repulsed by yeomanry who fired at them from the windows. The crowd dispersed, and did not assemble here in such numbers again.

As my friend and I walked out to see a sick neighbour, we looked with fearful curiosity over a wall inside of which we saw lying the youthful form of the murdered Richard Yeates. There he had been thrown after his death, his clothes undisturbed, but his bosom all bloody. For many days after I thought my food tasted of blood, and at night I was frequently awakened by my feelings of horror, and stretched forth my hand to feel if my husband was safe at my side.

All the horses which could be got were taken by the insurgents. A man came to me with a drawn sword in his hand, demanding my own mare. I told him that one of the Tyrone officers had borrowed her, and fortunately another man who knew me bore testimony to my veracity, so that I was left unharmed. When I saw how the fine horses were abused and galloped without mercy by the insurgents, I rejoiced that my Nell was not in their hands.

A man afterwards came, with a horse-pistol in his hand, to take my husband. My brother had been previously taken, together with some of his guests. They were all to be brought to the camp in the hollow side of the hill at the east, and when the soldiers came, they should be placed, the insurgents said, in the front of the battle, to stop a bullet if they would not fire one. This man, not finding my husband below, and thinking he was concealed, ran upstairs where our little children were in bed, with the huge pistol in his hand, swearing horribly that he would send the contents of it through his head if he did not go with him. I stood at the door, less terrified than I could have expected, and asked a young man who had accompanied the other if they meant to kill us. 'To kill you?' he repeated, in a tone expressive of surprise and sorrow at such a supposition. At length he prevailed on his angry companion to go away, threatening as he went, that if the Quakers did not take up arms their houses should be in flames, 'as Mr. Bayley's was.' I was sorry for the destruction of the Hall, but soon found that, though it had been attempted, the fire had been put out before much damage had been done. My husband, having been visiting my mother, was not found, and did not know he had been sought for. Many came to us weeping and trembling for their friends; and to the doctor, who, having much influence with the people, exerted it to do them good. We could do nothing.

The cars laden with goods from Dublin, which the carriers were bringing to our shopkeepers, were plundered, and a barricade made of them across the road leading down to the village. The insurgents talked boldly of forming a camp on the Curragh. All who were missing were reported to have fallen in the ambush in the wood, or in the encounter at the Bog-road. At both places many did fall. The wife of one of my brother's labourers was told that he lay dead in the wood; she hastened thither; but when she reached the spot, she found the face so disfigured with wounds that she could not recognize it. She examined the linen – it was not his; even this melancholy satisfaction was denied her. But what a satisfaction was in store for her! She met her husband alive and well, and brought him in triumph to the house of their master, whose young daughter, who had participated in the anguish of the supposed widow, now shared her joy with all the vivid warmth of her ardent nature. This young creature, still a child, was endued with uncommon courage and prudence in this time of trial. Her bodily powers were exerted in paying attention to her father's numerous guests; for over a hundred people sought refuge under his roof; and the strength of her mind seemed to invigorate all around her. A soldier lay ill of a fever in a house in the garden. It would have been death to him if his asylum were known to the insurgents; so she carefully attended to all his wants herself. Such was Betsy Shackleton.

Everyone seemed to think that safety and security were to be found in my brother's house. Thither the insurgents brought their prisoners, and thither, also, their own wounded and suffering comrades. It was an awful sight to behold in that large parlour such a mingled assembly of throbbing, anxious hearts – my brother's own family, silent tears rolling down their faces, the wives of the loyal officers, the wives of the soldiers, the wives and daughters of the insurgents, the numerous guests, the prisoners, the trembling women – all dreading to see the door open, lest some new distress, some fresh announcement of horrors should enter. It was awful; but every scene was now awful, and we knew not what a day might bring forth.

All our houses were thronged with people seeking refreshment and repose, and threatening to take possession for the purpose of firing upon the soldiery when they should come. Ours seemed peculiarly adapted for such a purpose, being a corner house, and in a central situation; so, believing its destruction was inevitable, I packed up in a small trunk such portable articles as I esteemed of most value, amongst which were some of my dear friends' letters, and made packages of clothes for my husband, myself, and the little ones. I wore two pair of pockets, wishing to preserve as much as I could; though in my heart I had not much fear of an engagement, believing that the spirit which had animated the insurgents had evaporated.

Young girls dressed in white, with green ribbons, and carrying pikes, accompanied the insurgents. They had patrols and a countersign, but it was long before they could decide upon the password. At length they fixed upon the word, 'Scourges.' Sentinels were placed in various parts of the village. One day, as I went to my brother's, a sentinel called to a man who walked with me not to advance on pain of being shot. The sentinel was my former friend, 'The Canny.' I approached him and asked would he shoot me if I proceeded. 'Shoot you!' exclaimed he, taking my hand and kissing it, adding a eulogium on the Quakers. I told him it would be well if they were all of our way of thinking, for then there would be no such work as the present. I thought I could comprehend 'The Canny's' incoherent answer, 'Aye, but you know our Saviour – the scourges, oh! the scourges!' With little exception, we were kindly treated, and the females amongst us were frequently encouraged to dismiss our fears, with hearty shakes of the hand, and assurances that they would 'burn those who would burn us.' We began to be familiarized with these dangers; and added our entreaties to the representations of our men that they should give up their arms, and resign the project which threatened them with destruction.

They had been mistaken as to their prospect of success. Dublin was safe, and at Naas and Kilcullen great slaughter of the insurgents had been made, though on Kilcullen-green many of the military had also fallen. An attack in the night had been made on Carlow, which was repulsed with slaughter, amounting almost to massacre. A row of cabins in which numbers of the defeated insurgents had taken shelter were set on fire, and the inmates burned to death. No quarter was given, – no mercy shown; and most of those who had escaped, burning with disappointment, rage, and revenge, joined the Wexford party. John Bewley, a man endued with wisdom, courage, and benevolence, exerted them all in behalf of the deluded people, along with my husband and brother; and as he was not exposed to the suspicion which attached to an inhabitant, he treated with Colonel Campbell on their behalf. The Colonel was willing to make favourable terms with the insurgents, most of whom were willing to come in to him, but a few still held out, and amongst these was a priest. John Bewley proposed to take another message to Colonel Campbell; the people at length consented; but so much time had been lost meanwhile that Colonel Campbell's terms were now less favourable. Six hostages were demanded to be sent before an appointed time, to guarantee the surrender of the arms before the noon of the next day. They could not decide upon the hostages, the hour passed by, and the fate of Ballitore was sealed!

We believed the hostages had been sent, for we perceived the people had begun to weary of ill-doing; and a stranger, who begged some refreshment wistfully, asked me when there would be peace. We got our beds replaced upon their steads, and sank into that quiet repose which for some nights we had not known, little imagining what the morrow was to bring forth. This eventful morrow was the 27th of Fifth-month (May). At three o'clock in the morning the intelligence that the army was near roused us from our beds. We saw the glitter of arms through the dust which the horses of the 9th Dragoons made, galloping along the high road from Carlow. We heard the shots repeatedly fired. We saw the military descend the hill, cross the bridge, and halt before our house, where some dismounted and entered, and asked for milk and water. As I handed it, I trembled; my spirits, which had risen superior to the danger till now, fell; the dragoon perceived my emotion, and kindly told me I need not fear, that they came to protect us, adding, 'It is well you were not all murdered!' Thus assured, I recovered my composure. I should not have recovered it so easily had I known that my brother and his friends had walked forth to meet the troops, who were commanded by Major Dennis. John Bewley, holding up a paper from Colonel Campbell, said, 'We are prisoners!' 'It is well for you,' said the Major, 'that you are prisoners, else I should have shot you, every man.' Then raising himself in his stirrups, he revoked the orders given to his men, to fire upon every man in coloured clothes. Oh, rash and cruel orders, which exposed to such danger lives of such value, which if thus sacrificed no regrets could have restored! Nothing can justify such commands.

I thought the bitterness of death was passed, but the work was not yet begun. Colonel Campbell's men, who had impatiently rested on their arms several hours, marched out of Athy. They took Narraghmore in their way, and directed their mistaken rage against the newly erected house of Colonel Keatinge, planting cannon to destroy the dwelling which so much worth had inhabited. They mortally wounded John Carroll, cousin to the Colonel. This party of soldiers entered Ballitore exhausted by rage and fatigue; they brought cannon. Cannon in Ballitore! The horse and foot had now met. Colonel Campbell was here in person and many other officers. The insurgents had fled on the first alarm, – the peaceable inhabitants remained. The trumpet was sounded, – and the peaceable inhabitants were delivered up for two hours to the unbridled license of a furious soldiery! How shall I continue the fearful narrative?

My mind never could arrange the transactions which were crowded into those two hours. Every house in the Burrow was in flames; a row of houses opposite to the School was also set on fire; none others were burnt immediately in the village, but a great many windows were broken, and when I heard this crash I thought it was cannon. We saw soldiers bending under loads of plunder. Captain Palmer came in to see me, and was truly solicitous about us, and insisted on giving us 'a protection.' Soldiers came in for milk; some of their countenances were pale with anger, and they grinned at me, calling me names which I had never heard before. They said I had poisoned the milk which I gave them, and desired me to drink some, which I did with much indignation. Others were civil, and one enquired if we had any United Irishmen in the house. I told them we had. In that fearful time the least equivocation, the least deception appeared to me fraught with danger. The soldier continued his enquiry – 'Had they plundered us?' 'No, except of eating and drinking.' 'On free quarters,' he replied, smiled, and went away.

A fine-looking man, a soldier, came in, in an extravagant passion; neither his rage nor my terror could prevent me from observing that this man was strikingly handsome; he asked me the same question in the same terms – and I made the same answer. He cursed me with great bitterness, and raising his musket presented it to my breast. I desired him not to shoot me. It seemed as if he had the will, but not the power to do so. He turned from me, dashed pans and jugs off the kitchen table with his musket, and shattered the kitchen window. Terrified almost out of my wits, I ran out of the house, followed by several women almost as much frightened as myself. When I fled, my fears gained strength, and I believed my enemy was pursuing; I thought of throwing myself into the river at the foot of the garden, thinking the bullet could not hurt me in the water. One of our servants ran into the street to call for help. William Richardson and Charles Coote, who kindly sat on their horses outside our windows, came in and turned the ruffian out of the house.

That danger passed, I beheld from the back window of our parlour the dark red flames of Gavin's house and others rising above the green of the trees. At the same time a fat tobacconist from Carlow lolled upon one of our chairs, and talked boastingly of the exploits performed by the military whom he had accompanied; how they had shot several, adding, 'We burned one fellow in a barrel.' I never in my life felt disgust so strongly; it even overpowered the horror due to the deed, which had been actually committed. The stupid cruelty of a man in civil life, which urged him voluntarily and without necessity to leave his home and bear a part in such scenes, was far more revolting than the fiery wrath of a soldier.

While Captain Palmer was with me, a soldier who had been previously quartered at my mother's came to him, to beg leave to go see 'the old mistress.' My dear mother, who was now in the stage of second childhood, in her unconsciousness of what was passing, had lost the timidity of her nature, mingled and conversed freely in her simplicity with all parties, and was treated by all with the greatest respect and tenderness; for amid the darkness of the tumult, some rays of light gleamed forth, some countenances expressed humanity and a weariness of the work of death.

I must be an egotist in these relations, for I can scarcely describe anything but what I saw and heard. I scarce had the guidance even of my own movements. Sometimes I found myself with my children, whom I had shut up in a back room; again I was below, enquiring for my husband. Our old gardener was discovered lying in the shrubbery, and the instrument of death which was aimed at his defenceless breast was arrested by his daughter, who, rushing forward, begged that her life might be taken instead. The soldier spared both, but poor Polly was ever after subject to fits, which reduced her to a deplorable situation, and by which she eventually lost her life, being seized with one as she crossed a stream. A carpenter in the village took his goods into the grave-yard, and hid himself and his family there. But in vain – this solemn retreat was violated, their goods were plundered, and the poor old man was murdered in wanton cruelty.

Owen Finn, the smith who had been imprisoned and liberated, felt himself secure because of his late acquittal, and could not be prevailed upon to conceal himself or leave his house. Alas! he was mistaken in expecting that rage reeking with blood would stop to discriminate. Owen was dragged out of his cottage; his pleadings were not listened to; his cottage, where industry had assembled many comforts, was pillaged and then set on fire. His wife ran through the crowd, to assure herself of her husband's safety. She beheld his bleeding and dead body: she threw herself with her infant upon the corpse, while those who had wrought her misery assaulted her with abusive language, and threatened to kill her also. 'And I wished,' said she, 'that they would kill me!'

Tom Duffy, called 'The Fairy,' had come from Dublin that morning to the house of his sister, whose husband was a yeoman, and had fallen in the battle of Kilcullen. The widow, though agonized with sorrow, found some little comfort in assuring herself and her children of protection by reason of her husband having suffered on the side of government. Her grief was mingled with astonishment heightened to frenzy when she found she had deceived herself. Her brother, poor Fairy Tom, was murdered; her son was murdered; her servant-boy was murdered; her house was plundered; her little daughter, on seeing her brother's dead body, fell into fits which caused her death; and her own reason gave way. Such are the horrors of civil war.

Our poor Doctor Johnson had suffered much from fatigue and anxiety during those days of terror; he ate and slept but little; and on the 26th, coming into Mary and Anne Doyle's, he declared his firm belief that he should fall by one party or the other, adding he did not care how soon. They wanted him to lie down and get a little rest, but his agitated mind would not permit him to take any. Next morning he was made prisoner, not endeavouring to conceal himself. I saw him walking in his yeomanry dress with a crowd of soldiers, and thought he was in friendship with them. I did not know that they pressed the ends of their muskets on his feet as he walked, and, by thus tormenting him, showed how little mercy he had to expect from them. The crowd stopped before Mary and Anne Doyle's shop; the tumult was loud; I believe they called it a court martial. An officer asked my husband had the doctor been at the battle of Narraghmore. He assured him he had not. Charles Coote stood by him, and begged to have him taken to the colonel. What his friends said was disregarded. Some young men, prisoners, passed by; Doctor Johnson appealed to them, but they passed on in silence. He was alone and unarmed, and I believe had never raised his hand to injure any one. Captain Sandys, who afterwards lost his life at Vinegar Hill, took the doctor's part in this business. So many swords and bayonets, and at length a musket, could not be long in taking the life of an unarmed man.

A short time before the end, a soldier came into our parlour, and, with a kind of bitter smile, told me they were going to hang the doctor. I said I hoped not, and went up to my children, trembling. One of our servants entered the room, and said the doctor was shot. I started up and contradicted her; just then the trumpet sounded a retreat. The window near my bedside had for some time caused me a dread which I could not account for, save by having heard of persons being shot through windows. But to this window I now went mechanically, and saw stretched before it, lying on his back, the friend I had known from childhood – my neighbour, my physician. His arms were extended; there was a large wound in the lower part of his face; and his once graceful form and intelligent countenance were disfigured with more than the horrors of death. I took but one look; I cried aloud; and Anne Doyle led me away. We went to the back apartments; the glass of the windows was hot from the reflection of burning houses, but I looked on them with a stupid composure. My only thought was, Is my husband safe? Had not our dwelling and offices been slated, we should have been probably houseless, for the unchecked flames rose in dreadful spires, and the crash of falling roofs caused a terrific sound. The morning was balmy, beautiful, and mild; bounteous Nature smiled sweetly upon us, rich with the treasures of a benign Creator. The unbridled passion of man alone deformed the scene!

Captain Palmer, naturally good-natured, was peculiarly desirous to preserve everybody and everything in the vale he loved so well. He learned the doctor's danger, and hastened from Athy to save him; but he came, alas! too late – too late for that purpose, but in time to rescue another who was in those hands reeking with blood, and ready to take his life, as, speechless with terror, he stood beholding the sad spectacle. Priest Cullen, justly apprehensive for his life, had applied to my brother for one of his coats wherewith to disguise himself, but dared not wait to put it on. He ran to Boakefield, and hid in one of the clumps of trees in the lawn, while several officers were refreshing themselves in the parlour, and soldiers were scattered about the house, who seemed to thirst for his blood.

After the trumpet had sounded a retreat, a soldier shot one of our pigs, for which he was tied to a car and lashed. Oh! how shocking that seemed to me! Commanded to take the precious human life – punished for taking that of a brute! The progress of the army on the way they went was impeded by trees purposely felled by the insurgents a day or two before. Some of the soldiers availed themselves of this delay to return to Ballitore, and renew the work of plunder. This alarmed Charles Coote on our account, as he justly feared the protections previously granted would not again avail. The soldiers were overloaded with their spoils, and had to throw some away. A paper was discovered in a work-bag, containing a list of names which roused suspicion. Charles Coote, on the watch, claimed to look at the paper, and quickly convinced the soldiers that their suspicions were unfounded; yet his heart was wrung in secret, for this paper, in my handwriting, contained the charades and rebuses with which we had amused ourselves on one of our past happy evenings, with a list of explanations. He feared lest those who had returned might plunder and murder us; and the anguish of such an apprehension was quickened by the contrast with the convivial hour. Thus Homer heightens our interest in the fate of Hector, by pointing him to our view as flying from his destroyer by those fountains,

> 'Where Trojan dames, ere yet alarmed by Greece,
> Washed their fair garments in the days of peace.'[1]

Now the blast was over – all was silent and sad. Our houseless tenants were sheltered under our roof; we sat down with Mary and Anne, – the closed windows concealing our dead friend from us. Mary, pale as death, shook the table on which she leaned with her excessive trembling; and when Anne saw the body carried along and thrown over the little wall at the corner where the elm tree once stood, her cry of grief was heart-piercing; – while I sate like a stone. The report of the soldiers intending to return made his neighbours afraid to shelter in their houses those dear remains. Here they were carefully watched, for the swine, snuffing blood, were waiting to make a horrid repast. For several months there was no sale for bacon cured in Ireland, from the well founded dread of the hogs having fed upon the flesh of men....

On the 29th, people ventured to seek for their friends, and to bury their dead. Whether it was that having so many companions in misfortune lightened the load, whether they considered those that had fallen as martyrs, or whether

> 'Vengeance, deep brooding o'er the slain,
> Had locked the source of softer woe,'[2]

there did not appear so much lamentation as one might have expected. The ruins of cars lay in some of the ditches at the entrance into Ballitore, and in another ditch lay the scull of the poor youth who had been burnt in the barrel where he sought refuge.

I saw moving along under the arching trees a few persons, chiefly women, bearing an empty coffin. I joined them in silence, and met in the grave-yard my husband and two or three more, about to open the grave in which the poor doctor was laid, and at his widow's desire to re-enter him in a coffin. I saw the earth being removed; I wished yet dreaded to see the body. A shroud was wanted; I hastened back to

---

1. *The Iliad*, tr. Alexander Pope, Book XXII, 'The Death of Hector', ll. 203–04.
2 Sir Walter Scott, *The Lay of the Last Minstrel* I. ix. 7–8.

Mary and Anne's for it; we hastily made it, and returned towards the grave-yard with it, till a boy met us who had been sent to fetch it; therefore the body had been washed, wrapped in its shroud, and laid in the coffin before we got there. I experienced strange and contradictory feelings while I stood at the grave-yard door, wishing and yet fearing to enter; Mary and Anne confessed to similar sensations, but we all regretted our irresolution when we heard the coffin lid screwed down. My husband, when he saw how it disturbed me, regretted that he had hastened to prevent our seeing so sad a sight, though the remains were little altered by having lain three days in the earth. The bloody waistcoat lay near, and the sight of it renewed our emotions of horror.

Timolin was attacked after Ballitore, and several houses in its suburbs burnt. Conway, a Protestant, was protected, or rather spared by one party of soldiers, but was cut down by another, and his house shared the fate of the other dwellings. The Dublin road for nearly four miles north of Ballitore exhibited a scene of desolation, few houses having escaped there; and about Narraghmore and Crookstown the same destruction was apparent. The street of Ballitore was strewed with broken glass and earthenware, ground by the trampling of the feet. We looked around at our altered village, and were ready to wonder that we yet lived. 'Surely the wrath of man shall praise Thee, the remainder of wrath wilt Thou restrain.'[1] We were sensible that a preserving Providence had restrained that wrath which threatened general destruction.

Hostages having been sent, the insurgents prepared to deliver up their arms on the 30th. A little boy was the herald, who with a bit of white paper stuck in his hat to announce his office, and secure his person, passed safely between the opposite parties, and we respected the little fellow for his courage. The appointed spot of our meeting was about half way between this and Athy, and there the insurgents were informed that those who had assembled on the Curragh for a similar purpose, had been, I suppose by some unfortunate mistake, fallen upon by a party commanded by Sir James Duff, and put to the sword. Terrified by this intelligence, many returned at full speed; but by my brother's and Ephraim Boake's exertions, representations, and offers to accompany them, they were prevailed upon to go back and conclude this disastrous business, by delivering up their arms, and obtaining pardon for their offences against government, though not for those committed against the laws of their country. Ephraim Boake was

---

1. Psalm 76: 10.

a wise old man; he was truly loyal to his king, but he did not think loyalty incompatible with mercy. 'Those who do not like this government,' he was wont to say, 'let them go and live under another; but while they are protected by this, let them not disturb it.'

The prisoners had gone away under the protection of the army – some of the soldiers leaving money to relieve the present distress of the poor. Indeed many characters were now developed; the sordid, the carnal, the selfish had gained opportunity of gratification; while brighter through the surrounding gloom beamed the candid, the liberal, the benevolent mind, and Captain Chenery and Captain Palmer will be long remembered in Ballitore.

SIR JONAH BARRINGTON (1760–1834)

Barrington was born in a Big House at Knapton, Co. Laois, the fourth of sixteen children. His description of the setting of his childhood is reminiscent of *Castle Rackrent** in its profligacy. He studied at Trinity College, Dublin, and was called to the Bar in 1788. He took silk in 1793, and became a judge in the admiralty in 1798. In 1790 he was returned to the Irish House of Commons for Tuam; he lost his seat in 1797, and was returned in 1798, representing Clogher until January 1800; he contested Dublin city unsuccessfully in 1802. He was knighted in May 1807. Barrington claimed that he had received an offer for the solicitor-generalship from Lord Clare in 1799 if he lent his support to the Act of Union, but he seems to have been less incorruptible, buying over members to the government side. His extravagant lifestyle brought him into debt, and he appropriated money that had been paid into his court – as was discovered in 1830. In 1815 he moved to France to escape his creditors, and he died in Versailles in 1834.

Barrington is the convivial historian of the raucously rombustious Protestant gentry before the Act of Union. His *Personal Sketches of His Own Times* (3 vols, 1827; 1832) portrays a society of barbarous civility, with heavy drinking, hardy fighting, sophisticated wit and political intrigue. In *The Rise and Fall of the Irish Nation* (1833) Barrington expressed his aversion for the Act of Union, exposing the political conspiracies that led to the Irish Parliament's voting itself out of existence.

From *Personal Sketches of His Own Times*

(1827)

IRISH BEAUTIES

It is singular enough, but at the same time true, that female beauty has of late years kept pace in improvement with modern accomplishments.

She who in the early part of my life would have been accounted a perfect beauty, whose touch upon a harpsichord or spinnet, accompanied by a simple air sung what they then called 'judgment' (in tune), would have constituted her at once a Venus and a Syren, would now be passed by merely as 'a pretty girl, but such a confounded *bore* with her music?' In fact, women fifty years since, and much later, not being, generally speaking, thrust into society till they had arrived at the age of maturity, were more respected, more beloved, and more sedulously attended than in these days, when the men seem to have usurped the ladies' corsets, to affect their voices, practise their gait, imitate their small talk, and in surtouts and trowsers hustle ladies off the footpaths, to save their own dog-skins from humidity.

This degradation of both sexes has arisen from various causes. Beauty is apparently become less rare, accomplishments more common, dress less distinguished, dignity worse preserved, and decorum less attended to than in former times. It is a great mistake in women not to recollect their own importance, and keep up that just medium between reserve and familiarity which constitutes the best criterion whereby to appreciate the manners of a gentlewoman. But women are too apt to run into extremes in everything, and overlook the fact, that neither personal beauty nor drawing-room display are calculated to form permanent attractions, even to the most adoring lover. The *breakfast-table* in the morning and *fireside* in the evening must be the ultimate touchstones of connubial comfort; and this is a maxim which any woman who intends to marry should never lose sight of.

To such lengths did respect for the sex extend, and so strong was the impression that men were bound to protect it even from accidental offence, that I remember if any gentleman presumed to pass between a lady and the wall in walking the streets of Dublin, he was considered as offering a personal affront to her escort; and if the parties wore swords, as was then customary, it is probable the first salutation to the offender would be, 'Draw, sir!' However, such affairs usually ended in an apology to the lady for inadvertence.

But if a man ventured to intrude into the boxes of the theatre in his surtout or boots, or with his hat on, it was regarded as a general insult to every lady present, and he had little chance of escaping without a shot or a thrust before the following night. Every gentleman then wore in the evening a sword, a queue, and a three-cocked hat – appointments rather too fierce looking for the modern dandy! whilst the morning dress consisted of what was then called a French frock, a waistcoat bordered with lace, and a *couteau de chasse,* with a short curved broad blade, the handle of green ivory, with a lion's head in silver or gilt at the end, and a treble chain dangling loose from its mouth, terminating at an ornamented cross or guard which surmounted the scabbard. Such was the Irish costume; but although either the male or female attire of that day might now appear rather grotesque, yet people of fashion had then the exclusive dress and air of such, and gentlewomen ran no risk of being copied in garb or manner by their pretty waiting-maids, now called 'young persons!'

The Irish court at that period was kept up with great state, and hence the parties who frequented it were more select. I recollect when the wives and daughters of attorneys, who now I believe are the general occupiers of the red benches, were never admitted to the vice-regal drawing-rooms. How far the present growing system of equality in appearance amongst different ranks will eventually benefit or injure society in general, is for casuists, not for me, to determine. I must, however, take occasion to own myself an admirer, and, whenever it is proper, a zealous contender for distinction of ranks; and to state my decided opinion, that nothing but superior talents, learning, military reputation, or some other quality which raises men by general assent, should be permitted to amalgamate society.

It is an observation I have always made, although it may be perhaps considered a frivolous one, that dress has a moral effect upon the conduct of mankind. Let any gentleman find himself with dirty boots, old surtout, soiled neck-cloth, and a general negligence of dress, he will in all probability find a corresponding disposition to negligence of address. He may, *en deshabille,* curse and swear, and speak roughly and *think* roughly; but put the same man into frill dress, powder him well, clap a sword by his side, and give him an evening coat, breaches, and silk stockings, he will feel himself quite another person! To use the language of the blackguard would then be out of character: he will talk smoothly, affect politeness, if he has it not, pique himself upon good manners, and respect the women; nor will the spell subside until returning home, the old *robe de chambre,* or its substitute surtout, with other slovenly appendages, make him lose again his brief consciousness of being a gentleman!

Some women mistake the very nature and purposes of dress: glaring abroad, they are slatterns at home. The husband detests in his *sposa* what he is too apt to practise himself: he rates a dirty wife, she retorts upon a ruffianly husband, and each of them detests the other for neglect which neither will take the trouble of avoiding.

Three ladies, about the period of my return from London, became very conspicuous for their beauty, though extremely different in all points both of appearance and manners. They still live. Two of them I greatly admired, not for beauty alone, but for an address the most captivating; and one of these, especially, for the kindest heart and the soundest sense, when she gave it fair play, that I have ever met with amongst females.

In admitting my great preference to this individual lady, I may, perhaps, by those who know her, be accused of partiality, less to herself than to a family: be it so! she is the wife of my friend, and I esteem her for his sake; but she is also an excellent woman, and I esteem her for her own.

Another of the parties alluded to, Lady M—— is a gentlewoman of high birth, and was then, though not *quite* a beauty, in all points attractive. She passed her spring in misfortune, her summer in misery, her autumn without happiness! but I hope the winter of her days is spent amidst every comfort. Of the third lady I have not yet spoken: though far inferior to both the former, she has succeeded better in life than either; and, beginning the world without any pretensions beyond mediocrity, is likely to end her days in ease and more than ordinary respectability.

My first knowledge of Lady M—— arose from a circumstance which was to me of singular professional advantage; and as it forms a curious anecdote respecting myself, I will proceed to relate it.

At the assizes of Wexford, whilst I was but young at the bar, I received a brief in a cause of Sir R—— M—— , Bart., against a Mr. H——. On perusal, I found it was an action brought by the baronet against the latter gentleman respecting his lady, and that I was retained as advocate for the lady's honour. It was my 'first appearance' in that town. But, alas! I had a senior in the business, and therefore was without opportunity of displaying my abilities. The illfated Bagenal Harvey[1] was that senior counsel, and he had prepared himself to make some exhibition in a cause of so much and such universal excitement. I felt dispirited, and would willingly have given up twenty fees in order to possess his opportunity.

The cause proceeded before Judge Kelly: the evidence was finished, and the proper time for the defence had arrived; everything as to the lady was at stake. Bagenal Harvey had gone out to take fresh air, and probably to read over some notes, or con some florid sentences and

---

1 An unfortunate friend of mine who was afterwards hanged, and his head stuck over the door of the same Court House. [*Barrington's note.*]

quotations with which he intended to interlard his elocution. At the moment the evidence closed, the judge desired me to proceed. I replied, that Mr. Harvey, my senior, would return into court directly.

Judge Kelly, who was my friend, and clearly saw my wish, said he would not delay public business one minute for anybody; and by a sort of instinct, or rather impulse, – I cannot indeed exactly say what it was, but certainly it was totally *impromptu*, – I began to state her ladyship's case. I always had words enough at command; the evidence afforded sufficient material for their exercise; and in fact, being roused by the cause into a sort of knight-errantry, I felt myself completely identified with it. If I should succeed, it would greatly serve me. I forgot poor Bagenal Harvey, and was just getting into the marrow and pathos of my case, when the crier shouted out, 'Clear the way for Counsellor Harvey!' Bagenal came in puffing and blowing, and struggling through the crowd, scarcely able to command utterance. I instantly stopped, and begged his pardon, adding that the judge had said the public time could wait for nobody! 'So,' continued I, 'let me just shew you where I left off!' turning over the leaves of my brief, 'there, begin there, it will be useless to repeat what I have already said, so begin there.' A loud laugh succeeded.

Bagenal became irritated as much as he was susceptible of being, and whispered me that he considered it as a personal insult; whilst old Judge Kelly gravely said, 'Go on, Mr. Barrington, go on, we can have no speeches by dividends, go on, sir!' So on I went, and I believe, because everybody told me so, that my impromptu speech was entirely successful. I discredited the witnesses by ridicule, destroyed all sympathy with the husband, and interested everybody for the wife. In short, I got the judge and jury into good humour. Yet, I know not by what means I should have ensured a verdict, had not a certain point of law, which I believe was then stated for the first time, occurred to me, and which, though rational in itself, and on that trial recognised by the judge, has since been overruled in terms, though it stands in substance, – namely, if a husband cannot truly aver that he has sustained mental injury by the loss of that comfort arising from the *society* of a wife, it is anomalous to say he has any claim to damages; and this averment can scarcely be made where the parties have been separated voluntarily and completely for years.[1]

1 This is, indeed, altogether a species of action maintained in no country but England, a money country. Why not transfer the offence to the *criminal* side of the courts of justice? All the rest of Europe ridicules our system. The idea entertained on the Continent upon such occasions is silence or death, if not the most lucrative, certainly the most *honourable* mode of procedure. [*Barrington's note.*]

The judge, the kindest-hearted man living, chuckled at this new point. The jury, who did not much admire the plaintiff, were quite pleased with my suggestion; and after the judge had given his charge, in a few minutes, to the utter discomfiture of the baronet, there was a verdict against him! His lips quivered, he stood pale and trembling with anger, and subsequently quitted the town with the utmost expedition.

Some time afterwards a reconciliation took place between the parties so far that her ladyship consented to live with him again – influenced much, I rather think, by having suffered great inconvenience, if not distress, from want of regularity in the receipt of her separate maintenance of £700 per annum. I had the pleasure of meeting her frequently at the Lady-Lieutenant's parties.

The conclusion of the renewed intercourse is too curious to be omitted. Sir R—— had taken a house in the city of Dublin, and it was thought possible that he and his wife might, at any rate, pass some time under the same roof: but fate decided otherwise.

Sir R—— was literally insane on all political subjects, his imagination being occupied night and day with nothing but papists, Jesuits, and rebels. Once in the dead of the night his lady was awakened by a sense of positive suffocation, and rousing herself, found that Sir R—— was in the very act of strangling her! – he had grasped her by the throat with all his might, and muttering heavy imprecations, had nearly succeeded in his diabolical attempt. She struggled, and at length extricated herself from his grasp; upon which he roared out, making a fresh effort, – 'You infernal papist rebel! you United Irishman! I'll never part from you alive, if you don't come quietly.'

In fact this crazy Orangeman had in his dream fancied that he was contesting with a rebel, whom he had better choke than suffer to escape, and poor Lady M—— was nearly sacrificed to his excess of loyalty. In her *robe de chambre* and slippers she contrived to get out of the house, and never more ventured to return, as she now clearly perceived that even her personal safety could not be calculated on in her husband's society.

*   *   *

PATRICIANS AND PLEBEIANS

I will now proceed to lay before the reader a brief but more general sketch of the state of Irish society at the period of my youth, reminding him of the principle which I have before assumed – namely, that of considering anecdotes, bon-mots, and such like, valuable only as they tend to exemplify interesting facts, relative to history or manners: many such I have inserted in these fragments; and as I have been careful throughout to avoid mere inventions, my reader need not by any means reserve their perusal for the study of his travelling carriage.

Miss Edgeworth, in her admirable sketch of *Castle Rackrent*, gives a faithful picture of the Irish character under the circumstances which she has selected; and the account that I am about to give may serve as a kind of supplement to that little work, as well as an elucidation of the habits and manners of Irish country society about the period Miss Edgeworth alludes to, and somewhat later.

In those days, then, the common people ideally separated the gentry of the country into three classes, and treated each class according to the relative degree of respect to which they considered it was entitled.

They generally divided them thus: –

1. *Half-mounted* gentlemen.
2. Gentlemen every *inch of them*.
3. Gentlemen to the *backbone*.

The first-named class formed the only species of independent yeomanry then existing in Ireland. They were the descendants of the small grantees of Queen Elizabeth, Cromwell, and King William; possessed about 200 acres of land each, in fee farm, from the Crown; and were occasionally admitted into the society of gentlemen, particularly hunters, living at other times amongst each other with an intermixture of their own servants, with whom they were always on terms of intimacy. They generally had good clever horses, which could leap over anything, but had never felt the trimming-scissors or curry-comb. The riders commonly wore buck-skin breeches, and boots well greased – blacking was never used in the country – and carried large thong whips heavily loaded with lead at the butt-end, so that they were always prepared either to horsewhip a man or knock his brains out, as circumstances might dictate. These half-mounted gentlemen exercised the hereditary authority of keeping the ground clear at horse-races, hurlings, and all public meetings, as the soldiers keep the line at a review. Their business was to ride round the inside of the ground, which they generally did with becoming spirit, trampling over some, knocking down others, and slashing everybody who encroached on the proper limits. Bones being but very *seldom* broken, and skulls still seldomer fractured, everybody approved of their exertions, because all the bystanders gained therefrom a full view of the sport which was going forward. A shout of merriment was always set up when a half-mounted gentleman knocked down an interloper; and some of the *poets* present, if they had an opportunity, roared out their verses[1] by way of a song to encourage the gentlemen.

The second class, or gentlemen every *inch of them*, were of excellent old families, whose finances were not in so good order as they might have been, but who were popular amongst all ranks. They were far above the first degree, somewhat inferior to the third, but had great influence, were much beloved, and carried more sway at popular elections and general county meetings than the other two classes put together.

The third class, or gentlemen to the *backbone*, were of the oldest families and settlers, universally respected, and idolized by the peasantry, although they also were generally a little out at elbows. Their word was law, their nod would have immediately collected an army of cottagers, or colliers, or whatever the population was composed of. Men, women, and children were always ready and willing to execute anything 'the squire' required, without the slightest consideration as to either its danger or propriety.

A curious circumstance, perhaps, rendered my family peculiarly popular. The common people had conceived the notion that the lord of Cullenaghmore had a right to save a man's life every summer assizes at Maryborough; and it did frequently so happen, within my recollection, that my father's intercession in favour of some poor deluded creatures (when the White Boy system was in activity) was kindly attended to by the Government; and, certainly, besides this number, many others of his tenants owed their lives to similar interference. But it was wise in the Government to accede to such representations, since their concession never failed to create such an influence in my father's person over the tenantry, that he was enabled to preserve them in perfect tranquillity, whilst those surrounding were in a constant state of insubordination to all law whatever.

---

1 I recollect an example of those good-humoured madrigals. A poet, called Daniel Bran, sang it aloud as he himself lay sprawling on the grass, after having been knocked down and ridden over by old Squire Flood, who showed no mercy in the 'execution of his *duty*'

> 'There was Despard so brave,
> That of the wave,
> And Tom Conway, the pride of the bower;
> But noble Squire Flood
> swore, G–d d–n his blood!
> But he'd drown them all in the Delower.'
> [*Barrigton's note.*]

87

I recollect a Mr. Tom Flinter, of Timahoe, one of the first-class gentlemen, who had speculated in cows and sheep, and everything he could buy up, till his establishment was reduced to one blunt faithful fellow, Dick Hennessy, who stuck to him throughout all his vicissitudes. Flinter had once on a time got a trifle of money, which was burning in his greasy pocket, and he wanted to expend it at a neighbouring fair! where his whole history, as well as the history of every man of his half-mounted contemporaries, was told in a few verses,[1] by a fellow called Ned the dog-stealer, but who was also a *great poet*, and resided in the neighbourhood.

In travelling through Ireland, a stranger is very frequently puzzled by the singular ways, and especially by the idiomatic equivocation, characteristic of every Irish peasant. Some years back, more particularly, these men were certainly originals – quite unlike any other people whatever. Many an hour of curious entertainment has been afforded me by their eccentricities; yet though always fond of prying into the remote sources of these national peculiarities, I must frankly confess that, with all my pains, I never was able to develop half of them, except by one sweeping observation – namely, that the brains and tongues of the Irish are somehow differently formed or furnished from those of other people.

One general hint which I beg to impress upon all travellers in Hibernia, is the following: that if they show a disposition towards kindness, together with a moderate familiarity, and *affect* to be *inquisitive*, whether so or not, the Irish peasant will outdo them tenfold in every one of these dispositions. But if a man is haughty and overbearing, he had better take care of himself.

---

1 They were considered as a standig joke for many years in that part of the country, and ran as follows:

DIALOGUE BETWEEN TOM FLINTER AND HIS MAN

Tom Flinter.	Dick! said he.
Dick Henesey.	What? said he
Tom Flinter.	Fetch me my hat, says he;
	For I will go, says he
	To Timahoe, says he;
	To buy the fair, says he;
	And all that's there, says he.
Dick Henesey.	Arrah! *pay what you owe!* said he;
	And *then* you may go, says he;
	To Timahoe, says he;
	To buy the fair, says he;
	And all that's there, says he;
Tom Flinter.	Well! by this and by that,, said he;
	Dick! *hang up my hat!* says he.

[*Barrigton's note.*]

I have often heard it remarked and complained of, by travellers and strangers, that they never could get a true answer from any Irish peasant as to *distances* when on a journey. For many years I myself thought it most unaccountable. If you meet a peasant on your journey and ask him how far, for instance, to Ballinrobe? he will probably say it is '*three short* miles.' You travel on, and are informed by the next peasant you meet, that it is '*five long* miles.' On you go, and the next will tell 'your honour' it is '*four miles*, or about that same.' The fourth will swear 'if your honour stops at *three* miles, you'll never get there!' But on pointing to a town just before you, and inquiring what place that is, he replies,

'Oh! plaze your honour, that's Ballinrobe, sure enough!'

'Why, you said it was more than three miles off!'

'Oh yes! to be sure and sartin, that's from my *own cabin*, plaze your honour. We're no scholards in this country. Arrah! how can we tell any distance, plaze your honour, but from our own *little cabins*? Nobody but the schoolmaster knows that, plaze your honour.'

Thus is the mystery unravelled. When you ask any peasant the distance of the place you require, he never computes it from where you *then are*, but from his *own* cabin, so that if you asked twenty, in all probability you would have as many different answers, and not one of them correct. But it is to be observed, that frequently you get no reply at all, unless you understand *Irish*.

In parts of Kerry and Mayo, however, I have met with peasants who speak Latin not badly. On the election of Sir John Brown for the County of Mayo, Counsellor Thomas Moore and I went down as his counsel. The weather was desperately severe. At a solitary inn, where we were obliged to stop for horses, we requested dinner, upon which the waiter laid a cloth that certainly exhibited every species of dirt ever invented. We called, and, remonstrating with him, ordered a clean cloth. He was a low fat fellow, with a countenance perfectly immovable, and seeming to have scarcely single muscle in it. He nodded, and on our return to the room, which we had quitted during the interval, we found, instead of a clean cloth, that he had only folded up the filthy one into the thickness of a cushion. We now scolded away in good earnest. He looked at us with the greatest *sang-froid*, and said sententiously: '*Nemo me impune lacessit*'.[1]

He kept his word; when we had proceeded about four miles in

---

1 *Nemo me impune lacessit*: 'No one injures me with impunity' – first used on coins of James VI of Scotland (James I of England).

deep snow, and through a desperate night, on a bleak road, one of the wheels came off the carriage, and down we went! We were at least two miles from *any* house. The driver cursed in Irish Michael the waiter, who, he said, had put a *new* wheel upon the carriage, which had turned out to be an *old* one, and had broken to pieces.

We had to march through the snow to a wretched cottage, and sit up all night to get a genuine *new wheel* ready for the morning.

The Irish peasant also never answers any questions directly: in some districts, if you ask him where such a gentleman's house is, he will point and reply, 'Does your honour see that large house there all amongst the trees, with a green field before it?' You answer, 'Yes'. 'Well,' says he, 'plaze your honour that's *not it*. But do you see the big brick house with the cowhouses by the side of that same, and a pond of water?' 'Yes!'

'Well, plaze your honour, *that's* not it. But, if you plaze, look quite to the right of that same house, and you'll see the top of a castle amongst the trees there, with a road going down to it betune the bushes.'

'Yes!'

'Well, plaze your honour, *that's not it* neither; but if your honour will come down this bit of a road a couple of miles, I'll show it you *sure enough* – and if your honour's in a hurry, I can run on *hot foot*,[1] and tell the squire your honour's *galloping after* me. Ah! Who shall I tell the squire, plaze your honour, is coming to see him? he's my own landlord, God save his honour day and night!'

From *The Rise and Fall of the Irish Nation*

(1833)

PREFATORY OBSERVATIONS

More than thirty summers have now passed by, since that disastrous measure called a 'Legislative Union' extinguished at one blow, the pride, the prosperity, and the independence of the Irish Nation.

A measure which, under the false colours of guarding for ever against a disunion of the empire, has taken the longest and surest stride to lead it to dismemberment.

---

1 A figurative expression for 'with all possible *speed*' – used by the Irish peasants; by taking short cuts, and fairly hopping along, a young peasant would beat any traveller. [*Barrington's note.*]

A measure which, instead of *'consolidating the strength and resources of the empire,'* as treacherously expressed from the throne of the Viceroy, has through its morbid operation, paralysed the resources of Ireland; whilst England is exhausting her own strength, squandering her own treasures, and clipping her own constitution, to uphold a measure effected by corruption, and maintained by oppression.

A measure which, pretending to tranquilize, has, in fact, excited more hostile, and I fear, interminable disgust, than had ever before existed between the two nations and has banished from both, that mutual and invigorating attachment, which was daily augmenting, under the continuance of the federative connexion.

The protecting body of the country gentlemen have evacuated Ireland, and in their stead, we now find official clerks, griping agents, haughty functionaries, and proud Clergy. The resident aristocracy of Ireland, if not quite extinguished, is hourly diminishing; and it is a political truism, that the co-existence of an oligarchy, without a cabinet, a resident executive, and an absent legislation, tenants without landlords, and magistrates without legal knowledge, must be, from its nature, a form of constitution at once incongruous, inefficient, and dangerous. The present is a state which cannot exist: it is a struggle that cannot continue, there is a 'tide' in the affairs of Empires, as well as of individuals; every fever has a crisis: Ireland is in one now, I am no fanatic, I am the partisan only of tranquillity, in the country where I drew my first breath.

The people of England, and also of some continental kingdoms, are fully aware of the distracted state of Ireland, but are at a loss to account for it; it is now, however, in proof, that thirty-three years of Union have been thirty-three years of beggary and disturbance, and this result, I may fairly say, I always foresaw....

CHAPTER XXVII

I. It is not possible to comprise in a single volume a tithe of the means and measures of every description, resorted to by the Viceroy and Secretary, not only to seduce the members, put to procure addresses favourable to their views, from every or any rank or description of people, from the first rank to the very lowest order; beggars, cottagers, tradesmen, every individual who could be influenced, were tempted to put in their names or marks to addresses, not one word of which they understood the intent, still less the ruinous results of. Even public instances were adduced, some mentioned in Parliament, and not denied, of felons in the gaols purchasing pardon, or transmutation, by signatures, or by forging names to Union eulogiums.

English generals, who, at a moment when martial law existed, or a recollection of its execution was still fresh in every memory, could not fail to have their own influence over proclaimed districts and bleeding peasantry; of course, their success in procuring addresses to Parliament, was not limited either by their power, their disposition, or their instructions.

The Anti-Union addresses, innumerable and fervid, in their very nature voluntary, and the signatures of high consideration, were stigmatized by the title of seditious and disloyal; whilst those of the compelled, the bribed, and the culprit were printed and circulated by every means that the treasury, or the influence of the Government, could effect.

Mr. Darby, High Sheriff of King's County, and Major Rogers of the artillery, had gone so far as to place two six-pounders towards the doors of the Court House, where the gentlemen and freeholders of the county were assembling to address as Anti-Unionists; and it is not to be wondered at, that the dread of grape-shot not only stopped those, but numerous meetings for similar purposes. Yet this was one of the means taken to prevent the expression of public meetings without, and formed a proper comparison for the measures – resorted to, within the walls of Parliament.

As this volume cannot detail the innumerable circumstances and episodes which a perfect history of those times would embody, it may be enough to say, that if the English readers of this work will imagine any act that an indefatigable, and, on this subject, the most corrupt Governments, could by possibility resort to, to carry a measure they had determined on, such readers cannot imagine acts more illegal, unconstitutional, and corrupt, than those of the Viceroy of Ireland, his Secretary and Under-Secretary employed, from the close of the session of 1799 to that of 1800. In the last of the Irish Parliaments every thing therefore is passed over, or but slightly touched on, till the opening of the last session.

II. Lords Cornwallis[1] and Castlereagh,[2] having made good progress during the recess, now discarded all secrecy and reserve. To excite the various acts of *simple metallic corruption* which were practised without any reserve, during the summer of 1799, are [*sic*] too numerous for this volume. It will be sufficient to describe the proceedings, with-

---

1 Charles, 1st Marquis and 2nd Earl of Cornwallis (1738–1805), Viceroy of Ireland (1798–1801).
2 Robert Stewart, Viscount Castlereagh, and 2nd Marquis of Londonderry (1769–1822), was Chief Secretary for Ireland in 1799.

out particularising the individuals. Many of the Peers, and several of the Commoners had the patronage of boroughs, the control of which was essential to the success of the Minister's project. These patrons Lord Castlereagh assailed by every means which his power and situation afforded. Lord Cornwallis was the remote, Lord Castlereagh the intermediate, and Mr. Secretary Cooke,[1] the immediate agents on many of these bargains. Lord Shannon, the Marquis of Ely, and several other Peers commanding votes, after much coquetry, had been secured during the first session, but the defeat of Government rendered their future support uncertain. The Parliamentary patrons had breathing time after the preceding session, and began to tremble for their patronage and importance; and some desperate step became necessary to Government to insure a continuance of the support of these personages. This object gave rise to a measure which the British nation will scarcely believe possible, its enormity is without parallel.

Lord Castlereagh's first object was to introduce into the House, by means of the Place Bill, a sufficient number of dependants to balance all opposition. He then boldly announced his intention to turn the scale, by bribes to all who would accept them, under the name of *compensation* for the loss of patronage and interest. He publicly declared, *first*, that every nobleman who returned members to Parliament, should be paid, in cash, £15,000 for every member so returned; *secondly*, that every member who had *purchased* a seat in Parliament should have his purchase-money repaid to him, by the Treasury of Ireland; *thirdly*, that all members of Parliament, or others, who were losers by an Union, should be fully recompensed for their losses, and that 1,500,000 should be devoted to this service; in other terms, all who supported his measure were, under some pretence or other, to share in this bank of corruption.

A declaration so flagitious and treasonable was never publicly made in any country; but it had a powerful effect in his favour; and, before the meeting of Parliament, he had secured a small majority (as heretofore mentioned,) of eight above a moiety of the members, and he courageously persisted.

After the debate on the Union in 1800, he performed his promise, and brought in a bill to raise one million and a half of money upon the Irish people, nominally to compensate, but really to bribe their representatives, for betraying their honour and selling their country. This Bill was but feebly resisted; the divisions of January and February

---

1 Edward Cooke (1775–1820), Under-Secretary for Ireland (1796–1804).

(1800) had reduced the success of the Government to a certainty, and all further opposition was abandoned. It was unimportant to Castlereagh, who received the plunder of the Nation; the taxes were levied, and a vicious partiality was effected in the partition.

The assent to the Bill by his Majesty, as King of Ireland, gives rise to perhaps the most grave consideration suggested in these memoirs....

SIR VERE HUNT (1761–1818)

Descended from Vere Hunt, a Cromwellian officer who settled in Curragh Chase in 1657, and whose grandmother, Jane de Vere, was daughter of Aubrey de Vere, second son of the fifteenth earl of Oxford, he became High Sheriff of Co. Limerick, and was created baronet in 1784. Lt-Colonel of the 135th Limerick Regiment of Foot, he was the father of Sir Aubrey de Vere*. MP for Askeaton, his seat had cost him £5,000 – a sum which he tried to recoup by voting for the Union. He purchased Lundy Island, in the Bristol Channel, which for years he tried to sell to the government. A heavy gambler, he spent months in the Fleet, the debtor's gaol.

From His Diaries

28 March 1798

The County[1] met at one over the Exchange. I proposed that it be recommended to landlords to give a temporary abatement to poor tenants on account of the fall of grain, and to pay tythes for those under £10 a year rent. It was negatived. A memorial was sent to the Lord Lieutenant signed by thirty-six Justices to proclaim the entire county as in a state of insurrection. Dined at Harry Fosbery's and got drunk.

23 May 1798 – Dublin

The town in great confusion and a rising expected every hour.... Went to the Castle,[2] saw Lord Edward Fitzgerald's uniform....[3] Lord Rossmore showed me an impression of the Great Seal found on Lord Edward.... People taken up every instant and flogged by military law to get confessions.... Determined to send my family off without delay, called with a hackney coach for Lady Hunt, Aubrey and Jenny Bindon, and set out for the *Prince of Wales* Packet. She could not sail,

---

1 *The County*: Co. Limerick.
2 the Castle: Dublin Castle, the centre of adminstration, housed the offices of the Chief Secretary, the law offices of the Crown. It was used by the Lord Lieutenant as his town residence; St Patrick's Hall was the venue for state occasions.
3 *Lord Edward Fizgerald* (1763–98), a gallant leader of the United Irishmen. He was arrested on 19th May, and died on 4 June, of wounds inflicted during his arrest.

the wind being foul, and we all slept on board. Heard from Captain Hill of the *Lady Fitzgibbon* that Frank Arthur, Dr Hargrove, Doctor Ross (all from Limerick) and others were apprehended, and from my Uncle William Hunt that his son Billy was taken up.

28 May 1813 – Dublin

Walked into town and met Major Sirr[1] near the Castle, who stopped me and told me exultingly, as if I had been, which God forbid, an enemy to Catholic Emancipation, that the question was lost, a majority of four being against it in the Commons. I surprised him not a little, when I replied I was most heartily concerned to hear it....Thence to Nick Mahon's where I dined sumptuously on fish, no meat as per following bill of fare: – Salmon, fresh herring, potato pudding, asparagus, sole, haddock epergue, turnips, asparagus, salt fish, turbot, removes, rice pudding, pies, cheese, etc. The company, three ladies, Doctor O'Shaughnessy, Catholic Bishop of Killaloe, Doctor Reynolds, Counsellor O'Gorman and his brother, the two Mr Everards and two or three others. Home at eleven, smoked a pipe and then to bed.

4 June 1813 – Dublin

Very fine day, and being the Kings birthday, the town was in bustle and hurry from morning till night. In the early part of the day a Review in the Phoenix Park, where all ranks and classes were crowded together to see poor soldiers sweating and stinking, and great Militia officers, from the mighty Colonel to the puny Ensigns, exhibiting their bravery and military acquirements. City Buckeens on hired horses and with borrowed boots and spurs; young misses slipping away from their mammas to meet their lovers; old maids taking snuff, and talking and thinking of old times; pickpockets waiting for a lob, and old bawds and whores for a cull; handkerchiefs in constant employ, wiping dust, sweat and dander from the face and head; coaches, landaus, gigs, curricles and jaunting cars in constant jostle and confusion in the backstreet to avoid paying money and the shops open to try to get some; mail coaches making a grand procession through the principal streets.

A Levée at the Castle, attended as usual by pimps, parasites, hangers-on, aidecamps, state-officers, expectant clergymen, hungry lawyers, spies, informers, and the various descriptions of characters that consti-

---

1 *Major Sirr*: Henry Charles Sirr (1764–1841) Dublin town major (1798–1808); he captured Lord Edward Fitzgerald in 1798 and Robert Emmet in 1803.

tute the herd of which the motley petty degraded and pretended Court of this poor fallen country is made up. Alas, poor Ireland.

I spent the day lounging about, seeing what was to be seen, and, in proud feelings of superior independence, looked down with utter contempt of the weakness of an administration, imbecile, evasive, and mouldering into contempt; and every loss of public opinion and respect ever must attend the paltry pretended administration of this despicable and degraded country.

After dinner take a rambling circuit over Westmoreland Street and up Anglesea Street. Lounge into booksellers' shops, then to Crow Street to see, according to ancient custom, all the blackguard boys collected to insult and pelt with small stones, gravel, periwinkles, etc. the ladies who go to the Play on this night. Boxes being free for the ladies, consequently it may be supposed what degree of respect is due to that class of the tender sex who avail themselves of enjoying a theatrical treat.

RICHARD ALFRED MILLIKEN (1767–1815)

Born in Castlemartyr, Co. Cork, the son of a Scottish Quaker, who had joined the Church of Ireland before he settled in Cork, Richard worked as an attorney, but devoted more time to the arts. He contributed verse to the Cork *Monthly Miscellany* in 1795, and started the short-lived magazine *The Casket* in 1797. He joined the Cork Royal Volunteers on the outbreak of the 1798 Rebellion. In 1807 he published *The Riverside*, a poem in blank verse; it was followed in 1810 by the short tale, *The Slave of Surinam*, and by a play, *Darby in Arms*. He is chiefly remembered as the author of 'The Groves of Blarney' (written in 1797 or 1798), the most famous example of Irish burlesque, based on the doggerel 'Castle Hyde',* attributed on its first appearance to an itinerant poet called Barrett. Milliken's mock-idyll has appeared in various versions, including one in *The Reliques of Father Prout*.* The idyll contains oblique references to the local undermining of established (pro-British) power.

The Groves of Blarney
(1797/98)

The groves of Blarney
They look so charming,
Down by the purling
    Of sweet silent streams,
Being banked with posies,
That spontaneous grow there,
Planted in order

By the sweet rock close.
'Tis there's the daisy
And the sweet carnanation,
The blooming pink,
 And the rose so fair
The daffodowndilly –
Likewise the lily,
All flowers that scent
 The sweet fragrant air.

'Tis Lady Jeffers[1]
That owns this station,
Like Alexander,
 Or Queen Helen fair;
There's no commander
In all the nation,
For emulation
 Can with her compare.
Such walls surround her,
That no nine pounder
Could dare to plunder
 Her place of strength;
But Oliver Cromwell,
Her he did pommell,
And made a breach
 In her battlement.

There's gravel walks there
For speculation,
And conversation
 In sweet solitude,
'Tis there the lover
May hear the dove, or
The gentle plover
 In the afternoon,
And if a lady

1 *Lady Jeffers*: This reference to Arabella Jeffereys holds the key to the poem's political innuendo. She was the eldest sister of John Fitzgibbon, 1st Earl of Clare (1749–1802), Attorney-General (1784–1789) and Lord Chancellor (1789–1802), who opposed Catholic Relief and patriotism. He supported tough measures against the United Irishmen in the time of the 1790s crises. Lord Westmorland described him as having 'no God but English government'. His sister, in contrast, was considered a sympathizer with the Whiteboys, whom she employed to drain the Blarney lake, much to the chagrin of her brother.

Would be so engaging
As to walk alone in
   Those shady bowers,
'Tis there the courtier
He may transport her
Into some fort, or
   All under ground.

For 'tis there's a cave where
No daylight enters,
But cats and badgers
   Are for ever bred;
Being mossed by nature,
That makes it sweeter
Than a coach-and-six,
   Or a feather-bed.
'Tis there the lake is,
Well stored with perches,
And comely eels in
   The verdant mud;
Besides the leeches,
And groves of beeches,
Standing in order
   For to guard the flood.

There's statues gracing
This noble place in –
All heathen gods
   And nymphs so fair:
Bold Neptune, Plutarch,
And Nicodemus,
All standing naked
   In the open air!
So now to finish
This brave narration,
Which my poor geni'
   Could not entwine;
But were I Homer,
Or Nebuchadnezzar,
'Tis in every feature
   I would make it shine.

[*Of the following verse, added by Father Prout, Samuel Lover* maintained that any editor who omitted it ought to be 'hung up to dry on his own lines'.*]

There is a boat on
The lake to float on,
And lots of beauties
    Which I can't entwine;
But were I a preacher,
Or a classic teacher,
In every feature
    I'd make 'em shine!
There is a stone there,
That whoever kisses,
Oh! he never misses
To grow eloquent;
'Tis he may clamber
To a lady's chamber,
Or become a member
    Of parliament.
A clever spouter
He'll soon turn out, or
An out-and-outer,
    To be let alone.
Don't hope to hinder him,
Or to bewilder him,
Sure he's a pilgrim
    From the Blarney Stone!

MARIA EDGEWORTH (1767–1849)

The third child of Richard Lovell Edgeworth by the first of his four wives, Maria Edgeworth was born in England, where she was educated. In 1782 she moved with her father to the family estate in Edgeworthstown, Co. Longford. He encouraged Maria's writing – she showed rough outlines of her novels to him and he commented on them, making sure she finished them. It was a fruitful partnership: he also taught her estate management – she was the eldest daughter of his twenty-two children. These children had to be educated, and Edgeworth was interested in education, not least in Rousseau's theories. She taught her younger stepbrothers and stepsisters, and collaborated with her father on formulating a progressive system of education based on the tenets of Jean Jacques Rousseau (set out in their *Practical Education* –

1798) and on the humane management of the estate. In 1800 she published *Castle Rackrent*, which was praised by Sir Walter Scott. It established Maria Edgeworth as the first regional – and the first Irish – novelist, and it offers a notoriously unreliable narrator in the servant Thady Quirk. The responsibility of the Irish landed gentry informs her novels *Ennui* (1809), *The Absentee* (1812) and *Ormond* (1817). After her father's death in 1817, Maria wrote less, but completed his *Memoirs*. During the Famine she worked tirelessly to relieve the plight of the peasants in the area.

From *Castle Rackrent*

(1800)

[*Castle Rackrent* is one of the first examples of regional fiction.[1] It is also the first Irish story presented by an unreliable protagonist. 'Poor, honest' Thady Quirk, servant at Castle Rackrent, witnesses the demise of three generations of his landlords, and the rise of his son Jason into their estate.]

... To go back to the day of the election, which I never think of but with pleasure and tears of gratitude for those good times; after the election was quite and clean over, there comes shoals of people from all parts, claiming to have obliged my master with their votes, and putting him in mind of promises which he could never remember himself to have made – one was to have a freehold for each of his four sons – another was to have a renewal of a lease – another an abatement – one came to be paid ten guineas for a pair of silver buckles sold my master on the hustings, which turned out to be no better than copper gilt – another had a long bill for oats, the half of which never went into the granary to my certain knowledge, and the other half were not fit for the cattle to touch; but the bargain was made the week before the election, and the coach and saddle-horses were got into order for the day, besides a vote fairly got by them oats – so no more reasoning on that head – but then there was no end to them that were telling Sir Condy he had engaged to make their sons excisemen, or high constables, or the like; and as for them that had bills to give in for liquor, and beds, and straw, and ribbons, and horses, and post-chaises for the gentlemen freeholders that came from all parts and other counties to vote for my master, and were not, to be sure, to be at any charges, there was no standing against all these; and, worse than all, the gentlemen of my master's committee, who managed all

---

1 The title of first Irish – regional – novel goes to the anonymous *Virtue Rewarded; or, the Irish Princess. A new Novel* (1693).

for him, and talked how they'd bring him in without costing him a penny, and subscribed by hundreds very genteelly, forgot to pay their subscriptions, and had laid out in agents and lawyers, fees and secret service money, to the Lord knows how much, and my master could never ask one of them for their subscription, you are sensible, nor for the price of a fine horse he had sold one of them, so it all was left at his door. He could never, God bless him again, I say, bring himself to ask a gentleman for money, despising such sort of conversation himself; but others, who were not gentlemen born, behaved very uncivil in pressing him at this very time, and all he could do to content 'em all was to take himself out of the way as fast as possible to Dublin, where my lady had taken a house as fitting for him, a Member of Parliament, to attend his duty in there all the winters. – I was very lonely when the whole family was gone, and all the things they had ordered to go and forgot sent after them by the stage. There was then a great silence in Castle Rackrent, and I went moping from room to room, hearing the doors clap for want of right locks, and the wind through the broken windows that the glazier never would come to mend, and the rain coming through the roof and best ceilings all over the house, for want of the slater whose bill was not paid; besides our having no slates or shingles for that part of the old building which was shingled, and burnt when the chimney took fire, and had been open to the weather ever since. I took myself to the servants' hall in the evening to smoke my pipe as usual, but missed the bit of talk we used to have there sadly, and ever after was content to stay in the kitchen and boil my little potatoes[1], and put up my bed there; and every post day I looked in the newspaper, but no news of my master in the house. – He never spoke good or bad – but, as the butler wrote down word to my son Jason, was very ill used by the government about a place that was promised him and never given, after his supporting them against his conscience very honorably, and being greatly abused for it, which hurt him greatly, he having the name of a great patriot in the country before. The house and living in Dublin too was not to be had for nothing, and my son Jason said Sir Condy must soon be looking out for a new agent, for I've done my part, and can do no more – if my lady had the bank of Ireland to spend, it would go all in one winter, and Sir Condy would never gainsay her, though he does not care the rind of a lemon for her all the while.

---

1 *My little potatoes* – Thady does not mean by this expression that his potatoes were less than other people's, or less than the usual size – *little* is here used only as an Italian diminutive, expressive of fondness. [*Edgeworth's note.*]

Now I could not bear to hear Jason giving out after this manner against the family, and twenty people standing by in the street. Ever since he had lived at the Lodge of his own he looked down, howsomever, upon poor old Thady, and was grown quite a great gentleman, and had none of his relations near him – no wonder he was no kinder to poor Sir Condy than to his own kith and kin[1]. – In the spring it was the villain that got the list of the debts from him brought down the custodiam, Sir Condy still attending his duty in Parliament; and I could scarcely believe my own old eyes, or the spectacles with which I read it, when I was shewn my son Jason's name joined in the custodiam; but he told me it was only for form's sake, and to make things easier than if all the land was under the power of a total stranger. – Well, I did not know what to think – it was hard to be talking ill of my own, and I could not but grieve for my poor master's fine estate, all torn by these vultures of the law; so I said nothing, but just looked on to see how it would all end.

It was not till the month of June that he and my lady came down to the country. – My master was pleased to take me aside with him to the brewhouse that same evening, to complain to me of my son and other matters, in which he said he was confident I had neither art nor part: he said a great deal more to me, to whom he had been fond to talk ever since he was my white-headed boy before he came to the estate, and all that he said about poor Judy I can never forget, but scorn to repeat. – He did not say an unkind word of my lady, but wondered, as well he might, her relations would do nothing for him or her, and they in all this great distress. – He did not take any thing long to heart, let it be as it would, and had no more malice or thought of the like in him than the child that can't speak; this night it was all out of his head before he went to his bed. – He took his jug of whiskey punch – my lady was grown quite easy about the whiskey-punch by this time, and so I did suppose all was going on right betwixt them, till I learnt the truth through Mrs. Jane, who talked over their affairs to the housekeeper, and I within hearing. The night my master came home, thinking of nothing at all, but just making merry, he drank his bumper toast 'to the deserts of that old curmudgeon my father-in-law, and all enemies at Mount Juliet's town.' – Now my lady was no longer in the mind she formerly was, and did no ways relish hearing her own friends abused in her presence, she said. –

---

1 *Kith and kin* – family or relations. *Kin* from kind – *Kith* from – we know not what. [*Edgeworth's note.*] (from Old English *cýð*—'couth').

'Then why don't they shew themselves your friends, (said my master,) and oblige me with the loan of the money I condescended, by your advice, my dear, to ask? – It's now three posts since I sent off my letter, desiring in the postscript a speedy answer by the return of the post, and no account at all from them yet.' – 'I expect they'll write to *me* next post,' says my lady, and that was all that passed then; but it was easy from this to guess there was a coolness betwixt them, and with good cause.

The next morning being post-day, I sent off the gossoon early to the post-office to see was there any letter likely to set matters to rights, and he brought back one with the proper post-mark upon it, sure enough, and I had no time to examine, or make any conjecture more about it, for into the servants' hall pops Mrs. Jane with a blue bandbox in her hand, quite entirely mad. – 'Dear Ma'am, and what's the matter?' says I. – 'Matter enough, (says she) 'don't you see my band-box is wet through, and my best bonnet here spoiled, besides my lady's, and all by the rain coming in through that gallery window, that you might have got mended, if you'd had any sense, Thady, all the time we were in town in the winter.' – 'Sure I could not get the glazier, Ma'am,' says I. – 'You might have stopped it up any how,' says she. – 'So I did, Ma'am, to the best of my ability, one of the panes with the old pillow-case, and the other with a piece of the old stage green curtain – sure I was as careful as possible all the time you were away, and not a drop of rain came in at that window of all the windows in the house, all winter, Ma'am, when under my care; and now the family's come home, and it's summer-time, I never thought no more about it to be sure – but dear, it's a pity to think of your bonnet, Ma'am – but here's what will please you, Ma'am – a letter from Mount Juliet's town for my lady.' With that she snatches it from me without a word more, and runs up the back stairs to my mistress; I follows with a slate to make up the window – this window was in the long passage, or gallery, as my lady gave out orders to have it called, in the gallery leading to my master's bed-chamber and her's, and when I went up with the slate, the door having no lock, and the bolt spoilt, was a-jar after Mrs. Jane, and as I was busy with the window, I heard all that was saying within.

'Well, what's in your letter, Bella, my dear? (says he) you're a long time spelling it over.' – 'Won't you shave this morning, Sir Condy,' says she, and put the letter in her pocket. – 'I shaved the day before yesterday, (says he) my dear, and that's not what I'm thinking of now – but any thing to oblige you, and to have peace and quietness, my dear' – and presently I had a glimpse of him at the cracked glass over the chimney-piece, standing up shaving himself to please my lady. – But she took no notice, but went on reading her book, and Mrs. Jane doing her hair behind. – 'What is it you're reading there, my dear? – phoo, I've cut myself with this razor; the man's a cheat that sold it me, but I have not paid him for it yet – What is it you're reading there? did you hear me asking you, my dear?' 'The sorrows of Werter,'[1] replies my lady, as well as I could hear. – 'I think more of the sorrows of Sir Condy, (says my master, joking like). – What news from Mount Juliet's Town?' – 'No news, (says she) but the old story over again; my friends all reproaching me still for what I can't help now.' – 'Is it for marrying me, (said my master, still shaving); what signifies, as you say, talking of that, when it can't be helped now?'

With that she heaved a great sigh that I heard plain enough in the passage. – 'And did not you use me basely, Sir Condy, (says she) not to tell me you were ruined before I married you?' – 'Tell you, my dear, (said he) did you ever ask me one word about it? and had not you friends enough of your own, that were telling you nothing else from morning to night, if you'd have listened to them slanders.' – 'No slanders, nor are my friends slanderers; and I can't bear to hear them treated with disrespect as I do, (says my lady and took out her pocket-handkerchief) – they are the best of friends, and if I had taken their advice – But my father was wrong to lock me up, I own; that was the only unkind thing I can charge him with; for if he had not locked me up, I should never have had a serious thought of running away as I did.' – 'Well, my dear, (said my master) don't cry and make yourself uneasy about it now, when it's all over, and you have the man of your own choice, in spite of 'em all.' – 'I was too young, I know, to make a choice at the time you ran away with me, I'm sure,' says my lady, and another sigh, which made my master, half shaved as he was, turn round upon her in surprise – 'Why, Bella, (says he) you can't deny what you know as well as I do, that it was at your own particular desire, and that twice under your own hand and seal expressed, that I should carry you off as I did to Scotland, and marry you there.' – 'Well, say no more about it, Sir Condy, (said my lady, pettish like) – I was a child then, you know.' – 'And as far as I know, you're little better now, my dear Bella, to be talking in this manner to your husband's *face*; but I won't take it ill of you, for I know it's something in that

---

1 The eponymous hero of Goethe's popular novel, *The Sorrows of Young Werther* (1774), commits suicide. Two English translations appeared in 1779, one by Daniel Malthus, the other by Richard Graves.

letter you put into your pocket just now, that has set you against me all on a sudden, and imposed upon your understanding.' – 'It is not so very easy as you think it, Sir Condy, to impose upon *my* understanding,' (said my lady) – 'My dear, (says he) I have, and with reason, the best opinion of your understanding of any man now breathing, and you know I have never set my own in competition with it; till now, my dear Bella, (says he, taking her hand from her book as kind as could be,) till now – when I have the great advantage of being quite cool, and you not; so don't believe one word your friends say against your own Sir Condy, and lend me the letter out of your pocket, till I see what it is they can have to say.' – 'Take it then, (says she,) and as you are quite cool, I hope it is a proper time to request you'll allow me to comply with the wishes of all my own friends, and return to live with my father and family, during the remainder of my wretched existence, at Mount Juliet's Town.'

At this my poor master fell back a few paces, like one that had been shot – 'You're not serious, Bella, (says he) and could you find it in your heart to leave me this way in the very middle of my distresses, all alone?' – But recollecting himself after his first surprise, and a moment's time for reflection, he said, with a great deal of consideration for my lady – 'Well, Bella, my dear, I believe you are right; for what could you do at Castle Rackrent, and an execution against the goods coming down, and the furniture to be canted, and an auction in the house all next week – so you have my full consent to go, since that is your desire, only you must not think of my accompanying you, which I could not in honour do upon the terms I always have been since our marriage with your friends; besides I have business to transact at home – so in the mean time, if we are to have any breakfast this morning, let us go down and have it for the last time in peace and comfort, Bella.'

Then as I heard my master coming to the passage door, I finished fastening up my slate against the broken pane, and when he came out, I wiped down the window seat with my wig[1], bade him a good-morrow as kindly as I could, seeing he was in trouble, though he strove

---

1 Wigs were formerly used instead of brooms in Ireland, for sweeping or dusting tables, stairs, &c. The Editor doubted the fact, till he saw a labourer of the old school sweep down a flight of stairs with his wig; he afterwards put it on his head again with the utmost composure, and said, 'Oh, please your honour, it's never a bit the worse.'

It must be acknowledged, that these men are not in any danger of catching cold by taking off their wigs occasionally, because they usually have fine crops of hair growing under their wigs. – The wigs are often yellow, and the hair which appears from beneath them black; the wigs are usually too small, and are raised up by the hair beneath, or by the ears of the wearers. [*Edgeworth's note.*]

and thought to hide it from me. – 'This window is all racked and tattered, (says I,) and it's what I'm striving to mend.' 'It *is* all racked and
tattered, plain enough, (says he) and never mind mending it, honest
old Thady,' says he, it will do well enough for you and I, and that's
all the company we shall have left in the house by and bye.' – 'I'm
sorry to see your honour so low this morning, (says I,) but you'll be
better after taking your breakfast.' – 'Step down to the servants' hall,
(says he) and bring me up the pen and ink into the parlour, and get a
sheet of paper from Mrs. Jane, for I have business that can't brook to
be delayed, and come into the parlour with the pen and ink yourself,
Thady, for I must have you to witness my signing a paper I have to
execute in a hurry.' – Well, while I was getting of the pen and ink-
horn, and the sheet of paper, I ransacked my brains to think what
could be the papers my poor master could have to execute in such a
hurry, he that never thought of such a thing as doing business afore
breakfast in the whole course of his life for any man living – but this
was for my lady, as I afterwards found, and the more genteel of him
after all her treatment.

I was just witnessing the paper that he had scrawled over, and was
shaking the ink out of my pen upon the carpet, when my lady came
in to breakfast, and she started as if it had been a ghost, as well she
might, when she saw Sir Condy writing at this unseasonable hour. –
'That will do very well, Thady,' says he to me, and took the paper I
had signed to, without knowing what upon the earth it might be, out
of my hands, and walked, folding it up, to my lady –

'You are concerned in this, my Lady Rackrent, (says he, putting it
into her hands,) and I beg you'll keep this memorandum safe, and shew
it to your friends the first thing you do when you get home, but put it
in your pocket now, my dear, and let us eat our breakfast, in God's
name.' – 'What is all this?' said my lady, opening the paper in great
curiosity. – 'It's only a bit of a memorandum of what I think becomes
me to do whenever I am able, (says my master); you know my situation,
tied hand and foot at the present time being, but that can't last always,
and when I'm dead and gone, the land will be to the good, Thady, you
know; and take notice it's my intention your lady should have a clear
five hundred a year jointure off the estate, afore any of my debts are
paid.' – 'Oh, please your honour, says I, I can't expect to live to see that
time, being now upwards of fourscore and ten years of age, and you a
young man, and likely to continue so, by the help of God.' – I was
vexed to see my lady so insensible too, for all she said was – 'This is very
genteel of you, Sir Condy – You need not wait any longer, Thady' – so

I just picked up the pen and ink that had tumbled on the floor, and heard my master finish with saying – 'You behaved very genteel to me, my dear, when you threw all the little you had in your own power, along with yourself, into my hands; and as I don't deny but what you may have had some things to complain of, (to be sure he was thinking then of Judy, or of the whiskey punch, one or t'other, or both); and as I don't deny but you may have had something to complain of, my dear, it is but fair you should have something in the form of compensation to look forward to agreeably in future; besides it's an act of justice to myself, that none of your friends, my dear, may ever have it to say against me I married for money, and not for love.' – 'That is the last thing I should ever have thought of saying of you, Sir Condy,' said my lady, looking very gracious. – 'Then, my dear, (said Sir Condy) we shall part as good friends as we met, so all's right.'

I was greatly rejoiced to hear this, and went out of the parlour to report it all to the kitchen. – The next morning my lady and Mrs. Jane set out for Mount Juliet's town in the jaunting-car; many wondered at my lady's chusing to go away, considering all things, upon the jaunting-car, as if it was only a party of pleasure; but they did not know till I told them, that the coach was all broke in the journey down, and no other vehicle but the car to be had; besides, my lady's friends were to send their coach to meet her at the cross roads – so it was all done very proper.

My poor master was in great trouble after my lady left us. – The execution came down, and every thing at Castle Rackrent was seized by the gripers,[1] and my son Jason, to his shame be it spoken, amongst them – I wondered, for the life of me, how he could harden himself to do it, but then he had been studying the law, and had made himself attorney Quirk; so he brought down at once a heap of accounts upon my master's head – To cash lent, and to ditto, and to ditto, and to ditto and oats, and bills paid at the milliner's and linen-draper's, and many dresses for the fancy balls in Dublin for my lady, and all the bills to the workmen and tradesmen for the scenery of the theatre, and the chandler's and grocer's bills, and tailor's, besides butcher's and baker's, and, worse than all, the old one of that base wine-merchant's, that wanted to arrest my poor master for the amount on the election day, for which amount Sir Condy afterwards passed his note of hand, bearing lawful interest from the date thereof; and the interest and compound interest was now mounted to a terrible deal on

---

1 *gripers*: extortioners.

many other notes and bonds for money borrowed, and there was besides hush-money to the sub-sheriffs, and sheets upon sheets of old and new attornies' bills, with heavy balances, *as per former account furnished*, brought forward with interest thereon; then there was a powerful deal due to the Crown for sixteen years arrear of quit-rent of the town lands of Carrickshaughlin, with driver's fees, and a compliment to the receiver every year for letting the quit-rent run on, to oblige Sir Condy and Sir Kit afore him. – Then there was bills for spirits, and ribbons at the election time, and the gentlemen of the Committee's accounts unsettled, and their subscriptions never gathered; and there was cows to be paid for, with the smith and farrier's bills to be set against the rent of the demesne, with calf and hay-money: then there was all the servants' wages, since I don't know when, coming due to them, and sums advanced for them by my son Jason for clothes, and boots, and whips, and odd monies for sundries expended by them in journeys to town and elsewhere, and pocket-money for the master continually, and messengers and postage before his being a parliament man – I can't myself tell you what besides; but this I know, that when the evening came on the which Sir Condy had appointed to settle all with my son Jason; and when he comes into the parlour, and sees the sight of bills and load of papers all gathered on the great dining-table for him, he puts his hands before both his eyes, and cries out – 'Merciful Jasus! what is it I see before me!' – Then I sets an arm chair at the table for him, and with a deal of difficulty he sits him down, and my son Jason hands him over the pen and ink to sign to this man's bill and t'other man's bill, all which he did without making the least objections; indeed, to give him his due, I never seen a man more fair, and honest, and easy in all his dealings, from first to last, as Sir Condy, or more willing to pay every man his own as far as he was able, which is as much as any one can do. – 'Well, (says he, joking like with Jason) I wish we could settle it all with a stroke of my grey-goose quill. – What signifies making me wade through all this ocean of papers here; can't you now, who understand drawing out an account, Debtor and Creditor, just sit down here at the corner of the table, and get it done out for me, that I may have a clear view of the balance, which is all I need be talking about, you know?' – 'Very true, Sir Condy, nobody understands business better than yourself,' says Jason. – 'So I've a right to do, being born and bred to the bar, (says Sir Condy) – Thady, do step out and see are they bringing in the tings[1]

---

1 *tings*: 'things'.

for the punch, for we've just done all we have to do for this evening.' – I goes out accordingly, and when I came back, Jason was pointing to the balance, which was a terrible sight to my poor master. – 'Pooh! pooh! pooh! (says he) here's so many noughts they dazzle my eyes, so they do, and put me in mind of all I suffered, larning of my numeration table, when I was a boy, at the day-school along with you, Jason – Units, tens, hundreds, tens of hundreds. – Is the punch ready, Thady?' says he, seeing me. – 'Immediately, the boy has the jug in his hand; it's coming up stairs, please your honour, as fast as possible,' says I, for I saw his honour was tired out of his life, but Jason, very short and cruel, cuts me off with – 'Don't be talking of punch yet a while, it's no time for punch yet a bit – Units, tens, hundreds,' goes he on, counting over the master's shoulder – 'units, tens, hundreds, thousands.' – 'A-a-agh! hold your hand, (cries my master,) where in this wide world am I to find hundreds, or units itself, let alone thousands?' – 'The balance has been running on too long, (says Jason, sticking to him as I could not have done at the time if you'd have given both the Indies and Cork to boot); the balance has been running on too long, and I'm distressed myself on your account, Sir Condy, for money, and the thing must be settled now on the spot, and the balance cleared off,' says Jason. 'I'll thank you if you'll only shew me how,' says Sir Condy. – 'There's but one way, (says Jason) and that's ready enough; when there's no cash, what can a gentleman do but go to the land?' – 'How can you go to the land, and it under custodiam to yourself already, (says Sir Condy) and another custodiam hanging over it? and no one at all can touch it, you know, but the custodees.' – 'Sure, can't you sell, though at a loss? – sure you can sell, and I've a purchaser ready for you,' says Jason. – 'Have ye so? (said Sir Condy) that's a great point gained; but there's a thing now beyond all, that perhaps you don't know yet, barring Thady has let you into the secret.' – 'Sarrah bit[1] of a sacret, or any thing at all of the kind has he learned from me these fifteen weeks come St. John's eve, (says I) for we have scarce been upon speaking terms of late – but what is it your honor means of a secret?' – 'Why, the secret of the little keepsake I gave my lady Rackrent the morning she left us, that she might not go back empty-handed to her friends.' – 'My Lady Rackrent, I'm sure, has baubles and keepsakes enough, as those bills on the table will shew, (says Jason); but whatever it is, (says he, taking up his pen) we must add it to the balance, for to be sure it can't be paid for.' – 'No,

---

1 *Sarrah bit*: 'not a bit' (Hiberno–English emphatic negative).

nor can't till after my decease, (said Sir Condy) that's one good thing.'
– Then colouring up a good deal, he tells Jason of the memorandum
of the five hundred a year jointure he had settled upon my lady; at
which Jason was indeed mad, and said a great deal in very high words,
that it was using a gentleman who had the management of his affairs,
and was moreover his principal creditor, extremely ill, to do such a
thing without consulting him, and against his knowledge and consent.
To all which Sir Condy had nothing to reply, but that, upon his conscience, it was in a hurry, and without a moment's thought on his part,
and he was very sorry for it, but if it was to do over again he would
do the same; and he appealed to me, and I was ready to give my evidence, if that would do, to the truth of all he said.

So Jason with much ado was brought to agree to a compromise. –
'The purchaser that I have ready (says he) will be much displeased to
be sure at the incumbrance on the land, but I must see and manage
him – here's a deed ready drawn up – we have nothing to do but to
put in the consideration money and our names to it. – And how much
am I going to sell? – the lands of O'Shaughlin's-town, and the lands
of Gruneaghoolaghan, and the lands of Crookagnawaturgh, (says he,
just reading to himself) – and – 'Oh, murder, Jason! – sure you won't
put this in' – the castle, stable, and appurtenances of Castle Rackrent
– Oh, murder! (says I, clapping my hands) this is too bad, Jason.' –
'Why so? (said Jason) when it's all, and a great deal more to the back
of it, lawfully mine, was I to push for it.' 'Look at him (says I, pointing to Sir Condy, who was just leaning back in his arm-chair, with his
arms falling beside him like one stupified) is it you, Jason, that can
stand in his presence and recollect all he has been to us, and all we
have been to him, and yet use him so at the last?' – 'Who will you find
to use him better, I ask you? (said Jason) – if he can get a better purchaser, I'm content; I only offer to purchase to make things easy and
oblige him – though I don't see what compliment I am under, if you
come to that; I have never had, asked, or charged more than sixpence
in the pound receiver's fees, and where would he have got an agent
for a penny less?' 'Oh, Jason! Jason! how will you stand to this in the
face of the county, and all who know you, (says I); and what will people tink[1] and say, when they see you living here in Castle Rackrent,
and the lawful owner turned out of the seat of his ancestors, without
a cabin to put his head into, or so much as a potato to eat?' – Jason,
whilst I was saying this and a great deal more, made me signs, and

---

1 *tink*: 'think'.

winks, and frowns; but I took no heed, for I was grieved and sick at heart for my poor master, and couldn't but speak.

'Here's the punch! (says Jason, for the door opened) – here's the punch!' – Hearing that, my master starts up in his chair and recollects himself, and Jason uncorks the whiskey – 'Set down the jug here,' says he, making room for it beside the papers opposite to Sir Condy, but still not stirring the deed that was to make over all. Well, I was in great hopes he had some touch of mercy about him, when I saw him making the punch, and my master took a glass; but Jason put it back as he was going to fill again, saying, 'No, Sir Condy, it shan't be said of me, I got your signature to this deed when you were half-seas over; you know, your name and hand-writing in that condition would not, if brought before the courts, benefit me a straw, wherefore let us set-tle all before we go deeper in the punch-bowl.' – 'Settle all as you will, (said Sir Condy, clapping his hands to his ears) but let me hear no more, I'm bothered to death this night.' – 'You've only to sign,' said Jason, putting the pen to him. – 'Take all, and be content,' said my master – So he signed – and the man who brought in the punch wit-nessed it, for I was not able, but crying like a child; and besides, Jason said, which I was glad of, that I was no fit witness, being so old and doating. It was so bad with me, I could not taste a drop of the punch itself, though my master himself, God bless him! in the midst of his trouble, poured out a glass for me and brought it up to my lips. – 'Not a drop, I thank your honor's honor as much as if I took it though,' and I just set down the glass as it was and went out; and when I got to the street door, the neighbours' childer who were playing at mar-bles there, seeing me in great trouble, left their play, and gathered about me to know what ailed me; and I told them all, for it was a great relief to me to speak to these poor childer, that seemed to have some natural feeling left in them: and when they were made sensible that Sir Condy was going to leave Castle Rackrent for good and all, they set up a whillalu that could be heard to the farthest end of the street; and one fine boy he was, that my master had given an apple to that morning, cried the loudest, but they all were the same sorry, for Sir Condy was greatly beloved amongst the childer[1] for letting them go a nutting in the demesne without saying a word to them, though my lady objected to them. – The people in the town who were the most of them standing at their doors, hearing the childer cry, would know the reason of it; and when the report was made known, the

---

1 This is the invariable pronunciation of the lower Irish. [*Edgeworth's note.*]

people one and all gathered in great anger against my son Jason, and terror at the notion of his coming to be landlord over them, and they cried, 'No Jason! No Jason! – Sir Condy! Sir Condy! Sir Condy Rackrent for ever!' and the mob grew so great and so loud I was frighted, and made my way back to the house to warn my son to make his escape, or hide himself for fear of the consequences. – Jason would not believe me, till they came all round the house and to the windows with great shouts – then he grew quite pale, and asked Sir Condy what had he best do? – 'I'll tell you what you had best do, (said Sir Condy, who was laughing to see his fright) finish your glass first, then let's go to the window and shew ourselves, and I'll tell 'em, or you shall if you please, that I'm going to the Lodge for change of air for my health, and by my own desire, for the rest of my days.' – 'Do so,' said Jason, who never meant it should have been so, but could not refuse him the Lodge at this unseasonable time. Accordingly Sir Condy threw up the sash and explained matters, and thanked all his friends, and bid 'em look in at the punch bowl, and observe that Jason and he had been sitting over it very good friends; so the mob was content, and he sent 'em out some whiskey to drink his health, and that was the last time his honor's health was ever drank at Castle Rackrent....

From *The Absentee*
(1812)

[While his mother, Lady Clonbrony, desperately tries to keep up with the *ton* of London, Lord Colambre returns to Ireland in order to explore the waning fortune of the absentee family's estate.]

The tide did not permit the packet to reach the Pigeon-house,[1] and the impatient lord Colambre stepped into a boat, and was rowed across the bay of Dublin. It was a fine summer morning. The sun shone bright on the Wicklow mountains. He admired, he exulted in the beauty of the prospect; and all the early associations of his childhood, and the patriotic hopes of his riper years, swelled his heart as he approached the shores of his native land. But scarcely had he touched his mother earth, when the whole course of his ideas was changed; and if his heart swelled, it swelled no more with pleasurable

---

1 *the Pigeon-house*: a prominent landmark in Dublin harbour, named after John Pigeon, who was employed there in 1786. In 1812 it was used as a fort or magazine, a barrack, and military port.

sensations, for instantly he found himself surrounded and attacked by a swarm of beggars and harpies, with strange figures and stranger tones; some craving his charity, some snatching away his luggage, and at the same time bidding him 'never trouble himself,' and 'never fear.' – A scramble in the boat and on shore for bags and parcels began, and an amphibious fight betwixt men, who had one foot on sea and one on land, was seen; and long and loud the battle of trunks and portmanteaus raged! The vanquished departed, clinching their empty hands at their opponents, and swearing inextinguishable hatred; while the smiling victors stood at ease, each grasping his booty; bag, basket, parcel, or portmanteau. – 'And, your honour, where *will* these go? Where *will* we carry 'em all to, for your honour?' – was now the question. Without waiting for an answer, most of the goods were carried at the discretion of the porter to the custom-house, where, to his lordship's astonishment, after this scene of confusion, he found that he had lost nothing but his patience; all his goods were safe, and a few *tinpennies* made his officious porters happy men and boys; blessings were showered upon his honour, and he was left in peace at an excellent hotel in —— street, Dublin. He rested, refreshed himself, recovered his good-humour, and walked into the coffee-house, where he found several officers, English, Irish, and Scotch. One English officer, a very gentlemanlike, sensible looking man, of middle age, was sitting reading a little pamphlet, when lord Colambre entered; he looked up from time to time, and in a few minutes rose, and joined the conversation; it turned upon the beauties and defects of the city of Dublin. Sir James Brooke, for that was the name of the gentleman, showed one of his brother officers the book which he had been reading, observing that, in his opinion, it contained one of the best views of Dublin, which he had ever seen, evidently drawn by the hand of a master, though in a slight, playful, and ironical style. It was '*An Intercepted Letter from China.*'[1] The conversation extended from Dublin to various parts of Ireland, with all which sir James Brooke showed that he was well acquainted. Observing, that this conversation was particularly interesting to lord Colambre; and quickly perceiving, that he was speaking to one not ignorant of books; sir James spoke of different representations and misrepresentations of Ireland. In answer to lord Colambre's inquiries, he named the works which had afforded him most satisfaction; and with discriminative, not superficial celerity, touched on all ancient and modern authors, from

1 *An Intercepted Letter from China: An Intercepted Letter from J——T——Esq.: Writer at Canton to his Friend in Dublin, Ireland* (1804), an anonymous satire on post-union Dublin.

Spenser and Davies, to Young and Beaufort. Lord Colambre became anxious to cultivate the acquaintance of a gentleman, who appeared so able and willing to afford him information. Sir James Brooke, on his part, was flattered by this eagerness of attention, and pleased by our hero's manners and conversation; so that, to their mutual satisfaction, they spent much of their time together, whilst they were at this hotel; and, meeting frequently in society in Dublin, their acquaintance every day increased and grew into intimacy; an intimacy which was highly advantageous to lord Colambre's views of obtaining a just idea of the state of manners in Ireland. Sir James Brooke had, at different periods, been quartered in various parts of the country – had resided long enough in each to become familiar with the people, and had varied his residence sufficiently to form comparisons between different counties, their habits, and characteristics. Hence he had it in his power to direct the attention of our young observer at once to the points most worthy of his examination, and to save him from the common errour of travellers; the deducing general conclusions from a few particular cases, or arguing from exceptions as if they were rules. – Lord Colambre, from his family connexions, had of course immediate introduction into the best society in Dublin, or rather into all the good society of Dublin. – In Dublin there is positively good company, and positively bad; but not, as in London, many degrees of comparison: not innumerable luminaries of the polite world, moving in different orbits of fashion, but all the bright planets of note and name move and revolve in the same narrow limits. Lord Colambre did not find that either his father's, or his mother's representations of society in Dublin resembled the reality, which he now beheld. Lady Clonbrony had, in terms of detestation, described Dublin such as it appeared to her soon after the Union; Lord Clonbrony had painted it with convivial enthusiasm, such as he saw it long and long before the Union, when *first* he drank claret at the fashionable clubs. This picture, unchanged in his memory, and unchangeable by his imagination, had remained and ever would remain the same. – The hospitality of which the father boasted, the son found in all it's warmth, but meliorated and refined; less convivial, more social; the fashion of hospitality had improved. To make the stranger eat or drink to excess, to set before him old wine and old plate, was no longer the sum of good breeding. The guest now escaped the pomp of grand entertainments; was allowed to enjoy ease and conversation, and to taste some of that feast of reason, and that flow of soul, so often talked of, and so seldom enjoyed. Lord Colambre found a spirit of improvement, a desire

for knowledge, and a taste for science and literature, in most companies, particularly among gentlemen belonging to the Irish bar: nor did
he in Dublin society see any of that confusion of ranks or predomi-
nance of vulgarity, of which his mother had complained. – Lady
Clonbrony had assured him, that, the last time she had been at the
drawing-room at the castle, a lady, whom she afterwards found to be
a grocer's wife, had turned angrily when her ladyship had accidentally trodden on her train, and had exclaimed with a strong brogue, 'I'll
thank you, ma'am, for the rest of my tail.'

Sir James Brooke, to whom lord Colambre, without *giving up his
authority*, mentioned the fact, declared, that he had no doubt the
thing had happened precisely as it was stated; but that this was one of
the extraordinary cases, which ought not to pass into a general rule,
that it was a slight instance of that influence of temporary causes,
from which no conclusions, as to national manners, should be drawn.

'I happened,' continued sir James, 'to be quartered in Dublin soon
after the Union took place; and I remember the great, but transient
change, that appeared. From the removal of both houses of parliament, most of the nobility, and many of the principal families among
the Irish commoners, either hurried in high hopes to London, or
retired disgusted and in despair to their houses in the country.
Immediately, in Dublin, commerce rose into the vacated seats of rank;
wealth rose into the place of birth. New faces and new equipages
appeared: people, who had never been heard of before, started into
notice, pushed themselves forward, not scrupling to elbow their way
even at the castle; and they were presented to my lord-lieutenant and
to my lady-lieutenant; for their excellencies, for the time being, might
have played their vice-regal parts to empty benches, had they not
admitted such persons for the moment to fill their court. Those of
former times, of hereditary pretensions and high-bred minds and
manners, were scandalised at all this; and they complained with justice, that the whole *tone* of society was altered; that the decorum, elegance, polish, and charm of society was gone: and I among the rest,'
said sir James, 'felt and deplored their change – But, now it is all over,
we may acknowledge, that, perhaps, even those things which we felt
most disagreeable at the time, were productive of eventual benefit.

'Formerly, a few families had set the fashion. From time immemo-
rial every thing had, in Dublin, been submitted to their hereditary
authority; and conversation, though it had been rendered polite by
their example, was, at the same time, limited within narrow bounds.
Young people, educated upon a more enlarged plan, in time grew up;

and, no authority or fashion forbidding it, necessarily rose to their just place, and enjoyed their due influence in society. The want of manners, joined to the want of knowledge, in the new set, created universal disgust: they were compelled, some by ridicule, some by bankruptcies, to fall back into their former places, from which they could never more emerge. In the mean time, some of the Irish nobility and gentry, who had been living at an unusual expense in London, – an expense beyond their incomes, were glad to return home to refit; and they brought with them a new stock of ideas, and some taste for science and literature, which, within these latter years, have become fashionable, indeed indispensable, in London. That part of the Irish aristocracy, who, immediately upon the first incursions of the vulgarians, had fled in despair to their fastnesses in the country, hearing of the improvements which had gradually taken place in society, and assured of the final expulsion of the barbarians, ventured from their retreats, and returned to their posts in town. So that, now,' concluded sir James, 'you find a society in Dublin, composed of a most agreeable and salutary mixture of birth and education, gentility and knowledge, manner and matter; and you see pervading the whole new life and energy, new talent, new ambition, a desire and a determination to improve and be improved – a perception, that higher distinction can now be obtained in almost all company, by genius and merit, than by airs and dress. . . . So much for the higher order. – Now, among the class of tradesmen and shopkeepers, you may amuse yourself, my lord, with marking the difference between them and persons of the same rank in London.'

Lord Colambre had several commissions to execute for his English friends, and he made it his amusement in every shop to observe the manners and habits of the people. He remarked, that there are in Dublin two classes of trades-people; one, who go into business with intent to make it their occupation for life, and as a slow, but sure means of providing for themselves and their families: another class, who take up trade merely as a temporary resource, to which they condescend for a few years; trusting that they shall, in that time, make a fortune, retire, and commence or recommence gentlemen. The Irish regular men of business are like all other men of business – punctual, frugal, careful, and so forth; with the addition of more intelligence, invention, and enterprise, than are usually found in Englishmen of the same rank. But the Dublin tradesmen *pro tempore* are a class by themselves: they begin without capital, buy stock upon credit, in hopes of making large profits, and, in the same hopes, sell upon credit. Now, if the credit they can obtain is longer than that which they are forced to give, they go on and prosper; if not, they break, turn bankrupts, and sometimes, as bankrupts, thrive. By such men, of course, every *short cut* to fortune is followed; whilst every habit, which requires time to prove it's advantage, is disregarded; nor with such views, can a character for *punctuality* have it's just value. In the head of a man who intends to be a tradesman to day, and a gentleman to morrow, the ideas of the honesty and the duties of a tradesman, and of the honour and the accomplishments of a gentleman, are oddly jumbled together, and the characteristics of both are lost in the compound.

He will *oblige* you, but he will not obey you; he will do you a favour, but he will not do you *justice*; he will do *any thing to serve you*, but the particular thing you order, he neglects; – he asks your pardon, for he would not for all the goods in his warehouse, *disoblige* you; not for the sake of your custom, but he has a particular regard for your family. – Economy, in the eyes of such a tradesman, is, if not a mean vice, at least a shabby virtue, which he is too polite to suspect his customers of, and particularly proud to prove himself superior to. Many London tradesmen, after making their thousands and their tens of thousands, feel pride in still continuing to live like plain men of business; but from the moment a Dublin tradesman of this style has made a few hundreds, he sets up his gig, and then his head is in his carriage, and not in his business; and when he has made a few thousands, he buys or builds a country-house – and then, and thenceforward, his head, heart, and soul are in his country-house, and only his body in the shop with his customers.

Whilst he is making money, his wife, or rather his lady, is spending twice as much out of town as he makes in it. At the word country-house, let no one figure to himself a snug little box, like that in which a *warm* London citizen, after long years of toil, indulges himself, one day out of seven, in repose – enjoying from his gazabo, the smell of the dust, and the view of passing coaches on the London road. No: these Hibernian villas are on a much more magnificent scale; some of them formerly belonged to Irish members of parliament, who are at a distance from their country-seats. After the Union these were bought by citizens and tradesmen, who spoiled, by the mixture of their own fancies, what had originally been designed by men of good taste.

Some time after lord Colambre's arrival in Dublin, he had an opportunity of seeing one of these villas, which belonged to Mrs. Raffarty, a grocer's lady, and sister to one of lord Clonbrony's agents, Mr. Nicholas Garraghty. Lord Colambre was surprised to find, that his father's agent resided in Dublin: he had been used to see agents, or stewards, as they are called in England, live in the country, and usually on the estate of which they have the management. Mr. Nicholas Garraghty, however, had a handsome house, in a fashionable part of Dublin. Lord Colambre called several times to see him, but he was out of town, receiving rents for some other gentleman, as he was agent for more than one property.

Though our hero had not the honour of seeing Mr. Garraghty, he had the pleasure of finding Mrs. Raffarty one day at her brother's house. Just as his lordship came to the door, she was going, on her jaunting car, to her villa, called Tusculum, situate near Bray.[1] She spoke much of the beauties of the vicinity of Dublin; found his lordship was going with sir James Brooke, and a party of gentlemen, to see the county of Wicklow, and his lordship and party were entreated to do her the honour of taking in his way a little collation at Tusculum.

Our hero was glad to have an opportunity of seeing more of a species of fine lady, with which he was unacquainted.

The invitation was verbally made, and verbally accepted, but the lady afterwards thought it necessary to send a written invitation in due form, and the note she sent directed to the *most right honourable* the lord viscount Colambre. On opening it he perceived, that it could not have been intended for him. It ran as follows:

My dear Juliana O'Leary,

I have got a promise from Colambre, that he will be with us at Tusculum on Friday the 20th, in his way from the county of Wicklow, for the collation I mentioned; and expect a large party of officers; so pray come early, with your house, or as many as the jaunting-car can bring. And pray, my dear, be *elegant*. You need not let it transpire to Mrs. O'G——, but make my apologies to miss O'G——, if she says any thing, and tell her I'm quite concerned I can't ask her for that day; because, tell her, I'm so crowded, and am to have none that day but *real quality*.

Yours ever and ever,
Anastasia Raffarty.

P.S. And I hope to make the gentlemen stop the night with me: so will not have beds. Excuse haste, and compliments, &c.

Tusculum, Sunday 15.

---

1 *Tusculum ... Bray*: Tusculum, a fashionable resort in ancient Rome, is a grand name for a house in the coastal town of Bray.

After a charming tour in the county of Wicklow, where the beauty
of the natural scenery, and the taste with which those natural beauties
had been cultivated, far surpassed the sanguine expectations lord
Colambre had formed, his lordship and his companions arrived at
Tusculum, where he found Mrs. Raffarty, and miss Juliana O'Leary,
very elegant, with a large party of the ladies and gentlemen of Bray,
assembled in a drawing-room, fine with bad pictures and gaudy gild-
ing; the windows were all shut, and the company were playing cards
with all their might. This was the fashion of the neighbourhood. In
compliment to lord Colambre and the officers, the ladies left the card-
tables; and Mrs. Raffarty, observing that his lordship seemed *partial*
to walking, took him out, as she said, 'to do the honours of nature
and art.'

His lordship was much amused by the mixture, which was now
exhibited to him, of taste and incongruity, ingenuity and absurdity,
genius and blunder; by the contrast between the finery and vulgarity,
the affectation and ignorance, of the lady of the villa. We should be
obliged to *stop* too long at Tusculum, were we to attempt to detail all
the odd circumstances of this visit; but we may record an example or
two, which may give a sufficient idea of the whole.

In the first place, before they left the drawing-room, miss Juliana
O'Leary pointed out to his lordship's attention a picture over the
drawing-room chimney-piece. 'Is not it a fine piece, my lord?' said
she, naming the price Mrs. Raffarty had lately paid for it at an auction. – 'It has a right to be a fine piece, indeed; for it cost a fine price!'
Nevertheless, this *fine* piece was a vile daub; and our hero could only
avoid the sin of flattery, or the danger of offending the lady, by
protesting that he had no judgment in pictures.

'Indeed! I don't pretend to be a connoisseur or conoscenti myself;
but I'm told the style is undeniably modern. – And was not I lucky,
Juliana, not to let that *Medona*[1] be knocked down to me? I was just
going to bid, when I heard such smart bidding; but fortunately, the
auctioneer, let out that it was done by a very old master – a hundred
years old. Oh! your most obedient, thinks I! – if that's the case, it's
not for my money: so I bought this, in lieu of the smoke-dried thing,
and had it a bargain.'

In architecture, Mrs. Raffarty had as good a taste and as much skill
as in painting. There had been a handsome portico in front of the
house: but this, interfering with the lady's desire to have a veranda,

1 *Medona*: 'Madonna'.

which she said could not be dispensed with, she had raised the whole portico to the second story, where it stood, or seemed to stand, upon a tarpaulin roof. But Mrs. Raffarty explained, that the pillars, though they looked so properly substantial, were really hollow and as light as feathers, and were supported with cramps, without *disobliging* the front wall of the house at all to signify.

'Before she showed the company any farther,' she said, 'she must premise to his lordship, that she had been originally stinted in room for her improvements, so that she could not follow her genius liberally; she had been reduced to have some things on a confined scale, and occasionally to consult her pocket-compass; but she prided herself upon having put as much into a light pattern as could well be; that had been her whole ambition, study, and problem, for she was determined to have at least the honour of having a little *taste* of everything at Tusculum.'

So she led the way to a little conservatory, and a little pinery, and a little grapery, and a little aviary, and a little pheasantry, and a little dairy for show, and a little cottage for ditto, with a grotto full of shells, and a little hermitage full of earwigs, and a little ruin full of looking-glass, 'to enlarge and multiply the effect of the gothic.' – 'But you could only put your head in, because it was just fresh painted, and though there had been a fire ordered in the ruin all night, it had only smoked.'

In all Mrs. Raffarty's buildings, whether ancient or modern, there was a studied crookedness.

'Yes,' she said, 'she hated every thing straight, it was so formal and *unpicturesque*. Uniformity and conformity,' she observed, 'had their day; but now, thank the stars of the present day, irregularity and difformity bear the bell, and have the majority.' –

As they proceeded and walked through the grounds, from which Mrs. Raffarty, though she had done her best, could not take that which nature had given, she pointed out to my lord 'a happy moving termination,' consisting of a Chinese bridge, with a fisherman leaning over the rails. On a sudden, the fisherman was seen to tumble over the bridge into the water. The gentlemen ran to extricate the poor fellow, while they heard Mrs. Raffarty bawling to his lordship, to beg he would never mind, and not trouble himself.

When they arrived at the bridge, they saw the man hanging from part of the bridge, and apparently struggling in the water; but when they attempted to pull him up, they found it was only a stuffed figure, which had been pulled into the stream by a real fish, which had seized hold of the bait.

Mrs. Raffarty, vexed by the fisherman's fall, and by the laughter it occasioned, did not recover herself sufficiently to be happily ridiculous during the remainder of the walk, nor till dinner was announced, when she apologised for 'having changed the collation, at first intended, into a dinner, which she hoped would be found no bad substitute, and which she flattered herself might prevail on my lord and the gentlemen to sleep, as there was no moon.'

The dinner had two great faults – profusion and pretension. There was, in fact, ten times more on the table than was necessary; and the entertainment was far above the circumstances of the person by whom it was given: for instance, the dish of fish at the head of the table had been brought across the island from Sligo, and had cost five guineas; as the lady of the house failed not to make known. But, after all, things were not of a piece; there was a disparity between the entertainment and the attendants; there was no proportion or fitness of things. A painful endeavour at what could not be attained, and a toiling in vain to conceal and repair deficiencies and blunders. Had the mistress of the house been quiet; had she, as Mrs. Broadhurst would say, but let things alone, let things take their course; all would have passed off with well-bred people: but she was incessantly apologizing, and fussing and fretting inwardly and outwardly, and directing and calling to her servants, – striving to make a butler, who was deaf, and a boy, who was hair-brained, do the business of five accomplished footmen of *parts and figure*. The mistress of the house called for 'plates, clean plates!——plates!'–

'But none did come, when she did call.'

Mrs. Raffarty called 'Lanty! Lanty! My lord's plate, there! – James! bread, to captain Bowles! – James! port wine, to the major! – James! James Kenny! James!'

'And panting James toiled after her in vain.'[1]

At length one course was fairly got through, and after a torturing half-hour, the second course appeared, and James Kenny was intent upon one thing, and Larry upon another, so that the wine-sauce for the hare was spilt by their collision; but what was worse, there seemed little

---

1 *And panting ... in vain*: Samuel Johnson, 'Prologue at the Opening of the Theatre in Drury Lane' (1747): 'And panting Time toiled after him in vain'.
2 *grass*: asparagus.

chance that the whole of this second course should ever be placed altogether rightly upon the table. Mrs. Raffarty cleared her throat, and nodded, and pointed, and sighed, and set Lanty after Kenny, and Kenny after Lanty; for what one did, the other undid; and at last, the lady's anger kindled, and she spoke.

'Kenny! James Kenny, set the sea-cale at this corner, and put down the grass² cross-corners; and match your macaroni yonder with *them* puddens, set – Ogh! James! the pyramid in the middle, can't ye?'

The pyramid, in changing places, was overturned. Then it was that the mistress of the feast, falling back in her seat, and lifting up her hands and eyes in despair, ejaculated; 'Oh, James! James!' –

The pyramid was raised by the assistance of the military engineers, and stood trembling again on its base; but the lady's temper could not be so easily restored to it's equilibrium.

The comedy of errours, which this day's visit exhibited, amused all the spectators. But lord Colambre, after he had smiled, sometimes sighed. – Similar foibles and follies in persons of different rank, fortune, and manner, appear to common observers so unlike, that they laugh without scruples of conscience in one case, at what in another ought to touch themselves most nearly. It was the same desire to appear what they were not; the same vain ambition to vie with superior rank and fortune, or fashion, which actuated lady Clonbrony and Mrs. Raffarty; and, whilst this ridiculous grocer's wife made herself the sport of some of her guests, lord Colambre sighed, from the reflection, that, what she was to them, his mother was to persons in a higher rank of fashion. – He sighed still more deeply, when he considered, that, in whatever station or with whatever fortune, extravagance, that is the living beyond our income, must lead to distress and meanness, and end in shame and ruin. In the morning, as they were riding away from Tusculum and talking over their visit, the officers laughed heartily, and rallying lord Colambre upon his seriousness, accused him of having fallen in love with Mrs. Raffarty, or with the *elegant* miss Juliana. Our hero, who wished never to be nice overmuch, or serious out of season, laughed with those that laughed, and endeavoured to catch the spirit of the jest. But sir James Brooke, who now was well acquainted with his countenance, and who knew something of the history of his family, understood his real feelings, and, sympathising in them, endeavoured to give the conversation a new turn.

'Look there, Bowles,' said he, as they were just riding into the town of Bray; 'Look at the barouche, standing at that green door, at the farthest end of the town. Is not that lady Dashfort's barouche?'

'It looks like what she sported in Dublin last year,' said Bowles; 'but you don't think she'd give us the same two seasons? Besides, she is not in Ireland, is she? I did not hear of her intending to come over again.'

'I beg your pardon,' said another officer; 'she will come again to so good a market, to marry her other daughter. I hear she said, or swore, that she will marry the young widow, lady Isabel, to an Irish nobleman.'

'Whatever she says, she swears, and whatever she swears, she'll do,' replied Bowles. 'Have a care, my lord Colambre; if she sets her heart upon you for lady Isabel, she has you. Nothing can save you. Heart, she has none, so there you're safe, my lord,' said the other officer; 'but if lady Isabel sets her eye upon you, no basilisk's is surer.'

'But if lady Dashfort had landed, I am sure we should have heard of it, for she makes noise enough wherever she goes; especially in Dublin, where all she said and did was echoed and magnified, till one could hear of nothing else. I don't think she has landed.'

'I hope to Heaven, they may never land again in Ireland!' cried sir James Brooke: 'one worthless woman, especially one worthless English woman of rank, does incalculable mischief in a country like this, which looks up to the sister country for fashion. For my own part, as a warm friend to Ireland, I would rather see all the toads and serpents, and venomous reptiles, that St. Patrick carried off in his bag, come back to this island, than these two *dashers*. Why, they would bite half the women and girls in the kingdom, with the rage for mischief, before half the husbands and fathers could turn their heads about. And, once bit, there's no cure in nature or art.'

'No horses to this barouche!' cried captain Bowles. – 'Pray, sir, whose carriage is this?' said the captain to a servant who was standing beside it.

'My lady Dashfort, sir, – it belongs to' – answered the servant, in rather a surley English tone – and turning to a boy, who was lounging at the door – 'Pat, bid them bring out the horses, for my ladies is in a hurry to get home.'

Captain Bowles stopped to make his servant alter the girths of his horse, and to satisfy his curiosity; and the whole party halted. Captain Bowles beckoned to the landlord of the inn, who was standing at his door.

'So, Lady Dashfort is here again? – This is her barouche, is not it?'

'Yes, sir, she is – it is.'

'And has she sold her fine horses?'

'Oh, no, sir – this is not her carriage at all – she is not here. – That is, she is here, in Ireland; but down in the county of Wicklow, on a visit! And this is not her own carriage at all; – that is to say, not that which she has with herself, driving; but only just the cast barouche like, as she keeps for the lady's maids.'

'For the lady's maids! that is good! that is new, faith! – Sir James, do you hear that?'

'Indeed, then, and it's true, and not a word of a lie!' said the honest landlord. – 'And this minute, we've got a directory of five of them abigails, sitting within in our house; as fine ladies, as great dashers, too, every bit as their principals; and kicking up as much dust on the road, every grain! – Think of them, now! The likes of them, that must have four horses, and would not stir a foot with one less! – As the gentleman's gentleman there, was telling and boasting to me about now, when the barouche was ordered for them, there at the lady's house, where lady Dashfort is on a visit – they said they would not get in till they'd get four horses; and their ladies backed them; and so the four horses was got; and they just drove out here, to see the points of view for fashion's sake, like their betters; and up with their glasses, like their ladies; and then, out with their watches, and 'Isn't it time to lunch?' So there they have been lunching within on what they brought with them; for nothing in our house could they touch, of course! They brought themselves a *picknick* lunch, with Madeira and Champagne to wash it down. Why, gentlemen! what do you think, but a set of them, as they were bragging to me, turned out of a boarding-house at Cheltenham, last year, because they had not peach-pies to their lunch! – But, here they come! shawls, and veils, and all! – streamers flying! But mum is my cue! – Captain, are these girths to your fancy, now?' said the landlord, aloud: then, as he stooped to alter a buckle, he said, in a voice meant to be heard only by captain Bowles, 'If there's a tongue, male or female, in the three kingdoms, it's in that foremost woman, Mrs. Petito.'

'Mrs. Petito!' repeated Lord Colambre, as the name caught his ear; and, approaching the barouche, in which the five abigails were now seated, he saw the identical Mrs. Petito, who, when he left London, had been in his mother's service.

She recognized his lordship, with very gracious intimacy; and, before he had time to ask any questions, she answered all she conceived he was going to ask, and with a volubility which justified the landlord's eulogium of her tongue.

'Yes, my lord! I left my lady Clonbrony, some time back – the day after you left town; and both her ladyship and Miss Nugent was charmingly, and would have sent their loves to your lordship, I'm sure, if they'd any notion I should have met you, my lord, so soon. And I was very sorry to part with them; but the fact was, my lord,' said Mrs. Petito, laying a detaining hand upon lord Colambre's whip, one end of which he unwittingly trusted within her reach; – 'I and my lady had a little difference, which the best friends, you know, sometimes have: so my lady Clonbrony was so condescending to give me up to my lady Dashfort, – and I knew no more than the child unborn, that her ladyship had it in contemplation to cross the seas. But, to oblige my lady, and as colonel Heathcock, with his regiment of militia, was coming for purtection in the packet at the same time, and we to have the government-yacht, I waived my objections to Ireland. And, indeed, though I was greatly frighted at first, having heard all we've heard, you know, my lord, from lady Clonbrony, of there being no living in Ireland, and expecting to see no trees nor accommodation, nor any thing but bogs all along; yet, I declare, I was very agreeably surprised; for, as far as I've seen at Dublin and in the vicinity, the accommodations, and every thing of that nature, now is vastly put-up-able with!'

'My lord,' said sir James Brooke, 'we shall be late.'

Lord Colambre, withdrawing his whip from Mrs. Petito, turned his horse away. She, stretching over the back of the barouche as he rode off, bawled to him,

'My lord, we're at Stephen's Green, when we're at Dublin.' But, as he did not choose to hear, she raised her voice to its highest pitch, adding,

'And where are you, my lord, to be found? – as I have a parcel of miss Nugent's for you.'

Lord Colambre instantly turned back, and gave his direction.

'Cleverly done, faith!' said the major. – 'I did not hear her say when lady Dashfort is to be in town,' said captain Bowles.

'What, Bowles! have you a mind to lose more of your guineas to lady Dashfort, and to be jockied out of another horse by lady Isabel?'

'Oh! confound it – no! I'll keep out of the way of that – I have had enough,' said captain Bowles; 'it is my lord Colambre's turn now; you hear, that Lady Dashfort would be very *proud* to see him. His lordship is in for it, and with such an auxiliary as Mrs. Petito, lady Dashfort has him for lady Isabel, as sure as he has a heart or hand.'

'My compliments to the ladies, but my heart is engaged,' said lord

Colambre, 'and my hand shall go with my heart, or not at all.'

'Engaged! engaged to a very amiable, charming woman, no doubt,' said sir James Brooke, 'I have an excellent opinion of your taste; and if you can return the compliment to my judgment, take my advice. Don't trust to your heart's being engaged, much less plead that engagement; for it would be lady Dashfort's sport, and lady Isabel's joy, to make you break your engagement, and break your mistress's heart; the fairer, the more amiable, the more beloved, the greater the triumph, the greater the delight, in giving pain. All the time love would be out of the question; neither mother nor daughter would care if you were hanged, or, as lady Dashfort would herself have expressed it, if you were d—d.'

'With such women, I should think a man's heart could be in no great danger,' said lord Colambre.

'There you might be mistaken, my lord; there's a way to every man's heart, which no man in his own case is aware of, but which every woman knows right well, and none better than these ladies, by his vanity.'

'True,' – said captain Bowles.

'I am not so vain as to think myself without vanity,' said lord Colambre; 'but love, I should imagine, is a stronger passion than vanity.'

'You should imagine! Stay till you are tried, my lord. Excuse me,' said captain Bowles, laughing.

Lord Colambre felt the good sense of this, and determined to have nothing to do with these dangerous ladies; indede, though he had talked, he had scarcely yet thought of them, for his imagination was intent upon that packet from miss Nugent, which Mrs. Petito said she had for him. – He heard nothing of it, or of her, for some days. He sent his servant every day to Stephen's Green, to inquire if lady Dashfort had returned to town. Her ladyship at last returned; but Mrs. Petito could not deliver the parcel to any hand but lord Colambre's own, and she would not stir out, because her lady was indisposed. No longer able to restrain his impatience, lord Colambre went himself – knocked at lady Dashfort's door – inquired for Mrs. Petito – was shown into her parlour. The parcel was delivered to him; but, to his utter disappointment, it was a parcel *for*, not *from* miss Nugent. It contained merely an odd volume of some book of miss Nugent's, which Mrs. Petito said she had put up along with her things *in a mistake*, and she thought it her duty to return it by the first opportunity of a safe conveyance.

Whilst lord Colambre, to comfort himself for his disappointment, was fixing his eyes upon miss Nugent's name, written by her own hand, in the first leaf of the book, the door opened, and the figure of an interesting looking woman, in deep mourning, appeared – appeared for one moment, and retired.

'Only my lord Colambre, about a parcel I was bringing for him from England, my lady – my lady Isabel, my lord,' said Mrs. Petito.

Whilst Mrs. Petito was saying this, the entrance and retreat had been made, and made with such dignity, grace, and modesty; with such innocence dove like eyes had been raised upon him, fixed and withdrawn; with such a gracious bend the lady Isabel had bowed to him as she retired; with such a smile, and with so soft a voice, had repeated 'lord Colambre!' that his lordship, though well aware that all this was mere acting, could not help saying to himself as he left the house:

'It is a pity it is only acting. There is certainly something very engaging in this woman. It is a pity she is an actress. And so young! A much younger woman than I expected. A widow before most women are wives. So young, surely she cannot be such a fiend as they described her to be!'

A few nights afterwards, lord Colambre was, with some of his acquaintance at the theatre, when lady Isabel and her mother came into the box, where seats had been reserved for them, and where their appearance instantly made that *sensation* which is usually created by the entrance of persons of the first notoriety in the fashionable world. Lord Colambre was not a man to be dazzled by fashion, or to mistake notoriety for deference paid to merit, and for the admiration commanded by beauty or talents. Lady Dashfort's coarse person, loud voice, daring manners, and indelicate wit, disgusted him almost past endurance. He saw sir James Brooke in the box opposite to him; and twice determined to go round to him. His lordship had crossed the benches, and once his hand was upon the lock of the door; but, attracted as much by the daughter as repelled by the mother, he could move no farther. The mother's masculine boldness heightened, by contrast, the charms of the daughter's soft sentimentality. The lady Isabel seemed to shrink from the indelicacy of her mother's manners, and appeared peculiarly distressed by the strange efforts lady Dashfort made, from time to time, to drag her forward, and to fix upon her the attention of gentlemen. Colonel Heathcock, who, as Mrs. Petito had informed lord Colambre, had come over with his regiment to Ireland, was beckoned into their box by lady Dashfort, by her squeezed into a seat next to lady Isabel; but lady Isabel seemed to feel sovereign contempt, properly repressed by politeness, for what, in a low whisper to a female friend on the other side of her, she called, 'the self-sufficient inanity of this sad coxcomb.' – Other coxcombs, of a more vivacious style, who stationed themselves round her mother, or to whom her mother stretched from box to box to talk, seemed to engage no more of lady Isabel's attention, than just what she was compelled to give by lady Dashfort's repeated calls of,

'Isabel! Isabel! colonel G——. Isabel! lord D—— bowing to you, Belle! Belle! sir Harry B——. Isabel, child, with your eyes on the stage! Did you never see a play before? Novice! major P—— waiting to catch your eye this quarter of an hour; and now her eyes gone down to her play-bill! Sir Harry, do take it from her.

'Were eyes so radiant only made to read?"[1]

Lady Isabel appeared to suffer so exquisitely and so naturally from this persecution, that lord Colambre said to himself,

'If this be acting, it is the best acting I ever saw. If this be art, it deserves to be nature.'

And with this sentiment, he did himself the honour of handing lady Isabel to her carriage this night, and with this sentiment he awoke next morning; and by the time he had dressed and breakfasted, he determined, that it was impossible all that he had seen could be acting. 'No woman, no young woman, could have such art.' Sir James Brooke had been unwarrantably severe; he would go and tell him so.

But sir James Brooke this day received orders for his regiment to march to quarters in a distant part of Ireland. His head was full of arms, and ammunition, and knapsacks, and billets, and routes, and there was no possibility, even in the present chivalrous disposition of our hero, to enter upon the defence of the lady Isabel. Indeed, in the regret he felt for the approaching and unexpected departure of his friend, lord Colambre forgot the fair lady. But just when sir James had his foot in the stirrup he stopped.

'By the by, my dear lord, I saw you at the play last night. You seemed to be much interested. Don't think me impertinent, if I remind you of our conversation when we were riding home from Tusculum; and if I warn you,' said he, mounting his horse, 'to beware of counterfeits, – for such are abroad.' Reining in his impatient steed,

---

1 George Lyttleton, 'Soliloquy of a Beauty in the Country', l. 42.

sir James turned again and added, '*Deeds not words*, is my motto. Remember, we can judge better by the conduct of people towards others, than by their manner towards ourselves.'

From *Memoirs of Richard Lovell Edgeworth*
(1820)

...At last came the dreaded news. The French, who landed at Killala, were, as we learned, on their march towards Longford. The touch of Ithuriel's spear[1] could not have been more sudden or effectual, than the arrival of this intelligence, in shewing people in their real forms. In some faces joy struggled for a moment with feigned sorrow, and then, encouraged by sympathy, yielded to the *natural* expression. Still my father had no reason to distrust those, in whom he had placed confidence; his tenants were steady; he saw no change in any of the men of his corps, though they were in the most perilous situation, having rendered themselves obnoxious to the rebels and invaders, by becoming yeomen, and yet standing without means of resistance or defence, their arms not having arrived.

The evening of the day, when the news of the success and approach of the French came to Edgeworth-Town, all seemed quiet; but early the next morning, September 4th, a report reached us, that the rebels were *up* in arms within a mile of the village, pouring in from the county of Westmeath, hundreds strong. Such had been the tranquillity of the preceding night, that we could not at first believe their report. – An hour afterwards it was contradicted. An English servant, who was sent out to ascertain the truth, brought back word, that he had ridden three miles from the village on the road described, and that he had seen only twenty or thirty men with green boughs in their hats, and pikes in their hands, who said, '*that they were standing there to protect themselves against the Orangemen, of whom they were in dread, and who, as they heard, were coming down to cut them to pieces.*' This was all nonsense; but no better sense could be obtained. Report upon report, equally foolish, was heard, or at least uttered. But this much being certain, that men armed with pikes were assembled, my father sent off an express to the next garrison town (Longford), requesting the commanding

---

1   Him [Satan] thus intent Ithuriel with his spear
              Touched lightly; for no falsehood can endure
              Touch of celestial temper, but returns
              Of force to its own likeness.
                          (*Paradise Lost*, iv. 810)

officer to send him assistance for the defence of this place. He desired us to be prepared to set out at a moment's warning. We were under this uncertainty, when an escort with an ammunition cart passed through the village, on its way to Longford. – It contained several barrels of powder, intended to blow up the bridges, and to stop the progress of the enemy. One of the officers of the party rode up to our house, and offered to let us have the advantage of his escort. But, after a few minutes deliberation, this friendly proposal was declined. My father determined, that he would not stir till he knew whether he could have assistance; and as it did not appear as yet absolutely necessary that we should go, we staid – fortunately for us!

About a quarter of an hour after the officer and the escort had departed, we, who were all assembled in the portico of the house, heard a report like a loud clap of thunder. The doors and windows shook with some violent concussion; a few minutes afterwards, the officer galloped into the yard, and threw himself off his horse into my father's arms almost senseless. The ammunition cart had blown up, one of the officers had been severely wounded, and the horses and the man leading them killed; the wounded officer was at a farm-house on the Longford road, at about two miles distance. The fear of the rebels was now suspended, in concern for this accident. Mrs. Edgeworth went immediately to give her assistance; she left her carriage for the use of the wounded gentleman, and rode back. At the entrance of the village she was stopped by a gentleman in great terror, who, taking hold of the bridle of her horse, begged her not to attempt to go further, assuring her that the rebels were coming into the town. But she answered, that she must and would return to her family. She rode on, and found us waiting anxiously for her. No assistance could be afforded from Longford; the rebels were reassembling, and advancing towards the village; and there was no alternative, but to leave our home as fast as possible. One of our carriages having been left with the wounded officer, we had but one at this moment for our whole family, eleven in number. No mode of conveyance could be had for some of the female servants; our faithful English housekeeper offered to stay till the return of the carriage, which had been left with the officer; and as we could not carry her, we were obliged, most reluctantly, to leave her behind to follow, as we hoped, immediately. As we passed through the village, we heard nothing but the entreaties, lamentations, and objurgations of those, who could not procure the means of carrying off their goods or their families: most painful when we could give no assistance.

Next to the safety of his own family, my father's greatest anxiety was for his defenceless corps. No men could behave better than they did at this first moment of trial. No one absented himself, though many, living at a distance, might, if they had been so inclined, have found plausible excuses for nonappearance. The bugle was not sounded to call them together, but they were in their ranks in the street the moment they had their captain's orders, declaring, that whatever he commanded they would do. He ordered them to march to Longford. The idea of going to Longford could not be agreeable to many of them, who were Catholics; because that town was full of those who called themselves – I would avoid using party names if I could, but I can not otherwise make the facts intelligible – who called themselves Orangemen, and who were not supposed to have favourable opinions of any of another religious persuasion. There was no reluctance shewn, however, by the Catholics of this corps to go among them. The moment the word *march* was uttered by their captain, they marched with alacrity. – One of my brothers, a youth of fifteen, was in their ranks; another, twelve years old, marched with them.

We expected every instant to hear the shout of the rebels entering Edgeworth-Town. When we had got about half a mile out of the village, my father suddenly recollected, that he had left on his table a paper, containing a list of his corps; and that, if this should come into the hand of the rebels, it might be of dangerous consequence to his men; it would serve to point out their houses for pillage, and their families for destruction. He turned his horse instantly, and galloped back for it. The time of his absence appeared immeasurably long, but he returned safely, after having destroyed the dangerous paper.

About two miles from the village was the spot, where the ammunition cart had been blown up; the dead horses, swollen to an unnatural bulk, were lying across the road. As we approached, we saw two men in an adjoining field looking at the remains of one of the soldiers, who had been literally blown to pieces. They ran towards us, and we feared, that they were rebels going to stop us. They jumped over the ditch, and seized our bridles; but with friendly intent. With no small difficulty they dragged us past the dead horses, saying, 'God speed you! and make haste any way!' We were very ready to take their advice. After this, on the six long miles of the road from Edgeworth-Town to Longford, we did not meet a human being. It was all silent and desert, as if every creature had fled from the cabins by the road side.

Longford was crowded with yeomanry of various corps, and with the inhabitants of the neighbourhood, who had flocked thither for protection. With great difficulty the poor Edgeworth-Town infantry found lodgings. We were cordially received by the landlady of a good inn. Though her house was, as she said, fuller than it could hold, as she was an old friend of my father's, she did contrive to give us two rooms, in which we eleven were thankful to find ourselves. All our concern now was for those we had left behind. We heard nothing of our housekeeper all night, and were exceedingly alarmed: but early the next morning, to our great joy, she arrived. She told us, that after we had left her, she waited hour after hour for the carriage: she could hear nothing of it, as it had gone to Longford with the wounded officer. Towards evening, a large body of rebels entered the village. – She heard them at the gate, and expected that they would have broken in the next instant. But one, who seemed to be a leader, with a pike in his hand, set his back against the gate, and swore, that, 'if he was to die for it the next minute, he would have the life of the first man, who should open that gate, or set enemy's foot within side of that place. He said the housekeeper, who was left in it, was a good gentlewoman, and had done him a service, though *she did not know him, nor he her*. He had never seen her face, but she had, the year before, lent his wife, when in distress, sixteen shillings, the rent of flax-ground, and he would stand her friend now.

He kept back the mob; they agreed to send him to the house with a deputation of six, *to know the truth*, and to ask for arms. The six men went to the back-door, and summoned the housekeeper; one of them pointed his blunderbuss at her, and told her, that she must fetch all the arms in the house; she said she had none. Her champion asked her to say if she remembered him – 'No; to her knowledge she had never seen his face.' He asked if she remembered having lent a woman money to pay her rent of flax-ground the year before? 'Yes,' she remembered that, and named the woman, the time, and the sum. His companions were thus satisfied of the truth of what he had asserted. He bid her not to be *frighted*, 'for that no harm should happen to her, nor any belonging to her; not a soul should get leave to go into her master's house; not a twig should be touched, nor a leaf harmed.' His companions huzzaed and went off. Afterwards, as she was told, he mounted guard at the gate during the whole time the rebels were in the town.

When the carriage at last returned, it was stopped by the rebels, who filled the street; they held their pikes to the horses and to the coachman's breast, accusing him of being an Orange-man, because, as they said, he wore the orange colours (our livery being yellow and brown). A painter, a friend of ours, who had been that day at our house, copying some old family portraits, happened to be in the street at that instant, and called out to the mob, '*Gentlemen, it is yellow! – gentlemen, it is not orange.*' In consequence of this happy distinction they let go the coachman; and the same man, who had mounted guard at the gate, came up with his friends, rescued the carriage, and surrounding the coachman with their pikes brought him safely into the yard. The pole of the carriage having been broken in the first onset, the housekeeper could not leave Edgeworth-Town till morning. She passed the night in walking up and down, listening and watching, but the rebels returned no more, and thus our house was saved by the gratitude of a single individual.

We had scarcely time to rejoice in the escape of our housekeeper, and safety of our house, when we found, that new dangers arose even from this escape. The house being saved created jealousy and suspicion in the minds of many, who at this time saw every thing through the mist of party prejudice. The dislike to my father's corps appeared every hour more strong. He saw the consequences, that might arise from the slightest breaking out of quarrel. It was not possible for him to send his men, unarmed as they still were, to their homes, lest they should be destroyed by the rebels; yet the officers of the other corps wished to have them sent out of the town, and to this effect joined in a memorial to government. Some of these officers disliked my father, from differences of electioneering interests; others, from his not having kept up an acquaintance with them; and others, not knowing him in the least, were misled by party reports and misrepresentations.

These petty dissensions were, however, at one moment suspended and forgotten in a general sense of danger. An express arrived late one night, with the news that the French, who were rapidly advancing, were within a few miles of the town of Longford. A panic seized the people. There were in the town eighty of the carabineers and two corps of yeomanry, but it was proposed to evacuate the garrison. My father strongly opposed this measure, and undertook, with fifty men, if arms and ammunition were supplied, to defend the gaol of Longford, where there was a strong pass, at which the enemy might be stopped. He urged, that a stand might be made there, till the king's army should come up. The offer was gladly accepted – men, arms, ammunition, all he could want or desire, were placed at his disposal. He slept that night in the gaol, with every thing prepared for its defence; but the next morning fresh news came, that the French had turned off from the Longford road, and were going towards Granard; of this, however, there was no certainty. My father, by the desire of the commanding officer, rode out to reconnoitre, and my brother went to the top of the court-house with a telescope for the same purpose. We (Mrs. Edgeworth, my aunts, my sisters, and myself) were waiting to hear the result in one of the upper sitting-rooms of the inn, which fronted the street. We heard a loud shout, and going to the window, we saw the people throwing up their hats, and heard huzzas. An express had arrived with news, that the French and the rebels had been beaten; that General Lake had come up with them at a place called Ballynamuck, near Granard; that 1,500 rebels and French were killed, and that the French generals and officers were prisoners.

We were impatient for my father, when we heard this joyful news; he had not yet returned, and we looked out of the windows in hopes of seeing him, but we could see only a great number of the people of the town, shaking hands with each other. This lasted a few minutes, and then the crowd gathered in silence round one man, who spoke with angry vehemence and gesticulation; stamping, and frequently wiping his forehead. We thought he was a mountebank haranguing the populace, till we saw, that he wore a uniform. Listening with curiosity to hear what he was saying, we observed, that he looked up towards us, and we thought we heard him pronounce the names of my father and brother in tones of insult. We could scarcely believe what we heard him say. Pointing up to the top of the court-house, he exclaimed, '*That* young Edgeworth ought to be dragged down from the top of that house.'

Our housekeeper burst into the room, so much terrified she could hardly speak.

'My master, ma'am! – it is all against my master, the mob say they will tear him to pieces, if they catch hold of him. They say he's a traitor, that he illuminated the gaol to deliver it up to the French.'

No words can give an idea of our astonishment. Illuminated! what could be meant by the gaol being illuminated? My father had literally but two farthing candles, by the light of which he had been reading the newspaper late the preceding night. These however were said to be signals for the enemy! The absurdity of the whole was so glaring, that we could scarcely conceive the danger to be real; but our pale landlady's fears were urgent, she dreaded that her house should be pulled down. We found, that the danger was not the less because the accusation was false; on the contrary, it was great in proportion to its absurdity, for the people who could at once be under such a perversion of intellects, and such an illusion of their senses, must indeed be in a state of frenzy.

The crowd had by this time removed from before the windows; but we heard, that they were gone to that end of the town, through which they expected Mr. Edgeworth to return.

We wrote immediately to the commanding officer, informing him of what we had heard, and requesting his advice and assistance. He came to us, and recommended, that we should send a messenger to warn Mr. E. of his danger, and to request, that he would not return to Longford this day. The officer added, that, in consequence of the rejoicings for the victory, his men would probably be all drunk in a few hours, and that he could not answer for them. This officer, a captain of yeomanry, was a good-natured, but inefficient man, who spoke under considerable nervous agitation, and seemed desirous to do all he could, but not to be able to do any thing. We wrote, instantly, and with difficulty found a man, who undertook to convey the note. It was to be carried to meet him on one road, and Mrs. Edgeworth and I determined to drive out to meet him on the other. We made our way down a back straircase into the inn yard, where the carriage was ready. Several gentlemen spoke to us as we got into the carriage, begging us not to be alarmed: Mrs. Edgeworth answered, that she was more surprised than alarmed. The commanding officer and the sovereign of Longford walked by the side of the carriage through the town; and as the mob believed, that we were going away not to return, we got through without molestation. We went a few miles on the road towards Edgeworth-Town, till at a tenant's house we heard, that my father had passed by half an hour ago; that he was riding in company with an officer, supposed to be of Lord Cornwalllis's or General Lake's army; that they had taken a *short cut*, which led into Longford by another entrance. Most fortunately not that at which an *armed* mob had assembled, expecting the object of their fury. Seeing him return to the inn with an officer of the king's army, they imagined, as we were afterwards told, that he was brought back a prisoner, and they were satisfied.

The moment we saw him safe, we laughed at our own fears, and again doubted the reality of the danger, more especially as he treated the idea with the utmost incredulity and scorn.

Major (now General) Eustace was the officer, who returned with him. He dined with us; every thing appeared quiet. The persons who had taken refuge at the inn were now gone to their homes, and it was supposed, that, whatever dispositions to riot had existed, the news of the approach of some of Lord Cornwallis's suite, or of troops who were to bring in the French prisoners, would prevent all probability of disturbance. In the evening the prisoners arrived at the inn; a crowd followed them, but quietly. A sun-burnt, coarse looking man, in a huge cocked hat, with a quantity of gold lace on his clothes, seemed to fix all attention; he was pointed out as the French General Homberg, or Sarrazin. As he dismounted from his horse, he threw the bridle over its neck, and looked at the animal as being his only friend.

We heard my father in the evening ask Major Eustace, to walk with him through the town to the barrack-yard to evening parade; and we saw them go out together without our feeling the slightest apprehension. We remained at the inn. By this time Col. Handfield, Major Cannon, and some other officers, had arrived, and they were at the inn at dinner in a parlour on the ground-floor, under our room. It being hot weather, the windows were open. Nothing now seemed to be thought of but rejoicings for the victory. Candles were preparing for the illumination; waiters, chambermaids, landlady, all hands were busy scooping turnips and potatoes for candlesticks, to stand in every pane of every loyal window.

In the midst of this preparation about half an hour after my father had left us, we heard a great uproar in the street. At first we thought the shouts were only rejoicings for victory, but as they came nearer we heard screechings and yellings, indescribably horrible. A mob had gathered at the gates of the barrack yard, and joined by many soldiers of the yeomanry on leaving parade, had followed Major Eustace and my father from the barracks. The major being this evening in colored clothes, the people no longer knew him to be an officer; nor conceived, as they had done before, that Mr. Edgeworth was his prisoner. The mob had not contented themselves with the horrid yells that we had heard, but had been pelting them with hard turf, stones, and brickbats. From one of these my father received a blow on the side of his head, which came with such force as to stagger, and almost to stun him; but he kept himself from falling, knowing that if once he fell he should be trampled under foot. He walked on steadily till he came within a few yards of the inn, when one of the mob seized hold of Major Eustace by the collar. My father seeing the windows of the inn open, called with a loud voice, 'Major Eustace is in danger!'

The officers, who were at dinner, and who till that moment had supposed the noise in the street to be only drunken rejoycings, immediately ran out, and rescued Major Eustace and my father. At the sight of British officers and drawn swords, the populace gave way, and dispersed in different directions.

The preparation for the illuminations then went on, as if nothing had intervened. All the panes of our windows in the front room were in a blaze of light by the time the mob returned through the street. The night passed without further disturbance.

As early as we could the next morning we left Longford, and returned homewards, all danger from rebels being now over, and the rebellion having been terminated by the late battle.

When we came near Edgeworth-Town, we saw many well known faces at the cabin doors, looking out to welcome us. One man, who was digging in his field by the road side, when he looked up as our horses passed, and saw my father, let fall his spade and clasped his hands; his face, as the morning sun shone upon it, was the strongest picture of joy I ever saw. The village was a melancholy spectacle; windows shattered, and doors broken. But though the mischief done was great, there had been little pillage. Within our gates we found all property safe; literally 'not a twig touched, not a leaf harmed.' Within the house every thing was as we had left it – a map that we had been consulting was still open on the library table, with pencils, and slips of paper containing the first lessons in arithmetic, in which some of the young people had been engaged the morning we had been driven from home; a pansy, in a glass of water, which one of the children had been copying, was still on the chimney-piece. These trivial circumstances, marking repose and tranquillity, struck us at this moment with an unreasonable sort of surprise, and all that had passed seemed like an incoherent dream. The joy of having my father in safety remained, and gratitude to Heaven for his preservation. These feelings spread inexpressible pleasure over what seemed to be a new sense of existence. Even the most common things appeared delightful; the green lawn, the still groves, the birds singing, the fresh air, all external nature, and all the goods and conveniences of life, seemed to have wonderfully increased in value, from the fear into which we had been put of losing them irrecoverably.

The first thing my father did, the day we came home, was to draw up a memorial to the Lord Lieutenant, desiring to have a court martial held on the sergeant, who by haranguing the populace, had raised the mob at Longford; his next care was to walk through the village, to examine what damage had been done by the rebels, and to order that repairs of all his tenants' houses should be made at his expense. A few days after our return, Government ordered, that the arms of the Edgeworth-Town infantry should be forwarded by the commanding officer at Longford. Through the whole of their hard week's trial, the corps had, without any exception, behaved perfectly well. It was perhaps more difficult to honest and brave men passively to bear such a trial, than any to which they could have been exposed in action.

When the arms for the corps arrived, my father, in delivering them to the men, thanked them publicly, for their conduct, assuring them, that he would remember it, whenever he should have opportunities of serving them, collectively or individually. In long after years, as occasions arose, each, who continued to deserve it, found in him a friend, and felt, that he more than fulfilled his promise. Now that he could look back upon suspicions and accusations, now that events had decided upon guilt and innocence, and had shown who were, and who were not, implicated in this rebellion, he had the satisfaction of feeling, that, though he had trusted much, he had not in *many* instances, trusted rashly. In some few cases he was deceived. – Who in Ireland at that time can boast, that he was not? Some few, very few indeed, of his tenantry, on a remote estate – alas too near Ballynamuck, did join the rebels! These persons were never readmitted on my father's estate.

In some cases it was difficult to know what ought to be done: for instance, with regard to the man who had saved his house from pillage, but who had joined the rebels. It was the wise policy of Government, to pardon those, who had not been ringleaders in this rebellion; and who, repenting of their folly, were desirous to return to their allegiance, and to their peaceable duties. My father sent for this man, and said he would apply to Government for a pardon for him. The man smiled, and clapping his pocket said, 'I have my *Corny* here safe already, I thank your Honor – else sure I would not have been such a fool, as to be shewing myself without I had a *purtection.*' – A pardon, signed by the Lord Lieutenant, Lord Cornwallis, in their witty spirit of abbreviation they called a *Corny.*

We observed, and thought it an instance of Irish acuteness and knowledge of character, that this man was sure my father never would *forget him*, though he gave him nothing at this time. When my father said, that, though we were obliged to him for saving the house, he could not *reward* him for being a rebel; he answered, 'Oh, I know that I could not expect it, nor look for any thing at all, but what I got – *thanks.*' With these words he went away satisfied.

A considerable time afterward my father, finding that the man conducted himself well, took an opportunity of serving him. Rewards my father thought fully as necessary and as efficacious as punishments, for the good government of human creatures: therefore he took especial care, not only to punish those who had done ill, but to reward, as far as he could, all who had done well.

Before we quit this subject, it may be useful to record, that the French generals, who headed this invasion, declared they had been completely deceived as to the state of Ireland. They had expected to find the people in open rebellion, or, at least, in their own phrase, *organized* for insurrection; but to their dismay, they found only raga-muffins, as they called them, who, in joining their standard, did them infinitely more harm than good. It is a pity, that the lower Irish could not hear the contemptuous manner, in which the French, both officers and soldiers, spoke of them and of their country. The generals described the stratagems, which had been practised upon them by their good allies. The same rebels frequently returning with different tones and new stories, to obtain double and treble provisions of arms, ammuni-tion, and uniforms – selling the ammunition for whiskey, and running away at the first fire in the day of battle. The French, detesting and despising those by whom they had been thus cheated, pillaged, and deserted, called them beggars, rascals, and savages. They cursed also without scruple their own Directory for sending them, after they had, as they boasted, conquered the world, to be at last beaten in an Irish bog. Officers and soldiers joined in swearing, that they would never return to a country, where they could find neither bread, wine, nor dis-cipline; and where the people lived on roots, whiskey, and lying.

These, as my father observed, were comfortable words for Ireland. National antipathy, thus felt and expressed between the invaders and the Irish malecontents, would be better security for the future quiet and safety of the country even than the victory. Full of these thoughts, unconcerned about himself, and in excellent spirits, he succeeded in turning our attention to new objects. The Longford mob completely vanished from our imagination. Reflecting upon what had passed, my father drew from it one useful conclusion for his own future conduct – that he ought to mix more with society, and make himself more gen-erally known in Ireland....

ARTHUR WELLESLEY, DUKE OF WELLINGTON (1769-1852)

Born in Dublin, he was educated at Eton, Brighton, and the School of Equitation, Angers, France. He was MP for Trim in the Irish House of Commons (1790-1795); he commanded the 33rd Foot in India (1797), and was commander of the British armies in Spain from 1808 until the abdication of Napoleon in 1814. For his services he was created the first Duke of Wellington. After Napoleon's return, he was appointed Commander-in-Chief of the British and Dutch-Belgian forces, and defeated him at Waterloo on 18 June 1815. He served three terms as Prime Minister (1828-1830, 1834 and 1841-1846); in his first term in office, Catholic Emancipation, which he had resisted, became law. He became the *eminence grise* of the Tory party.

from A Speech in the House of Lords, 27 June 1850

ABOLITION OF THE LORD-LIEUTENANCY OF IRELAND

I will not trouble your lordships with details; but I will advert to one or two circumstances which will show clearly to your lordships what may be the consequences of putting down this great office of the lord-lieu-tenant. Among the first operations I had to contemplate after being appointed to the office which I have the honour to hold, were the meas-ures necessary to be adopted to put an end to what were called by the individual who promoted them the 'monster meetings' in Ireland.[1] There were several important legal as well as political questions involved in the consideration of those measures. Upon every one of these it was essen-tial to refer to my noble friend Earl de Grey, then the Lord-lieutenant of Ireland; and it was also necessary that he should be in close communi-cation with the military authorities. Those measures could not have been adopted, proceeded with, or carried into execution, without the con-stant communication and conference of the two authorities—the civil and political authority—the lord-lieutenant and the military officer com-manding the troops; and it was likewise necessary that there should be communications with the government in this country. I say, then, that no part of these proceedings could have been adopted if you had not had an officer in Ireland with the constitutional power and authority of the lord-lieutenant. Since that time there has been a constant series of mili-tary operations in the course of being carried on in Ireland. The persons who rendered those operations necessary adopted the usual course of modern revolutionists, of publishing their designs, so that they were known to those who were to oppose them as well as to themselves; and though these designs were not so formidable as others that have been seen, yet it was very necessary to attend to them, to oppose the barri-cading of the streets, the interruption of the communications, and other proceedings, which, if they had succeeded, would have occasioned very great inconvenience, if not disastrous consequences. The requisite meas-ures of precaution were necessarily to be discussed by the military authorities with the lord-lieutenant and the civil authorities of the gov-

---

1 *the individual...* ' Daniel O'Connell.

ernment, no part of which could have been carried into execution without the knowledge, consideration, and full concurrence of the lord-lieutenant. Withdraw the lord-lieutenant from Ireland, and who becomes the chief civil authority in different parts of the country? In Dublin the chief civil authority would be the lord-mayor. Now I think that, in less than three months after the adoption of the measure to put down the monster meetings in Ireland, I had the honour of attending her majesty at court, and there I saw Mr. O'Connell as Lord-mayor of Dublin, followed by some of his suite, presenting an address to her majesty on the throne. Now, will any one say that the military authorities would have ventured to concert any military operations with the then lord-mayor of Dublin, elected by the democratic corporation created by a recent act of parliament? I will take another case. I had afterwards to provide against barricades in the streets of Dublin, to take measures for attacking them if they should be formed, and to secure the free passage of the streets. For this purpose it was necessary to have confiendial communications with the secretary of state here and with the Lord-lieutenant of Ireland. Could I have ventured to do this with the Lord-mayor of Dublin? Could I have written a line on the subject without ordering the commander-in-chief on the spot in Dublin to take care that the lord-mayor and the gentlemen of the Dublin corporation should know nothing about the matter? I will give you another instance. The Corporation Act passed some years ago enabled the corporations in the country parts of Ireland to elect their mayors, and some very nice mayors they have elected. It was necessary some time ago to carry on military operations in the very neighbourhood of Kilkenny. Who was the elected mayor there at that time? Dr. Cane. And what became of Dr. Cane? Why, before the operations of Kilkenny were over, he was in prison under the provisions of the act for the suspension of the *habeas corpus*. And yet such was the gentleman with whom the general officer, carrying on his operations with his troops, must have consulted in the absence of the Lord-lieutenant of Ireland.... I entreat noble lords opposite to consider well this proposition for abolishing the office of lord-lieutenant, and let them reflect whether it would be expedient, with the view of saving some £20,000 a year, or any paltry sum of that kind, to remove from a country in such a state of constant disturbance as Ireland is in, has been in, and possibly may continue to be in for some time, the authority which is required to put down this state of disturbance by taking advantage of every favourable opportunity to secure tranquillity. I entreat noble lords to consider well the difficulty of carrying on the government under such circumstances.

TIGHE, MARY (1772-1810)

B orn in Co. Wicklow, the daughter of Theodosia Tighe, a founding-member of Irish Methodism, and the Rev. William Blachford, a keeper of Marsh's Library, who died in her infancy, she was educated by her mother, and began to write poetry at an early age. She was unhappily married to her cousin Henry Tighe, MP, of Woodstock, Co. Kilkenny. Her Spenserian allegory on love and the soul, was published privately in 1805. It is believed to have influenced Keats's *Endymion*.

From *Psyche, or the Legend of Love*
(1805)

from CANTO VI

Now as with languid stroke they ply the oars,
While the dense fog obscures their gloomy way;
Hymen, well used to coast these dangerous shores,
Roused from the dreaming trance in which he lay,
Cries to the knight in voice of dread dismay,
'Steer hence thy bark, oh! yet in time beware;
Here lies Petrea, which with baneful sway
Glacella rules, I feel the dank cold air,
I hear her chilling voice, methinks it speaks despair!'

Even while he speaks, behold the vessel stands
Immoveable! in vain the pilot tries
The helm to turn; fixed in the shallow strands,
No more obedient to his hand, it lies,
The disappointed oar no aid supplies
While sweeping o'er the sand it mocks their force.
The anxious knight to Constance now applies,
To his oft tried assistance has recourse,
And bids his active mind design some swift resource.

Debating doubtfully awhile they stood,
At length on their united strength rely,
To force the bark on the supporting flood;
They rouse the seamen, who half slumbering lie,
Subdued and loaded by the oppressive sky.
Then wading mid the fog, with care explore
What side the deepest waters may supply,

And where the shallows least protect the shore,
While through their darksome search the star sheds light before.

Mean time deep slumbers of the vaporous mist
Hang on the heavy eye-lids of the fair;
And Hymen too, unable to resist
The drowsy force of the o'erwhelming air,
Laid at her feet at length forgets his care.
When lo! Glacella's treacherous slaves advance,
Deep wrapt in thickest gloom; the sleeping fair
They seize, and bear away in heedless trance,
Long ere her guardian knight suspects the bitter chance.

Thus the lorn traveller imprudent sleeps
Where his high glaciers proud Locendro shews;
Thus o'er his limbs resistless torpor creeps,
As yielding to the fatal deep repose
He sinks benumbed upon the Alpine snows,
And sleeps no more to wake; no more to view
The blooming scenes his native vales disclose,
Or ever more the craggy path pursue,
Or o'er the lichened steep the chamois chase renew.

Lo! to their queen they bear their sleeping prey,
Deep in her ice-built castle's gloomy state,
There on a pompous couch they gently lay
Psyche, as yet unconscious of her fate,
And when her heavy eyes half opening late
Dimly observe the strange and unknown scenes,
As in a dream she views her changed estate,
Gazing around with doubtful, troubled mien
Now on the stupid crowd, now on their dull proud queen.

With vacant smile, and words but half exprest,
In one ungracious, never-varying tone,
Glacella welcomes her bewildered guest,
And bids the chief supporter of her throne
Approach and make their mighty mistress known,
Proud Selfishness, her dark ill-favoured lord!
Her gorgeous seat, which still he shared alone,
He slowly leaves obedient to her word,

And ever as he moved the cringing train adored.

Nought of his shapeless form to sight appears,
Impenetrable furs conceal each part;
Harsh and unpleasing sounds in Psyche's ears
That voice which had subdued full many a heart;
While he, exerting every specious art,
Persuades her to adore their queen's control;
Yet would he not Glacella's name impart,
But with false title, which she artful stole
From fair Philosophy, deludes the erring soul.

'Rest, happy fair!' he cries, 'who here hast found
From all the storms of life a safe retreat,
Sorrow thy breast henceforth no more shall wound
Nor care invade thee in this quiet seat:
The voice of the distressed no more shall meet
The sympathizing ear; another's woes
Shall never interrupt the stillness sweet,
Which here shall hush thee to serene repose,
Nor damp the constant joys these scenes for thee disclose.

'Fatigue no more thy soft and lovely frame
No deep heaved sigh shall here thy pity claim,
Nor hateful want demand thy wealth to share;
For thee shall Independence still prepare
Pleasures unmingled, and for ever sure;
His lips our sovereign's peaceful laws declare,
Centre existence in thyself secure,
Nor let an alien shade thy sunshine e'er obscure.'

He spoke, and lo! unnumbered doors unfold,
And various scenes of revelry display;
Here Grandeur sunk beneath the massive gold;
Here discontented Beauty pined away,
And vainly conscious asked her promised sway;
Here Luxury prepared his sumptuous feast,
While lurking Apathy behind him lay
To poison all the insipid food he drest,
And shake his poppy crown o'er every sated guest.

The hireling minstrels strike their weary lyre,
And slumber o'er the oft-repeated strain;
No listless youth to active grace they fire:
Here Eloquence herself might plead in vain,
Nor one of all the heartless crowd could gain:
And thou, oh! sweeter than the Muses song,
Affection's voice divine! with cold disdain
Even thou art heard, while mid the insulting throng
The daunted, shivering form moves timidly along!

Thus o'er the oiled surface softly slides
The unadmitted stream, rapid it flows,
And from the impervious plain pellucid glides;
Repulsed with gentle murmurs thus it goes,
Till in the porous earth it finds repose,
Concealed and sheltered in its parents breast: –
Oh! man's best treasure in this vale of woes!
Still cheer the sad, and comfort the distrest,
Nor ever be thy voice by selfishness opprest!

Psyche with languid step he leads around,
And bids her all the castle's splendour see.
Here Dissipation's constant sports abound,
While her loose hand in seeming bounty free,
Her scentless roses, painted mimicry,
Profusely sheds; here Pride unheeded tells
To nodding crowds his ancient pedigree;
And Folly with reiterated spells
To count her spotted cards the yawning group compels.

'See how, attentive to her subject's ease,
To their reluctant prey', exclaims her guide,
'Each fleeting joy of life she bids them seize,
Anxious for each gay pastime to provide;
See her fast spreading power increasing wide,
Adored and worshipped in each splendid dome!
Lo! Beauty glows for ever at her side,
She bids her cheek the unvarying rose assume;
And Bacchus sees for her his votive ivy bloom.

'Is aught then wanting in this fairy bower?

Or is there aught which yet thy heart can move?'
That heart, unyielding to their sovereign's power,
In gentle whispers sighing answers, 'Love!'
While scornful smiles the fond reply reprove,
Lo!' he exclaims, 'thy vanquished Cupid view;
He oft with powerful arms had vainly strove
Our sovereign's rocky fortress to subdue,
Now, subject to her reign, he yields obedience due.'

Wondering she gazed around, and where he points,
An idiot child in golden chains she spies,
Rich cumbrous gems load all his feeble joints,
A gaudy bandage seels his stupid eyes,
And foul Desire his short-lived torch supplies:
By the capricious hand of Fashion led,
Her sudden starts with tottering step he tries
Submissive to attend: him had she bred,
And Selfishness himself the nursling ever fed.

With lustre false his tinsel arms to deck
Ungraceful ornaments around him shone,
Gifts of his sportive guide; she round his neck
A glittering cord insultingly had thrown,
Loading its pendent purse with many a stone
And worthless dross, and ever as he went,
His leaden darts, with wanton aim unknown,
Now here, now there, in careless chance she sent,
That oft their blunted force in empty air was spent.

Shocked, from the gross imposture Psyche turned
With horror and disgust her fearful eye;
Her fate forlorn in silent anguish mourned,
And called her knight with many a hopeless sigh.
But see, the crowds in sudden tumult fly!
The doors, fast closing to exclude some foe,
Proclaim to Psyche's hopes her hero nigh:
Escaping from her guard she flies, when lo!
His form the bursting gates in awful beauty shew.

'Fly from these dangerous walls,' his page exclaims;
Swift let us haste our floating bark to gain!

See thy knight's wondrous dart in terror flames;
Soon shall these ice-built walls no shape retain!
Nor can their Queen his dreaded sight sustain.'
Scarcely she heard while rapidly she fled,
Even as a bird, escaped the wily train
The fowler with destructive art had spread,
Nor panting stays its flight, nor yet foregoes its dread.

See how astonished now the crowd supine,
Roused by his potent voice, confused arise;
In tottering masses o'er their heads decline
Dissolving walls; they gaze with wild surprise,
And each affrighted from the ruin flies: –
Pitying he views the vain unfeeling band
Beneath his care, a vile and worthless prize,
Their Queen alone his vengeful arms demand,
But unknown force was hers his terrors to withstand.

A shield she had of more than Gorgon power,
And whom she would she could transform to stone,
Nor ever had it failed her till that hour:
She proves his form invincible alone,
And calls its force petrific on her own.
Amazed he sees the indurated train,
The callous tenants of the silent throne,
And all the marble subjects of their reign,
Inviolably hard, their breathless shape retain.

The magic shield he thence in triumph bore,
Resolved, in pity to the human race,
Her noxious hands its might should guide no more,
And bade the seas conceal its Hydra face:
Oh! kindly meant, though much-defeated grace!
For though the o'erwhelming weight of sounding waves
Conceal its rugged orb a little space,
Snatched by Glacella from the dark deep caves,
Once more the arm of Love with potent spell it braves.

But Psyche, rescued from their cruel scorn,
Urges her knight to hasten from the shore:
The buoyant vessel on the billows borne

147

Rides proudly o'er the mounting surge once more;
Again they spread the sails, the feathered oar
Skims with impatient stroke the sparkling tide;
The blushing Hymen now their smiles restore
Again to frolic gaily at their side,
Though still their playful taunts reproach their slumbering guide.

DANIEL O'CONNELL (1775-1847)

'The Great Liberator', 'the Uncrowned King of Ireland', he was Ireland's dominant political figure in the first half of the nineteenth century. Born in Cahirciveen, eldest son of Morgan O'Connell, of Carhen House, Cahirciveen, Co. Kerry, the scion of an ancient Gaelic family, he was educated at a local hedge-school, adopted by his uncle Maurice 'Hunting Cap' O'Connell, sent to Father Harrington's school at Redington, Co. Cork, and in 1791 to the English College of St. Omer. The following year, he was transferred to Douai. At the suppression of the college, he went to London, attended a private school, and entered Lincoln's Inn. He was called to the Irish bar in 1798. He married his cousin Mary in 1802. In his first public speech, in 1800, to a meeting of Catholics in the Royal Exchange, Dublin, in protest against the Act of Union, he argued that religious questions were subordinate to matters of national importance (he would later claim that this speech contained all the principles of his political career). He opposed Vatican interference in Irish politics, and protested against the veto of Catholic appointments by the British government. In 1821 he issued an *Address to the Catholics of Ireland* calling for a collective Repeal of the Union by all religious denominations. With the founding of the Catholic Association (1823) he became head of a movement that achieved Emancipation in 1829 (through the 'Catholic Rent', he allowed ordinary people to join the association for a penny per month, and in five years raised over £15,000). He was returned for Clare in 1828, but was not allowed to take his seat until he was re-elected after Emancipation, in 1830, becoming the first Catholic to sit in the House of Commons. He supported the Reform Act of 1832, which increased the electorate, and was returned for Dublin, heading by 1835 a thirty-five strong parliamentary grouping (comprising his three sons, two sons-in-law and a brother-in-law) which supported the Whig Government in return for reforms of the tithe system, and of municipal government (he became Lord Mayor of Dublin in 1841).

In 1840, anticipating the return of a Tory government, he founded the Repeal Association. It attracted support from the Young Irelanders, who, in their popular paper *The Nation* promulgated a cultural ideology of nationalism (other press support came from the *Pilot*). Marshalling supporters of Father Mathew's Temperance Movement, O'Connell organised a series of 'Monster Meetings' at historic places (with bands, banners, processions and even triumphal arches), which attracted in all over one quarter of the population of the southern provinces. Some 800,000 people supposedly attended the meeting at Tara on 15 August 1843. O'Connell, the mob-orator, was not averse to crying in public for Ireland (Yeats called him 'The Great Comedian'). The last of these rallies in the 'Repeal Year' of 1843 was called for Clontarf in October; it was proscribed by Sir Robert Peel's government, and cancelled by O'Connell as hundreds of thousands made their way to the site. Following his call for arbitration courts to replace the courts of justice, O'Connell was arrested and sentenced for sedition by a packed jury in 1844. After four months, the House of Lords ordered his release. He resumed his seat in parliament, seeking new allegiances with Whigs, for a while supporting federalism over Repeal, but he had lost his mental and physical agility. His opposition to the 1845 Provincial Colleges Act, which established three Queen's colleges to meet the Catholic demand for university education, led to a rift with the Young Irelanders, whose increasing militancy O'Connell opposed. In his last Commons speech, he pleaded, barely audibly, for aid for his starving country. He died on his way to Rome. O'Connell's courage and prowess became the subject of folklore (it was, for instance, told that you could not throw a stick over a workhouse wall without hitting one of his bastard children).

From His Letters

TO HIS WIFE

Dublin, Monday, 29 November [1802]

How like a journal I begin the date of my letter, and the fact is that I mean it so, for I will indulge myself this night too in writing to my dearest darling, to the sweetest and most beloved of her sex.... Should I not be a little angry with my *best* of girls for desiring me not to write to her when I am hurried by business – as if my first business and my only sweet duty was not to endeavour to please you. Indeed, Mary, it is so. The God of Nature in whose presence we were united, is the witness I call to attest the sincerity of my assertion when I declare that you are my only study. To make you happy, to engage your affections is my only business....

As for the child, darling, I insist on it that it must be a daughter.[1] I *will* have it a daughter. I am the father and can not bear to have it anything but a daughter, a girl like her dear sweet mother, very fair and *cherry* cheeked, *beautiful* fair hair, a saucy nose a little cocked, white teeth very even but a little advanced, thin lips, breath sweeter than all

---

1 The child was a boy, whom they christened Maurice.

nature. Small person but full in its shapes, and legs exquisitely well formed. There now is exactly the form of the little girl I will have from you. Recollect now, I bespeak just such a one. As for the mind of this little darling, it will copy its mother. I will say to it when the reason begins to expand: 'Resemble your mother. You, my child, have only to unite every amiable and endearing quality and you then be like her. She is modest, she is sweet-tempered, she is most virtuous, she is affectionate, attentive, tender, charitable and therefore she is beloved.'... Darling Mary, one of the powerful motives which first attracted me to you was that I saw in you greater capability of every thing that is great and really virtuous in the extended meaning of that word than any other young woman I met with. Your heart, I am sure, meets mine when I say you feel the conviction that in virtue alone is there any happiness. If we act well we are rewarded; and love is perhaps the first as it is the only reward of those who think as we do. Let us however endeavour to merit that reward by devoting our lives not to the gloomy parts of religion but to its more solid objects – the doing of good. I am running into a kind of sermon, for the fact really is that since our marriage I have grown somewhat more serious on these subjects. I always had a kind of meditative piety but it has grown alive and in some measure. [Be] sure you pray for me, Angel, I cannot tell what pleasure I feel in thus pouring out my mind to you. I have a great delight in thus simply placing my thoughts before you. Darling goodnight.

TO RICHARD BARRETT

Ennis, 19 May 1831

Private

My dear Barrett,

I came in here yesterday from Tralee. My brother, with several others, preceded me. We found the county polled out but O'Gorman Mahon[1] keeping the poll open for mere purposes of vexation, and causing expense. His career has been one of the most extraordinary that ever yet was exhibited. No other human being but himself would have dared to attempt it. *First*, he canvassed as a 'Terry-Alt'[2] and con-

---

1 Charles James Patrick, the O'Gormon Mahon (1800–91). At O'Connell's urging he successfully ran for Clare in 1828, but he was unseated on charges of bribery and succeeded by Maurice O'Connell. He again contested the seat in 1831 without O'Connell's support.
2 An agrarian secret society called the Terry-Alts was active in Co. Clare and neighbouring areas at the time.

tinued to do so until the day of election. Even his speech, *as reported by himself*, is full of that strain. His failure is, however, a proof that the influence of the miscreants of that party is not paramount but it did a great deal for him. It is probable that, without the aid of the Terry-Alt system, he could not poll one hundred votes by all his other exertions. Secondly, finding that the system of terror became insufficient, some of his friends resorted to the plan by which he got in before – namely, bribery. They, one way or the other (and it is believed chiefly by committing to his utter ruin his unfortunate youngest brother), raised between them some twelve *hundred pounds* and made a desperate effort with that sum on Monday. It was, however, soon exhausted and with it ended all hope of success. On Tuesday he polled but sixteen, on Wednesday but six; and yet, as the law allows him to keep open the poll this day, he does keep it open without having one single voter to produce. Thirdly, being defeated in their system of terror and exhausted in funds, so that there could be no more bribery, he resorted to rousing at his side the spirit of – what think you? – Orange bigotry! It is certainly a fact. He determined to 'put down the priests'. Such were his words, but infinitely more virulent, as I understand. Indeed nothing, it is said, could exceed the coarseness of his expressions. He got circulars written to all the parsons and to several of the Brunswick high party, promising to oppose the bill!!! and put down priestly domination. But although these circulars were in a great measure supported and indeed backed by a fat attorney of the name of Greene, one of the oldest Orangemen in Ireland, and by the noted Thomas Mahon, of biblical and Kildare Place celebrity,[1] yet they so totally failed as not to produce one single vote. The parsons and the Brunswickers were too keen to be deluded with the proffered support of a man who, having been untrue to every other party and especially to his own, could not possibly be true to them; they rejected him with scorn. *The last attempt* came then. I hope and wish to believe that there was no kind of intention of carrying it to a murderous or felonious extent; but the facts appear to be that on Wednesday afternoon late he made a violent harangue and, as Gibbon says, 'his peroration was peculiarly eloquent' because he concluded by giving the butchers a 30 shilling note to drink whiskey, which they accordingly did, and in about half an hour the butchers appeared in the streets in a formidable state because, although their number was

---

1 Thomas Mahon (b. 1787), a director of the Bible Society, Dublin, and the Kildare Place Society.

not great, they were armed with long knives and hatchets. This, of course, created the utmost terror and dismay. I do not think that more than two persons were cut. It became necessary to call out the garrison. The butchers were put to flight, six or seven of them lodged in gaol, and a charge was exhibited against O'Gorman Mahon of having instigated the riot, before Major Vignolles, whose conduct on this, as on many other occasions during the elections, deserves the highest praise. Having thus failed in every attempt, and Major McNamara having a majority of more than 500 and Mr O'Connell a majority of 104, he was driven to desperation. He attacked Major McNamara in the streets, called him all manner of abusive names. The Major heard him with silent contempt. There was an immediate meeting of the friends of the Major, who at once decided that he was not only not to have any message sent to him[1] for his unprovoked insult but he was not even to be prosecuted but was to be treated with total contempt and disregard. So ends his career.... Such then is the result of this mad campaign; but what else would you expect from a man who has acted the part he has? He cannot do any more mischief. In future he will be perfectly harmless.

[P.S.] O'Gorman Mahon has resigned. I have instituted a prosecution against his brother.[2] I am a trustee for the public and cannot allow any man to carry an election by sheer violence or to make a second election by what would be assassination.

TO THE EDITOR, *NORTHAMPTON MERCURY*

Strictly private

London, 11 February 1832

Sir,

Some person kindly sent me your paper containing very well written strictures on my public conduct.[3] There is much of that commentary which I am bound to confess is very flattering to my vanity and for *that* you will easily believe I feel thankful. But perhaps I ought to

---

1 A challenge to a duel.

2 William Richard Mahon was alleged to have struck Maurice O'Connell in the street in Ennis. Shortly after, friends of the O'Connells arrived in Ennis from Kerry and Tipperary, heavily armed, to act as Maurice's body-guard.

3 This refers to an editorial in the weekly *Northampton Mercury*, dated 11 February 1832, which commended O'Connell for refusing to fight duels while arguing that his refusal should oblige him to refrain from making verbal attacks which lead to duels.

be more grateful for the passages that imply censure as they also suggest good advice....

... I feel myself most strictly bound to speak nothing of any *public* man but what I deem accurately true. I do not think myself at liberty to suppress the truth respecting a *public* man in his *public* conduct merely because I am determined not to attend to any challenge to fight a duel. I act in that respect precisely as I hope I should if under the terror of duelling. I speak the truth – and *I speak the whole truth* – which is a duty respecting the acts and *selfish motives* of public men.

But if I go one jot beyond the truth I am most ready to atone by public apology and public retractation. This readiness I have avowed and *published* over and over again. I never assail private vices if they exist but public crimes I expose with all my energy taking every preliminary precaution to ascertain the truth – and being ready to correct the error if after such precaution I exceed. Such is my principle, such is my practice. I am not to spare the enemy of the people merely because I am not ready to shoot him or to be shot for doing my duty. But I am ready and most unfeignedly anxious to repair any mistake I may fall into, and that at the expence of any humiliation or what may be called disgrace. It is a debt I have to pay and I ought not to shrink from paying that debt even at the expence of the greatest personal suffering.

You accuse me of political timidity. Alas, I had to steer the vessel that bore 'freedom of conscience' through stormy seas and amidst shoals, sands and rocks – rocks scarcely showing their summits above the treacherous waves.

To avoid figurative language – I had to conduct a public cause *against* an adverse and most vigilant press prompt to misrepresent every act and to exaggerate every fault, *against* corrupt and bigotted judges ready to exercise the utmost vengeance of the law, *against* the certainty of a packed jury requiring only permission to convict, against hollow and deceiptful friends and cordial and unequivocal enemies. One bold dashing blow would have defeated my exertions for ever because my reputation as a leader depended on keeping my party safe from prosecution and I could not keep them safe without keeping myself so. Yet I was twice prosecuted by the most outrageous stretch of arbitrary power.

To be useful I must have preserved my reputation as a leader.

I owe you an apology for trespassing thus on your patience. You may differ from me on principle but you now know mine.

I might arraign your judgment on my political fortitude but I do not. I only remind you that I a working barrister *opposed* the judges, *opposed* the Chancellor, *opposed* the party that constituted the special juries, *taunted* and ridiculed the Law officers of the Crown, *opposed* the ministry and their minions, *opposed* the prejudices, passions and power of the then powerful and most vindictive Orange faction , *opposed* the servility and corruption of the Catholic aristocracy and the treachery of fellow agitators.

You think I was *timid*. I think I was only *prudent*. Who shall decide between us. One thing only is certain that no person can be more unfit to decide than he who has the honour to be

Your obedient and graceful servant,

Daniel O'Connell

Speech at Tara (15 August 1843)

It would be the extreme of affectation in me to suggest that I have not some claims to be the leader of this majestic meeting. It would be worse than affectation – it would be drivelling folly, if I were not to feel the awful responsibility of the part I have taken in this majestic movement imposed upon me (*hear, hear.*) I feel responsibility to my country, responsibility to my Creator. Yes, I feel the tremulous nature of that responsibility – Ireland is aroused, is aroused from one end to another. Her multitudinous population have but one expression and one wish, and that is the extinction of the Union, the restoration of her nationality.

Suddenly, someone cried, 'there will be no compromise.'

Who is it that talks of compromise? I am not here for the purpose of making anything like a schoolboy's attempt at declamatory eloquence; I am not here to revive in your recollection any of those poetic imaginings respecting the spot on which we stand, and which have really become as familiar as household words; I am not here to exaggerate the historical importance of the spot on which we are congregated – but it is impossible to deny that Tara has historical recollections that give to it an importance, relatively, to other portions of the land, and deserves to be so considered by every person who comes to it for political purposes, and gives it an elevation and point of impression in the public mind that no other part of Ireland can possibly have. History may be tarnished by exaggeration, but the fact is undoubted that we are at Tara of the Kings. We are on the spot where the monarchs of Ireland were elected, and where the chieftains of Ireland bound themselves by the sacred pledge of honour and the tie of religion to stand by their native land against the Danes or any other stranger (*cheers*). This is emphatically the spot from which emanated the social power – the legal authority – the right to dominion over the furthest extremes of the island, and the power of concentrating the force of the entire nation for the purpose of national defence. On this important spot I have an important duty to perform. I here protest in the face of my country, in the face of my Creator – in the face of Ireland and her God, I protest against the continuance of the unfounded and unjust Union. My proposition to Ireland is that the Union is not binding upon us; it is not binding, I mean, upon conscience it is void in principle. It is void as matter of right and it is void in constitutional law. I protest everything that is sacred, without being profane, to the truth of my assertion there is really no union between the two countries.

My proposition is that there was no authority vested in any person to pass the Act of Union. I deny the authority of the Act, I deny the competency of the two legislatures to pass that Act. The English legislature had no such competency – that must be admitted by every person. The Irish legislature had no such competency; and I arraign the Union, therefore, on the ground of the incompetency of the bodies that passed it. No authority could render it binding but the authority of the Irish people, consulted individually through the counties, cities, towns, and villages; and if the people of Ireland called for the Union, then it was binding on them, but there was no other authority that could make it binding. The Irish Parliament had no such authority; they were elected to make laws and not legislatures, and it had no right to the authority which alone belonged to the people of Ireland. The trustee might as well usurp the right of the person who trusts him; the servant might as well usurp the power of the master; the Irish Parliament were elected as our trustees, we were their masters – they were but our servant and they had no right to transfer us to any other power on the face of the earth. This doctrine is manifest, and would be admitted by every person; if it were applied to England, would any person venture to assert that the Parliament of England should have the power to transfer its privileges to make laws from England to the legislative chamber of France? Would any person be so insane as to admit it, and that insanity would not be misstated even if they were allowed to send over their representatives to France? Yes, every person would admit in that case that the Union was void.

I have no higher affection for England than for France. They are both foreign authorities to me. The highest legal authority in England has declared us aliens in blood, aliens in religion, and aliens in language from the English. Let no person groan him – I thank him for the honesty of the expression. I never heard of any other act of honesty on his part, and the fact of his having committed one act of honesty ought to recommend him to your good graces. I can refer you to the principle of constitutional law, and to Locke on government, to show that the Irish Parliament had no power or authority to convey itself away.[1] I will only detain you on that point by citing the words of Lord Chancellor Plunket.[2] He declared in the Irish House of Commons that they had no right to transfer the power of legislation from the country. He called upon them to have his words taken down, and he defied the power of Lord Castlereagh[3] to have him censured for the expression, limiting the authority of Parliament. He said to them that they could not transfer their authority, that the maniacal suicide might as well imagine that the blow by which he destroyed his miserable body could annihilate his immortal soul, as they to imagine they could annihilate the soul of Ireland, her constitutional right. The illustration is a happy one. I am here the representative of the Irish nation, and in the name of that great, that virtuous, that moral, temperate, brave, and religious nation, I proclaim the Union a nullity, for it is a nullity in point of right. Never was any measure carried by such iniquitous means as the Union was carried. The first thing that taints it in its origin, and makes it, even if it were a compact, utterly void, is the fraud committed in fermenting discord in the country, and encouraging the rebellion until it broke out, and in making that rebellion and the necessity for crushing it the means of taking from Ireland her constitution and her liberties. There was this second fraud committed on her, that at the time of the passing of the Act of Union Ireland had no legal protection; the habeas corpus was suspended, martial law was proclaimed, trial by jury was at an end, and the lives and liberties of all the King's subjects in Ireland were at the mercy of the courts martial. Those among you who were old enough at the

---

1 *Locke on government ... away*: 'Of the Dissolution of Government', in *Essay Concerning the true original, extent, and end of Civil Government* by John Locke (1632–1704). Locke's essay epitomises Whig ideology.
2 William Conyngham, 1st Baron Plunket (1764–1854), Lord Chancellor (1830–41). He had supported Catholic Relief.
3 Robert Stewart, Viscount Castlereagh, 2nd Marquis of Londonderry (1769–1822).

time remember when the shriek from the triangle was heard from every village and town, and when the troops would march out from Trim and lay desolate the country for nine or ten miles around. The military law was established in all its horrors throughout every district of the country and the people were trampled in the dust under the feet of the yeomanry, army, and fencibles. The next fraudulent device to which England had recourse in order to carry this infamous measure, and to promote her own prosperity on the ruins of Irish nationality, was to take the most effective means in order to prevent the Irish people from meeting to remonstrate against the insult and the injury which was about to be inflicted upon them. The Union was void no less from the utter incompetency of the contracting parties to enter into any such contract than by reason of the fact, that it was carried into operation by measures most iniquitous, atrocious and illegal; the habeas corpus act was suspended, torture, flogging, pitch caps, and imprisonment were the congenial agencies whereby England endeavored to carry her infamous designs, and executions upon the gallows for no other crime than that of being suspected to be suspicious, were of daily occurrence in every part of the kingdom. Thus it was that they endeavored to crush the expression of the people's feelings, whom they resolved to plunder and degrade. The people were not permitted to assemble together for the purpose of remonstrating against the Union. Meetings convened by the officers of justice – by the high sheriffs of counties, were dispersed at the point of the bayonet. The people were not permitted to meet together for remonstrance, but they got up petitions in every direction, to testify their feelings upon the subject, and although no less than seven hundred and seven thousand signatures were signed to petitions against the Union, despite of all the corrupt influence of the Government, more than three thousand wretches could not be found to sign a petition in favour of the measure.

The next impeachment which I bring against the Union is that it was brought about not only by physical force, but by bribery the most unblushing and corruption the most profligate. One million two hundred and seventy-five thousand pounds were expended upon the purchase of rotten boroughs alone, and no less a sum than two millions of money were lavished upon peculation unparalleled, and bribery the most enormous and most palpable that ever yet disgraced the annals of humility. There was not an office, civil, military, or ecclesiastical in the county, which was not flung open to the Unionist as the pence and wages of his political depravity. Six or seven judges bought their seats upon the bench by giving in their adhesion to the Union; and having no claim to wear the ermine other than that which was to be derived from the fact of their being recreants to their country, they continued in right of this during their lives to inflict the effects of their iniquity upon the people whom they betrayed. Twelve bishops obtained their seats by voting for the Union, for the spirit of corruption spared nothing. Men were made prelates, generals, admirals, commissioners for supporting the ministry in this infamous design, and every office in the revenue and customs was placed at the disposal of those who were base enough to sell their country for a mess of pottage. In fact, corruption was never known to have been carried before or since to such excess in any country of the world, and if such a contract, if contract it could be called, was to be binding on the Irish nation, there was no longer any use for honesty or justice in the world. But strong as was the influence of corruption on the human mind, the victory which the English ministry achieved was slow and by no means easy of accomplishment, for the intimidation to the death upon the one hand, and bribery on the other, were impotent to procure a majority for them in the Irish House of Commons in the first session, when the bill was introduced. On the contrary, when the first attempt was made to frustrate our liberties, there was a majority of eleven against the Union Bill. But the despoiler was not easy to be foiled, nor was he apt to be disheartened by a single failure. The work of corruption was set on foot with redoubled energy, and the wretches who were not so utterly abandoned as to suffer themselves to be bribed for the direct and positive purpose of giving their vote for the Union, accepted bribes on the condition of withdrawing from the House altogether, and accordingly they vacated their seats, and in their place stepped in Englishmen and Scotchmen who knew nothing of Ireland, and who were not impeded by any conscientious scruples whatever from giving their unqualified sanction to any plot of the English, how infamous so ever, to oppress and plunder the country. By these accumulated means the Union was carried and the fate of Ireland sealed. But the monster evil of the Union is the financial robbery which by its means was practiced upon Ireland. A scandalous injustice thus inflicted would be in itself sufficient even in the absence of other arguments – even if other arguments were wanting – to render the Union void and of no effect. At the passing of that fatal act – badge of our ruin and disgrace – Ireland owed only twenty millions, England owed four hundred and forty six millions, and the equitable terms on which the contract was based, whereby both countries were to be allied and identified – identified indeed! – were these, that England was generously to undertake the liability of one-half of her national debt, on condition that we would undertake the responsibility of one-half of hers. This is not a befitting time nor season to enter into minute details relative to the particulars of this financial swindle, but I may be permitted to direct your attention to this very obvious fact, that whereas England has only doubled her debt since the passing of the Union, the increase of the national debt of Ireland during the same period cannot with justice be estimated on a different ratio, and that consequently Ireland, at the very highest calculation, cannot in reality and as of her own account, owe a larger sum than forty millions; and I will tell you, my friends, that never will we consent to pay one shilling more of a national debt than that. I say it in the name and on behalf of the Irish nation. But I will tell you this, as a secret, and you may rely upon it as a truth, that in point of fact we do not owe one farthing more than thirty millions; and in proof of the truth of this assertion, I beg leave to refer you to a work published by a very near and dear relative of mine – my third son, the member for Kilkenny[1] – who, by the most accurate statistical calculations, and by a process of argument intelligible to the humblest intellect, has made the fact apparent to the world, that according to the terms of honest and equitable dealing, as between both countries, Ireland's proportion of the national debt cannot be set down at a larger sum than I state, thirty millions. I am proud that there is a son of mine who, after the Repeal shall have been carried, will be able to meet the cleverest English financier of them all, foot to foot and hand to hand, and prove by arguments most incontestable how grievous and intolerable is the injustice which was inflicted upon our country in this respect by the Union. The project of robbing Ireland by joining her legislatively with England was no new scheme which entered the minds of the English for the first time about the year, 1800. It was a project which was a favourite theme of dissertation with all the English essayists for years previous to the period when it was carried into practical effect, and the policy towards Ireland, which their literary men were continually urging upon the English people for their adoption, was similar to that of the avaricious housewife who killed the goose who laid her golden eggs. Yes, such was the course they pursued towards Ireland, and you will deserve the reputation of being the lineal descendants of that goose if you be such ganders as not to

---

1 John O'Connell (1810–58), 'The Young Liberator', was MP for Kilkenny from 1841 to 1847.

declare in a voice of thunder that no longer shall this system of plunder be permitted to continue.

My next impeachment of the Union is founded upon the disastrous effects which have resulted therefrom to our commercial and manufacturing interests, as well as to our general national interests. Previous to the Union, the county Meath was filled with the seats of noblemen at Semen! What a contrast does its present state present! I, on Monday read at the Association a list of the deserted mansions which are now to be found ruined and desolate in your country. Even the spot where the Duke of Wellington – famed the world over for his detestation of his country – drew his first breath, instead of bearing a noble castle, or splendid mansion, presented the aspect of ruin and desolation, and briars and nettles adequately marked the place that produced him.[1] The county of Meath was at one time studded thickly with manufactories in every direction, and an enormous sum was expended yearly in wages, but here, as in every other district of the country, the eye was continually shocked with sights which evidenced with but too great eloquence the lamentable decay which has been entailed upon our country by the Union. The linen trade at one period kept all Ulster in a state of affluence and prosperity. Kilkenny was for ages celebrated for its extensive blanket manufactures and Cork also – and Carrick-on-Suir, and in a thousand other localities, too numerous to mention, thousands were kept in constant and lucrative employment, at various branches of national industry, from year's end to year's end, before the passing of the Union. But this is no longer the case, and one man is not now kept in employment for a thousand who were employed before the Union. The report of the English commissioners themselves has declared this appalling fact to the world that one-third of our population are in a state of actual destitution; and yet, in the face of all this, men may be found who, claiming to themselves the character of political honesty, stand up and declare themselves in favour of the continuance of the Union. It is no bargain; it was a base swindle. Had it, indeed, been a fair bargain, the Irish would have continued faithful to it to the last, regardless of the injuries which it might have entailed upon them for the Irish people have been invariably faithful to their contracts; whereas England never yet made a promise which she did not violate, nor ever entered into a contract which she did not shamelessly and scandalously outrage. Even the Union itself, beneficial as it is to England, is but a living lie to Ireland.

---

1 Arthur Wellesley, Duke of Wellington (1769–1852). His place of birth is uncertain; the nurse claimed that he was born on 6 March at Dangan Castle, Co. Meath. He was believed to have been born in a stable.

Everybody now admits the mischief that the Union has produced to Ireland. The very fact of its not being a compact is alone sufficient to nullify the Union, and on that ground I here proclaim, in the name of the Irish nation, that it is null and void. It is a union of legislators, but not a union of nations. Are you and I one bit more of Englishmen now than we were twenty or forty years ago? If we had a Union would not Ireland have the same parliamentary franchise that is enjoyed by England? But calling it a Union, could anything be more unjust on the part of England than to give her own people a higher and more extensive grade of franchise? And to the Irish people a more limited and an extinguishing and perishing franchise. She has given to her people an extended municipal reform, and to Ireland a wretched and miserable municipal reform. Even within the last week a plan was brought forward by Lord Elliot and the [*sneers*] Attorney-General Smith, that will have the effect of depriving one-third of those who now enjoy the franchise of its possession. No, the Union is void, but it is more peremptorily void on the ground of the ecclesiastical revenues of the courts being left to support a church of a small portion of the people. In England the ecclesiastical revenues of the country are given to the clergy that the majority of the people believe to teach the truth. In Scotland the ecclesiastical revenues are, or at least were up to a late period, paid to the clergy of the majority of the people; but the Irish people are compelled to pay the clergy of a small minority, not amounting to more than the one-tenth of the people of the entire island. The Union was effected against all constitutional principle by the most atrocious fraud – by the most violent and most iniquitous exercise of force, by the most abominable corruption and bribery, by the shifting of Irish members out of their seats, and the putting of Englishmen and Scotchmen into their places; and that was followed by the destruction of our commerce, by the annihilation of our manufactures, by the depreciation of our farmers – and you know I speak the truth when I talk of the depression of the farming interests by financial robbery, on an extensive scale to be sure, but a robbery on that very account, only the more iniquitous, fiendish, and harsh. I contend, therefore, that the Union is a nullity; but do I, on that account, advise you to turn out against it? No such thing. I advise you to act quietly and peaceably and in no other way.

Then a voice cried, 'any way you like.'

Remember that my doctrine is that 'the man who commits a crime gives strength to the enemy,' and you should not act in any manner that would strengthen the enemies of your country. You should act peaceably and quietly, but firmly and determinedly. You may be certain that your cheers here today will be conveyed to England.

The vast assemblage here commenced cheering in the most deafening and enthusiastic manner, and the distant lines of people on the limits of the assembly were seen waving their hats and handkerchiefs in response.

Yes, the overwhelming majestic of your multitude will be taken to England, and will have its effect there. The Duke of Wellington began by threatening us. He talked of civil war, but he does not say a single word of that now. He is now getting eyelet holes made in the old barracks, and only think of an old general doing such a thing, just as if we were going to break our heads against stone walls. I am glad to find that a great quantity of brandy and biscuits has been latterly imported, and I hope the poor soldiers get some of them. But the Duke of Wellington is not now talking of attacking us, and I am glad of it; but I tell him this – I mean no disrespect to the brave, the gallant, and the good conducted soldiers that compose the Queen's army; and all of them that we have in this country are exceedingly well conducted. There is not one of you that has a single complaint to make against any of them. They are the bravest army in the world and therefore I do not mean to disparage them at all, but I feel it to be a fact, that Ireland, roused as she is at the present moment, would, if they made war upon us, furnish women enough to beat the entire of the Queen's forces. At the last fight for Ireland, when she was betrayed by having confided in England's honour, but oh! English honour will never again betray our land, for the man will deserve to be betrayed who would confide again in England. I would as soon think of confiding in the cousin-german of a certain personage having two horns and a hoof. At that last battle, the Irish soldiers, after three days fighting, being attacked by fresh troops, faltered and gave way, and 1,500 of the British army entered the breach. The Irish soldiers were fainting and retiring when the women of Limerick threw themselves between the contending forces, and actually stayed the progress of the advancing enemy. I am stating matter of history to you, and the words I use are not mine, but those of Parson Story, the chaplain of King William, who describes the siege, and who admits that the Limerick women drove back the English soldiers from fifteen to thirty paces. Several of the women were killed, when a shriek of horror resounded from the ranks of the Irish. They cried out, 'Let us rather die to the last man than that our women should be injured,' and then they threw themselves forward, and, made doubly valiant by the bravery of the women, they scattered the Saxon and the Dane before them. Yes, I have women enough in Ireland to beat them if necessary; but, my friends, it is idle to imagine that any statesman ever existed who could resist the cry that Ireland makes for justice....

We will break no law. See how we have accumulated the people of Ireland for this Repeal Year. When, on the 2nd of January, I ventured to call it the Repeal Year, every person laughed at me. Are they laughing now? It is our turn to laugh at present. Before twelve months more, the Parliament will be in College Green. I said the Union did not take away from the people of Ireland their legal rights. I told you that the Union did not deprive the people of that right, or take away the authority to have self-legislation. It has not lessened the prerogatives of the Crown, or taken away the rights of the Sovereign, and amongst them is the right to call her Parliament wherever the People are entitled to it, and the people of Ireland are entitled to have it in Ireland. And the Queen has only tomorrow to issue her writs and get the Chancellor to seal them, and if Sir Edward Sugden does not sign them she will soon get an Irishman that will, to revive the Irish Parliament. The towns which sold their birthright have no right to be reckoned amongst the towns sending members to Parliament. King James the First, in one day, created forty boroughs in Ireland, and the Queen has the same right as her predecessor to do so. We have a list of the towns to return members according to their population, and the Queen has only to order writs to issue, and to have honest ministers to advise her to issue those wants, and the Irish Parliament is revived by its own energy, and the force of the Sovereign's prerogative. I will only require the Queen to exercise her perogative, and the Irish people will obtain their nationality again. If, at the present moment, the Irish Parliament was in existence, even as it was in 1800, is there a coward amongst you – is there a wretch amongst you so despicable that would not die rather than allow the Union to pass?

Another voice interrupted him, 'Yes, to the last man.'

Let every man who, if we had an Irish Parliament, would rather die than allow the Union to pass lift up his hands. Yes, the Queen will call that Parliament; you may say it is the act of her ministry, if you please. To be sure it would be the act of her ministry, and the people of

Ireland are entitled to have their friends appointed to the ministry. The Irish Parliament will then assemble, and I defy all the generals, old and young, and all the old women in pantaloons. Nay, I defy all the chivalry of the earth to take away that Parliament from us again. Well, my friends, may I ask you to obey me in the course of conduct I point out to you, when I dismiss you to-day; when you have heard the resolutions put, I am sure you will go home with the same tranquillity with which you came here, every man of you; and if I wanted you again, would you not come again to Tara Hill for me? Remember me, I lead you into no peril. If danger existed, it would arise from some person who would attack us, for we will attack nobody; and if that danger exists you will not find me in the rear rank. The Queen will be able to restore our Parliament to us. The absentee drains, which caused the impoverishment of the country, will be at an end – the wholesale ejectment of tenants and turning them out on the highway — the murdering of tenants by the landlords will be at an end. The rights of the landlords will be respected, but their duties shall be enforced – an equitable tenure will take the place of the cruel tyranny of the present code of laws, and the protection of the occupying tenants of Ireland be inscribed on the banner of Repeal. Carry home with you my advice. Let there be peace and quiet, law and order, and let every one of you enroll yourselves Repealers – men, women, and children. Give me three millions of Repealers, and I will soon have them. The next step is being taken, and I announce to you from this spot, that all the magistrates that have been deprived of the communion of the peace shall be appointed by the Association to settle all the disputes and differences in their neighbourhood. Keep out of the petty sessions court, and go to them on next Monday. We will submit a plan to choose persons to be arbitrators to settle the differences of the people without expense, and I call upon every man that wishes to be thought the friend of Ireland, to have his disputes settled by the arbitrators, and not again to go to the petty sessions. We shall shortly have the preservative society to arrange the means of procuring from her Majesty the exercise of her prerogative, and I believe I am able to announce to you that twelve months cannot possibly elapse without having a hurrah for our Parliament in College Green. Remember, I pronounce the Union to be null – to be obeyed, as an injustice must be obeyed, when it is supported by law until we have the royal authority to set the matter right, and substitute our own Parliament. I delight at having this day presided over such an assemblage on Tara Hill. Those shouts that burst from you were enough to recall to life the Kings and Chiefs of Ireland. I almost fancy that the spirits of the mighty dead are hovering over us, that the ancient Kings and Chiefs of Ireland are from yonder clouds listening to us. Oh, what a joyous and cheering sound is conveyed in the chirrup for Old Ireland! It is the most beautiful, the most fertile – the most abundant, the most productive country on the face of the earth. It is a lovely land, indented with noble harbours, intersected with transcendent, translucent streams divided by mighty estuaries. Its harbours are open at every hour for every tide, and are sheltered from every storm that can blow from any quarter of Heaven. Oh, yes, it is a lovely land and where is the coward that would not dare to die for it! Yes, our country exhibits the extreme of civilization, and your majestic movement is already the admiration of the civilised world. No other country could produce such an amount of physical force, coupled with so much decorum and propriety of conduct. Many thousands of persons assembled together, and, though they have force sufficient to carry any battle that ever was fought, they separate with the tranquillity of schoolboys breaking up in the afternoon. I wish you could read my heart, to see how deeply the love of Ireland is engraven upon it, and let the people of Ireland, who stood by me so long, stand by me a little longer, and Ireland shall be a nation again.

SYDNEY OWENSON, LADY MORGAN (?1776–1859)

Sydney Owenson's life is infused with a whiff of the romantic spirit that characterizes her fiction. It is alleged that she was born on the Irish Sea, but she herself claimed Dublin as her place of birth. Her father, of Catholic descent, was actor-manager at the Theatre Royal and the Fishamble Street Theatre, and specialized in stage-Irish parts. Her mother, Jane Hill, was an English Methodist. After her death, Sydney was sent to a Huguenot boarding school in Clontarf. Her father's career was affected by financial ineptitude. In the 1790s he was forced to tour the country as a wandering actor; Sydney accompanied him. In her mid-twenties, she relieved the family's insolvency by taking up positions as a governess. Her literary career was launched modestly with a volume of poetry in 1801, and two novels, *St Claire, or the Heiress of Desmond* (1803) and *The Novice of Dominick* (1805; 1806). But success came, almost instantly, with *The Wild Irish Girl* (1806). The novel went into seven editions in two years. In *The Book of the Boudoir* (1829), she describes, with characteristic Romantic aplomb, her entrée into London society, 'freshly launched from the barony of Tireragh in the province of Connaught,' while 'not many days before, I had danced a jig, on an earthen floor, with an O'Rourke, prince of Brefney.' Other 'National Tales' ensued – *O'Donnel* (1814), *Florence Macarthy* (1818) and *The O'Briens and the O'Flahertys* (1827) – receiving great popular demand. In 1809 she became a member of the Marquis of Abercorn's entourage, and three years later married her patron's surgeon, Sir Charles Morgan. In 1837 she became the first woman to receive a literary pension from the British government. She was a champion of Catholic Emancipation, although she was suspicious of Daniel O'Connell's pragmatism, which was at variance with her Romantic zeal. Disillusioned with events in Ireland, she moved to London in 1837, writing little thereafter.

The Wild Irish Girl relates the conversion of Horatio, son of the Earl of M --, from a life of cosmopolitan dissipation to Irish feudal sensibility. His father packs Horatio off for correction to his Connaught estate; here he meets the impoverished Gaelic Prince of Inismore, whose forebears were banished from their demesne by Horatio's forefathers. Horatio falls in love with Glorvina, the Prince's daughter (an idealized version of Sydney Owenson); she gives him a good grind in the ceremony and innocence of ancient Irish culture. They marry. With its glorification of Irish stereotypes (including the harp), the novel has proved a welcome source for cultural criticism.

From *The Wild Irish Girl*
(1806)
Letter V.

To J.D. Esq. M.P.

Castle of Inismore, Barony of —

Aye, 'tis even so – point your glass, and rub your eyes, 'tis all one; here I am, and here I am likely to remain for some time. But whether a prisoner of war, or taken up on a suspicion of espionage, or to be offered as an appeasing sacrifice to the *manes*[1] of the old Prince of Inismore, you must for a while suspend your patience to learn.

According to the *carte du pays* laid out for me by the fisherman, I left the shore and crossed the summit of a mountain that 'battled o'er the deep,' and which after an hour's ascension, I found sloped almost perpendicularly down to a bold and rocky coast, its base terminating in a peninsula, that advanced for near half a mile into the ocean. Towards the extreme western point of this peninsula, which was wildly romantic beyond all description, arose a vast and grotesque pile of rocks, which at once formed the scite and fortifications of the noblest

---

1 *manes*: 'The deified souls of departed ancestors' (O.E.D.).

mass of ruins on which my eye ever rested. Grand even in desolation, and magnificent in decay – it was the Castle of Inismore. The setting sun shone brightly on its mouldering turrets, and the waves which bathed its rocky basis, reflected on their swelling bosoms the dark outlines of its awful ruins.[1]

As I descended the mountain's brow, I observed that the little isthmus which joined the peninsula to the mainland, had been cut away, and a curious danger-threatening bridge was rudely thrown across the intervening gulf, flung from the rocks on one side to an angle of the mountain on the other, leaving a yawning chasm of some fathoms deep beneath the foot of the wary passenger. This must have been a very perilous pass in days of civil warfare; and in the intrepidity of my daring ancestor, I almost forgot his crime. Amidst the interstices of the rocks which skirted the shores of this interesting peninsula, patches of the richest vegetation were to be seen, and the trees, which sprung wildly among its venerable ruins, were bursting into all the vernal luxuriancy of spring. In the course of my descent, several cabins of a better description than I had yet seen, appeared scattered beneath the shelter of the mountain's innumerable projections; while in the air and dress of their inhabitants (which the sound of my horse's feet brought to their respective doors), I evidently perceived a something original and primitive, I had never noticed before in this class of persons here.

They appeared to me, I know not why, to be in their holiday garb, and their dress, though grotesque and coarse, was cleanly and characteristic. I observed that round the heads of the elderly dames were folded several wreaths of white or coloured linen,[2] that others had handkerchiefs[3] lightly folded round their brows, and curiously fastened under the chin; while the young wore their hair fastened up with wooden bodkins. They were all enveloped in large shapeless mantles of blue frize, and most of them had a rosary hanging on their arm, from whence I inferred they were on the point of attending vespers at the chapel of Inismore. I alighted at the door of a cabin a few

---

1 Those who have visited the Castle of Dunluce, near the Gaints' Causeway, may, perhaps, have some of its striking features in this rude draught of the Castle of Inismore. [*Morgan's note.*]

2 'The women's ancient head-dress so perfectly resembles that of the Egyptian Isis, that it cannot be doubted but that the modes of Egypt were preserved among the Irish.' – *Walker on the Ancient Irish Dress*, page 62.

The Author's father, who lived in the early part of his life in a remote skirt of the Province of Connaught, remembers to have seen the heads of the female peasantry encircled with folds of linen in form of a turban. [*Morgan's note.*]

3 These handkerchiefs they call *Binnogues*: it is a remnant of a very ancient mode. [*Morgan's note.*]

paces distant from the Alpine bridge, and entreated a shed for my horse, while I performed my devotions. The man to whom I addressed myself, seemed the only one of several who surrounded me, that understood English, and appeared much edified by my pious intention, saying, 'that God would prosper my Honour's journey, and that I was welcome to a shed for my horse, and a night's lodging for myself into the bargain.' He then offered to be my guide, and as we crossed the draw-bridge, he told me I was out of luck by not coming earlier, for that high mass had been celebrated that morning for the repose of the soul of a Prince of Inismore, who had been murdered on this very day of the month. 'And when this day comes round,' he added, 'we all attend dressed in our best; for my part, I never wear my poor old grandfather's *berrad* but on the like occasion,' taking off a curious cap of a conical form, which he twirled round his hand, and regarded with much satisfaction.[1]

By heavens! as I breathed this region of superstition, so strongly was I infected, that my usual scepticism was scarcely proof against my inclination to mount my horse and gallop off, as I shudderingly pronounced,

'I am then entering the Castle of Inismore, on the anniversary of that day on which my ancestors took the life of its venerable Prince!'

You see, my good friend, how much we are the creatures of situation and circumstance, and with what pliant servility the mind resigns itself to the impressions of the senses, or the illusions of the imagination.

We had now reached the ruined cloisters of the chapel; I paused to examine their curious but delapidated architecture when my guide, hurrying me on said, 'if I did not quicken my pace, I should miss getting a good view of the Prince,' who was just entering by a door opposite to that we had passed through. Behold me then mingling among a group of peasantry, and, like them, straining my eyes to that magnet which fascinated every glance.

And sure, Fancy, in her boldest flight, never gave to the fairy vision of poetic dreams, a combination of images more poetically fine, more strikingly picturesque, or more impressively touching. Nearly one half of the chapel of Inismore has fallen into decay, and the ocean breeze, as it rushed through the fractured roof, wafted the torn banners of the family which hung along its dismantled walls. The red beams of the

---

1 A few years back, Hugh Dugan, a peasant of the County of Kilkenny, who affected the ancient Irish dress, seldom appeared without his *berrad*. [*Morgan's note.*]

sinking sun shone on the glittering tabernacle which stood on the altar, and touched with their golden light the sacerdotal vestments of the two officiating priests, who ascended its broken steps at the moment that the Prince and his family entered.

The first of this most singular and interesting group, was the venerable Father John, the chaplain. Religious enthusiasm never gave to the fancied form of the first of the Patriarchs, a countenance of more holy expression, or divine resignation; a figure more touching by its dignified simplicity, or an air more beneficently mild – more meekly good. He was dressed in his pontificals, and with his eyes bent to earth, his hands spread upon his breast, he joined his coadjutors.

What a contrast to this saintly being now struck my view; a form almost gigantic in stature, yet gently thrown forward by evident infirmity; limbs of Herculean mould, and a countenance rather furrowed by the inroads of vehement passions, than the deep trace of years. Eyes still emanating the ferocity of an unsubdued spirit, yet tempered by a strong trait of benevolence; which, like a glory, irradiated a broad expansive brow, a mouth on which even yet the spirit of convivial enjoyment seemed to hover, though shaded by two large whiskers on the upper lip,[1] which still preserved their ebon hue; while time or grief had bleached the scattered hairs, which hung their snows upon the manly temple. The drapery which covered this striking figure was singularly appropriate, and, as I have since been told, strictly conformable to the ancient costume of the Irish nobles.[2]

The only part of the under garment visible, was the ancient Irish *truis*, which closely adhering to the limbs from the waist to the ancle, includes the pantaloon and hose, and terminates in a kind of buskin, not dissimilar to the Roman *perones*. A triangular mantle of bright *scarlet* cloth, embroidered and fringed round the edges, fell from his shoulders to the ground, and was fastened at the breast with a large circular golden broach,[3] of a workmanship most curiously beautiful; round his neck

---

1 'I have been confidently assured, that the grandfather of the present Rt. Hon. John O'Neil, (great grandfather to the present Lord O'Neil), the elegant and accomplished owner of Shanes Castle, wore his beard after the *prohibited* Irish mode.' – *Walker*, p. 62. [*Morgan's note.*]

2 The Irish mantle, with the fringed or shagged borders sewed down the edges of it, was not always made of frize and such coarse materials, which was the dress of the lower sort of people, but, according to the rank and quality of the wearer, was sometimes made of the finest cloth, bordered with silken fringe of scarlet, and various colours – *Walker*, vol. ii. p. 75. [*Morgan's note.*]

3 Several of these useful ornaments (in Irish, *dealg fallain*), some gold, some silver, have been found in various parts of the kingdom, and are to be seen in the cabinets of our national *virtuosi*. Joseph Cooper Walker, Esq. to whose genius, learning, and exertions, Ireland stands so deeply indebted, speaking of a broach he had seen in the possession of R. Ousley, Esq. says – 'Neither my pen or pencil can give an adequate idea of the elegant gold filligree work with which it is composed.' [*Morgan's note.*]

hung a golden collar, which seemed to denote the wearer of some order of knighthood, probably hereditary in his family; a dagger, called a *skiene* (for my guide explained every article of the dress to me), was sheathed in his girdle, and was discerned by the sunbeam that played on its brilliant haft. And as he entered the chapel, he removed from his venerable head a cap, or berrad, of the same form as that I had noticed with my guide, but made of velvet, richly embroidered.

The chieftain moved with dignity – yet with difficulty – and his colossal, but infirm frame, seemed to claim support from a form so almost impalpably delicate, that as it floated on the gaze, it seemed like the incarnation of some pure etherial spirit, which a sigh too roughly breathed would dissolve into its kindred air; yet to this sylphid elegance of spheral beauty was united all that symmetrical *contour* which constitutes the luxury of human loveliness. This scarcely 'mortal mixture of earth's mould,'[1] was vested in a robe of vestal white, which was enfolded beneath the bosom with a narrow girdle embossed with precious stones.

From the shoulder fell a mantle of scarlet silk, fastened at the neck with a silver bodkin, while the fine turned head was enveloped in a veil of point lace, bound round the brow with a band, or diadem, ornamented with the same description of jewels as encircled her arms.[2]

Such was the *figure* of the Princess of Inismore! – But Oh! not once was the face turned round towards that side where I stood. And when I shifted my position, the envious veil intercepted the ardent glance which eagerly sought the fancied charms it concealed: for was it possible to doubt the face would not 'keep the promise which the form had made.'

The group that followed was grotesque beyond all powers of description. The ancient bard, whose long white beard

'Descending, swept his aged breast,'[3]

the incongruous costume – half modern, half antique – of the bare-

---

1 John Milton, *Comus*, 244–45: 'Can any mortal mixture of earth's mould / Breathe such divine enchanting ravishment?'.

2 This was, with little variation, the general costume of the female *noblesse* of Ireland from a very early period. In the 15th century the veil was very prevalent, and was termed fillag, or scarf, the Irish ladies, like those of ancient and modem Greece, seldom appearing unveiled. As the veil made no part of the Celtic costume, its origin was probably merely oriental.

The great love of ornaments betrayed by the Irish ladies of other times,—'the beauties of the heroes of old,' are thus described by a quaint and ancient author.- 'Their necks are hung with chains and carkanets—their arms wreathed with many bracelets.' [*Morgan's note.*]

3 *Descending ... breast:* Oliver Goldsmith, *The Deserted Village*, 149.

footed domestics; the ostensible air of the steward, who closed the procession – and above all, the dignified importance of the *nurse,* who took the lead in it immediately after her young lady: her air, form, countenance, and dress, were indeed so singularly fantastic and *outré,* that the genius of masquerade might have adopted her figure as the finest model of grotesque caricature.

Conceive for a moment a form whose longitude bore no degree of proportion to her latitude; dressed in a short jacket of brown cloth, with loose sleeves from the elbow to the wrist, made of red camblet, striped with green, and turned up with a broad cuff – a petticoat of scarlet frize, covered by an apron of green serge, longitudinally striped with scarlet tape, and sufficiently short to betray an ancle that sanctioned all the libels ever uttered against the ancles of the Irish fair – true national brogues set off her blue worsted stockings, and her yellow hair, dragged over an high roll, was covered on the summit with a little coiff, over which was flung a scarlet handkerchief, which fastened in a large bow under her rubicund chin.[1]

As this singular and interesting group advanced up the centre aisle of the chapel, reverence and affection were evidently blended in the looks of the multitude, which hung upon their steps; and though the Prince and his daughter seemed to lose in the meekness of true religion all sense of temporal inequality, and promiscuously mingled with the congregation, yet *that* distinction they humbly avoided, was reverentially forced on them by the affectionate crowd, which drew back on either side as they advanced – until the chieftain and his child stood alone, in the centre of the ruined choir – the winds of Heaven playing freely amidst their garments – the sun's setting beam enriching their beautiful figures with its orient tints, while he, like Milton's ruined angel,

> 'Above the rest,
> In shape and feature proudly eminent,
> Stood like a tower;'[2]

and she, like the personified spirit of Mercy, hovered round him, or supported more by her tenderness than her strength, him from whom she could no longer claim support.

---

1 Such was the dress of Mary Morgan, a poor peasant, in the neighbourhood of Drogheda, in 1786. 'In the close of the last century Mrs Power, of Waterford, vulgarly called the *Queen of Credan,* appeared constantly in this dress, with the exception of ornaments being gold, silver and fine Brussels lace.'—See *Walker's Essay on Ancient Irish Dress, p. 73.* [*Morgan's note.*]
2 *Above the rest ... tower*: Milton's description of Satan in *Paradise Lost,* Book I, 589–91 (for 'feature' read 'gesture').

Those grey-headed domestics too – those faithful though but nominal vassals, who offered that voluntary reverence with their looks, which his repaid with fatherly affection, while the anguish of a suffering heart hung on his pensive smile, sustained by the firmness of that indignant pride which lowered on his ample brow!

What a picture!

As soon as the first flush of interest, curiosity, and amazement, had subsided, my attention was carried towards the altar; and then I thought, as I watched the impressive avocation of Father John, that had I been the Prince, I would have been the *Caiphas*[1] too.

What a religion is this! How finely does it harmonize with the weakness of our nature; how seducingly it speaks to the senses; how forcibly it works on the passions; how strongly it seizes on the imagination; how interesting its forms; how graceful its ceremonies; how awful its rites. – What a captivating, what a *picturesque* faith! Who would not become its proselyte, were it not for the stern opposition of reason – the cold suggestions of philosophy!

The last strain of the vesper hymn died on the air as the sun's last beam faded on the casements of the chapel; and the Prince and his daughter, to avoid the intrusion of the crowd, withdrew through a private door, which communicated by a ruinous arcade with the castle.

I was the first to leave the chapel, and followed them at a distance as they moved slowly along. Their fine figures sometimes concealed behind a pillar, and again emerging from the transient shade, flushed with the deep suffusion of the crimsoned firmament.

Once they paused, as if to admire the beautiful effect of the retreating light, as it faded on the ocean's swelling bosom; and once the Princess raised her hand and pointed to the evening star, which rose brilliantly on the deep cerulean blue of a cloudless atmosphere, and shed its fairy beam on the mossy summit of a mouldering turret.

Such were the sublime objects which seemed to engage their attention, and added their *sensible* inspiration to the fervour of those more abstracted devotions in which they were so recently engaged. At last they reached the portals of the castle, and I lost sight of them. Yet still spell-bound, I stood transfixed to the spot from whence I had caught a last view of their receding figures.

While I felt like the victim of superstitious terror when the spectre of its distempered fancy vanishes from its strained and eager gaze, all I

---

1 *Caiphas*: Caiaphas, the high priest who, after interrogating Jesus, condemns him for claiming to be the son of God.

had lately seen revolved in my mind like some pictured story of romantic fiction. I cast round my eyes; all still seemed the vision of awakened
imagination – Surrounded by a scenery grand even to the boldest
majesty of nature, and wild even to desolation – the day's dying splen-
dours awfully involving in the gloomy haze of deepening twilight – the
grey mists of stealing night gathering on the still faintly illumined surface of the ocean, which awfully spreading to infinitude, seemed to the
limited gaze of human vision to incorporate with the heaven whose last
glow it reflected – the rocks, which on every side rose to Alpine elevation, exhibiting, amidst the soft obscurity, forms savagely bold or
grotesquely wild; and those finely interesting ruins which spread grand-
ly desolate in the rear, and added a moral interest to the emotions excited by this view of nature in her most awful, most touching aspect.

Thus suddenly withdrawn from the world's busiest haunts, its
hackneyed modes, its vicious pursuits, and unimportant avocations –
dropt as it were amidst scenes of mysterious sublimity – alone – on
the wildest shores of the greatest ocean of the universe; immersed
amidst the decaying monuments of past ages; still viewing in recollection such forms, such manners, such habits (as I had lately beheld),
which to the worldly mind may be well supposed to belong to a race
long passed beyond the barrier of existence, with 'the years beyond
the flood,' I felt like the being of some other sphere newly alighted on
a distant orb. While the novel train of thought which stole on my
mind seemed to seize its tone from the awful tranquillity by which I
was surrounded, and I remained leaning on the fragment of a rock, as
the waves dashed idly against its base, until their dark heads were sil-
vered by the rising moon, and while my eyes dwelt on her silent
progress, the castle clock struck nine. Thus warned, I arose to depart,
yet not without reluctance. My soul, for the first time, had here held
commune with herself; the 'lying vanities' of life no longer intoxicating my senses, appeared to me for the first time in their genuine
aspect, and my heart still fondly loitered over those scenes of solemn
interest, where some of its best feelings had been called into existence.

Slowly departing, I raised my eyes to the Castle of Inismore, and
sighed, and almost wished I had been born the Lord of these beautiful
ruins, the Prince of this isolated little territory, the adored Chieftain of
these affectionate and natural people. At that moment a strain of music
stole by me, as if the breeze of midnight stillness had expired in a manner on the Eolian lyre. Emotion, undefinable emotion, thrilled on every
nerve. I listened. I trembled. A breathless silence gave me every note.
Was it the illusion of my now all awakened fancy, or the professional

exertions of the bard of Inismore? Oh, no! for the voice it sym-
phonized; the low wild tremulous voice, which sweetly sighed its soul
of melody o'er the harp's responsive chords, was the voice of a
woman!

Directed by the witching strain, I approached an angle of the building from whence it seemed to proceed; and perceiving a light which
streamed through an open casement, I climbed, with some difficulty,
the ruins of a parapet wall, which encircled this wing of the castle,
and which rose so immediately under the casement as to give me,
when I stood on it, a perfect view of the interior of that apartment to
which it belonged.

Two tapers which burned on a marble slab, at the remotest extremity of this vast and gloomy chamber, shed their dim blue light on the
saintly countenance of Father John; who, with a large folio open
before him, seemed wholly wrapt in studious meditation; while the
Prince, reclined on an immense gothic couch, with his robe thrown
over the arm that supported his head, betrayed by the expression of
his countenance, those emotions which agitated his soul, while he listened to those strains which spoke once to the heart of the father, the
patriot, and the man – breathed from the chords of his country's
emblem – breathed in the pathos of his country's music – breathed
from the lips of his apparently inspired daughter! The 'white rising of
her hands upon the harp;'[1] the half-drawn veil, that imperfectly discovered the countenance of a seraph; the moonlight that played
round her fine form, and partially touched her drapery with its silver
beam – her attitude! her air! But how cold – how inanimate – how
imperfect this description! Oh! could I but seize the touching features
– could I but realize the vivid tints of this enchanting picture, as they
then glowed on my fancy! By heavens! you would think the mimic
copy fabulous; the 'celestial visitant' of an over-heated imagination.
Yet as if the independent witchery of the lovely minstrel was not in
itself all, all-sufficient, at the back of her chair stood the grotesque figure of her antiquated nurse. O! the precious contrast. And yet it
heightened, it finished the picture.

While thus entranced in breathless observation, endeavouring to
support my precarious tenement, and to prolong this rich feast of the
senses and the soul, the loose stones on which I tottered gave way
under my feet, and impulsively clinging to the wood-work of the casement, it mouldered in my grasp. I fell – but before I reached the earth

---

1 James Macpherson, *Temara: An Epic Poem*, Book VII.

I was bereft of sense. With its return I found myself in a large apartment, stretched on a bed, and supported in the arms of the Prince of Inismore! His hand was pressed to my bleeding temple; while the priest applied a styptic to the wound it had received; and the nurse was engaged in binding up my arm, which had been dreadfully bruised and fractured a little above the wrist. Some domestics, with an air of mingled concern and curiosity, surrounded my couch; and at her father's side stood the Lady Glorvina, her looks pale and disordered – her trembling hands busily employed in preparing bandages, for which my skilful doctress impatiently called.

While my mind almost doubted the evidence of my senses, and a physical conviction alone *painfully* proved to me the reality of all I beheld, my wandering, wondering eyes met those of the Prince of Inismore! A volume of pity and benevolence was registered in their glance; nor were mine, I suppose, inexpressive of my feelings, for he thus replied to them: –

'Be of good cheer, young stranger; you are in no danger; be composed; be confident; conceive yourself in the midst of friends; for you are surrounded by those who would wish to be considered as such.'

I attempted to speak, but my voice faultered; my tongue was nerveless; my mouth dry and parched. A trembling hand presented a cordial to my lip. I quaffed the philtre, and fixed my eyes on the face of my ministering angel. – That angel was Glorvina! – I closed them, and sunk on the bosom of her father.

'Oh, he faints again!' cried a sweet and plaintive voice.

'On the contrary,' replied the priest, 'the weariness of acute pain something subsided, is lulling him into a soft repose; for see, the colour re-animates his cheek, and his pulse quickens.'

'It indeed beats most wildly;' returned the sweet physician – for the pulse which responded to her finger's thrilling pressure, moved with no languid throb.

'Let us retire,' added the priest, 'all danger is now, thank heaven, over; and repose and quiet the most salutary requisites for our patient.'

At these words he arose from my bed-side; and the Prince gently withdrawing his supporting arms, laid my head upon the pillow. In a moment all was death-like stillness, and stealing a glance from under my half-closed eyes, I found myself alone with my skilful doctress, the nurse; who, shading the taper's light from the bed, had taken her distaff and seated herself on a little stool at some distance.

This was a golden respite to feelings wound up to that vehement excess which forbade all expression, which left my tongue powerless, while my heart overflowed with emotion the most powerful.

Good God! I, the son of Lord M——, the hereditary object of hereditary detestation, beneath the roof of my implacable enemy! Supported in his arms; relieved from anguish by his charitable attention; honored by the solicitude of his lovely daughter; overwhelmed by the charitable exertions of his whole family; and reduced to that bodily infirmity that would of necessity oblige me to continue for some time the object of their beneficent attentions.

What a series of emotions did this conviction awaken in my heart! Emotions of a character, an energy, long unknown to my apathized feelings; while gratitude to those who had drawn them into existence, combined with the interest, the curiosity, the admiration, they had awakened, tended to confirm my irresistible desire of perpetuating the immunities I enjoyed, as the guest and patient of the Prince and his daughter. And while the touch of this Wild Irish Girl's hand thrilled on every sense – while her voice of tenderest pity murmured on my ear, and I secretly triumphed over the prejudices of her father, I would not have exchanged my broken arm and wounded temple for the strongest limb and soundest head in the kingdom; but the same chance which threw me in the supporting arms of the irasible Prince, might betray to him in the person of his patient, the son of his hereditary enemy: it was at least probable he would make some inquiries relative to the object of his benevolence, and the singular cause which rendered him such; it was therefore a necessary policy in me to be provided against this scrutiny.

Already deep in adventure, a thousand seducing reasons were suggested by my newly awakened heart, to go on with the romance, and to secure for my future residence in the castle, that interest, which, if known to be the son of Lord M——, I must eventually have forfeited, for the cold aversion of irreclaimable prejudice. The imposition was at least innocent, and might tend to future and mutual advantage; and after the ideal assumption of a thousand fictitious characters, I at last fixed on that of an itinerant artist, as consonant to my most cultivated talent, and to the testimony of those witnesses which I had fortunately brought with me, namely, my drawing book, pencils, etc. etc. – self-nominated *Henry Mortimer,* to answer the initials on my linen, the only proofs against me, for I had not even a letter with me.

I was now armed at all points for inspection; and as the Prince lived in a perfect state of isolation, and I was unknown in the country, I entertained no apprehensions of discovery during the time I should remain at the castle; and full of hope, strong in confidence, but wearied by incessant cogitation, and something exhausted by pain, I fell into that profound slumber I did before but feign.

The mid-day beam shone brightly through the faded tints of my bed curtains before I awakened the following morning, after a night of such fairy charms as only float round the couch of

'Fancy trained in bliss.'

The nurse, and the two other domestics, relieved the watch, at my bed-side during the night; and when I drew back the curtain, the former complimented me on my somniferous powers, and in the usual mode of inquiry, but in a very unusual accent and dialect, addressed me with much kindness and good-natured solicitude. While I was endeavouring to express my gratitude for her attentions, and what seemed most acceptable to her, my high opinion of her skill, the Father Director entered.

To the benevolent mind, distress or misfortune is ever a sufficient claim on all the privileges of intimacy; and, when Father John seated himself by my bed-side, affectionately took my hand, lamented my accident, and assured me of my improved looks, it was with an air so kindly familiar, so tenderly intimate, that it was impossible to suspect the sound of his voice was yet a stranger to my ear.

Prepared and collected, as soon as I had expressed my sense of his and the Prince's benevolence, I briefly related my feigned story; and in a few minutes I was a young Englishman, by birth a gentleman, by inevitable misfortunes reduced to a dependence on my talents for a livelihood, and by profession an artist. I added, that I came to Ireland to take views, and seize some of the finest features of its landscapes; that having heard much of the wildly picturesque charms of the north-west coasts, I had penetrated thus far into this remote corner of the province of Connaught; that the uncommon beauty of the views surrounding the castle, and the awful magnificence of its ruins, had arrested my wanderings, and determined me to spend some days in its vicinity: that having attended divine service the preceding evening in the chapel, I continued to wander along the romantic shores of Inismore, and in the adventuring spirit of my art, had climbed part of the mouldering ruins of the castle, to catch a fine effect of light and shade, produced by the partially-veiled beams of the moon, and had then met with the accident which now threw me on the benevolence of the Prince of Inismore; an unknown in a strange country, with a fractured limb, a wounded head, and an heart oppressed with the sense of gratitude under which it laboured.

'That you were a stranger and a traveller, who had been led by curiosity or devotion to visit the chapel of Inismore,' said the priest, 'we were already apprised of, by the peasant who brought to the castle last night the horse and valise left at his cabin, and who feared, from the length of your absence, some accident had befallen you. What you have yourself been kind enough to detail, is precisely what will prove your best letter of recommendation to the Prince. Trust me, young gentleman, that your standing in need of his attention, is the best claim you could make on it; and your admiration of his native scenes, of that ancient edifice, the monument of that decayed ancestral splendour still dear to his pride; and your having so severely suffered through an anxiety by which he must be flattered, will induce him to consider himself as even *bound* to administer every attention that can meliorate the unpleasantness of your present situation.'

What an idea did this give me of the character of him whose heart I once believed divested of all the tender feelings of humanity. Every thing that mine could dictate on the subject, I endeavoured to express, and borne away by the vehemence of my feelings, did it in a manner that more than once fastened the eyes of Father John on my face, with that look of surprise and admiration which, to a delicate mind, is more gratifying than the most finished verbal eulogium.

Stimulated by this silent approbation, I insensibly stole the conversation from myself to a more general theme; one thought was the link to another – the chain of discussion gradually extended, and before the nurse brought up my late breakfast, we had ranged through the whole circle of *sciences*. I found that this intelligent and amiable being, had trifled a good deal in his young days with chemistry, of which he still spoke like a lover who, in mature life fondly dwells on the charms of that object who first awakened the youthful raptures of his heart. He is even still an enthusiast in botany, and as free from monastic pedantry as he is rich in the treasures of classical literature, and the elegancies of belles lettres. His feelings even yet preserve something of the ardour of youth, and in his mild character, evidently appears blended, a philosophical knowledge of human nature, with the most perfect worldly inexperience, and the manly intelligence of an highly-gifted mind, with the sentiments of a recluse, and the simplicity of a child. His still ardent mind seemed to dilate to the correspondence of a kindred intellect, and two hours bed-side chit chat, with all the unrestrained freedom such a situation sanctions, produced a more perfect intimacy, than an age would probably have effected under different circumstances.

After having examined and dressed the wounded temple, which he declared to be a mere scratch, and congratulated me on the apparent convalescence of my looks, he withdrew, politely excusing the length of his visit, by pleading the charms of my conversation as the cause of his detention. There is, indeed, an evident vein of French suavity flowing through his manners, that convinced me he had spent some years of his life in that region of the graces. I have since learned that he was partly educated in France; so that, to my astonishment, I have discovered the manners of a gentleman, the conversation of a scholar, and sentiments of a philanthropist, united in the character of an Irish priest.

While my heart throbbed with the natural satisfaction arising from the consciousness of having awakened an interest in those whom it was my ambition to interest, my female Esculapius[1] came and seated herself by me; and while she talked of fevers, inflammations, and the Lord knows what, insisted on my not speaking another word for the rest of the day. Though by no means appearing to labour under the same Pythagorean restraint[2] she had imposed on me; and after having extolled her own surgical powers, her celebrity as the best bone-setter in the barony, and communicated the long list of patients her skill had saved, her tongue at last rested on the only theme I was inclined to hear.

'Arrah! now jewel,' she continued, 'there is our Lady Glorvina now, who with all her skill, and knowing every leaf that grows, why she could no more set your arm than she could break it. Och! it was herself that turned white, when she saw the blood upon your face, for she was the first to hear you fall, and hasten down to have you picked up; at first, faith, we thought you were a robber; but it was all one to her; into the castle you must be brought, and when she saw the blood spout from your temple – Holy Virgin! she looked for all the world as if she was kilt dead herself'

'And is she,' said I, in the selfishness of my heart, 'is she always thus humanely interested for the unfortunate?'

'Och! it is she that is tender-hearted for man or beast,' replied my companion. 'I shall never forget till the day of my death, *nor then* either, faith, the day that Kitty Mulrooney's cow was bogged: you must know, honey, that a bogged cow...

Unfortunately, however, the episode of Kitty Mulrooney's cow

---

1 *Esculapius*: Greek God of medcine.
2 *Pythagorean restraint*: Pythagorus and his followers abstained from eating meat.

was cut short, for the Prince now entered, leaning on the arm of the priest.

Dull indeed must be every feeling, and blunted every recollective faculty, when the look, the air, the smile, with which this venerable and benevolent Chieftain, approaching my bed, and kindly taking me by the hand, addressed me in the singular idiom of his expressive language.

'Young man,' said he, 'the stranger's best gift is upon you, for the eye that sees you for the first time, wishes it may not be the last; and the ear that drinks your words, grows thirsty as it quaffs them. So says our good Father John here; for you have made him your friend ere you are his acquaintance; and as *the friend of my friend,* my heart opens to you – you are welcome to my house, as long as it is pleasant to you; when it ceases to be so, we will part with you with regret, and speed your journey with our wishes and our prayers.'

Could my heart have lent its eloquence to my lip – but that was impossible; very imperfect indeed was the justice I did to my feelings; but as my peroration was an eulogium on these romantic scenes and interesting ruins, the contemplation of which I had nearly purchased with my life, the Prince seemed as much pleased as if my gratitude had poured forth with *Ciceronian* eloquence,[1] and he replied,

'When your health will permit, you can pursue here uninterrupted your charming art. Once, the domains of Inismore could have supplied the painter's pencil with scenes of smiling felicity, and the song of the bard – with many a theme of joy and triumph; but the harp can now only mourn over the fallen greatness of its sons; and the pencil has nothing left to delineate, but the ruins which shelter the grey head of the last of their descendants.'

These words were pronounced with an emotion that shook the debilitated frame of the Prince, and the tear which dimmed the spirit of his eye, formed an associate in that of his auditor. He gazed on me for a moment with a look that seemed to say, 'you feel for me then – yet you are an Englishman;' and taking the arm of Father John, he walked towards a window which commanded a view of the ocean, whose troubled bosom beat wildly against the castle cliffs.

'The day is sad,' said he, 'and makes the soul gloomy: we will summons O'Gallagher to the hall, and drive away sorrow with music.'

Then turning to me, he added, with a faint smile, 'the tones of an Irish harp have still the power to breathe a spirit over the droop-

---

1 *Ciceronian eloquence*: Marcus Tullius Cicero (106–43BC), Roman orator renowed for his rhetorical eloquence.

ing soul of an Irishman; but if its strains disturb your repose, command its silence: the pleasure of the host always rests in that of his guest.'

With these words, and leaning on the arm of his chaplain, he retired; while the nurse, looking affectionately after him, raised her hands, and exclaimed,

'Och! there you go, and may the blessing of the Holy Virgin go with you, for it's yourself that's the jewel of a Prince!'

The impression made on me by this brief but interesting interview, is not to be expressed. You should see the figure, the countenance, the dress of the Prince; the appropriate scenery of the old Gothic chamber, the characteristic appearance of the priest and the nurse, to understand the combined and forcible effect the whole produced.

Yet, though experiencing a pleasurable emotion, strong as it was novel there was still one little wakeful wish throbbing vaguely at my heart.

Was it possible that my chilled, my sated misanthropic feelings, still sent forth one sigh of wishful solicitude for woman's dangerous presence! No, the sentiment the daughter of the Prince inspired, only made a *part* in that general feeling of curiosity, which every thing in this new region of wonders continued to nourish into existence. What had I to expect from the unpolished manners, the confined ideas of this Wild Irish Girl? Deprived of all those touching allurements which society only gives; reared in wilds and solitudes, with no other associates than her nurse, her confessor, and her father; endowed indeed by nature with some personal gifts, set off by the advantage of a singular and characteristic dress, for which she is indebted to whim and natural prejudice, rather than native taste: – I, who had fled in disgust even from those to whose natural attraction the bewitching blandishments of education, the brilliant polish of fashion, and the dazzling splendour of *real* rank, contributed their potent spells.

And yet, the roses of Florida, though the fairest in the universe, and springing from the richest soil, emit no fragrance; while the mountain violet, rearing its timid form from a steril bed, flings on the morning breeze the most delicious perfume.

While given up to such reflections as these – while the sound of the Irish harp arose from the hall below, and the nurse muttered her prayers in Irish over her beads by my side, I fell into a gentle slumber, in which I dreamed that the Princess of Inismore approached my bed, drew aside the curtains, and raising her veil, discovered a face I had hitherto rather guessed at, than seen. Imagine my horror – it was the face, the head, of a *Gorgon!*[1]

Awakened by the sudden and terrific motion it excited, though still almost motionless, as if from the effects of a night-mare (which in fact, from the position I lay in, had oppressed me in the form of the Princess), I cast my eyes through a fracture in the old damask drapery of my bed, and beheld – not the horrid spectre of my recent dream, but the form of a cherub hovering near my pillow – it was the Lady Glorvina herself! Oh! how I trembled lest the fair image should only be the vision of my slumber: I scarcely dared to breathe, lest it should dissolve.

She was seated on the nurse's little stool. Her elbow resting on her knee, her cheek reclined upon her hand; for once the wish of Romeo appeared no hyperbola.

Some snow-drops lay scattered in her lap, on which her downcast eyes shed their beams; as though she moralized over the modest blossoms, which, in fate and delicacy, resembled herself. Changing her pensive attitude, she collected them into a bunch, and sighed, and waved her head as she gazed on them. The dew that trembled on their leaves seemed to have flowed from a richer source than the exhalation of the morning's vapour – for the flowers were faded – but the drops that gem'd them were fresh.

At that moment the possession of a little kingdom would have been less desirable to me, than the knowledge of that association of ideas and feelings which the contemplation of these honoured flowers awakened. At last, with a tender smile, she raised them to her lip, and sighed; and placed them in her bosom; then softly drew aside my curtain. I feigned the stillness of death – yet the curtain remained unclosed – many minutes elapsed – I ventured to unseal my eyes, and met the soul dissolving glance of my sweet attendant spirit, who seemed to gaze intently on her charge. Emotion on my part the most delicious, on hers the most modestly confused, for a moment prevented all presence of mind; the beautiful arm still supported the curtain – my ardent gaze was still rivetted on a face alternately suffused with the electric flashes of red and white. At last the curtain fell, the priest entered, and the vision, the sweetest, brightest, vision of my life, dissolved!

Glorvina sprung towards her tutor, and told him aloud, that the nurse had entreated her to take her place, while she descended to dinner.

---

1 *the head, of a Gorgon!*: in Greek mythology, one of three sisters who had the power to turn anyone who looked at her to stone. She is depicted with snakes for her hair.

'And no place can become thee better, my child,' said the priest, 'than that which fixes thee by the couch of suffering and sickness.'

'However,' said Glorvina, smiling, 'I will gratify you by resigning for the present in your favour;' and away she flew, speaking in Irish to the nurse, who passed her at the door.

The benevolent confessor then approached, and seated himself beside my bed, with that premeditated air of chit-chat sociality, that it went to my soul to disappoint him. But the thing was impossible. To have tamely conversed in mortal language on mortal subjects, after having held 'high communion' with an ethereal spirit; when a sigh, a tear, a glance, were the delicious vehicles of our souls' secret inter-course – to stoop from this 'coloquy sublime!' I could as soon have delivered a logical essay on identity and diversity, or any other subject equally interesting to the heart and imagination.

I therefore closed my eyes, and breathed most sonorously; the good priest drew the curtain and retired on tip-toe, and the nurse once more took her distaff, and for her sins was silent.

These good people must certainly think me a second Epimenides,[1] for I have done nothing but sleep, or feign to sleep, since I have been thrown amongst them.

From *The Lay of an Irish Harp*

(1807)

To him who said, 'You live only for the world'

> 'Vivons pour nous....
> Que l'amitié qui nous unit
> Nous tienne lieu du monde
> VOLTAIRE

Oh! no I live not for the throng
Thou seest me mingle oft among.
    By fashion driven.
Yet one *may* snatch in this same world
Of noise and din, where one is hurl'd,
    Some glimpse of heaven!

When *gossip* murmurs rise around,

---

1 *Epimenides*: Cretan poet and prophet; legend has it that as a boy he slept for 57 years.

And all is empty shew and sound,
    Of *vulgar* folly,
How sweet! to give wild fancy play,
Or bend to thy dissolving sway.
    Soft melancholy.

When silly beaux around one flutter,
And silly belles gay nonsense utter,
    How sweet to steal
To some lone corner *(quite perdue)*
And with the dear elected *few*
    Converse and *feel!*

When forced for tasteless crowds to sing,
Or listless sweep the trembling string,
    Say, when we meet
The eye whose beam alone inspires,
And wakes the warm soul's latent fires,
    Is it not sweet?

Yes, yes, the dearest bliss of any
Is that which midst the blissless many
    So oft *we* stole:
Thou knowst 'twas midst much cold parade
And idle crowds, we each betray'd
    To each – a soul.

THE REV. PATRICK BRONTË (1777–1861)

Born in Co. Down, the son of a small farmer, his family came originally from Co. Fermanagh and was called Brunty, Prunty or O'Prunty. He worked as a blacksmith, then taught at Glascar before going to Cambridge, where he graduated in 1806. He was a curate in Essex and in various parishes in Yorkshire and became perpetual curate of Haworth in 1820. He married Maria Branwell in 1812, and was the father of seven children, whom he survived. Charlotte, Emily and Anne became famous novelists; their brother Branwell, though gifted, died at 31. Brontë wrote mainly didactic poems and stories as well as evangelical sermons. The poem included was written to Mrs Buckworth when her dog Robin Tweed was pining for his mistress who, with her husband, was away from Dewsbury and Patrick had taken up his duties at Hartshead.

Tweed's Letter to his Mistress

(1811)

Ah! Mistress, dear,
Pray lend an ear,
To simple Robin Tweed;
I've been to you,
Both kind and true,
In every time of need.
I have no claim,
To rank or name,
Amongst the barking gentry;
No spaniel neat,
Nor greyhound fleet,
To grace the street, or entry.
But then, you know,
I still can shew,
A bonny spotted skin,
Can watch the house,
Kill rat or mouse,
And give you, 'welcome in'.
How oft have I,
With watchful eye,
And fondly wagging tail,
And bark, and whine,
And frisk so fine,
Said: 'Mistress dear, all hail'.
Rap! at the door –
I soiled the floor,
With capering, and with jumping,
Whilst on my back,
With lusty thwack
Fierce Esther, was a thumping!
My love for you,
Still bore me through,
Whatever my disaster;
If you said 'Tweed'! –
And stroked my head,
Each wound had then a plaster.
Each night I lie
    With sleepless eye,

And longing wait the morrow:
And poke my nose,
And smell your clothes,
And howl aloud for sorrow!
The other night,
By clear fire-light,
I saw your gown a drying,
So, on the stones,
I stretched my bones,
And spent the night in sighing!
But all in vain!
   I thus complain,
Alas! there's none to heed me,
     You have not sent,
     As you were went,
To Esther for to feed me.
Hard is my lot!
Since I'm forgot,
By one I'll love forever! –
But mankind change,
As round they range –
A dog, he changes, never!
A long farewell! –
The gloomy knell,
Will soon inform the neighbours,
     That Tweed is dead,
     And has got rid,
     of all his cares and labours.

Your kind, trusty, and humble dog, Robin Tweed, at my kennel
near the Vicarage, Dewsbury, the 11th June 1811.

ROBERT EMMET (1778-1803)

Born at St. Stephen's Green, Dublin, the youngest son of the physician to the Viceroy in Ireland, he was educated at private schools in Dublin and at Trinity College, Dublin, where he became a prominent member of the College Historical Society, and befriended Thomas Moore (upon hearing 'Let Erin remember the day' Emmet exclaimed 'Oh that I were at the head of twenty thousand men, marching to that air!'). He left the college when in 1798 Lord Clare investigated the students' sympathies with the United Irishmen. He travelled on the continent, meeting Irishmen in exile (including his brother Thomas Addis Emmet). He met Talleyrand and Napoleon in 1802; the latter promised to invade England in August of the following year. Emmet's doubts of Napoleon's sincerity did not prevent him from planning a bold rising; he purchased arms, surrounded himself with a small band of conspirators, and set up arms depots. An explosion in the Patrick Street depot on 16 July 1803 accelerated the Rising. On 23 July, Emmet, wearing a green coat, white breeches and a cocked hat with feathers, marched towards Dublin Castle at the head of a mob which chanced upon the carriage of the Lord Chief Justice Kilwarden, whom they murdered with their pikes. Emmet fled, disheartened by the violence. The rising was quashed by the ordinary guard. Emmet refused to leave Dublin until he had met his fiancée, Sarah Curran. He was captured by Major Sirr in his hiding place in Harold's Cross. He was convicted of treason by a special court under Lord Norbury; he was hanged outside St. Catherine's Church, Thomas Street, on 20 September 1803, and then beheaded. His grave is unknown.

Arbor Hill[1]

No rising column marks this spot,
    Where many a victim lies;
But oh! The blood that here has streamed,
    To heaven for justice cries.

It claims it on the oppressor's head,
    Who joys in human woe,
Who drinks the tears by misery shed,
    And mocks them as they flow.

It claims it on the callous judge,
    Whose hands in blood are dyed,
Who arms injustice with the sword,
    The balance throws aside.

It claims it for his ruined isle,
    Her wretched children's grave;
Where withered Freedom droops her head,
    And man exists – a slave.

O sacred justice! free this land
    From tyranny abhorred;

---

1 Arbour Hill, in Dublin, is the site of a military prison. Its burial grond contains the remains of many of the insurgents of the 1798 Rising. R. R. Madden, in *Life and Times of Robert Emmet* (1840), claims that Emmet wrote this poem in invisible ink in 1797.

Resume thy balance and thy seat –
    Resume – but sheathe thy sword.

No retribution should we seek –
    Too long has horror reigned?
By mercy marked may Freedom rise,
    By cruelty unstained.

Nor shall a tyrant's ashes mix
    With those our martyred dead;
This is the place where Erin's sons
    In Erin's cause have bled.

And those who here are laid at rest,
    Oh! hallowed be each name;
Their memories are forever blest –
    Consigned to endless fame.

Unconsecrated is this ground,
    Unblest by holy hands;
No bell here tolls its solemn sound,
    No monument here stands.

But here the patriot's tears are shed,
    The poor man's blessing given;
These consecrate the virtuous dead,
    These waft their fame to heaven.

Speech from the Dock, 19 September 1803

I am asked what I have to say why sentence of death should not be pronounced on me, according to law. I have nothing to say that can alter your pre-determination, nor that it will become me to say, with any view to the mitigation of that sentence which you are to pronounce and I must abide by. But I have that to say which interests me more than life and which you have laboured to destroy. I have much to say why my reputation should be rescued from the load of false accusation and calumny which has been cast upon it. I do not imagine that, seated where you are, your minds can be so free from prejudice as to receive the least impression from what I am going to utter.

I have no hope that I can anchor my character in the breast of a court constituted and trammeled as this is.

I only wish, and that is the utmost that I can expect, that your lordships may suffer it to float down your memories untainted by the foul breath of prejudice, until it finds some more hospitable harbour to shelter it from the storms by which it is buffeted. Were I only to suffer death, after being adjudged guilty by your tribunal, I should bow in silence, and meet the fate that awaits me without a murmur; but the sentence of the law which delivers my body to the executioner will, through the ministry of the law, labour in its own vindication, to consign my character to obloquy; for there must be guilt somewhere, whether in the sentence of the court or in the catastrophe – time must determine. A man in my situation has not only to encounter the difficulties of fortune, and the force of power over minds which it has corrupted or subjugated, but the difficulties of established prejudice. The man dies, but his memory lives. That mine may not perish, that it may live in the respect of my countrymen, I seize upon this opportunity to vindicate myself from some of the charges alleged against me. When my spirit shall be wafted to a more friendly port, when my shade shall have joined the bands of those martyred heroes who have shed their blood on the scaffold and in the field in defense of their country and of virtue, this is my hope: I wish that my memory and my name may animate those who survive me, while I look down with complacency on the destruction of that perfidious government which upholds its domination by blasphemy of the Most High; which displays its power over man as over the beasts of the forest; which sets man upon his brother, and lifts his hand in the Name of God, against the throat of his fellow who believes or doubts a little more or a little less than the government standard, a government which is steeled to barbarity by the cries of the orphans and the tears of the widows it has made.

Here Lord Norbury[1] interrupted Emmet, saying that 'the mean and wicked enthusiasts who felt as he did, were not equal to the accomplishment of their wild designs.'

I appeal to the immaculate God, I swear by the Throne of Heaven,

---

1 John Toler, 1st Earl of Norbury (1745–1831); staunch supporter of the Anglo-Irish Ascendancy. As attorney-general he conducted the prosecution of the rebels of the '98 Rising. When he was made Chief Justice in 1800, Lord Clare is said to have remarked, 'Make him a bishop, or even an archbishop, but not a chief justice'.

before which I must shortly appear, by the blood of the murdered patriots who have gone before me, that my conduct has been, through all this peril, and through all my purposes, governed only by the conviction which I have uttered, and by no other view than that of the emancipation of my country from the super-inhuman oppression under which she has so long and too patiently travailed; and I confidently hope that, wild and chimerical as it may appear, there is still union and strength in Ireland to accomplish this noblest of enterprises. Of this I speak with confidence, with intimate knowledge, and with the consolation that appertains to that confidence. Think not, my lords, I say this for the petty gratification of giving you a transitory uneasiness. A man who never yet raised his voice to assert a lie will not hazard his character with posterity by asserting a falsehood on a subject so important to his country, and on an occasion like this. Yes, my lords, a man who does not wish to have his epitaph written until his country is liberated, will not leave a weapon in the power of envy, or a pretense to impeach the probity which he means to preserve, even in the grave to which tyranny consigns him.

Here he was again interrupted by Norbury.

Again I say that what I have spoken was not intended for your lordship, whose situation I commiserate rather than envy – my expressions were for my countrymen. If there is a true Irishman present, let my last words cheer him in the hour of his affliction.

Here he was again interrupted. Lord Norbury said he did not sit there to hear treason.

I have always understood it to be the duty of a judge, when a prisoner has been convicted, to pronounce the sentence of the law. I have also understood that judges sometimes think it their duty to hear with patience, and to speak with humanity; to exhort the victim of the laws, and to offer, with tender benignity, their opinions of the motives by which he was actuated in the crime of which he was adjudged guilty. That a judge has thought it his duty so to have done, I have no doubt; but where is the boasted freedom of your institutions, where is the vaunted impartiality, clemency and mildness of your courts of justice if an unfortunate prisoner, whom your policy and not justice is about to deliver into the hands of the executioner, is not suffered to explain his motives sincerely and truly, and to vindicate the principles by which he was actuated? My lord, it may be a part of the system of angry justice to bow a man's mind by humiliation to the purposed ignominy of the scaffold; but worse to me than the purposed shame or the scaffold's terrors would be the shame of such foul and unfounded imputations as have been laid against me in this court. You, my lord, are a judge; I am the supposed culprit. I am a man; you are a man also. By a revolution of power we might exchange places? Though we never could change characters. If I stand at the bar of this court and dare not vindicate my character, what a farce is your justice! If I stand at this bar and dare not vindicate my character, how dare you calumniate it? Does the sentence of death, which your unhallowed policy inflicts on my body, condemn my tongue to silence and my reputation to reproach? Your executioner may abridge the period of my existence; but while I exist I shall not forebear to vindicate my character and motives from your aspersion; and as a man to whom fame is dearer than life, I will make the last use of that life in doing justice to that reputation which is to live after me, and which is the only legacy I can leave to those I honour and love and for whom I am proud to perish. As men, my lords, we must appear on the great day at one common tribunal; and it will then remain for the Searcher of all hearts to show a collective universe, who was engaged in the most virtuous actions or swayed by the purest motives my country oppressor, or –

Here he was interrupted and told to listen to the sentence of the court.

My lords, will a dying man be denied the legal privilege of exculpating himself in the eyes of the community from an undeserved reproach, thrown upon him during his trial, by charging him with ambition and attempting to cast away for paltry consideration the liberties of his country? Why did your lordships insult me? Or rather, why insult justice, in demanding of me why sentence of death should not be pronounced against me? I know my lords, that form prescribes that you should ask the question, the form also presents the right of answering. This, no doubt, may be dispensed with, and so might the whole ceremony of the trial, since sentence was already pronounced at the Castle before the jury was impaneled. Your lordships are but the priests of the oracle, and I insist on the whole of the forms.

I am charged with being an emissary of France. An emissary of France! And for what end? It is alleged that I wished to sell the independence of my country. And for what end? Was this the object of my ambition? And is this the mode by which a tribunal of justice reconciles contradiction? No, I am no emissary; and my ambition was to hold a place among the deliverers of my country, not in power nor in profit, but in the glory of the achievement. Sell my country's independence to France! And for what? Was it a change of masters? No, but for my ambition. O, my country, was it a personal ambition that could influence me? Had it been the soul of my actions, could I not by my education and fortune, by the rank and consideration of my family, have placed myself amongst the proudest of your oppressors. My country was my idol. To it I sacrificed every selfish, every endearing sentiment, and for it I now offer up myself, O God! No, my lords; I acted as an Irishman, determined on delivering my country from the yoke of a foreign and unrelenting tyranny and the more galling yoke of a domestic faction, which is its joint partner and perpetrator in the patricide, from the ignominy existing with an exterior of splendour and a conscious depravity. It was the wish of my heart to extricate my country from this doubly riveted despotism; I wished to place her independence beyond the reach of any power on earth. I wished to exalt her to that proud station in the world. Connection with France was, indeed, intended, but only as far as mutual interest would sanction or require. Were the French to assume any authority inconsistent with the purest independence, it would be the signal for their destruction. We sought their aid and we sought it as we had assurance we should obtain it as auxiliaries in war and allies in peace. Were the French to come as invaders or enemies uninvited by the wishes of the people, I should oppose them to the utmost of my strength. Yes, my countrymen, I should advise you to meet them upon the beach with a sword in one hand and a torch in the other. I would meet them with all the destructive fury of war. I would animate my countrymen to immolate them in their boats, before they had contaminated the soil of my country. If they succeeded in landing, and if forced to retire before superior discipline, I would dispute every inch of the ground, burn every blade of grass, and the last entrenchment of liberty should be my grave. What I could not do myself, if I should fall, I should leave as a last charge to my countrymen to accomplish; because I should feel conscious that life, any more than death, is unprofitable when a foreign nation holds my country in subjection. But it was not as an enemy that the soldiers of France were to land. I looked, indeed, for the assistance of France; but I wished to prove to France and to the world that Irish men deserved to be assisted; that they were indignant at slavery, and ready to assert the independence and liberty of their country. I wished to procure for my country the guarantee which Washington procured for

America; to procure an aid which, by its example would be as important as its valour disciplined, gallant, pregnant with science and experience, that of a people who would perceive the good and polish the rough points of our character. They would come to us as strangers and leave us as friends, after sharing in our perils and elevating our destiny. These were my objects; not to receive new task-masters, but to expel old tyrants. It was for these ends I sought aid from France; because France, even as an enemy, could not be more implacable than the enemy already in the bosom of my country.

Here he was interrupted by the court.

I have been charged with that importance in the emancipation of my country as to be considered the keystone of the combination of Irishmen; or, as your lordships expressed it, 'the life and blood of the conspiracy.' You do me honour over much; you have given to the subaltern all the credit of a superior. There are men engaged in this conspiracy who are not only superior to me, but even to your own conceptions of yourself, my lord; men before the splendour of whose genius and virtues I should bow with respectful deference and who would think themselves disgraced by shaking your blood-stained hand.

Here he was interrupted.

What! my lord, shall you tell me on the passage to the scaffold, which that tyranny (of which you are only the intermediary executioner) has erected for my murder, that I am accountable for all the blood that has been shed and will be shed in this struggle of the oppressed against the oppressor; shall thou tell me this, and must I be so very a slave as not to repel it? I do not fear to approach the Omnipotent Judge to answer for the conduct of my whole life; and am I to be appalled and falsified by a mere remnant of mortality here? By you, too, although if it were possible to collect all the innocent blood that you have shed in your unhallowed ministry in one great reservoir, your lordship might swim in it.

Here the judge interrupted.

Let no man dare, when I am dead, to charge me with dishonour; let no man taint my memory by believing that I could have engaged in any cause but that of my country's liberty and independence; or that

I could have become the pliant minion of power in the oppression of my country. The Proclamation of the Provisional Government speaks for our views; no inference can be tortured from it to countenance barbarity or debasement at home, or subjection, humiliation or treachery from abroad. I would not have submitted to a foreign oppressor, for the same reason that I would resist the foreign and domestic oppressor. In the dignity of freedom I would have fought upon the threshold of my country, and its enemy would enter only by passing over my lifeless corpse. And am I who lived but for my country, and have subjected myself to the dangers of the jealous and watchful oppressor, and the bondage of the grave, only to give my countrymen their rights and my country her independence, am I to be loaded with calumny and not suffered to resent it? No; God forbid!

Here Norbury told the prisoner that his sentiments and language disgraced his family and education, but more particularly his father, Dr. Robert Emmet, who was a man that would, if alive, discountenance such opinions. To which Emmet replied:

If the spirit of the illustrious dead participate in the concerns and cares of those who were dear to them in this transitory life, O, ever dear and venerated shade of my departed father, look down with scrutiny upon the conduct of your suffering son and see if I have even for a moment, deviated from those principles of morality and patriotism which it was your care to instill into my youthful mind, and for which I am now about to offer up my life! My lords, you are impatient for the sacrifice. The blood which you seek is not congealed by the artificial terrors which surround your victim; it circulates warm and unruffled through the channels which God created for noble purpose, but which you are now bent to destroy for purposes so grievous that they cry to heaven. Be yet patient! I have but a few more words to say. I am going to go to my cold and silent grave. My lamp of life is nearly extinguished. My race is run. The grave opens to receive me and I sink into its bosom. I have but one request to ask at my departure from this world. It is the charity of its silence. Let no man write my epitaph; for as no man who knows my motives dare now vindicate them, let not prejudice or ignorance asperse them. Let them and me rest in obscurity and peace; and my tomb remain uninscribed and my memory in oblivion until other times and other men can do justice to my character. When my country takes her place among the nations of the earth, then, and not till then let my epitaph be written. I have done.

WILLIAM HAMILTON DRUMMOND (1778–1865)

Born in Larne, Co. Antrim, Drummond was educated at the Belfast Academical Institute and at Glasgow University. He was ordained minister to the Second Belfast Congregation in 1800, and graduated DD in 1810. From 1815 he ministered at Strand Street, Dublin. His early verse publications include *Juvenile Poems* (1795), *The Man of Age* (1797), *Hibernia* (1797), followed by *The Battle of Trafalgar* (1806) and a metrical translation of the *First Book of Lucretius* (1808). The poem *The Giant's Causeway* (1811) was written in support of the 'Neptunian' theory of marine erosion in rocks. *The Doctrine of the Trinity* (1827) is a prose defence of Unitarianism. His interest in national history is borne out in the poems *Clontarf* (1822) and *Bruce's Invasion of Ireland* (1826). He contributed verse translations to Hardiman's *Irish Minstrelsy** (1831) – 'Gerald Nugent's Ode on Leaving Ireland' won praise from Samuel Ferguson*. He issued his own *Ancient Irish Minstrelsy* (1852), containing verse translations of poems from the Fionn cycle, based on transliterations supplied by Eugene O'Curry*, Nicholas O'Kearney, and Hardiman.

From *Bruce's Invasion of Ireland: A Poem*
(1826)

PREFACE

Edward Bruce's invasion forms an important event in the history of Ireland. Wearied and exhausted by sanguinary wars, of which they could foresee no termination, the Irish chiefs became anxious to participate in the blessings of a well-constituted government, and to be admitted, with their people, to the rights and privileges of English subjects. An application to this effect was made to Ufford, the chief governor, accompanied by an offer of 8000 marks for the service of the king. Sound policy would have dictated compliance with a proposal so reasonable, and so advantageous to England as the voluntary submission of 'a high-minded and generous people.' King Edward himself was of this opinion, and evinced a desire to comply with their request, on the easy terms of their supplying a body of infantry whenever his affairs should require their assistance. The subject, however, being referred to the Irish Parliament, they were of a different sentiment. They employed every art to prevent a convention of the king's barons and subjects in Ireland to decide on this weighty point, and affirmed that the supplication of the Irish chieftains could not be granted without great prejudice to the king and his government. This parliament of 'perjured adventurers,' as they are indignantly styled in a letter of Columbanus, thirsting for confiscations, saw a termination to their rapacious schemes in the proposed settlement, and the desire of the Irish people, was 'fatally counteracted by those whose duty it was to promote a measure so well calculated for the benefit of the country.'

The chiefs, mortified and disappointed by the rejection of their reasonable entreaties, had recourse to their last and only alternative, the sword. But the spirit of discord was among them, and that redemption of their country, which their zealous co-operation might have accomplished, was frustrated by their disunion. At length, to end the mutual jealousies and rival claims of contending competitors for supremacy, some of the principal potentates agreed to elect a foreign prince to be their sovereign. They heard, with undissembled joy, of the illustrious achievements of King Robert Bruce. He had overcome the might of England in the memorable field of Bannockburn, and was now firmly seated on the Scottish throne. His brother Edward became the just object of their admiration, for by his military prowess he had acquired the name and the renown of a hero. He was descended from their ancient kings, and was therefore deemed worthy to ascend their throne. They accordingly invited him to be their monarch, made a pathetic representation to the cruel sufferings, and implored his aid in behalf of an oppressed people, ready to make every exertion to throw off the yoke of their common enemy, and every sacrifice to confirm his possession of the kingdom. Thus was the leopard solicited to protect the fold which had been already wasted by the wolf and the bear.

Such a proposal was too flattering not to be readily embraced. The conquest of Ireland was an object suited to the high and chivalrous spirit of Edward Bruce. King Robert fully accorded in the scheme, and furnished a fleet of three hundred vessels, with an army of six thousand men, the flower of the Scottish forces, under the command of valiant and experienced leaders.

The armament sailed from Ayr, and arrived in 'Wyking's frith,' the harbour of Larne, in the County of Antrim, on the 25th of May, 1315. The successes of Bruce were rapid and brilliant. He spread the terror of his arms through Ulster, and leaving a force to conduct the siege of Carrickfergus, advanced to Dundalk, where he was crowned king of Ireland. Hence pursuing his conquests, and having threatened the metropolis itself, he carried his victorious arms to the gates of Limerick. After a series of adventures, in which he had to struggle with famine and the sword, he was at last obliged to retreat. He took his last stand at Faughard, in the neighbourhood of Dundalk, where, in a desperate conflict with Lord John Birmingham, he fell, surrounded by the bravest of his troops.

Thus terminated an expedition which, if conducted with more prudence, might have had a very different result. Had Edward possessed the calm virtues of his brother Robert, he might have established himself on the throne of Ireland. But robbery, conflagration, and murder, are not the means of subduing nations, much less of securing their gratitude and loyalty. The horrible barbarities and rapacity of the Scotch army soon alienated the minds of his Irish allies, and gave them alarming proofs of what they were to expect from a change of masters. When the frogs besought a new king from Jupiter, the stork came and swallowed them up. The Scottish thistle was to Ireland as the bramble which threatened to send forth fires that would devour the cedars of Lebanon....

from CANTO SECOND

The Rising Of Erin – And Albyn's Retreat

> Unblest is the land where the fell Faction prevails;
> From Justice she wrests both the sword and the scales;
> All counsels of wisdom perverts to the wrong,
> And saps to its basis the might of the strong.

> Erin, wherefore did nature smile sweet on thy birth,
> When first from dark chaos sprang heaven and earth,
> Airs of Paradise redolent breathe o'er thy breast,
> And form thee a type of that land of the blest
> Which poets once sung, and which poets would choose
> Where to breathe inspiration and rove with the muse?
> What boot thy fair valleys, thy bright-blooming hills,
> Thy corn-covered fields and thy crystalline rills,
> If those valleys and hills but re-echo thy screams,
> While the sword reaps thy crops, and blood purples thy streams?
> Vain are nature's best blessings, if discord, more dire
> Than famine and plague and the elements' ire,
> Lets them ne'er be enjoyed; – but with wrath-kindled flame
> Turns thy song to a dirge – and thy glory to shame.
> Oh! didst thou but know thy own bliss and pursue –
> If to thy own cause thou wert loyal and true,

All nations would hail thee of isles the renowned,
A queen among queens with prosperity crowned;
Thy sons gathered round thee, an adamant pale,
Or a rampart of fire, that no foeman dared scale,
In accord with thy harp loud their voices would raise
In pæans of joy – or in anthems of praise.
But by thy own fires thou art wasted and burned –
Against thy own bosom thy faulchion[1] is turned;
Low, low art thou fallen, heart-stricken and sore,
Rent, plundered, and bleeding at every pore.
Breathes a spirit within thee? Oh! better to die,
Than thus crushed and trampled ingloriously lie.
Are thy warriors all slain? – Or dispersed far and wide,
In mountains and caverns their terrors to hide,
While their wives and their daughters become the sad spoil
Of the ruthless invaders that widow thy soil?

    Where now is the might of Clanrickard's brave line,
De Clare, and Fitz-Thomas, and stout Geraldine,
And Butler, and Desmond, that oft in the strife
For glory, have sported with treasure and life?
Ferns, where is thy Bishop? – On what mission sent[2]
In the dead of the night, did he seek Bruce's tent?
In sooth it behoves not the shepherd to hide,
When the wolf through the fold spreads his ravages wide.
But, mayhap, holy man! through the foes he has passed
To shrive some lorn penitent breathing his last;
Up the heaven-ward way to direct his poor soul,
And anoint the car-wheels ere he starts for the goal.

---

1 *Faulchion*: poetic name for a sword.
2 *Ferns, where is thy bishop?*: 'Adam of Northampton was consecrated Bishop of Ferns on Trinity Sunday, 1312. While he sat in this see, Ferns and the castle of it was plundered and set on fire by the rebels. He adhered some time to the Scotch invaders, and the Irish rebels who fought under them; whether through fear or force, or for what other cause, I know not. For we find a writ dated and issued against him on the 6th of August, 1317, to Roger Mortimer, Earl of March, and justice or customs of Ireland, commanding him to secure the bishop, and bring him to account for his treason in adhering to Edward Bruce, on his arrival in those parts, and afterwards to Robert Bruce his brother, and in furnishing them with provisions, arms, and men.' – *Ware*, 442.

    Fitz John, Bishop of Ossory, was a severe sufferer by Bruce, insomuch that 'Edward II recommended him to the Pope as an object of compassion; and on the 20th of January, 1320, wrote to his holiness very movingly in his behalf, to procure instalments for the payment of some debts due by his see to the court of Rome, on account of the irreparable damages he sustained by the devastations of Bruce and the Scots.'—*Ware*. [*Drummond's note.*]

And where are the Lacies? – Have they too turned good,[1]
Doffed target and sword for the cassoc and hood,
And gone to the Bruce, by entreaty and prayer,
To bend his stern soul bleeding Erin to spare?
Well! let them beware of the scaffold and block,
Though the seas bar them round in the heart of a rock!

Where now are the bards, once so potent to warm
The cold heart of fear, and the coward to arm?
Amergin, and Conla, and Moran, whose lays
In the soul a high tempest of passion could raise,
Have your harp-string in sorrow, in spite, or disdain,
Burst asunder, and sworn ne'er to vibrate again?
O spirit of Ossian! thou sweet soul of song,
Sire of Oscar the brave, son of Fionn the strong,
In hall and in bower must thy harp's thrilling sound
In the drone of that cursed Highland bagpipe be drowned?
From thy dark airy hall, as thou sailest on high,
Hear the groans of the land, and terrors come nigh.
These wasters behold of thy harp's native soil,
Who e'en of thy glory would Erin despoil.

---

1 *And where are the Lacies?*: The conduct of the Lacies was a tissue of treason throughout.
Though they joined the standard of Mortimer, when he marched against Bruce, they were the
first to desert the field. After the assembling of parliament, which did nothing for the peace of
the country, Sir Walter Lacy came to Dublin to clear himself of treasonable imputations, and
after the example of other lords, to tender hostages for his loyalty. By an inquisition which they
procured to be held on their conduct relative to the Scots, they were acquitted; they obtained a
charter of the king's peace, and took an oath, which they confirmed by the sacrament, to be true
to the King of England, and endeavour to destroy the Scots. But in violation of their oath, they
joined Bruce on his approach to Dublin, conducted his march, and gave him counsel. When
Mortimer took his journey to Tredagh, and thence to Trim, he sent letters to the Lacies to appear
before him, and on their contemptuous refusal to come, he sent Sir Hugh Crofts to treat with
them, and him they slew. After this, Mortimer marched in arms against them, seized their goods
and cattle, slew many of their adherents, and obliged themselves to seek refuge in Connaught.
Sir Walter, it was said, went to Ulster to join Bruce, and he with his brother Hugh, were
proclaimed seducers and felons to the king, because they had advanced their banner against the
peace of the King of England. John Lacy, it appears, had been imprisoned, for on Sunday, a
month after Easter, he was led forth of the castle at Dublin, and brought to Trim to be arraigned,
and receive judgement. He was adjudged to be strait dieted, and so he died in prison.

Hugh de Lacy, the younger, was, for various treasons, condemned to be drawn with horses,
afterwards to be hanged and quartered, one quarter, with his head, to be set up in Dublin, and
the others in Drogheda, Dundalk, and Trim, and his bowels to be burned.But the Archbishop of
Armagh and others interceding with the lord justice to respite his execution until the king's
pleasure might be known, his body was delivered for safe custody to Richard Taafe, Esq. sheriff
of the county of Louth, who kept him until he was ordered to be hanged at Drogheda.—
Camden—Lodge.

Three of the Lacies, viz. Sir Walter, Sir Robert, and Sir Aumer, were in the camp of Bruce,
during his last conflict at Dundalk, and with great difficulty escaped. [*Drummond's note.*]

Rough, prickly, and horrid, wherever they tread,
The thistle springs up in the shamrock's green bed.
Thou whose was the boast that if hell kept thy sire,
Thou dar'st with Clan-Boske to storm e'en hell-fire,[1]
And the captive restore, or that realm make thy own;
Let the strength of thy arm to these rovers be known –
With hail-shower and torrent, with tempest and night,
With the meteor's red flash, with the thunderbolt's might,
Haste and sweep them, in wrath, from the land of thy birth:
Through the bards, that are now but mere water and earth,
Shoot the life-giving lightning – that, daringly bold,
They may feel as they felt in the good days of old;
Send them forth in defence of their dear father-land,
With a sword by their side, and a harp in their hand,
Replete with thy spirit, again to re-start,
In accord with its own, all the strings of the heart.
Let this be thy song –

                      'Men of Erin arise!
Your country invokes you with agonized cries,
By her tears and her groans, plundered altars and graves,
Awake! or sleep on, and for ever be slaves.
Black shame to the coward, who hears not the sound –
Transfix him, ye darts of the brave, to the ground!
Or bear him, ye tempests, to some desert wild,
Where the dew never fell, where the sun never smiled,
To lap the foul puddle, to browse the bare thorn,[2]
And the flee as a hare flees the hound and the horn!

---

1 *Thou dar'st with Clan-Boske to storm e'en hell-fire*: In an Irish poem, entitled the Prayer of Ossian, published by Dr. Young, in the first volume of the Transactions of the Royal Irish Academy, Ossian says –

    'Na bithad clanna Baosga asteach,
    'S clanna Moran ne feached treun,
    Bherrmuid Fionn amach ar,
    No bhith an teach aguin fein.'

'If the clan of Boisgne were alive, and the descendant Morne of valiant deeds, we would force Finn out of hell, or house would be our own.' [*Drummond's note.*]

2 *To lap the foul puddle, to browse the bare thorn*: 'Here some man happly thinke it not correspondent to the gravitie of this worke, if I should by relate what a ridiculous opinion hath fully possessed the minds of a number of the Irishress, yea, and perswaded them verily to beleeve that he who in that barbarous Pharoh, and outcry of the soldiers which, with great straining of their voice, they use to set up when they joine battaile, doth not cry and shout as the doe, is suddenly caught up from the ground, and carried as it were, flying in the aire, into those desart vallies (in the County of Kerry) out of any country of Ireland, whatsoever: where he eateth grasse, lappeth water, knoweth not in what state he is, good or bad, hath some use of reason, but not of speech, but shall be caught at length with the help of houndes, and hunters, and brought home to their owne homes.' – *Camden*. [*Drummond's note.*]

'Erin once had a sword never tarnished with rust,
And men that would trample her foes in the dust,
And hearts that, to slavery ere they would bow,
Would bleed – and would burst – but oh! where are they now?
Weak, heartless, inglorious, of manhood the shame,
Ye women of Erin, ye men but in name!
Sit down – fold your arms – bow your necks – and your lives,
Though worthless, redeem with your children and wives.
Hew wood and draw water, to please your proud foes;
Let them dance in your halls – in your chambers repose.
Ere ye shrink form their lash, and be bound with their thongs,
Let the lance and the sword in their blood wreak your wrongs.
If yet in your bosoms a chord may be found,
At the dear name of country to trill and rebound,
If honour, and feeling, and shame have not fled,
And left you as clods, soulless, torpid, and dead,
Ere ye hear her last groans, her last agonies see,
Rise, with swords in your hands, still undaunted and free.
Up! up! grasp your spears, and in martial array,
Away, men of Erin, to battle away!'

THOMAS MOORE (1779-1852)

Moore enjoyed more fame during his life than any Irish poet, and became a shibboleth for later generations. He was born in Dublin, the son of a grocer and wine merchant from Kerry, he was educated at the grammar school of Samuel Whyte, who had taught Richard Brinsley Sheridan*, and, from 1794, at Trinity College, Dublin, the ban on Catholics attending the college having been removed the previous year. Here he formed an intimate friendship with Robert Emmet*. Moore was not impressed by TCD; he called its Fellows 'scoundrelly monks'. He set about translating Anacreon, the sixth-century poet of wine, women and song. *The Odes of Anacreon*, dedicated to the Prince of Wales, appeared in 1800, a year after he received his BA degree. The following year he published *The Poetical Works of Thomas Little, Esq.*, amorous lyrics in the seventeenth century cavalier tradition, which induced Byron, who knew them by heart at the age of 15, to write poetry. His playing and singing opened doors to aristocratic mansions. In 1803 he was appointed admiralty registrar of Bermuda. After some time there, he appointed a deputy, and made a tour of America. On his return he published *Epistles, Odes and Other Poems* (1806), which contains some savage attacks on American society; the book was slated by Jeffrey in *The Edinburgh Review*. Moore challenged him to a duel, but the Bow Street Runners intervened, and the two became life-long friends.

The following year Moore embarked upon an undertaking which would turn him into a pop-idol and the national lyricist of Ireland. Inspired by Bunting's *General Collection of the Ancient Music of Ireland* (1796), he wrote lyrics of personal and national loss and languor, which were set to music by Sir John Stevenson. *Irish Melodies* appeared in two volumes in 1808. Hazlitt condemned the *Melodies* for turning 'the wild Harp of Erin into a musical snuff-box', but his was not the popular verdict. A further eight volumes were published up to 1834. Moore received a hundred guineas for each of the songs. The contract with his London and Dublin publisher stipulated that Moore promote the songs himself – and with his graceful presence behind the piano in Holland House he ensured the sympathetic reception of 'the misfortunes of a people'. They led to a series of *National Airs* (6 vols, 1818–28) based on folksong from other traditions. While producing these melancholy airs with their wavering rhythm, and sure sense of music, Moore wrote a number of biting satires which received scant attention, including *Corruption and Intolerance* (1808), about the Act of Union.

The hopes of Catholic Emancipation when the Prince of Wales became regent in 1811 were soon dashed. Moore wrote a series of lampoons on the court, collected in 1813 as *The Two-Penny Post Bag*, which echoed popular sentiment. In 1811 he married Elizabeth Dyke, a 16-year-old actress, to whom he remained devoted for the rest of his life. That year he signed a contract with Longmans for a staggering £3,000 for a long poem. The Orient was in fashion; Moore immersed himself in the East, hit upon *Lalla Rookh*, writing about opulent wealth as financial disaster hit England. The book was published in 1817; by 1841 it had run through twenty editions.

In 1818, Moore learnt that his deputy in Bermuda had embezzled £6,000, forcing him to live in Paris, from 1819 to 1822. His debt was relieved at £1,000 by the intervention of Lord Palmerston. In Venice Byron gave him the manuscript of his *Memoirs*. This Moore would burn in 1824 in a dispute over his projected life of Byron. He would publish the *Letters and Journals of Lord Byron, with Notices of his Life* (2 vols, 1830). In 1822 he returned to England, publishing *The Love of Angels* (1822), a poem on original sin. For his *Life and death of Lord Edward [Fitzgerald]* (2 vols, 1821) he interviewed the notorious Major Sirr, who had shot the United Irishman. *Memoirs of Captain Rock, the Celebrated Irish Chieftain* (1824), purportedly the manuscript autobiography of the Irish 'leader', edited by a protestant missionary, details the effects of English misrule in Ireland. His *Memoirs of the Life of the Right Honourable Richard Brinsley Sheridan* (1825) was condemned by George IV.

In 1832, Moore was asked to stand as the Repeal candidate for Limerick, but refused. His four-volume *History of Ireland* (1835–46), written for Lardner's *Cabinet Cyclopædia*, was lacking in coherent scholarship, and was not well received. In 1841 *The Poetical Works of Thomas Moore* appeared in ten volumes, collected by himself. The death of his four daughters and his son caused severe depression. Moore suffered and died from senile dementia.

Preface to The Poetical Works of Thomas Moore, Collected by Himself. In Ten Volumes

(1841)

To the zeal and industry of Mr. Bunting his country is indebted for the preservation of her old national airs. During the prevalence of the Penal code, the music of Ireland was made to share in the fate of its people. Both were alike shut out from the pale of civilised life; and seldom any where but in the huts of the proscribed race could the sweet voice of the songs of other days be heard. Even of that class, the itinerant harpers, among whom for a long period our ancient music had been kept alive, there remained but few to continue the precious tradition; and a great music-meeting held in Belfast in the year 1792, at which the two or three still remaining of the old race of wandering harpers assisted, exhibited the last public effort made by the lovers of Irish music to preserve to their country the only grace and ornament left to her, out of the wreck of all her liberties and hopes....

But for the zeal and intelligent research of Mr. Bunting, at that crisis, the greater part of our musical treasures would probably have been lost to the world. It was in the year 1796 that this gentleman published his first volume; and the national spirit and hope then wakened in Ireland, by the rapid spread of the democratic principle throughout Europe, could not but insure a most cordial reception for such a work....

It was in the year 1797 that, through the medium of Mr. Bunting's book, I was first made acquainted with the beauties of our native music [through a] young friend of our family, Edward Hudson... About the same period I formed an acquaintance, which soon grew into intimacy, with young Robert Emmet, I found him in full reputation, not only for his learning and eloquence, but also for the blamelessness of his life, and the grave suavity of his manners....There elapsed no very long time before I was myself the happy proprietor of a copy of the work and, though never regularly instructed in music, could play over the airs with tolerable facility on the pianoforte. Robert Emmet used sometimes to sit by me, when I was thus engaged; and I remember one day his starting up as from a reverie, when I had just finished playing that spirited tune called the Red Fox ['Let Erin Remember the Days of Old'] and exclaiming, 'Oh that I were at the head of twenty thousand men marching to that air!'... it was, I am ashamed to say, in dull and turgid prose, that I made my first appearance in print as champion of the popular cause. Towards the latter end of the year of 1797, the celebrated newspaper *The Press* was set up by Arthur O'Connor, Thomas Addis Emmet, and others, of the United Irish conspiracy, with the view to preparing and ripening the public mind for the great crisis then fast approaching....

To those unread in the painful history of this period, it is right to mention that almost all the leaders of the United Irish conspiracy were Protestants. Among those companions of my own alluded to in these pages, I scarcely remember one Catholic....

FROM *THE POETICAL WORKS*
(1812)

The Kiss

Illa nisi in leco nusquam potuere doceri
Ovid, lib. ii. eleg. 5.[1]

Give me, my love, that billing kiss
   I taught you one delicious night,
When, turning epicures in bliss,
   We tried inventions of delight.

Come, gently steal my lips along,
   And let your lips in murmurs move. –
Ah, no! – again – that kiss was wrong,–
   How can you be so dull, my love?

'Cease, cease!' the blushing girl replied –
   And in her milky arms she caught me –
'How can you thus your pupil chide;
   You know *'twas in the dark* you taught me!'

FROM *THE POETICAL WORKS*
(1840–41)

From Juvenile Poems

TO ....

When I loved you, I can't but allow
   I had many an exquisite minute;
But the scorn that I feel for you now
   Hath even more luxury in it.

---

1 Ovid, *Amores* II. v, 61: 'Such lessons could only have been taught in bed'.

Thus, whether we're on or we're off,
    Some witchery seems to await you;
To love you is pleasant enough
    And oh! 'tis delicious to hate you!

FROM *IRISH MELODIES*
(1808–1834)

Oh! Breathe Not His Name

Oh! breathe not his name,[1] let it sleep in the shade,
Where cold and unhonoured his relics are laid:
Sad, silent, and dark, be the tears that we shed,
As the night-dew that falls on the grass o'er his head.

But the night-dew that falls, though in silence it weeps,
Shall brighten with verdure the grave where he sleeps;
And the tear that we shed, though in secret it rolls,
Shall long keep his memory green in our souls.

When He, Who Adores Thee

When he, who adores thee, has left but the name
    Of his fault and his sorrows behind,
Oh say! wilt thou weep when they darken the fame
    Of a life that for thee was resign'd?
Yes, weep, and however my foes may condemn,
    Thy tears shall efface their decree;
For Heaven can witness, though guilty to them,
    I have been but too faithful to thee.

With thee were the dreams of my earliest love;
    Every thought of my reason was thine;
In my last humble prayer to the Spirit above
    Thy name shall be mingled with mine.
Oh! blest are the lovers and friends who shall live
    The days of thy glory to see;
But the next dearest blessing that Heaven can give
    Is the pride of thus dying for thee.

---

1 *breathe not his name*: Robert Emmet*, who in his speech from the dock implored, 'When my country takes her place among the nations of the earth, then, and not till then let my epitaph be written.'

The Harp That Once Through Tara's Halls

The harp that once through Tara's halls
    The soul of music shed,
Now hangs as mute on Tara's walls,
    As if that soul were fled. –
So sleeps the pride of former days,
    So glory's thrill is o'er,
And hearts, that once beat high for praise,
    Now feel that pulse no more.

No more to chiefs and ladies bright
    The harp of Tara swells;
The chord alone, that breaks at night,
    Its tale of ruin tells.
Thus Freedom now so seldom wakes,
    The only throb she gives,
Is when some heart indignant breaks,
    To show that she still lives.

The Meeting of the Waters[1]

There is not in the wide world a valley so sweet
As that vale in whose bosom the bright waters meet;[2]
Oh! the last rays of feeling and life must depart,
Ere the bloom of that valley shall fade from my heart.

Yet it *was* not that Nature had shed o'er the scene
Her purest of crystal and brightest of green;
'Twas *not* her soft magic of streamlet or hill,
Oh! no, – it was something more exquisite still.

'Twas that friends, the belov'd of my bosom, were near,
Who made every dear scene of enchantment more dear,
And who felt how the best charms of nature improve,
When we see them reflected from looks that we love.

---

1 'The Meeting of the Waters' forms a part of that beautiful scenery which lies between Rathdrum and Arklow, in the county of Wicklow, and these lines were suggested by a visit to this romantic spot, in the summer of the year 1807. [*Moore's note.*]
2 The rivers Avon and Avoca.

Sweet vale of Avoca! how calm could I rest
In thy bosom of shade, with the friends I love best,
Where the storms that we feel in this cold world should cease,
And our hearts, like the waters, be mingled in peace.

Let Erin Remember The Days Of Old

Let Erin remember the days of old,
    Ere her faithless sons betray'd her;
When Malachi wore the collar of gold[1],
    Which he won from her proud invader,
When her kings, with standards of green unfurl'd,
    Led the Red-Branch Knights to danger[2]; –
Ere the emerald gem of the western world
    Was set in the crown of a stranger.

On Lough Neagh's bank, as the fisherman strays,
    When the clear cold eve's declining,
He sees the round towers of other days
    In the wave beneath him shining;
Thus shall memory often, in dreams sublime,
    Catch a glimpse of the days that are over;
Thus, sighing, look through the waves of time
    For the long-faded glories they cover.[3]

---

1 'This brought on an encounter between Malachi (the Monarch of Ireland in the tenth century) and the Danes, in which Malachi defeated two of their champions, whom he encountered successively, hand to hand, taking a collar of gold from the neck of one, and carrying off the sword of the other, as trophies of his victory.'—Warner's *History of* Ireland, vol. i. book ix. [*Moore's note.*]

2 'Military orders of knights were very early established in Ireland: long before the birth of Christ we find an hereditary order of Chivalry in Ulster, called *Curaidhe na Craiobhe ruadh*, or the Knights of the Red Branch, from their chief seat in Emania, adjoining to the palace of the Ulster kings, called *Teagh na Craoibhe ruadh*, or the Academy of the Red Branch; and contiguous to which was a large hospital, founded for the sick knights and soldiers, called *Bronnbhearg*, or the House of the Sorrowful Soldier.'—O Halloran's Introduction, &c., part i. chap. 5. [*Moore's note.*]

3 It was an old tradition, in the time of Giraldus, that Lough Neagh had been originally a fountain, by whose sudden overflowing the country was inundated, and a whole region, like the Atlantis of Plato, overwhelmed. He says that the fishermen, in clear weather, used to point out to strangers the tall ecclesiastical towers under the water. *Piscatores aqua illius turres ecclesiasticas, quæ more patriæ arctæ sunt et altæ, necnon et rotundæ, sub undis manifeste sereno tempore conspiciunt, et extraneis transeuntibus, reique causus admirantibus, frequenter ostendunt.*—Topogr. Hib. dist. 2. c. 9. [*Moore's note.*]

The Song of Fionnuala[4]

Silent, oh Moyle, be the roar of thy water,
    Break not, ye breezes, your chain of repose,
While, murmuring mournfully, Lir's lonely daughter
    Tells to the night-star her tale of woes.
When shall the swan, her death-note singing,
    Sleep, with wings in darkness furl'd?
When will heaven, its sweet bell ringing,
    Call my spirit from this stormy world?

Sadly, oh Moyle, to thy winter-wave weeping,
    Fate bids me languish long ages away;
Yet still in her darkness doth Erin lie sleeping
    Still doth the pure light its dawning delay.
When will that day-star, mildly springing,
    Warm our isle with peace and love?
When will heaven, its sweet bell ringing,
    Call my spirit to the fields above?

Believe Me, If All Those Endearing Young Charms

Believe me, if all those endearing young charms,
    Which I gaze on so fondly to-day,
Were to change by to-morrow, and fleet in my arms,
    Like fairy-gifts fading away,
Thou wouldst still be ador'd, as this moment thou art,
    Let thy loveliness fade as it will,
And around the dear ruin each wish of my heart
    Would entwine itself verdantly still.

It is not while beauty and youth are thine own,
    And thy cheeks unprofan'd by a tear,
That the fervour and faith of a soul can be known,

---

1 To make this story intelligible in a song would require a much greater number of verses than any one is authorised to inflict upon an audience at once; the reader must therefore be content to learn, in a note, that Fionnuala, the daughter of Lir, was, by some supernatural power, transformed into a swan, and condemned to wander, for many hundred years, over certain lakes and rivers in Ireland, till the coming of Christianity, when the first sound of the mass-bell was to be the signal of her release. – I found this fanciful fiction among some manuscript translations from the Irish, which were begun under the direction of that enlightened friend of Ireland, the late Countess of Moira. [*Moore's note.*]

To which time will but make thee more dear;
No, the heart that had truly lov'd never forgets,
But as truly loves on to the close,
As the sun-flower turns on her god, when he sets,
The same look which she turn'd when he rose.

Before The Battle

By the hope within us springing,
    Herald of to-morrow's strife;
By that sun, whose light is bringing
    Chains or freedom, death or life –
Oh! Remember life can be
No charm for him, who lives not free!
    Like the day-star in the wave,
    Sinks the hero in his grave,
Midst the dew-fall of a nation's tears.

Happy is he o'er whose decline
The smiles of home may soothing shine,
And light him down the steep of years: –
    But oh, how blest they sink to rest,
    Who close their eyes on victory's breast!

O'er his watch-fire's fading embers
    Now the foeman's cheek turns white,
When his heart that field remembers,
    Where we tam'd his tyrant might.
Never let him bind again
A chain, like that we broke from then.
    Hark! the horn of combat calls –
    Ere the golden evening falls,
May we pledge that horn in triumph round![1]

Many a heart that now beats high,
In slumber cold at night shall lie,
Nor waken even at victory's sound: –
    But oh, how blest that hero's sleep,
    O'er whom a wond'ring world shall weep!

---

1 'The Irish Corna was not entirely devoted to martial purposes. In the heroic ages, our ancestors quaffed Meadh out of them, as the Danish hunters do their beverage at this day.' — *Walker.* [*Moore's note.*]

After The Battle

Night clos'd around the conqueror's way,
    And lightnings show'd the distant hill,
Where those who lost that dreadful day,
    Stood few and faint, but fearless still.
The soldier's hope, the patriot's zeal,
    For ever dimm'd, for ever crost –
Oh! who shall say what heroes feel,
    When all but life and honour's lost?

The last sad hour of freedom's dream,
    And valour's task, moved slowly by,
While mute they watch'd, till morning's beam,
    Should rise and give them light to die.
There's yet a world where souls are free,
    Where tyrant's taint not nature's bliss; –
If death that world's bright opening be,
    Oh! who would live a slave in this?

'Tis The Last Rose Of Summer

'Tis the last rose of summer
    Left blooming alone;
All her lovely companions
    Are faded and gone;
No flower of her kindred,
    No rosebud is nigh,
To reflect back her blushes,
    Or give sigh for sigh.

I'll not leave thee, thou lone one!
    To pine on the stem;
Since the lovely are sleeping,
    Go, sleep thou with them.
Thus kindly I scatter
    Thy leaves o'er the bed,
Where thy mates of the garden
    Lie scentless and dead.

So soon may *I* follow
    When friendships decay,

And from Love's shining circle
    The gems drop away.
When true hearts lie wither'd
    And fond ones are flown,
Oh! who would inhabit
    This bleak world alone?

The Young May Moon

The young May moon is beaming, love,
The glow-worm's lamp is gleaming, love,
        How sweet to rove
        Through Morna's grove[1]
When the drowsy world is dreaming, love!
Then awake! – the heavens look bright, my dear
'Tis never too late for delight, my dear,
        And the best of all ways
        To lengthen my days,
Is to steal a few hours from the night, my dear!

Now all the world is sleeping, love,
But the Sage, his star-watch keeping, love,
        And I, whose star,
        More glorious far,
Is the eye from that casement peeping, love.
Then awake! – till rise of sun, my dear,
The Sage's glass we'll shun, my dear,
        Or, in watching the flight
        Of bodies of light
He might happen to take thee for one, my dear.

The Minstrel-Boy

The Minstrel-Boy to the war is gone,
        In the ranks of death you'll find him;
His father's sword he has girded on,
        And his wild harp slung behind him. –
'Land of song!' said the warrior-bard,

---

1 'Steals silently to Morna's grove.' – See, in Mr. Bunting's collection, a poem translated from the Irish, by the late John Brown, one of my earliest college companions and friends, whose death was as singularly melancholy and unfortunate as his life had been amiable, honourable, and exemplary. [*Moore's note.*]

'Tho' all the world betrays thee,
  '*One* sword, at least, thy rights shall guard,
    '*One* faithful harp shall praise thee!'

The Minstrel fell! – but the foeman's chain
  Could not bring his proud soul under;
The harp he lov'd ne'er spoke again,
  For he tore its chords asunder;
And said, 'No chain shall sully thee,
  'Thou soul of love and bravery!
'Thy songs were made for the pure and free,
  They shall never sound in slavery.'

The Time I've Lost in Wooing

The time I've lost in wooing,
In watching and pursuing
  The light, that lies
  In woman's eyes,
Has been my heart's undoing.
Tho' Wisdom oft has sought me,
I scorn'd the lore she brought me,
  My only books
  Were woman's looks,
And folly's all they've taught me.

Her smile when Beauty granted,
I hung with gaze enchanted,
  Like him, the Sprite[1],
  Whom maids by night
Oft meet in glen that's haunted.
Like him, too, Beauty won me,
But while her eyes were on me,
  If once their ray
  Was turn'd away,
Oh! winds could not outrun me.

---

1 This alludes to a kind of Irish fairy, which is to be met with, they say, in the fields at dusk. As long as you keep your eyes upon him, he is fixed, and in your power; — but the moment you look away (and he is ingenious in furnishing some inducement) he vanishes. I had thought that this was the sprite which we call the Leprechaun; but a high authority upon such subjects, Lady Morgan, (in a note upon her national and interesting novel, *O'Donnel,*) has given a very different account of that goblin. [*Moore's note.*]

And are those follies going?
And is my proud heart growing
    Too cold or wise
    For brilliant eyes
Again to set it glowing?
No, vain, alas! th' endeavour
From bonds so sweet to sever;
    Poor Wisdom's chance
    Against a glance
Is now as weak as ever.

Dear Harp of My Country!

Dear Harp of my Country! in darkness I found thee,
    The cold chain of silence had hung o'er thee long[1],
When proudly, my own Island Harp, I unbound thee,
    And gave all thy chords to light, freedom, and song!
The warm lay of love and the light note of gladness
    Have waken'd thy fondest, thy liveliest thrill;
But, so oft has thou echo'd the deep sigh of sadness,
    That ev'n in thy mirth it will steal from thee still.

Dear Harp of my Country! farewell to thy numbers,
    This sweet wreath of song is the last we shall twine!
Go, sleep with the sunshine of Fame on thy slumbers,
    Till touch'd by some hand less unworthy than mine;
If the pulse of the patriot, soldier, or lover,
    Have throbb'd at our lay, 'tis thy glory alone;
I was *but* as the wind, passing heedlessly over,
    And all the wild sweetness I wak'd was thy own.

As Slow Our Ship

As slow our ship her foamy track
    Against the wind was cleaving,

---

1 In that rebellious but beautiful song, 'When Erin first rose,' there is, if I recollect right, the following line: –
    'The dark chain of Silence was thrown o'er the deep.'
The chain of Silence was a sort of practical figure of rhetoric among the ancient Irish. Walker tells us of 'A celebrated contention for precedence between Finn and Gaul, near Finn's palace at Almhain, where the attending Bards, anxious, if possible, to produce a cessation of hostilities, shook the chain of Silence, and flung themselves among the ranks.' See also the *Ode to Gaul, the Son of Morni,* in Miss Brooke's *Reliques of Irish Poetry.* [*Moore's note.*]

Her trembling pennant still look'd back
　　To that dear isle 'twas leaving.
So loath we part from all we love,
　　From all the links that bind us;
So turn our hearts, as on we rove,
　　To those we've left behind us.

When, round the bowl, of vanish'd years
　　We talk with joyous seeming, –
With smiles that might as well be tears,
　　So faint, so sad their beaming;
While mem'ry brings us back again
　　Each early tie that twined us,
Oh, sweet's the cup that circles then
　　To those we've left behind us.

And when, in other climes, we meet
　　Some isle, or vale enchanting,
Where all looks flow'ry, wild, and sweet,
　　And nought but love is wanting;
We think how great had been our bliss,
　　If Heav'n had but assigned us
To live and die in scenes like this,
　　With some we've left behind us!

As trav'llers oft look back at eve,
　　When eastward darkly going,
To gaze upon that light they leave
　　Still faint behind them glowing, –
So, when the close of pleasure's day
　　To gloom hath near consign'd us,
We turn to catch one fading ray
　　Of joy that's left behind us.

Remember Thee

Remember thee? yes, while there's life in this heart,
It shall never forget thee, all lorn as thou art;
More dear in thy sorrow, thy gloom, and thy showers,
Than the rest of the world in their sunniest hours.

Wert thou all that I wish thee, great, glorious, and free,
First flower of the earth, and first gem of the sea,
I might hail thee with prouder, with happier brow,
But oh! how could I love thee more deeply than now?

No, thy chains as they rankle, thy blood as it runs,
But make thee more painfully dear to thy sons –
Whose hearts, like the young of the desert-bird's nest,
Drink love in each life-drop that flows from thy breast.

FROM *NATIONAL AIRS*

(1818)

Oft, in the Stilly Night
(SCOTCH AIR.)

Oft, in the stilly night,
  Ere Slumber's chain has bound me,
Fond Memory brings the light
  Of other days around me;
    The smiles, the tears,
    Of boyhood's years,
  The words of love then spoken;
    The eyes that shone,
    Now dimm'd and gone,
  The cheerful hearts now broken!
Thus, in the stilly night,
  Ere Slumber's chain has bound me,
Sad Memory brings the light
  Of other days around me.

When I remember all
  The friends, so link'd together,
I've seen around me fall,
  Like leaves in wintry weather,
    I feel like one,
    Who treads alone
Some banquet-hall deserted,
    Whose lights are fled,
    Whose garlands dead,

And all but he departed!
Thus, in the stilly night
   Ere Slumber's chain has bound me,
Sad Memory brings the light
   Of other days around me.

FROM *BALLADS, SONGS, MISCELLANEOUS POEMS, ETC.*

Oh, Call It by Some Better Name

Oh, call it by some better name,
   For Friendship sounds too cold,
While Love is now a worldly flame,
   Whose shrine must be of gold;
And Passion, like the sun at noon,
   That burns o'er all he sees,
Awhile as warm, will set as soon –
   Then, call it none of these.

Imagine something purer far,
   More free from stain of clay
Than Friendship, Love, or Passion are,
   Yet human still as they:
And if thy lip, for love like this,
   No mortal word can frame,
Go, ask of angels what it is,
   And call it by that name!

FROM *MISCELLANEOUS POEMS*

To My Mother
WRITTEN IN A POCKET-BOOK, 1822

They tell us of an Indian tree,
   Which, howsoe'er the sun and sky
May tempt its boughs to wander free,
   And shoot, and blossom, wide and high,
Far better loves to bend its arms
   Downward again to that dear earth,
From which the life, that fills and warms
   Its graceful being, first had birth.

'Tis thus, though woo'd by flattering friends,
   And fed with fame (*if* fame it be),
This heart, my own dear mother, bends
   With love's true instinct back to thee!

FROM *ODES UPON CASH, CORN, CATHOLICS, AND OTHER MATTERS*

(1828)

Dialogue Between a Sovereign and a One-Pound Note
(1826)

['*O ego non felix, quam tu fugis, ut pavet acres
Agna lupos, capreæque leones*' – *Horace*[1]]

Said a Sov'reign to a Note,
   In the pocket of my coat,
Where they met in a neat purse of leather,
   'How happens it, I prithee,
   That though I'm wedded *with* thee,
Fair Pound, we can never live together?

   'Like your sex, fond of *change*,
   With silver you can range,
And of lots of young sixpences be mother;
   While with *me* – upon my word
   Not my Lady and my Lord
Of W——stm——th see so little of each other!'

The indignant Note replied
   (Lying crumpled by his side),
'Shame, shame, it is *yourself* that roam, Sir –
   One cannot look askance,
   But, whip! you're off to France,
Leaving nothing but old rags at home, Sir.

   Your scampering began
   From the moment Parson Van,

---

1 Horace, *Epode* 12, 25–26 (slightly misquoted):
'O woe is me, that you flee me as the lamb fears the wolves and the roe fears the lions'.

Poor man, made us *one* in Love's fetter;
  "For better or for worse"
  Is the usual marriage curse,
But ours is all "worse" and no "better."

  In vain are laws pass'd,
  There's nothing holds you fast
Tho' you know, sweet Sovereign, I adore you –
  At the smallest hint in life,
  Your forsake your lawful wife,
As *other* Sovereigns did before you.

  I flirt with Silver, true –
  But what can ladies do,
When disown'd by their natural protectors?
  And as to falsehood, stuff!
  I shall soon be *false* enough,
When I get among those wicked Bank Directors.'

  The Sovereign, smiling on her,
  Now swore, upon his honour,
To be henceforth domestic and loyal;
  But, within an hour or two,
  Why – I sold him to a Jew,
And he's now at No. 10, Palais Royal.

FROM *SATIRICAL AND HUMOROUS POEMS*

Paddy's Metamorphosis[1]
(1833)

About fifty years since, in the days of our daddies,
  That plan was commenced which the wise now applaud,
Of shipping off Ireland's most turbulent Paddies,
  As good raw materials for *settlers*, abroad.

Some West-Indian island, whose name I forget,
  Was the region then chos'n for this scheme so romantic;
And such the success the first colony met,

---

1 I have already, in a preceding page, referred to this squib, as being one of those wrung from me by the Irish Coercion Act of my friends, the Whigs. [*Moore's note.*]

That a second, soon after, set sail o'er th'Atlantic.

Behold them now safe at the long look'd-for shore,
 Sailing in between banks that the Shannon might greet,
And thinking of friends whom, but two years before,
 They had sorrow'd to lose, but would soon again meet.

And, hark! from the shore a glad welcome there came –
 'Arrah, Paddy from Cork, is it you, my sweet boy?'
While Pat stood astounded, to hear his own name
 Thus hail'd by black devils, who caper'd for joy!

Can it possibly be? – half amazement – half doubt,
 Pat listens again – rubs his eyes and looks steady;
Then heaves a deep sigh, and in horror yells out,
 'Good Lord! only think – black and curly already!'

Deceived by that well-mimick'd brogue in his ears,
 Pat read his own doom in these wool-headed figures,
And thought, what a climate, in less than two years,
 To turn a whole cargo of Pats into niggers!

MORAL.
'Tis thus, – but alas! – by a marvel more true
 Than is told in this rival of Ovid's best stories, –
Your Whigs, when in office a short year or two,
 By a *lusus naturæ*,[1] all turn into Tories,

And thus, when I hear them 'strong measures' advise,
 Ere the seats that they sit on have time to get steady,
I say, while I listen, with tears in my eyes,
 'Good Lord! only think, – black and curly already!'

CHARLES ROBERT MATURIN (1780–1824)

Maturin came from a French Huguenot family which had settled in Ireland, and taken orders in the Church of Ireland (his grandfather succeeded Swift* as Dean of St. Patrick's.). His father held an important post under government. Maturin was born in Dublin, and educated at Trinity College, Dublin, from which he graduated in 1800. He took orders in 1803, becoming curate at Loughrea, Co. Galway,

1 *lusus naturæ*: 'play of nature.'

which served as the setting for his novels, *The Wild Irish Boy* (1808) and *The Milesian Chief* (1812), written under the name of Dennis Jasper Murphy. In 1805 he became curate at St. Peter's Parish, Dublin, a post which he held for the rest of his life – a dutiful clergyman, he was denied preferment because of his eccentricities (summed up by John Anster's 'Maturin! Maturin! what an odd hat you're in!'). Maturin's stipend was modest; after his father lost his position in the General Post Office, his family had slender means, which were further compromised when a friend for whom Maturin had gone security went bankrupt, forcing him to write for money. He turned to Sir Walter Scott, who had written a favourable review of *The Fatal Revenge, or the Family of Montorio* (1807). Scott recommended the tragedy *Bertram* to Byron; the play was produced at Drury Lane in 1816, and was a financial success. His next two tragedies, *Manuel* (1817) and *Fredolfo* (1819) did not meet with similar popular approval, and Maturin returned to novel writing. The highly romantic *Women; or Pour et Contre* (1818) was the first novel to deal with an undergraduate's love affair. He followed it with his masterpiece, the Gothic, and manic *Melmoth the Wanderer* (1820). The eponymous fiend, a mixture of Faust and the Wandering Jew fascinated various European writers. Balzac wrote a sequel, *Melmoth reconcilié* (1835 – it in turn informed Mangan's story, 'The Man in the Cloak'), and Goethe tried his hand at a translation. Oscar Wilde took up the name 'Sebastian Melmoth' after his release from Reading Gaol. In the year of his death Maturin published *The Albigenses*, a Gothic history of the thirteenth century campaign of Simon de Monfort, and *Five Sermons of the Errors of the Roman Catholic Church*, in which he yet again vilifies monasticism. His death, it was said, was hastened by taking a wrong medicine.

FROM *WOMEN; OR, POUR ET CONTRE*

(1818)

[Charles De Courcy, the orphan heir to property in southern Ireland, rescues a girl called Eva Wentworth from her mad maternal grandmother, and becomes engaged to her. He meets Zaira Dalmatiani, a famous actress and singer, and is attracted to her genius. He proposes to her, but she suggests they first visit the Continent for a year, as companions. During their tour, he discovers that she has been married, and has a child. He abandons her in Paris. This chapter describes how Zaira then follows him to Dublin, and by chance finds her mother (Eva's grandmother).]

Chapter VIII.

– et Tyrios desertà quærere terrâ

VIRGIL[1]

Zaira arrived in Ireland; – what a different arrival from her first,

1 Virgil, *Aeneid* IV. 468, 'and seeking her [Dido's] Tyrians in a land forlorn'.

when, as De Courcy was accustomed to say, she made her *avatar* there! It was September when she landed; the fading light and short-ening days were now congenial to her feelings, and as she sat on the deck, and viewed the shore through the dim twilight of a hazy evening, that made every thing appear pale, cold, and colourless, she felt as if she was approaching the shores of the 'undiscovered coun-try' – 'the land of shadows,' where all things are forgotten.

She took a house at a little distance from Dublin, under an assumed name, saw no society, and never appeared in public. She was soon dis-covered, however, and the conductors of some charitable institution waited on her to intreat her to exert her talents at some concert or play that was to be performed for its benefit. This application appeared to give her great agony; – she was unable, for a considerable time, to return an answer. At length she said, – 'I would assist those unhappy persons with the sacrifice of half my fortune sooner than appear in public again.' The persons who conducted the charity, distressed by the effect of their application, retired. She sent a liberal donation, and immediately changed her residence, to escape similar persecutions. Her life was very monotonous, but calm. There was a dull weight on her senses and her faculties, an obtuse sense of pain never very excruciating, but never for a moment remitting. She said to herself perpetually, – 'It will soon be over, it will soon cease.' When we thus try to impose on ourselves, when we talk to ourselves as to another whom we try to pacify, the imposition is not more vain than it is melancholy. Still a sense of fatality, connected with her return to Ireland, operated at the bottom of her heart. She was like one of those in ancient times who is directed to visit an oracle, and who sits down before the doors of the temple till they unclose and there, overcome by grief and weariness, falls asleep. She could have said, with Lee's unfortunate hero,[1] to the prophet Tiresias –

> 'Therefore instruct us what remains *to do*,
> *Or suffer* – for I feel a sleep like death
> Upon me, and I long to be at rest.'

This state, which mentions *doing* and *suffering* in the same breath, and almost as the same thing, which expects no relief from fortitude, passive or active, is a fine image of a mind broken down by grief.

*   *   *

---

1 Presumably a reference to the *Oedipus* (1678) of John Dryden and Nathaniel Lee.

221

She walked incessantly during the day; she said it was to deaden the sense of inward pain; perhaps it was because she hoped somewhere to meet De Courcy. She did see him sometimes; she saw his figure at a distance; she trod with frantic fondness where his shadow had passed, but when she approached him, the beating of her heart amounted almost to suffocation. She shuddered, – she paused; and shocked at this public exposure of her weakness, she was compelled to grasp the rails of a house for support till he was out of sight. It was singular enough, that, during this period, she bore the loathsome, horrible spectacles of mendicity, misery, and vice, with which the streets of Dublin are almost putrid, with a kind of wretched patience almost approaching to satisfaction. The sight of physical suffering is at once a balance and consolation to the victim of internal pain. Misery is certainly very misanthropic in its simple operations.

The beautiful buildings of the city, its bay, its mountains – she never looked on them now; – she walked constantly through the streets – there was enough there to feed her mood. The perpetual spectacle of intoxication that occurred at every step, seemed to shock or terrify her no longer. Misery seeks misery every where, from the irresistible desire for comparison or analysis. When she saw these wretched objects raving or grovelling in the mire, she said, – 'Life is insupportable without some species of intoxication; I wish I could share the delirium of those wretches, without their brutalizing degradation. The lowest class of life seeks physical intoxication to forget its miseries; the higher seeks mental intoxication. The highest class of all tries the desperate intoxication of the heart, irrecoverable and incureable; whose delirium is "sweet madness," – whose waking is "despair".'

Zaira's knowledge or memory worked with terrible perverted industry in aid of the false theory of predominant misery. Spencer, she thought, tells of the miserable inhabitants of Ireland in the reign of Elizabeth, that they take snuff to 'beget fresh spirits.' The inhabitants of the Isles of the South-Sea produce this excitation by gliding along the surf in their light canoes; and some writers tell us of a more savage people, who try to attain it by standing on their heads till they arrive at stupefaction. How enviable! – Such were the miserable wanderings of a mind broke from its moorings, and driving before that storm which perhaps no human mind can ride out without 'tackle torn,' inglorious, dismasted, and disarrayed. When she saw the crowds of beggars that pollute and infest the streets of the 'beautiful city,' the same perverted feeling ministered fuel to the fire that was

consuming her. Mendicity, she thought with herself, is always the con-
comitant of a certain religion – it abounds to loathsomeness in countries professedly Catholic – it is diminished in England under the
influence of the established religion, and almost disappears under that
of Presbyterianism in Scotland. To what is this vast increase of
diminution of human misery, this fluctuation of the vast tide of
calamity, to be ascribed? – Merely to climate, to a cause in which man
has no share. The religion of the south of Europe is universally
Catholic, that of the north generally Protestant; this must be purely
physical. Well, then, the religion of men depends on their climate, and
on their religion depends a large portion of their external comforts,
of their human destiny, which is, doubtless, connected with their
future and immortal one; and all this is brought about by their being
natives of a certain climate. Had I been born in another country, had
other causes operated on my constitution and my feelings, what a different being might I have been!

Thus she strengthened herself in bad metaphysics, and worse sentiment. A singular contrast took place, (perceptibly to herself,)
between her sensibility of objects that give pleasure, and of objects
that give pain. She had formerly lived among every object that could
exalt the mind, and delight the senses; her heart favoured her creed
of optimism; her life was passed in a kind of refined and dignified
voluptuousness. Now she sought out the spectacle of wretchedness
every where with anxious and mischievous avidity. She left the fair
mountain to batten on the moor.

On her arrival in Dublin the preceding spring, she had been much
delighted by the picturesque situation and architectural beauty of the
city. Now, her sentiments were changed, and her senses appeared
changed along with them; undoubtedly the music of the soul is most
exquisite only when both are in harmony. A friend reminded her of
the admiration with which the beauty of the city impressed her a few
months before.

'Its beauty continues,' said Zaira, 'but it is the frightful lifeless
beauty of a corse; and the magnificent architecture of its public buildings seems like the skeleton of some gigantic frame, which the inhabiting spirit has deserted; like the vast structure of the bones of the
Behemoth, which has ceased to live for ages, and around whose
remains modern gazers fearfully creep and stare. We can bear the
ruins of a city long deserted by human inhabitants, but it is awful to
observe the inhabitants stealing from a city whose grandeur they can
no longer support. Thus the Dauphin (father of Louis XVI) saw with

his dying eyes the furniture thrown from the windows into the court of the castle where he lay, from the impatience of the attendants to quit it the moment he expired. I walk through the streets of this fine city – I pause at the gate of its superb university – I see a few sizars[1] and porters lounging there – I ask where are the 'illustrious men and ingenuous youths,' whom the *eloquent patriot* greeted in other times? – Its ingenuous youth are all gone to Oxford, or Cambridge, and the day might be marked with a cretic[2] note, when a gown with a gold, or even a silver tassel, is seen *a purpureus pannus*[3] amid the beggary of its deserted walls.

'Opposite to it I behold a building which would have embellished Athens in the purest days of its architectural pride – It was the Senate-house of Ireland – It is now *the Bank*; and along those steps, worthy of a temple of Minerva or of Jupiter, the inhabitants of this impoverished city, without trade and without wealth, are crawling to pay bills; and among those splendid passages which once echoed to the eloquence of a Flood, a Grattan, a Foster, and a Plunkett,[4] is heard the jargon of runners and tellers; and in that splendid apartment of the House of Peers still hung with the triumphs of William, the directors meet to ascertain dividends, and strike a bonus. I seek the residences of the nobility in this beautiful city; they are easily pointed out; their altered destination is enough to mark them. The palace of the Duke of Leinster (the only Duke in Ireland) belongs to the Dublin Academy;[5] the mansion of the Powerscourt family has become the station of the Stamp-office; the residence of Lord Glerawly has been levelled for the erection of a catholic chapel; that of the Cowper family has been purchased by the trustees of a charter-school; and the splendid modern house of Lord Aldborough (built within twenty years) is become the seat of the seminary of Professor Feinagle. Woe to the land where the mansions of her nobility have become the receptacles of office, or the palaces of pedagogues!'

Whether these observations are just or not, it is certain they did not occur to Zaira on her former arrival in Dublin. With the Old

---

1 *Sizars*: undergraduates of Trinity College, Dublin who received an allowance from the college.
2 *Cretic*: chalk-like (*obs.*)
3 *purpureus annus*: 'a purple patch', Horace, *Ars Poetica*, 14–15.
4 *a Flood, a Grattan, a Foster, and a Plunkett*: Henry Flood (1732–91), Henry Grattan (1746–1820), John Foster, Baron Oriel (1740–1828), William Conyngham, 1st Baron Plunket (1764–1854)), accomplished members of 'Grattan's Parliament'.
5 *the palace of the Duke of Leinster ... Dublin Academy*: Kildare House (now known as Leinster House, the seat of Dail Eireann, the Irish parliament) was sold in 1815 to the Dublin Society, and subsequently became the home of the National Gallery.

Marquis in Gil Blas,[1] perhaps, she was beginning to suspect that even the peaches of the latter time were degenerating. It is very terrible when grief, by destroying our sensibility, both of nature and art, deprives us of those auxiliaries against its power of which it has reduced us to the utmost need. It is like sending one to carry on war in a country which the enemy has already wasted with fire and sword before us.

One day she wandered to a very obscure part, called Swift's-alley; there is a dissenting meeting-house there.[2] The sight of it awoke many recollections in her mind; – her heart grew full, and she paused in the vain hope of being relieved by tears. An old woman who observed her, offered her a seat in her humble dwelling; she was involuntarily interested by that beautiful figure which could interest every heart but De Courcy's. She believed her ill. The poor, who know little but of physical sufferings, are apt to ascribe all signs of emotion to the one cause, they seldom suspect one of grief. Zaira accepted the offer; and with the remains of her former sweetness, made some inquiries about her hostess. She was a very old woman, nearly eighty years old, upwards of sixty of which had been passed in her present abode, a small building close to the meeting-house; she had a small pittance for keeping the keys of it, and seeing that it was cleansed and aired on the day of public worship. She had outlived her immediate relations, and perhaps forgotten her remote descendants; no one ever came to see her, nor did she perhaps wish for it, and her infirmities prevented her from going abroad. Her room contained a chair, a bed, a table, Bunyan's Holy War,[3] and a Bible. The latter she could no longer read, so that her habitation seemed as sterile as her existence. This hermitage, in a populous city, certainly presents a singular image. There have been persons who became enamoured of solitude, because it was embellished by the exquisite attractions of nature; this, one may say, is a sensuality so refined as almost to approach intellectual pleasure. It is a glorified body, whose sensibilities are no longer physical or impure. But there was nothing of this kind here; before, around, and above the dwelling of this woman, rose high and heavy walls of the darkest stone. The sun could so seldom shine on the narrow pave-

---

1 *Histoire de Gil Blas de Santiliane*: novel by Alain-René Lesage (1668–1747); in Chapter VII the old Count of Asamur remarks that in his time the peaches were much larger than they are now.

2 *A dissenting meeting-house*: the only Baptist chapel in Dublin was built in Swift's-alley in 1730.

3 John Bunyan, *The Holy War. Made by Shaddai upon Diabolus for the Regaining of the Metropolis of the World, or, The Losing and Taking Again of the Town of Mansoul* (1682).

ment before her door, that there was no verdure forcing its way between the stones – a few withered squalid blades of grass only, that seemed as if they had mistaken the place for a tombstone, there they grew like the forbidden enjoyments of life, struggling for their abode in a heart devoted to religion. The building itself, the only object she saw throughout the day, had the rigidity of Calvinism in every feature of it; it stood there like the substantial image of an abstract religion, without grace or embellishment, imparting its own sternness to the heart and the manners.

Zaira thought of the decorative splendour of the churches on the continent; and she remembered the rebuke of Jesus to the Pharisee, – 'Mine head with oil thou did'st not anoint; thou gavest me no water,'[1] &c. Would it not have been better if she had reflected, – 'He dwelleth not in temples made by hands.'[2] ——

'Gorgeous – yet love I not this pomp of prayer,'[3]

says one of our first poets.[3] Certainly in churches, architectural magnificence and luxurious embellishment are rather a sacrifice to the pride of man than to the glory of God, and the worshipper seems to come there rather to boast of what he has done for the Deity, than to shew what the Deity has done for him.

Zaira was withdrawn from her musings by the talking (for it could not be called conversation) of the old woman. 'She had remembered better days,' she said. – 'the days of famous preachers, long dead, when the meeting-house was so crowded, that there was not room for half that came to hear the Word of Life; when there was a talk about forty years ago of *enlarging* it,' (and as she spoke she stretched out her withered arms, as if the idea was too vast for her mind, unless she relieved it by a corresponding gesture.) – 'Now,' she said, 'things are very different.' And to hear her, one would imagine that the salvation of all mankind were dependent on the fullness of the congregation at an obscure meeting-house in Dublin. In her mind, a member of that meeting, and a Christian, were evidently synonimous terms, and inseparable ideas. Zaira enquired a little further, and learned, that at the time when the meeting was so much crowded, her fees had been very considerable. 'But people have all left off going the right way,'

---

1 *Mine head with oil ... '*: an Amalgamation of Luke 7: 46 & :44
2 *He dwelleth not in temples made by hands'*: Acts 17: 24.
3 *Gorgeous – yet love I not this pomp of prayer*: George Croly, 'Paris in 1815' XLI. I (for 'Gorgeous', read 'Pompous').

said the old woman. This was a wretched discovery; it is horrid to find littleness of soul in the dying, or in those who make religious pretensions, whom we nearly identify with the former. They both belong, in our minds, to another world.

This woman revived in Zaira's memory the idea of the old nun in the convent near Paris. There was the same sterility, vacancy, and uniformity in their characters. A person unacquainted with religious distinctions, would scarce have known one from the other; yet, in one respect, they were antipodes to each other – Catholicism and Calvinism placed an immeasurable distance between them. Had either heard of the other, she would have considered her as a being devoted to the devil and his angels, placed under the concentrated and immitigable wrath of the Almighty for ever and ever. Singular mixture of inanity and ferocity in the same mind!

Zaira then recollected a door-keeper at one of the foreign theatres; he was so old that he was called the patriarch, and highly amusing from the importance he attached to his situation. To hear him 'magnify his office,' one would think him an apostle, and that the duties of the drama were quite on a level with the duties of religion. He remembered the times of Senesino, Farinelli, Faustina, Cuzzoni, &c.;[1] and it was singular enough, that, in speaking of them, and of the crowded houses assembled to hear them, he used exactly the same language that the humble portress of Swift's Alley Meeting-house did, when recalling the departed glories of former days. Their sentences were constructed and expressed exactly in the same style of deliberate enthusiasm. The interests of the stage and the preaching of the gospel made the only difference between them.

This coincidence, that might have suggested, to a mind more happily disposed, a useful speculation, operated very differently on Zaira's. She compared the different characters and situations, and she said to herself, ' there is no difference, but that of habit.' When she once entered on this subject, she sunk deeper and deeper, plunging amid, billows that came

'Booming and buzzing o'er her sinking head.'[2]

She imagined there must be rest at the bottom – it was the rest of a

---

1 *Senesino, Farinelli, Faustina, Cuzzoni*: Italian singers who all performed in Handel's operas in London.
2 Cf. Sir James Bland, (1752–1824), 'The Exodiad' (1807–1808), 32–3: 'The eddying waves / Boom o'er his sinking head'.

sunk wreck, over which a thousand storms have passed, and the ocean pours its waves in fathomless silence. She thought, and was worse for every thought that passed through her mind. There is an atrophy of the soul, as well as of the body, and the mind when diseased can convert the most wholesome nutriment into actual poison.

That evening while pursuing her usual restless walk, (more like the wanderings of an 'unlaid spirit,' than the activity of a human being), she felt more misery than usual. She gave alms to the miserable objects that obstructed her path in every direction; she felt for the first time that the action was quite mechanical, she had no pleasure from it now. This sensation increased her wretchedness greatly ; she began to feel that she was losing the only feeling that made life supportable. How little she knew of the state of her heart at that moment! It is said in Ulloa's Voyages,[1] that, in the severest climate of North America, the spirits were frozen through the bottle – they were all ice; but the spirit retreating to the centre, formed a column of actual fire, that burned the lips that tasted them. Zaira's heart was frozen thus; the external surface was hard and cold, but the centre contained one burning drop. De Courcy's image glowed there still more strongly from the intensity of the surrounding and encroaching cold.

She was now near Island-bridge, when a heavy shower drove her (rather from consideration for her servant than herself) to seek for shelter. She went into a small shop, where was a great appearance of neatness and industry. The frequent calls of customers, and the pleased assiduity of the shopkeeper, gave token that things were going on prosperously. In a back room his wife was instructing her children; and the eager, happy voice of childhood, proud of newly-acquired intelligence, sounded delightfully in the ear. It gave no pleasure to *her* – she trembled at the sight of happiness – she felt as Adam did, perhaps, when, on the evening of his expulsion from Paradise, he might have wandered near its beloved limits, and drank the fragrance of its forbidden sweets, wafted to him by airs he must never breathe again; then looking up, saw the naming sword of exclusion turning every way against him.

In a few moments, the officious, but not servile attentions of the man forced themselves on her notice. She did not recognize him, till at last, unable to struggle any longer with the fullness of his heart, he told her he was the person whom she had assisted with such generosity before she quitted Ireland; that her liberality had enabled him to

---

1 *Ulloa's Voyages*: Antonio de Ulloa, *A Voyage to South America* (1772 [1748]).

recommence business, in which he was succeeding so well, that, as he said with Irish enthusiasm, 'he believed there was a blessing on all she did.'

At these words, which went too near her heart, she fixed her eyes on him with a look of such ghastly incredulity, that the man paused, fearful he had offended, though not understanding how. She was silent; and he resumed the subject in a lower voice. He hoped that the young gentleman, who was the means of introducing him and his distress to her notice, was well and happy. This was too much. Zaira struggled in vain to answer him. The man then found out that something (he knew not what) was wrong, and became silent, 'though it was pain and grief to him.'

Zaira rose to depart, and then he could contain [himself] no longer; he followed her to the door with blessings and thanks, and continued them till she was out of sight. These blessings, these prayers for our happiness and long life, are terrible to those who feel life a curse, and happiness an impossibility. Language, black with execration and horror, would be less painful to them. She hurried on to escape the insult of gratitude, and she felt as if she was doomed to go on, like Ladurlad, with 'a fire in her heart and a fire in her brain,'[1] condemned to do good without a share in it herself – blessing, but unblessed.

Again compelled to stop by the violence of the weather, an autumnal storm of wind and rain, she took shelter in a cabin, and directed her servant to go forward, and send the carriage for her, that she might 'return home.' Home! – what a word for the unhappy to use – a place where they meet nothing but that desolate heart which they brought out with them. In a few minutes her attention was drawn to an obscure corner of the cabin by groans that issued from it at long intervals. It was so dark, that it was long before she discovered there what had been a bed, on which was stretched something squalid, hagard, spent, and moaning.

'It is a poor creature,' said the woman who owned the cabin, 'that came in here for a night's lodging – bytimes I think she is only *half and half*, and she is not *expected* now, any how.'

Zaira approached the bed; and to her inexpressible horror recognized in the sunk, but wild features, the feeble, but singularly-modulated voice of the dying object, those of the madwoman whom she had thrice before encountered under circumstances so extraordinary.

---

1 Robert Southey, *The Curse of Kehama* (1810) I. 163–6: 'Thou shalt live in thy pain / While Kehama shall reign, / With a fire in thy heart, / And a fire in thy brain'.

The woman appeared to recognize her too; she raised her hollow and livid looks to Zaira.

'Oh, my eyes are dim!' said she, 'but I know you well – and are you come at last – come to hear the secret none knows but me – come to close the eyes of your —— '

And she stretched out her withered arms to Zaira. Zaira recoiled with an impulse she could not account for; she had never before thus shrunk from wretchedness and death. She was even hastening from the cabin, when the maniac, sitting up in her bed, called out to the woman to detain her.

'Stop her!' she cried, in a voice hollow but piercing; 'bid her stop, if she would shun the curse of—— '

'*Of* whom?' cried Zaira.

'*Of her mother!*' said the maniac, sinking back on her bed, and extending her clasped hands towards Zaira.

The latter approached the bed, trembling and subdued; her former recollections suggested the terrible possibility that this intelligence was true.

' Tell me,' said the old woman, 'are you not Irish by birth? Are you not the daughter of——of——, in the county of Fermanagh? And tell me the truth, for I am passing fast.'

'I am,' said Zaira.

'Then I am your mother – though when I saw you before I had not the power to tell you so.'

'My mother! – and in this hovel, and in these rags – Oh, merciful Heaven!'

'Ay, Heaven is merciful, or I would not be spared to tell you even this.'

'Oh, let me remove you from this wretched place.'

'Hush!' said her mother, raising her withered hand; 'what matters it to a soul going to judgment, whether it parts from straw or from down? – Listen to me. You had a child?'

'I had.'

'Well, that child is still alive, and I can tell you where.'

'Oh, speak, for God's sake, speak!'

'Not a word – not another word tonight, if the world was kneeling there. To-night *I must make my soul*,[1] and that's enough for a parting sinner to have to do.'

---

1 *i.e* Perform my religious duties. [*Maturin's note.*] In Ireland the phrase is sometimes used by people to describe their preparation for death.

No supplication, no adjuration of Zaira's agony was powerful enough to extort another syllable from her mother, beyond the bare permission to see her the next evening, if she lived.

'Oh, you will, you must live!' said Zaira, as she quitted the hovel, in emotion unutterable.

To explain this interview, it will be necessary to lay before the reader, the letter which it was mentioned Zaira wrote to Madame St Maur, on her *first* arrival in Ireland, and which contained the particulars of her former life. After stating the agitation with which she revisited Ireland, the emotion with which she beheld the sea that bore her, and listened to the breeze that wafted her there; she adds, 'it is the privilege of poetry and of grief alike to invest inanimate things with consciousness. Joy, full of itself, needs no sympathy from external things. To the happy every day is bright. But grief, like superstition, makes even the physical creation populous, and converts every object into an agent of consolation or of reproach.

'When in the morning we came within sight of the bay, – when I got on deck, and saw the blue mountains of my country bright on the left, and the bay, with its sweeping shores, and the city shrouded in the western mist, marking the horizon with its thin grey line, that trembled on the vapoury skirts of the morning, – when I felt what none but those who had left it long, and who perhaps return to find suffering not respited, but renewed, can feel, I clasped my hands on my heart; I almost thought its beatings would betray me. – I tried to utter some prayers, but I felt that my lips moved without articulating. The ocean lay as calm around me as if it had never borne the weight of suffering on its waves. The joy of the passengers, the short technical answers of the sailors, and the still colder language of the captain, who answered every question as if the progress of the elements had never affected human happiness or suffering, made a strange contrast to all I felt. Strange indifference, that is produced by a constant intercourse with the most awful phenomena! Thus, the more physical our existence is, the more tranquillity it enjoys; it is intellect alone that is always agitated, and almost always by pain. Singular awardment, whether it be the result of inconsistency or of deliberation – whether it proceed from an intelligent or an unintelligent cause! But from whatever source insensibility arises, how enviable does it seem to those who suffer? Thus, those who witness the Falls of Niagara are stunned by a crash that seems capable of uprooting nature; while those who dwell near it, deafened by the habitual roar, soon lose all impression; and here alone, dear Delphine, have I courage to relate the events of my former life to you. We have the same dread to retrace misfortune that we have to expose a wound; but we have more reason, for it is the wounds of the mind alone that are exempt from ever closing.

'Even here, I hesitate to begin to tell what I have been. Misfortune always seems to females like disgrace. I am, what none of my continental friends but you know, a native of Ireland. – I am the illegitimate daughter of a man of fortune in the west of Ireland, whose least error, perhaps, was his being the parent of a number of unfortunate nameless beings, none of whom he acknowledged or noticed but me. The singular beauty of my mother, I have heard, entitled me to this distinction. She possessed more influence over him than any other of his temporary favourites, and might have retained it but for a singular circumstance. Though she had sacrificed all that is valuable in the female character, she cherished a strong devotion for the catholic religion, perhaps with a view of palliating her other errors, and was so outraged by my father's avowed profession of the most daring infidelity, that even when I was an infant she declared she would rather see me perish than brought up under the roof of a monster, who defied both heaven and hell. After several attempts to take me from my father, whose fondness to me probably grew from opposition, she was detected in one, and after a dreadful altercation, she was driven from the house, with an injunction never again to be seen in the neighbourhood. I have heard, that as the servants forced her out, she broke from them, and, kneeling in the hall poured on my father and me a curse, the most solemn, bitter, and wild that ever passed the lips of a human being. On one of us, at least, it was fulfilled. Perhaps no curse could be more effectually accomplished than by my being left with the parent I was. He was a man of intellectual powers superior to most I have known, a 'scholar, and a ripe one;'[1] but he pressed every power he possessed into the service of obdurate scepticism. He called himself a philosophical unbeliever, but he did not disdain to borrow the aid of sophistry, invective, sneer, cavil; – all the light as well as heavy armed troops were at his service, and he had a full command of them all. His rage for converts was beyond that of the Pharisees; his scepticism had made him miserable, and, perhaps, he thought to communicate misery was to lessen it; his genius and eloquence in the evil cause were indeed enough to draw after him the third part of the host.

---

1 Cardinal Wolsey, in Shakespeare's *King Henry VIII* is described by Griffith as 'a scholar, and a ripe and good one' (IV. ii. 58).

'My education, which, next to the dissemination of infidelity, was his principal object, was beyond what most women receive. I had teachers of every language, masters in every art, instructors in every science, and my father illustrating, condensing, and harmonizing every thing into one vast mass of intellectual discipline. I was taught to know every thing but the one thing needful; I was permitted to read every thing but the Bible. My father was not the fool who saith in his heart, 'There is no God;' but he had so many objections against his power, goodness, or wisdom, drawn either from the physical constitution of things, or from the state of man, and his knowledge was so various, his reasoning powers so strong, and his resources so exhaustless, that those who encountered him were soon unequal to the task, and, weary of defending the attributes of the Deity against endless objections, were contented to compromise for His existence, which was generally allowed them; this, at least, was my case when I was permitted to reason with him. His wish to make me a prodigy in literature and the arts was rapidly fulfilling, as far as it could be fulfilled by a girl not fourteen. Singular and perversed ambition! In depriving me of heaven, he wished to multiply my ties to earth; and while he took away my birth-right, aggravated its value by the price he seemed anxious to give for it, as if one world could ever be a balance for the other. One dark cloud hung over me from the earliest period – one image haunted me from the commencement of my life, – it was that of my mother, whom the frightful tales of the servants still described as wandering about the house at night in stormy weather, and repeating her maledictions in a voice 'not of this world.' Her disappearance, my total ignorance of her situation, or whether she was yet alive, and that terrible sensation so common in the imaginations of the Irish, of a being whom we believe not to be alive, yet know not to be dead – who holds a kind of hovering intermediate existence between both worlds, and combines the passions of human existence with the power of a spirit, all produced in me a species of indefinite feeling towards this awful being, that neither reason or change of situation has ever been able to remove.

'The mythology of all countries has admitted and favoured the existence of such, from Thomas of Ercildoun[1] to Wordsworth's Lucy Gray.[2] Perhaps the cause of such wild imagery exists in the very nature of the human mind, and its unknown relation to futurity. We have

---

1 Thomas de Ercildoun (Thomas the Rhymer) was a thirteenth-century scholar, poet and prophet.
2 'Lucy Gray, Or Solitude', a ballad by William Wordsworth (1770–1850).

never trod the confines of human existence with feet that felt the landmark; of the boundaries of the future world we know still less; and we are therefore compelled to admit the existence of beings, whose state, partaking of both, can at least be arrayed in the images borrowed from one, while the rest of its shadowy existence fades away in the impermeable gloom of the other. Perhaps the loathsome superstition of the vampire, and our representation of Death by his physical form, both have this origin. Those who said they saw my unhappy mother, described her as wandering near the house in the stormy twilight of a winter's evening. – She was meagre, ragged, and bloody, and they gave dark hints of my father's passions.

Sometimes I have heard strange sounds under my window at night Do not wonder at this superstition of infidelity; – the widest extremes have been found to meet at last, as the Spaniards, in sailing round the globe, first expressed their wonder when, after long pursuing what they thought a direct course, it brought them to the point from which they had set out. The vacillations of the human mind are incessant, and the strongest impulse, given in a direction contrary to our natural one, only makes us return again with augmented velocity. The human mind may be said naturally to gravitate towards religion. But I was allowed no choice.

'Among the talents which my father was most anxious to cultivate, and which nature developed earliest in me, were my extraordinary vocal powers and musical enthusiasm, which have been the cause of so much suffering, and so much celebrity to me. My father, liberal in every thing, was extravagant in the cultivation of this darling art, that may well be called 'the Poetry of the Sciences.' The first teachers were engaged, at an enormous expense, to attend at his remote residence; and among them was a young Italian, who had made a conspicuous *debut* on the foreign stages, but whose voice, failing from disproportionate exertion, compelled him to adopt the profession of a teacher. Many things recommended him to my father; his musical skill was profound: even Frederic of Prussia would have found him no less invincible than he did Mara.[1] His *camera voce* was still delightful, though he could no longer fill theatres. He was well acquainted with the literature of his own country; and, above all, he was an atheist, vehement and declamatory; though, by a singular, but not inexplicable contrast, he always carried about him a portrait of the Virgin, and

---

1 *Mara*: Gertrud Elisabeth Mara (1749–1833), the daughter of a poor musician. She became the greatest German soprano and was a favourite of the music-loving Prussian Court.

always crossed himself when he heard a peal of thunder; – dreadful preceptor for a girl of fourteen to be consigned to, intoxicated with his delightful art, and incapable of being alarmed by his principles.

My father (oh, what a father!) left me for hours alone with this man, to listen to his brilliant and seductive picture of Italy, a land of palaces and flowers, a. land where the luxuries of art were combined with classic memorials; and the relaxation of manners was alike favourable to the indolence of literary enjoyment, and the silent felicities of the heart.

'Let me hurry over this miserable period of my existence. We were married by a catholic priest, but our marriage was kept secret from my father; for though he professed himself master of a splendid patrimony in his native country, he still seemed fearful of my father's displeasure. After some time it was necessary to disclose it: I was about to become linked to society by more than one tie. Oh! that dreadful disclosure! – Fioretti quitted the house, and left me to make it alone. The undivided, unmitigated storm of my father's fury burst on me, and stunned me. He cursed me, he spurned me; and I have heard would have killed me, but for the interposition of the terrified but merciful female servants, whom, however, he forced to bear me, still insensible, from his house, and from his sight for ever!

'In his rage of malediction, he cursed me as a monster destitute of principle; yet he had taught me none; and had torn me when an infant from my knees, when he saw a domestic attempting to teach me to form a prayer. He cursed me for a wretch and fool, ignorant of the duties of life; yet he had taught me, and his example justified his instructions, that to obey our passions was the only rule of human life. He cursed my disobedience as a child; yet he had taught me, that the only tie between parent and child was a temporary convention formed by mutual interest, and dissoluble when that interest ceased to exist.

'An old woman, in compassion, sheltered me in her wretched hovel (but I was insensible of its wretchedness) till my husband was apprized of my having now no other abode. He came; and still I wonder how even youth and obstinate health sustained my existence after that interview, which fully developed his motives and his character. After wasting hours in imprecations on me, whose bitterness was aggravated by the foreign language that used to be the vehicle of such different sentiments, till within the few last miserable hours, he left me, telling me, with a laugh more frightful than a curse, to be ready to accompany him in a few hours to the continent.

'I had no preparation to make. We set out on our melancholy journey to Dublin. He was silent the whole time, and this was like a relief to me; for early wretchedness is jealous of imaginary consolation, while confirmed misery rejects even real. I tried to reason myself into excuses for his disappointment, for his temper, for the vehemence of his national character; I tried to hope that my submission, my helplessness, and perhaps the exertion of the talent that he had cultivated and admired, might at some future time procure me his compassion, if not his affection. I had ceased to love him, but it is hard to disbelieve the only source of protection that humanity affords us. I even hoped that his child – his child! – Ah, Heaven! how much less would I have suffered, had I been its grave before I was its parent!

'We arrived in Dublin; and he was expediting our departure, when I felt that to depart immediately was impossible; with difficulty I was allowed an attendant. My sufferings were very great; they gave me a great quantity of laudanum; I know not whether it is usual at such times, still less do I know what might have been its effect. I was insensible for many hours.

*   *   *

'I asked for my child; it was hours before I could obtain an answer; the women about me wept. At length my husband, the father of my child, told me, I never should see it more. 'Do you not think,' said he, talking himself by passion into a justification of his unnatural crime, 'that the incumbrance of a wife is sufficient? Must I have a screaming brat to remind me of my wretchedness every where ? – You will never see it more – you must prepare yourself for another destiny.'

'I was insensible of all that he said afterwards. He had torn my child from me – a child from a mother of fifteen, dying to clasp to her heart a being almost like herself in helplessness and weakness. I would have forgiven him every thing – I would have worshipped him – I am unable to go on.

'A dismal light, like twilight, seemed to surround me for months – forms hovered around me, but I could not distinguish them – voices spoke to me, but I knew not what they meant – thoughts, too, were with me, of which I hardly comprehended the depth or the darkness, but they suited my desperation – despair unenlightened by religion, unsustained by hope – they haunt me still – they have been with me in solitude and in crowds – you have witnessed them, and started at their effect, when even I believed I had forgotten them – forget them – yes, I might, I would – but they never forget me.

236

'No one heeded me, no one comforted me; and perhaps to this I owe my life and reason – the torturing of officious consolation would have irritated me to madness – I never had a gleam of recollection till the bright sun of Italy glared on me like unwelcome light on a feverish sleeper, waking him to pain. I was not allowed a long respite – I wondered, knowing my husband's hatred, that he had not killed me, (*it is easy to crush a flower in the bud*, – it would have been so easy, for I could have made no resistance, and would have expressed no reluctance. I did not know *then* how much *his interest was connected with my existence*.

'We were now in Italy. He watched me, not with the interest of affection, not with the feeling of humanity, not even with the naked instinct of compassion, but with the hungry cupidity of avarice. He seized almost the first moment of my recovered reason to inform me, that his only object in bringing me there was to compel me to exhibit my musical talents publicly, or, in plainer language, to go on the stage.

*   *   *

'At times I feel it impossible to proceed – Such degradation, such misery! I have before said, a woman always feels a tale of shame like a tale of guilt.

*   *   *

'The first night of my public appearance seems to me like a dream – I went on the stage in a state of absolute stupefaction – the lights, the crowd, my terrors, my former sufferings, the appalling novelty of my situation, bewildered me. I moved in a kind of dazzling mist – the exertion of my powers was quite involuntary, and the enthusiastic applauses with which they were received, I returned with bursts of hysterical laughter. Habit, that never could reconcile me to my situation, reconciled me at last to its circumstances. Fioretti's avarice (the only passion he had) strongly excited by my success, prompted him to every measure that could ensure its lustre or its permanency. The study of my profession, both as a singer and actress, by occupying my time, began at length to occupy my mind. He easily discovered that my intelligence of the graces of the poetry I recited gave me an obvious advantage over his illiterate country-women. I was furnished with a library; the love of literature revived in my heart; that heart had no other object to love. My mornings were passed in study and seclusion, and in the evenings Fioretti attended me to the theatre, and prevented, by his constant presence, the expression of that admiration which I was said to have excited. Thus, in the midst of the dissipated cities of the continent, I lived a life of almost vestal retirement. The monotonous simplicity of this mode of existence was singularly contrasted with the brilliant applauses that attended my public exertions. I have often felt when I heard them as if they were not addressed to me.

'Fioretti died; and though I could not feel unhappy, I felt desolate at his loss. It was then, that, for the first time, a hope trembled through my heart, that seemed to add a new pulse to its beatings, – a hope of communication with my father, perhaps with my child. Days after days have I passed writing on my knees, and bathed in tears letters that I hoped might touch his heart, and tearing them because no language could supply me with words, submissive, piercing, and supplicating enough. I humbled myself even to the dust before him, and implored him to allow me to prostrate myself at his feet, if it were only to be spurned. Years passed on in these fruitless struggles; and, in the mean time, my public exertions were unremitting, for I felt I was acquiring a fortune and reputation that might one day be my child's. Oh, that child! – How have I sat hour after hour, trying to imagine its features, its growth, the tones of its voice, till my reason was almost lost from the intoxicating indulgence.

'This year I received a letter for the first time from my father; it told me that my child still lived, and that though he could not yet prevail on himself to forgive me, he would consent to see me before his death, and inform me of the name and situation of my child. He permitted me to come to Ireland, on condition of my appearing still as a public character, concealing my birth and connexions, and never intruding into his presence till summoned by himself. I came – all conditions were easy to me – my child was still alive – I lingered for a month in a breathless hope of momentary intelligence; it came *last night*; my father died suddenly, without disclosing the name – the – I cannot go on. What have I now to do in this country? What have I to do in life ? Even you, Delphine, cannot feel for me; you have never been a mother.'

*　　*　　*

It was after the receipt of the letter alluded to, that Zaira had fainted on one of her earlier nights of meeting with De Courcy.

Charles Robert Maturin

From *Melmoth the Wanderer*

(1820)

Chapter I.

Alive again? Then show me where he is;
I'll give a thousand pounds to look upon him.

SHAKESPEARE[1]

In the autumn of 1816, John Melmoth, a student in Trinity College, Dublin, quitted it to attend a dying uncle on whom his hopes for independence chiefly rested....

The beauty of the country through which he travelled (it was the county Wicklow) could not prevent his mind from dwelling on many painful thoughts, some borrowed from the past, and more from the future. His uncle's caprice and moroseness, – the strange reports concerning the cause of the secluded life he had led for many years, – his own dependent state, – fell like blows fast and heavy on his mind....

...The men, with the national deference of the Irish to a person of superior rank, all rose at his approach, (their stools chattering on the broken flags), and wished his honor 'a thousand years, and long life to the back of that; and would not his honor take something to keep the grief out of his heart;' and so saying, five or six red and bony hands tendered him glasses of whiskey all at once. All this time the Sibyl sat silent in the ample chimney-corner, sending redoubled whiffs out of her pipe. John gently declined the offer of spirits, received the attentions of the old housekeeper cordially, looked askance at the withered crone who occupied the chimney corner, and then glanced at the table, which displayed other cheer than he had been accustomed to see in his 'honor's time.' There was a wooden dish of potatoes, which Old Melmoth would have considered enough for a week's subsistence. There was the salted salmon, (a luxury unknown even in London. *Vide* Miss Edgeworth's Tales, 'The Absentee').

There was the *slink-veal*,[2] flanked with tripe; and, finally, there were lobsters and *fried* turbot enough to justify what the author of the tale asserts, 'suo periculo',[3] that when his great grandfather, the Dean of Killala, hired servants at the deanery, they stipulated that they should not be required to eat turbot or lobster more than twice a-

---

1 *II Henry VI.* III iii. 13–14.
2 *slink-veal*: premature calf.
3 *suo periculo*: 'at his own peril'.

week. There were also bottles of Wicklow ale, long and surreptitiously borrowed from 'his honor's' cellar, and which now made their first appearance on the kitchen hearth, and manifested their impatience of further constraint, by hissing, spitting, and bouncing in the face of the fire that provoked its animosity. But the whiskey (genuine illegitimate potsheen, smelling strongly of weed and smoke, and breathing defiance to excisemen) appeared, the 'veritable Amphitryon'[1] of the feast; every one praised, and drank as deeply as he praised....

The sound of the bell produced its full effect. The housekeeper rushed into the room, followed by a number of women, (the Irish præficae[2]); all ready to prescribe for the dying or weep for the dead, – all clapping their hard hands, or wiping their dry eyes. These hags all surrounded the bed; and to witness their loud, wild, and desperate grief, their cries of 'Oh! he's going, his honor's going, his honor's going,' one would have imagined their lives were bound up in his, like those of the wives in the story of Sinbad the Sailor, who were to be interred alive with their deceased husbands....

She read with great solemnity, – it was a pity that two interruptions occurred during the performance, one from old Melmoth, who, shortly after the commencement of the prayers, turned towards the old housekeeper, and said in a tone scandalously audible, 'Go down and draw the niggers of the kitchen fire closer, and lock the door, and let me *hear it locked*. I can't mind any thing till that's done.' The other was from John Melmoth gliding into the room, hearing the inappropriate words uttered by the ignorant woman, taking quietly as he knelt beside her the prayer-book from her hands, and reading in a suppressed voice part of that solemn service which, by the forms of the Church of England, is intended for the consolation of the departing.

... The old man grasped his hand, drew him close to his bed, cast a threatening yet fearful eye round the party, and then whispered in a voice of agonized constraint, 'I want a glass of wine, it would keep me alive for some hours, but there is not one I can trust to get it for me, – *they'd steal a bottle, and ruin me.*' John was greatly shocked. 'Sir, for God's sake, let *me* get a glass of wine for you.' 'Do you know where?' said the old man, with an expression in his face John could not understand. 'No, Sir; you know I have been rather a stranger here, Sir.' 'Take this key,' said old Melmoth, after a violent spasm;

---

1 *veritable Amphitryon*: a king of Thebes whom Zeus impersonated – his wife giving birth to Hercules. (From Molière's 'Le veritable Amphitryon est l'Amphitryon ou l'on dine,' (*Amphitryon* III. 5) the phrase was used to refer to a 'true host'.)
2 præficae: 'hired mourners'.

'take this key, there is wine in that closet, – *Madeira*. I always told them there was nothing there, but they did not believe me, or I should not have been robbed as I have been. At one time I said it was whiskey, and then I fared worse than ever, for they drank twice as much of it.'

John took the key from his uncle's hand; the dying man pressed it as he did so, and John, interpreting this as a mark of kindness, returned the pressure. He was undeceived by the whisper that followed, 'John, my lad, don't drink any of that wine while you are there.' 'Good God!' said John, indignantly throwing the key on the bed; then, recollecting that the miserable being before him was no object of resentment, he gave the promise required, and entered the closet, which no foot but that of old Melmoth had entered for nearly sixty years. He had some difficulty in finding out the wine, and indeed staid long enough to justify his uncle's suspicions, – but his mind was agitated, and his hand unsteady. He could not but remark his uncle's extraordinary look, that had the ghastliness of fear superadded to that of death, as he gave him permission to enter his closet. He could not but see the looks of horror which the women exchanged as he approached it. And, finally, when he was in it, his memory was malicious enough to suggest some faint traces of a story, too horrible for imagination, connected with it. He remembered in one moment most distinctly, that no one but his uncle had ever been known to enter it for many years.

Before he quitted it, he held up the dim light, and looked around him with a mixture of terror and curiosity. There was a great deal of decayed and useless lumber, such as might be supposed to be heaped up to rot in a miser's closet; but John's eyes were in a moment, and as if by magic, riveted on a portrait that hung on the wall, and appeared, even to his untaught eye, far superior to the tribe of family pictures that are left to moulder on the walls of a family mansion. It represented a man of middle age. There was nothing remarkable in the costume, or in the countenance, but *the eyes*, John felt, were such as one feels they wish they had never seen, and feels they can never forget. Had he been acquainted with the poetry of Southey, he might have often exclaimed in his after-life,

> Only the eyes had life,
> They gleamed with demon light. – THALABA.[1]

---

1 *Only the eyes … light*: Robert Southey, 'Thalaba the Destroyer' (1801) V. 10–11.

From an impulse equally resistless and painful, he approached the portrait, held the candle towards it, and could distinguish the words on the border of the painting, – Jno. Melmoth, anno 1646. John was neither timid by nature, or nervous by constitution, or superstitious from habit, yet he continued to gaze in stupid horror on this singular picture, till, aroused by his uncle's cough, he hurried into his room. The old man swallowed the wine. He appeared a little revived; it was long since he had tasted such a cordial, – his heart appeared to expand to a momentary confidence. 'John, what did you see in that room?' 'Nothing, Sir.' 'That's a lie; everyone wants to cheat or to rob me.' 'Sir, I don't want to do either.' 'Well, what did you see that you – you took notice of?' 'Only a picture, Sir.' 'A picture, Sir! – the original is still alive.' John, though under the impression of his recent feelings, could not but look incredulous. 'John,' whispered his uncle; 'John, they say I am dying of this and that; and one says it is for want of nourishment, and one says it is for want of medicine, – but, John,' and his face looked hideously ghastly, 'I am dying of a fright. That man,' and he extended his meagre arm towards the closet, as if he was pointing to a living being; 'that man, I have good reason to know, is alive still.' 'How is that possible, Sir?' said John involuntarily, 'the date on the picture is 1646.' 'You have seen it, – you have noticed it,' said his uncle. 'Well,' – he rocked and nodded on his bolster for a moment, then, grasping John's hand with an unutterable look, he exclaimed, 'You will see him again, he is alive.' Then, sinking back on his bolster, he fell into a kind of sleep or stupor, his eyes still open, and fixed on John....

John, greatly shocked, retired from the bed-side, and sat down in a distant corner of the room. The women were again in the room, which was very dark. Melmoth was silent from exhaustion, and there was a death-like pause for some time. At this moment John saw the door open, and a figure appear at it, who looked round the room, and then quietly and deliberately retired, but not before John had discovered in his face the living original of the portrait. His first impulse was to utter an exclamation of terror, but his breath felt stopped. He was then rising to pursue the figure, but a moment's reflection checked him. What could be more absurd, than to be alarmed or amazed at a resemblance between a living man and the portrait of a dead one! The likeness was doubtless strong enough to strike him even in that darkened room, but it was doubtless only a likeness; and though it might be imposing enough to terrify an old man of gloomy and retired habits, and with a broken constitution, John resolved it should not produce the same effect on him.

But while he was applauding himself for this resolution, the door opened, and the figure appeared at it, beckoning and nodding to him, with a familiarity somewhat terrifying. John now started up, determined to pursue it; but the pursuit was stopped by the weak but shrill cries of his uncle, who was struggling at once with the agonies of death and his housekeeper. The poor woman, anxious for her master's reputation and her own, was trying to put on him a clean shirt and nightcap, and Melmoth, who had just sensation enough to perceive they were taking something from him, continued exclaiming feebly, 'They are robbing me, – robbing me in my last moments, – robbing a dying man. John, won't you assist me, – I shall die a beggar; they are taking my last shirt, – I shall die a beggar.' – And the miser died.

JAMES HARDIMAN (1782–1855)

Born in Connaught, the son of a small landowner in Westport, Co. Mayo, he was reared as a native Irish speaker. According to John O'Donovan, he relinquished his studies for the priesthood because of blindness in one eye. He studied law in Dublin, and, from 1811, worked as a sub-commissioner in the Public Records Office. In 1820 he published his well-researched *History of the County and Town of Galway*; ten years later he settled in Galway. His influential *Irish Minstrelsy or Bardic Remains of Ireland, with English Poetical Translations* (2 vols, 1831) contained metrical versions by Furlong*, D'Alton*, and others, of Irish poetry, from ancient relics to the work of contemporaries such as Carolan*, whose literary remains he had collected. The book elicited a vehement reaction from Samuel Ferguson*, who queried Hardiman's Catholic militancy, calling him a 'literary Ribbonman'. His next publications were *An Account of two Irish Wills* and *The Statute of Kilkenny* (1843). Soon after its foundation he became Librarian of Queen's College, Galway, turning down the Chair of Irish.

From *Irish Minstrelsy, or Bardic Remains of Ireland* (1831)

Introduction

After ages of neglect and decay, the ancient literature of Ireland seems destined to emerge from obscurity. Those memorials which have hitherto lain so long unexplored, now appear to awaken the attention of the learned and the curiosity of the public; and thus, the literary remains of a people once so distinguished in the annals of learning, may be rescued from the oblivion to which they have been so undeservedly consigned. That the ancient Irish possessed ample stores in their native language, capable of captivating the fancy, enlarging the understanding, and improving the heart, is well known to those acquainted with the mouldering membranes which have survived to our times. The historical importance of our annals has been acknowledged by the most learned men of Europe for the last three centuries. They are written in the language of the first inhabitants of Europe; and, with a simplicity of detail which truth only can confer, they record the primæval state of this island, the origin of its early inhabitants, their history, religion, and laws, and the arts known amongst them for several generations. Former writers have brought discredit on our history by injudiciously blending with it the fictions of romance; and succeeding authors, unable or unwilling to separate the truth from the fable, became contented copyists, and thus encreased the evil which they pretended to remedy. Eager for temporary applause, which they mistook for permanent fame, they forced on the world their crude essays, which were remarkable only for distortion of fact and boldness of conjecture. The original documents, which would have guided them to truth, were wholly neglected, or but partially explored. Hence, the imperfect state of our early history, and the erroneous opinions entertained of it by many, even of the learned, at the present day. The difficulty of procuring the documents alluded to, and the still greater difficulty of deciphering them when procured, may be alleged as an excuse for the indolence, or ignorance, of which our countrymen have reason to complain in the generality of their historical writers. But this is a plea that cannot be admitted. Those chroniclers of error ought to have rendered themselves competent, or have remained for ever silent. What is true of the past will apply equally to the future. Until the difficulties alluded to shall be overcome, all attempts to illustrate, with certainty or authority, the earlier parts of our history must prove abortive. – Having judged it necessary to make the few foregoing observations on the most important use to be made of those neglected muniments, it now remains to ascertain what information they afford on the subject at present under consideration – the ancient poetry of Ireland.

That this country, from an early period, was famous for the cultivation of the kindred arts of poetry and music, stands universally admitted. The works of the prejudiced Cambrensis,[1] and the annals of Wales and Scotland, might be adduced in evidence of the fact; but we require not the aid of foreign proof, our domestic records supply abundant information on the subject. Although most of the records of the days of paganism were destroyed by the zeal of the first Christian Missionaries, and much of what then escaped, with many of later times, met with a similar fate from the barbarity of the Danes, and the destructive policy of the English, yet sufficient remains to enable us to trace those arts to a remote period in Ireland. The early settlers, afterwards distinguished by the name of Milesians, derived their origin from that part of the earth, where poetry and music appear coeval with the formation of society. Accordingly we find the poet and musician numbered in the train of these celebrated invaders. The bards AMERGIN, the son of their leader, and LUGAD, the son of ITH, are particularly named. The latter is called, in old writings, 'The first poet of Ireland,' ... and there still remain, after a lapse of nearly three thousand years, fragments of these ancient bards, some of which will be found included in the following pages, with proofs of their authenticity. After these, but anterior to the Christian era, flourished ROYNE FILE, or the poetic, and FERCEIRTNE, a bard and herald; some of whose remains will also be found with the foregoing. LUGAR and CONGAL lived about the birth of Our Redeemer, and many of their verses, particularly those of the latter, are still extant. The subjects and language of these insular poems afford internal evidence of an antiquity transcending that of any literary monument in the modern languages of Europe.

In that remote period the cultivation of music kept pace with the progress of poetry. The *Dinn Seanchas,* compiled by AMERGIN MAC AMALGAID, A.D. 544, relates that in the time of GEIDE, monarch of Ireland, A.M. 3143, 'the people deemed each others voices sweeter than the warblings of a melodious harp, such peace and concord reigned among them, that no music could delight them more than the sound of each others voice: *Temur* (*Tarah*) was so called from its celebrity for melody, above the palaces of the world. *Tea,* or *Te,* signifying melody or sweet music, and *mur, a* wall. *Te-mur,* the wall of music.' In the same ancient tract, music is again alluded to, in the relation of a youthful dream or vision of CAHIREMORE, monarch of Ireland, which, amongst other things, describes, 'a delightful hill, sur-

---

1 *Giraldus Cambrensis* (c. 1146–?1223) wrote two books on Ireland, *Topographia Hibernica* (1188) (*The Topography and History of Ireland*) and *Expugnatio Hibernica* (1189) (*The Conquest of Ireland*).

passing all others in height, whereon stood hosts; and there grew a most beautiful and stately tree, like gold, whose variegated and luxuriant foliage, when moved by the wind, yielded the most melodious music ever heard, and on it grew delicious fruit, pleasing to every one's taste.' The royal druid Bree, thus, interpreted the dream: 'You are the tree who shall rise high to the sovereignty, over all the nation; the wind blowing on the leaves, and producing harmony, is the sweetness of your words in giving laws and ordinances to the people; and the fruit you saw, are the many blessings that shall come on your subjects in your reign.' The first of these extracts contains the earliest allusion to the harp which I have met with, though it is frequently mentioned in Irish poems ascribed to Columba, and others of the sixth century. It is considered needless to multiply extracts, to shew the early knowledge and progress of music in Ireland. Proved to have existed as far back as the most ancient annals extend, its origin, like that of our round towers, must be sought for in the East.

The music of Ireland is better known to the world, at the present day, than its poetry. In the sweetest strains of natural feeling, the former found its ready way to every heart, and became endenizened in every clime, while the latter, wrapped in an ancient and expressive but proscribed and insulated language, has been generally neglected, particularly since the spread of the English tongue amongst us, and the downfall of the Milesians. Men there were, no doubt, who, knowing and valuing its beauties, have protected and cherished it amidst every vicissitude, as a precious depository of the genius of former times. But these generations have passed away. The few who inherit their spirit are gradually disappearing, and thus Irish poetry, with all its charms, may be left to linger awhile, and then sink into oblivion, unless rescued by the timely interposition of those who still retain some respect for the ancient honour of their country.

The nature and value of this venerable deposit now remain for investigation. Some ancient bards, anterior to the Christian era, have been already noticed. Thence, to a recent period, a numerous host of the principal 'sons of song,' whose names may appear uncouth to our modern ears, will pass, in tedious, perhaps, but necessary review, before the reader. These men's works are stamped with genius and learning, and are preserved in various records of the highest authority. In the second century CIOTHRUADH, the bard, addressed a poem to the monarch CON, which is preserved in the book of Munster. FINGIN, in the same reign, produced a poem, on the approaches to Tarah, preserved in the Dinn Seanchas – *Lecan*, f. 289. Some fragments of

LUACHNA, another bard of that period, and of FERGUS FIONBELL, or the 'Sweet-voiced,' who lived in the third century, are found in the same record. The bard OISIN is here omitted, for although there appear some poems ascribed to him in many old manuscripts, yet strong doubts are entertained of their authenticity. In the fourth and fifth centuries flourished the nervous and poetic TORNA, one of whose poems is given in the following collection; and DUBTHACH, the son of LUGAR, a bard who embraced the Christian faith in the time of St. Patrick. Two curious poems of the latter, on the privileges and duties of his order, and of the royal rights and duties of the King of Tarah, as monarch of Ireland, are preserved in the *Leabhar na Cceart*. A hymn to the Redeemer, by Dubthach, after his conversion, is found in the *Felire Anguis*, a poetical calendar, compiled about the end of the eighth century, and preserved in the *Leabhar Brac*, or 'Speckled Book,' a valuable miscellany, now in the library of the Royal Irish Academy. The foregoing are the most noted Pagan bards, whose poems and rhapsodies have descended to our times. The names and works of others have been handed down; and there can be no doubt but that more will be brought to light when the Irish MSS. scattered throughout these islands, and on the continent of Europe, as before alluded to, shall be recovered.

The introduction of Christianity gave a new and more exalted direction to the powers of poetry. Among the numerous bards, who dedicated their talents to the praises of the Deity, during the three succeeding centuries, the most distinguished are, FEICH, the bishop, whose poem, first published by the learned Colgan, is in the hands of every Irish scholar; AMERGIN, author of the *Dinn Seanchas;* the famous COLUMCILLE; DALLAN and SEANCHAN, some of whose minor poems are contained in this collection; CINFAELA, the learned, who revised the *Uraicepht*, or 'Primer of the Bards,' preserved in the book of Ballimote, and in the library of Trinity College, Dublin; the celebrated ADAMNAN; and ANGUS, the pious author of the *Felire*, or Hierology in verse, already mentioned. Most of these poems afford internal evidence that their construction is founded on the traditional rythmical songs of the Pagan bards. Their metre and their jingle are national. They follow a long established practice well known to the bards of former times. After the death of ANGUS, about the year 800, the incursions of the Danes, for a time, silenced the Muses, yet some famous bards flourished between that period and the arrival of the English. In 884, died, according to the annals of the Four Masters, MAOLMURA (MILES) of Fathan, described, in the Book of Invasions, as 'a skilful and truly learned poet,' whose works are distinguished for loftiness of thought, and strength of expression. Three valuable historical poems, by Maolmura, are preserved in the Books of Invasions and Lecan. Contemporary with him was FLANN, the son of LONAN, a graceful and elegant writer, who is called, in the annals of the Four Masters, the 'Virgil of Ireland.' Within the next century, we find the bards CORMACAN and KENETH O'HARTIGAN, whose valuable poems, particularly those of the latter, are inserted in the Book of Invasions, and the Dinn Seanchas; MAC GIOLLA CAOIMH, a sweet poet, one of whose elegies will be found in this collection; and the learned EOCHY O'FLOINN, who died in 984, and whose invaluable historical poems are preserved in the Books of Lecan, Ballimote, and Invasions. About the beginning of the eleventh century lived MAC LIAG, (Secretary and Biographer of the patriotic Monarch Brian, killed at Clontarf, A.D. 1014,) whose pathetic poems, on the death of his royal master, are given in the present collection. The originals of these, and other pieces by this bard, are contained in the *Leabhar Oiris.* The learned historical poems of CUAN O'LOCHAN, FLAN of Bute, and GIOLLA KEVIN, (who flourished in this century,) preserved in the records so often mentioned, shew that the general gloom of ignorance, which at that time overspread the rest of Europe, had not reached this island. The poems of the latter bard have been published by Doctor O'Conor, in his *Rerum Hibernicarum Scriptores,* vol. I., with translations and notes, of great value to the Irish historian. In the early part of the twelfth century flourished O'MULCONRY, the annalist and poet, who sung of the aboriginal tribes of Ireland in sweetly flowing verse, preserved in the Book of Lecan; the learned O'CASSIDY, abbot of Ardbracken in Meath, whose well known historical poem, 'Sacred Erin! Island of Saints,' is printed in the work above alluded to; and O'DUN, chief bard to the Prince of Leinster, who died in 1160, and whose historical poems are preserved in the valuable volumes of *Lecan, Ballimote,* and other ancient MSS. – Such were the *principal* bards of Ireland down to the Anglo-Norman invasion. Not imaginary personages, like many, called into fabulous existence by the zeal of some neighbouring nations, in asserting claims to early civilization and literature, but men long celebrated in the annals of their country, and whose works, still extant, are pointed out with as much perspicuity as the limits of these pages would allow. The nature and character of these works are deserving of peculiar attention. They do not possess any of the wild barbarous fervor of the Scandinavian Scalds; nor yet the effeminate softness of the professors of the 'gay science,' the *Troubadours* and *lady-bards* of the period to which we are now arrived. The simplicity of expression, and dignity of thought, which characterize the Greek and Roman writers of the purest period, pervade the productions of our bards: and, at the present day, they are particularly valuable for the important aids which they furnish, towards elucidating the ancient state of this early peopled and interesting island.

For two centuries after the invasion of Henry II. the voice of the muse was but feebly heard in Ireland. The genius of the nation withered at the approach of slavery. The bards were few, but among them were some of considerable eminence. The pious and highly gifted DONOGH O'DALY, abbot of Boyle, in Roscommon, was called the Ovid of Ireland, from the sweetness of his verse. He died in 1244, leaving several excellent poems, chiefly on divine subjects, which, even to *the present day,* are familiarly repeated by the people in various parts of the country. CONWAY, a bard of the O'Donnells of Tyrconnell, about the same time, poured forth some noble effusions to celebrate the heroic actions of that powerful sept. One of the most distinguished writers of this period was JOHN O'DUGAN, (chief poet of O'Kelly, Prince of Imania, in Conaught,) who died in the year 1372, and whose name and works are still remembered and repeated by the people. His topographical poem, describing the principal Irish families of Conaught, Meath, and Ulster, at the time of the English invasion, is particularly valuable. Not a line of these bards has ever been printed. The limits here prescribed preclude the possibility of particularizing the poets of the two succeeding centuries. If they evinced less talent, let it be remembered that they were more oppressed than their predecessors. They fell with their country; and like the captive Israelites, hung their untuned harps on the willows. Well might they exclaim, with the royal psalmist:

> Now while our harpes were hanged soe,
>   The men, whose captives then we lay,
> Did on our griefs insulting goe,
>   And more to grieve us thus did say:
> You that of musique make such show,
>   Come sing us now a Sion lay;
> O no, we have nor voice nor hand,
>   For such a song, in such a land.[1]

---

1 Mary Herbert (1561–1621), *The Psalms of the Countess of Pembroke*, Psalm 137.

But the spirit of patriotism at length aroused the bards from their slumbers, and during the cruel reign of Elizabeth, many men of genius started up throughout Ireland, who devoted their talents to the vindication of their suffering country. Of these, the most considerable were MAOLIN OGE MAC BRODIN, the most eminent poet of his time; O'GNIVE of Claneboy, who distinguished himself by several compositions to excite the natives against the English, and whose spirited poem on the 'Downfall of the Gael' is included in this collection; TEIGE DALL O'HIGGIN, brother to Maolmuire, archbishop of Tuam, whose genius was of a superior order, and whose poems are amongst the best in our language; O'MULCONRY, whose fine poem, in the Phœnician dialect of the Irish, addressed to the chieftain O'ROURKE of Briefny, is contained in this work; and the learned and philosophic MAC DAIRE of Thomond, and his gifted contemporary O'CLERY of Donegal, whose talents shine so conspicuously, as opposite leaders, in the *Iomarba,* or *'Contention of the Bards,'* about the year 1600.... Here I close the series of ancient bards, having arrived at the period which may now be considered as dividing our ancient and modern history. The estimation in which they were at all times held by their countrymen, may be learned from an English writer of the reign of Elizabeth, the accomplished Sir Philip Sidney, who, in his defence of poesy, tells us that 'In Ireland their poets are held in devout reverence.' A love of poetry has always distinguished our countrymen. No people have ever been more ready, according to the injunction of the sacred pensman, to honour such as by their skill found out musical tunes and published verses in writing: and if patriotism, genius, and learning, are entitled to regard amongst mankind, no men were ever more deserving of national honour than the ancient bards of Ireland.

It now remains to consider their successors to recent times; and here it may be necessary to observe, that the only poets mentioned throughout this work, are such as wrote solely in their native language.... It has been so long fashionable to decry that persecuted body, that the writer regrets it has not fallen to others more competent to vindicate them against the ignorance and prejudice by which they have been assailed, particularly during the last century. But their defence even in the humblest hands, must prove triumphant. What was their crime? – for, shame to humanity, in Ireland it was deemed a crime! – to love their country. What brought down on them the vengeance of the persecutor? their invincible attachment to the ancient faith, and to the ancient, though fallen, families of the land. If these be crimes, then were they guilty; if not, it is time to make reparation to the memory of these injured men, whose learning and genius would have been cherished and honoured, and held in 'devout reverence' in any country under heaven except their own. Richly did they possess those brilliant qualities of mind, the exercise of which, in later and comparatively better days, have placed their more fortunate, though not more talented, countrymen *Curran*, *Sheridan*, *O'Leary*, and others, in the foremost ranks of mankind. But the bards were "mere Irish." They thought and spoke and wrote in Irish. They were, invariably, Catholics, patriots, and jacobites. Even their broad Celtic surnames they disdained to submit to the polish of Saxon refinement. Hence they have been erroneously considered, and by many of the educated of their country are still considered, as rude rural rhymsters, without any claim either to talents or learning. So it was with the prince of Latin poets, when be first visited Rome. His countrymen could not discern the noble genius which lay hid under his rustic garb.

> —————————————rideri possit, eo quod
> Rusticius tonso toga defluit, et male laxus
> In pede calceus hæret. —————————
> —————————————at ingenium ingens
> Inculto latet hoc sub corpore. ———
>
> HOR.[1]

But, lest the charge of national partiality may be alleged against the character here given, let us hear the description of a writer, who cannot lie under that imputation. Doctor Parsons, *an Englishman*, author of a curious antiquarian treatise, entitled the 'Remains of Japhet,' tells us, in that work, that about the middle of the last century he 'spent several years of his life in Ireland, and there attained to a tolerable knowledge of the very ancient tongue of that country.' Speaking of the bards, he says, 'They repeat their poems in a stile that, for its beauty and fine sentiments, has often struck me with amazement; for I have been many times obliged, by many of these natural bards, with the repetition of as sublime poems upon love, heroism, hospitality, battles, &c. as can be produced in any language. Homer and Virgil have laid the ground of their noble tissue upon the basis of historical facts, and the Irish poets *of our times* write in the very same strain. It is the genius of the people, and their language is susceptible of it,

---

1 Horace, *Satires*, I. 3. 30–4: 'He can be ridiculed for his countrified haircut, the way his toga hangs carelessly, and his shoe dangles loosely on his foot – yet a mighty genius lies hidden under this rough exterior.'

more naturally than any other extant. There are numbers of them capable of composing extemporaneous eulogiums and poems of considerable length upon any subject, surprisingly elegant, and full of fine sentiments.' Doctor Parsons, moreover, states that he was personally acquainted with the bards whom he has thus described, and whose names are already given in the margin. Speaking of these men, even James Macpherson, in his Dissertation on the poems of Ossian, says, 'Their love sonnets, and their elegies on the death of persons worthy or renowned, abound with simplicity, and a wild harmony of numbers. The beauty of these species depends so much on a certain *curiosa* [*sic*] *felicitas* of expression in the original, that they must appear much to disadvantage in another language.'[1] Lord Byron and Sir Walter Scott have recorded their opinions of Irish poetry in terms which may enable us to conjecture what these distinguished men would have thought, could they have tasted the beauties of our bards in their original compositions. Many of the love sonnets and elegies alluded to by Macpherson will be found in the present collection, with some notices of their authors, whose names are thus brought to the remembrance of their countrymen, under a hope that this humble effort to awaken national attention towards these neglected sons of genius and their works, may be pursued by others better qualified to do justice to their memory.

For the course of education prescribed for the bards, in ancient and modern times, the reader is referred to the works in the margin. The language invariably used in their compositions, was that of the country. To it they were attached for many reasons, independent of nationality. The most learned men of Europe, since the revival of letters, have been loud in its praise. Usher has ranked it among the first for richness and elegance, and Leibnitz and Lluyd[2] have left on record their opinions of its value. The latter observes, that "The Irish have preserved their letters and orthography beyond all their neighbouring nations." The ancient language was very different from that spoken at the present day. It was divided into several dialects, of which the *Bearla Feine,* or *Phœnician,* was in highest estimation, and without a knowledge of that dialect it is impossible to understand the early poets. The introduction of Christianity, and Latin, had not that effect on this primordial language, which might be supposed. For a long

---

1 'A Dissertation concerning the poems of Ossian' (1797–edn.). Hardiman quotes selectively.
2 *Usher ... Leibnitz and Lluyd*: James Ussher (1581–1656), Archbishop of Armagh, author of *The Annals of the World* (1650; 1654); Baron Gottfried Wilhelm von Leibnitz (1646–1716), mathematician, philosopher *and* philologist; Edward Lluyd (1660–1709), Celtic scholar and naturalist – his *Archæologia Britannica* Vol. I (1707) contains a 'comparative etymology of the Celtic languages.

period after, it suffered no material alteration. At length, in the sixteenth century, our learned men began to turn their thoughts to the subject; and if they had not been impeded by the jealous interference of the English, it is probable that it would have undergone a change similar to that of most of the other dialects of Europe. How far that circumstance is now to be regretted, by one who contemplates the present, and probable future political amalgamation of the interests of these islands, it may be difficult to determine. From the days of Henry VIII. the English rulers were bent upon the total annihilation of our national language, but time has shewn the folly of the undertaking. The late Bishop Heber, in his life of Bedell, has stigmatized it as 'narrow and illiberal policy, which, though it has in part succeeded, has left a division in the national heart, far worse than that of the tongue.' Most grants of lands from the crown, in the reigns of Henry and his successors to Charles I., contained special provisoes, for the disuse of the native, and the encouragement of the English tongue. But all these efforts would have proved abortive, were it not for the fatal disasters of the seventeenth century. Immediately before the civil war of 1641, a momentary gleam of hope lightened over this devoted language. The learned antiquaries of Donegal associated to collect and publish the remains of our ancient literature; but their patriotic intentions were unhappily frustrated by the succeeding troubles, and the language which had withstood the shock of so many ages, at length sunk in the general wreck. Thenceforth it was banished from the castle of the chieftain, to the cottage of his vassal, and, from having been the cherished and cultivated medium of intercourse between the nobles and gentry of the land, it became gradually limited to the use of the uneducated poor. No wonder, then, that it should have been considered harsh and unpolished when thus spoken, but it was as unjust to estimate our language by such a standard, as it would be to judge of the English by the jargon of Yorkshire. The measure of its vicissitudes was not yet, however, full. In the last century, the inquisitors of the Irish parliament denounced it as the dialect of that phantom of their political frenzy, popery. According to a favorite mode of native reasoning, it was resolved to reduce the poor Catholics to a state of mental darkness, in order to convert them into enlightened protestants. A thick cloud of ignorance soon overspread the land; and the language of millions ceased to be a medium of written communication. To these circumstances, perhaps, may be attributed its preservation from the written corruptions which pervade the present Gaelic of Scotland. The bards of modern times were the principal scribes in Irish. In it they were educated; to its orthography and grammatical structure they carefully attended; and in this last stage of its eventful history, it appears in their writings in a degree of purity, which, considering the disadvantages under which they laboured, is truly remarkable.

In our poems and songs, but particularly in those exquisite old tales and romances, which for originality of invention, and elegance of expression, vie with the Eastern stories that have so long delighted Europe, the beauties of our language are fully displayed. In lyrical composition, which forms so large a portion of the present collection, its superiority even over the Italian, has been repeatedly asserted. On this point, a late favorite melodist says, 'I have in another place observed, that the Irish was superior even to the Italian, in lyrical composition. I know a contrary opinion is held by many, *but by very few capable of judging as to both languages.*'[1] Voltaire has observed, that a people may have a music and poetry, pleasing only to themselves, and yet both good. But Irish music has been admired wherever its melting strains have been heard. Handel, and the first-rate composers of Italy, have been loud in its praise. If it be permitted to argue, as Sir William Jones did on the language and music of Persia, that the natural and affecting melodies of that people, must have a language remarkable for its softness, and the strong accentuation of words, and for the tenderness of the songs written in it, it would follow, that the original songs, so long associated with the Irish melodies, would prove equally pleasing, if more generally known. Many of them are contained in the present volumes, and they will be found replete with the simplicity and natural feeling which will ever posses power over the human heart. Should these sweet original lyrics, therefore, attract the attention of future melodists, and be introduced on the stage, a circumstance, not at all unlikely, they may, when accompanied with their native melodies, and sung by our 'sweet singers,' prove no mean rivals to the dearly purchased warblings of Italy.

The metrical structure of ancient Irish poetry, must be considered with reference to its musical accompaniments. The voice of the bard retrenched, or supplied, the quantity of long or short syllables, in order to adapt them to the sound or melody. This license required many rules to restrain it. Hence the hundred kinds of verse mentioned by *Ferceirtne* in the *Uraicepht* or 'primer of the bards;' and the declaration of *O'Molloy*[2] in his prosody, that the rules of Irish verse were

---

1 *Reminiscences of Michael Kelly*, London, 1826. Introduction.
2 Francis O'Molloy (?1614–1684), professor of theology, author of *Grammatica Latino-Hibernica* (1677).

'the most difficult under the sun.' The latter writer describes 'a popular kind of poetry, much used in his time, called Ubhpʌn,' or 'sweet verse.' This he censures, as a deviation from the ancient rules; but it seems to have been devised as a middle course, between the strictness of the regular metre, and the license too generally taken by the voice of the bard. Some of our most admired lyrical compositions are in this measure. The *Octava Rima*, or eight line stanza of Italy, was borrowed from the Spaniards, who had it themselves from the *Troubadours* and Italians, perhaps not earlier than the end of the fifteenth century, and in it have been composed some of our finest songs.

The borrowed term 'Minstrelsy' is used in the title of this collection, only because it is familiar to the public ear, for others more appropriate might be found in our language. Aware of the influence of popular song on public morals, no verses, of even a doubtful tendency, have been admitted into the following pages; if some rigid moralist may not perhaps deem the *Chansons de boire* of our favourite bard CAROLAN exceptionable. It will be observed, that in the Irish originals all contractions are rejected, 'pro faciliori captu, et modo legendi addiscendique hanc linguam.' – *O'Molloy.*[1] With the same view the letter h is invariably inserted in place of its usual representative the aspirate point. Against this it may be urged that that letter was not anciently written; and, moreover, that its insertion may create a difficulty in the way of the mere Irish reader's acquiring its true pronunciation in English. It is not, however, an innovation, for the first objection is proved groundless by various old manuscripts; and even supposing the latter entitled to consideration, it was deemed more important to facilitate the reading of the originals.

With respect to the origin and progress of the present publication, a few words may be necessary for the satisfaction of the reader. It has long been a subject of regret, with the writer, that the remains of our national bards, of those men who, according to James Macpherson, 'have displayed a genius worthy of any age or nation,' should be consigned to obscurity at home, while a neighbouring nation derived so much literary fame from a few of those remains, boldly claimed and published as its own. Several societies formed among ourselves, for the purpose of preserving our ancient literature, having successively failed, the task seemed abandoned to individual exertion. This consideration induced the writer to devote his few leisure moments to the

---

1 *Grammatica Latino-Hibernica* (1677): 'For an easier way to aquire, read and make progress in, this language'.

collection of some of those neglected remnants of genius, with a hope that, at a future period, they might be rescued from the oblivion to which they were daily hastening. To this undertaking he adhered with a perseverance proportioned to his idea of its importance; and the first fruits of his humble labours are now respectfully presented to his countrymen....

JAMES WARREN DOYLE (1786–1834)

Born near New Ross, the posthumous son of a small farmer, he witnessed, aged eleven, the horrors of the '98 Rising in New Ross. In 1800 he entered the local seminary, taking his vows in 1806. His studies at the University of Coimbra in Portugal were interrupted by the Napoleonic invasion, and Doyle enlisted in the army of Sir Arthur Wellesley (later Duke of Wellington), acting as interpreter for the forces. He returned to Ireland in 1808, and was ordained at Enniscorthy. In 1813 he went to Carlow College, taking the chair of rhetoric, then of humanity, and finally of theology. He was elected to the see of Kildare and Leighlin in 1819. He established schools in every parish. When Magee, the protestant archbishop of Dublin, at his primary visitation in St. Patrick's Cathedral in 1822 asserted that 'the catholics had a church without a religion, and the dissenters a religion without a church,' Doyle retorted, under the signature 'J.K.L.' (James, Kildare and Leighlin), with a vehement attack on the established church. In 1823 he published the trenchant *Vindication of the Religious and Civil Principles of the Irish Catholics*. It was followed by *Letters on the State of Ireland* (1824-25). He served as a formidable witness at parliamentary committees on Catholic Emancipation, eliciting the observation from the Duke of Wellington that it was not the peers who were examining Dr Doyle, but Dr. Doyle who was examining the peers. Championing the cause of the poor, he was at first supported by O'Connell, but then opposed, not least for advocating a union of the Churches of England with the Church of Rome. His polemical writings contributed to the Disestablishment. He died at his residence, Braganza, near Carlow, and was buried in front of the altar at the cathedral in Carlow which was built under his aegis.

From *A Vindication of the Religious and Civil Principles of the Irish Catholics*

(1823)

It was the creed, my Lord, of a Charlemagne and of a St. Louis, of an Alfred and an Edward, of the monarchs of the feudal times as well as of the Emperors of Greece and Rome; it was believed at Venice and at Genoa, in Lucca and the Helvetic nations in the days of their freedom and greatness: all the barons of the middle ages, all the free cities of later times professed the religion we now profess. You well know, my Lord, that the Charter of British freedom, and the common law of England, have their origin and source in Catholic times. Who framed the free constitutions of the Spanish Goths? Who preserved science and literature, during the long night of the middle ages? Who imported literature, from Constantinople, and opened for her an asylum at Rome, Florence, Padua, Paris, and Oxford? Who polished Europe by art, and refined her by legislation? Who discovered the new world and opened a passage to another? Who were the masters of architecture, of painting, and of music? Who invented the compass, and the art of printing? Who were the poets, the historians, the jurists, the men of deep research and profound literature? Who have exalted human nature, and made man appear again little less than the angels? Were they not almost exclusively the professors of our creed? Were they who created and professed freedom under every shape and form unfit for her enjoyment? Were men, deemed even now, the lights of the world, and the benefactors of the human race, the deluded victims of a slavish superstition? But what is there in our creed which renders us unfit for freedom? Is it the doctrine of passive obedience? No, for the obedience we yield to authority, is not blind, but reasonable; our religion does not create despotism; it supports every established constitution, which is not opposed to the laws of nature, unless it be altered by those who are entitled to change it. In Poland it supported an elective monarchy; in France, an hereditary sovereign; in Spain, an absolute or constitutional king indifferently; in England, when the houses of York and Lancaster contended, it declared that he who was king *de facto*, was entitled to the obedience of the people. During the reign of the Tudors, there was a faithful adherence of the Catholics to their prince, under trials the most severe and galling; because the constitution required it: the same was exhibited by them to the ungrateful race of Stuart; but since the expulsion of James (foolishly called an abdication), have they not adopted with the nation at large, the doctrine of the revolution, 'that the crown is held in trust for the benefit of the people; and that should the monarch violate his compact, the subject is freed from the bond of his allegiance.' Has there been any form of government ever devised by man, to which the religion of Catholics had not been accommodated? Is there any obligation, either to a prince or to a constitution, which it does not enforce?...

What, my Lord! is the allegiance of the man divided who gives to Cæsar what belongs to Cæsar, and to God what belongs to God? Is the allegiance of the priest divided who yields submission to his bishop and his king? — of the son who obeys his parent and his prince? And yet their duties are not more distinct than those which we owe our sovereign and our spiritual head. Is there any man in society who has not distinct duties to discharge? May not the same person be the head of a corporation and an officer of the king? a justice of the peace, perhaps, and a bankrupt surgeon, with half his pay? And are the duties thus imposed upon him incompatible with one another? If the Pope can define that the Jewish Sabbath is dissolved, and the Lord's day to be sanctified, may not this be believed without prejudice to the act of settlement, or that for the limitation of the crown? If the Church decree that on Fridays her children shall abstain from flesh-meat, are they thereby controulled from obeying the king when he summons them to war?

No, I conclude it is impossible that any rational man could suppose that the Catholics, under equal laws, would be less loyal, less faithful subjects, than any others.

From *Letters on the State of Ireland*
(1825)

My Dear Sir;

The object of this Letter is to give you some idea of the state of parties in Ireland, their composition and ulterior views, and to throw some light on the character of our gentry....

The country is divided into three great parties, the Orangemen, the Catholics, and the Government party, besides a vast mass of inert matter, of what Swift would call *prudent men*, who, solely intent on their own interest, whisper away the characters of all the others, pass judgment in secret upon whatever occurs, are never pleased with anything, and are ready to pray with Cromwell or cry with Charles, but not until the contest between them is decided....

The orange party are next to the Government in the paucity of their numbers, in their knowledge of court discipline, in the array of their responsible officers, in their legal forms and proceedings, in the formality of their attitude, in the show and circumstance of their dignity, in keeping up a standing army, in administering oaths of allegiance, in having a council of state, plenipotentiaries, and envoys, with a public press to publish and defend their proceedings.

This party would be even stronger than it is, and more than able to cope with either of the other two, if it were not overbearing, haughty, insolent, and cruel. Monopoly and injustice are written on its standards, oppression is its watchword, falsehood and slander are its heralds; it has no reason or justice with it, but it is so clamorous and so menacing and unblushing as to overwhelm or confound whomsoever would approach it with argument, or seek to treat with it on a basis just, useful, or honourable....

This party, like Catiline and Cethegus,[1] has collected into its ranks every spendthrift, every idler, every punished or unpunished malefactor, every public robber and private delinquent, all the gamblers, all those whom gluttony or extravagance has reduced to want; in fine, all who love commotion, and who hope to live by corruption, or to rebuild their broken fortunes on the ruins of their country....

There is also a large class of saints or fanatics, another of conscientious Protestants, a third of traders in education, with almost the entire body of the Established Clergy, who, through fear orangemen: these classes form, in appearance, a neutral power, but constitute in reality the force which sustains the warfare in this country....

...Government should exist for the sake of the people, and not the people for those who govern them. The forms of speech to which we are accustomed sanction this mode of expression, and we may suppose, therefore, that the Government here is formed and carried on for the good of the community. The Catholics, therefore, who are, morally speaking, the people of this country, should engross the principal attention of our rulers; their interests in the state of Ireland should be considered like those of other subjects. Their rank or station or property, however respectable, should not be so much contemplated as their numbers; for just laws make no distinction in providing for the happiness and security of the rich more than of the poor. To treat of the Catholics, then, as of a party in Ireland, is not altogether correct, according to this theory; nor again, is it just in point of law; for such is the profound wisdom of our laws, that they almost ignore the existence of the people, and contemplate as subjects men who are no where to be found....

The Catholics, then, under the fostering care of penal statutes, and quite unnoticed by the laws made to protect and foster the faithful subjects of this part of the realm, have grown at least into a party....

This party is kept in a state of constant excitement; they are goaded by the orangemen, they are insulted by the press, they are taunted with

1 The dissolute and depraved Sergius Catilina surrounded himself with the dregs of humanity and, aided by Caius Cethegus, designed to overthrow the government and to murder Cicero (c. 65–63BC).

insult by the education societies, the distributors of Bibles, and itinerant saints; they are stripped naked and almost starved by the Squirarchy and church; the legislature does not attend to them; the Government does not protect them; the judges, who would not give a stone to them for bread, are generally inaccessible to them; they are reduced to such a state, that thousands upon thousands of them look to death for repose, as the exhausted traveller looks to the shadow of a great rock in a land fainting from heat. Add to these causes of excitement the harangues of their own leaders, the recollection of their former greatness, the history of their country, recollections 'pleasing and mournful to the soul,' and which are known by reading or by tradition to them all; but, above all, we should add, their enthusiastic attachment to the faith of their fathers; a faith rendered more and more dear to them by being daily and hourly reviled. When you have considered all these things, you may judge of the state of feeling which pervades the Catholic population....

Should it be suffered to continue, should this party or this people, whichever it may be called, remain neglected by the legislature; should their grievances be left unredressed – should their poor be left to perish – should their children be left a prey to evangelicals and methodists – should their religion continue to be insulted – should the agent, and the tithe-proctor, and the church-warden, like the toads and locust, come still in succession to devour the entire fruit of their industry – should their blood when wantonly spilled go unrevenged, we need no Pastorini[1] to foretell the result. We have only to refer to our own history, or open the volume of human nature, in order to ascertain it. A Police Bill, and a Tithe-composition Bill, and an Insurrection Bill,[2] and fifty thousand bayonets, may repress disturbances, but who can contemplate a brave and generous people so abused? – Who can dwell in a country so accursed? What man can appear before his God who has looked patiently at much wrong, or who has not contributed by every legal means to relieve his fellow-creatures from sufferings so intense?...

---

1 *Pastorini*: pseudonym of Bishop Charles Walmsley (1722–1797), who in his *General History of the Christian Church* (1771) predicted the apocalyptic victory of Catholicism over the plague of Protestantism. His millenarianism was disseminated throughout Ireland in chapbook editions of the *Prophecies of Pastorini*. Its impact is recorded in some of the fiction of Carleton* and the Banims*, and in some of Mangan's* poetry.

2 *A Police Bill, and Tithe-composition Bill, and Insurrection Bill*: Bill for Appointment of Constables, and to secure effectual Performance of their Duties, in Ireland (1822), Bill to provide for establishing of Compositions for Tithes in Ireland (1823), Bill, intituled, Act to continue Act for suppressing Insurrections, and preventing Disturbances of Public Peace in Ireland (1824).

How often have I perceived in a congregation of some thousand persons how the very mention from my own tongue of the penal code caused every eye to glisten and every ear to stand erect! The trumpet of the last judgment, if sounded, would not produce a more perfect stillness in any assemblage of Irish peasantry than a strong allusion to the wrongs we suffer. And there are men who think that the country can be improved whilst such a temper continues, or that this temper will cease whilst emancipation is withheld. Vain and silly thought! Men who reason so know nothing of human nature, or if they do, they know nothing of the nature of Irishmen.

This gentry has as many grades as there were steps in Jacob's ladder. Those of them who are possessed of large estates, and whose education and rank should lift them above local prejudices, and bless them with a knowledge of men and things, are for the greater part absent from the country; they know not the condition of their tenantry, unless from the reports of their agents, some of whom, to my knowledge, are most excellent men; whilst others of them are unfeeling extortioners, who exercise over the tenantry an inconceivable tyranny, and are the very worst description of oppressors....

I have the honour to remain,

Dear Sir, &c. &c.

J. K. L.

The Irish are, morally speaking, not only religious, like other nations, but entirely devoted to religion. The geographical position of the country, its soil and climate, as well as the state of society, have a strong influence in forming the natural temperament of the people; they are more sanguine than the English, less mercurial than the French; they seem to be compounded of both these nations, and more suited than either to seek after and indulge in spiritual affections. When it pleased God to have an Island of Saints upon the earth, he prepared Ireland from afar for this high destiny. Her attachment to the faith once delivered to her was produced by many concurrent causes, as far as natural means are employed by Providence to produce effects of a higher kind. The difference of language, the pride of a nation, the injustice and crimes of those who would introduce amongst us a second creed, are assigned as the causes of our adhesion to that which we first received. These causes have had their influence, but there was another and a stronger power labouring in Ireland for the faith of the Gospel; there was the natural disposition of the people suited to a religion which satisfied the mind and gratified the affections, whilst it turned them away from one whose origin, as it appeared to us, was tainted, and which stripped worship of substance and solemnity. Hence, the aboriginal Irish are all Catholics, for the few of them who have departed from the faith of their fathers only appear '*rari nantes in gurgite vasto.*'[1]

To these are joined, especially with the ancient pale, great numbers who have descended from the first settlers, and who in process of time have become more Irish than the Irish themselves; every year, also, adds considerably to their numbers, not only, as we suppose, through the influence of divine grace, but also by that attractive power which abides in the multitude; so that were it not for the emoluments and pride attached to Protestantism, and the artificial modes resorted to for recruiting its strength, there would not remain in three provinces of Ireland, amongst the middling and lower classes, more than a mere remnant of the modern faith. These Catholics have for nearly three centuries been passing through an ordeal of persecution more severe than any recorded in history. I have read of the persecutions by Nero, Domitian, Genseric, and Atilla, with all the barbarities of the sixteenth century; I have compared them with those inflicted in my own country, and I protest to God that the latter, in my opinion, have exceeded in duration, extent, and intensity, all that has ever been endured by mankind for justice sake.... The Irish Catholics are obliged to sweat and toil for those very ministers of another religion who contributed to forge their chains. Their hay and corn, their fleece and lambs, with the roots on which they feed, they are still compelled to offer at an altar which they deem profane. They still are bound to rebuild and ornament their own former parish church and spire, that they may stand in the midst of them as records of the right of conquest, or of the triumph of law over equity and the public good. They still have to attend the bailiff when he calls with the warrant of the church-wardens to collect their last shilling (if one should happen to remain) that the empty church may have a stove, the clerk a surplice, the communion-table elements to be sanctified, though perhaps there be no one to partake of them; they have also to pay a singer and a sexton, but not to toll a bell for them, with a school-master perhaps, but one who can teach the lilies how to grow, as he has no pupils. Such is their condition; while some half-thatched cabin or unfurnished house collects them on Sundays to render thanks to God for even these blessings, and to tell their woes to heaven.

---

1 Virgil, *Aeneid* I. 118: 'Some few [are seen] swimming in the vast flood'.

SIR AUBREY DE VERE HUNT (1788–1846)

He was born in Curragh Chase, Limerick, the eldest son of Sir Vere Hunt, whose baronetcy had been created in 1784. The family was descended from a Cromwellian officer who settled in the Curragh in 1657. Aubrey de Vere was educated at Harrow, a contemporary of Byron and Peel. In 1807 he married Mary Rice of Mount Trenchard, Co. Limerick, sister to Lord Monteagle. The couple had five sons (the third was the poet, Aubrey Thomas de Vere*) and three daughters. De Vere led a quiet life on the family estate, and was an enlightened landlord. He was a life-long friend of Wordsworth, who called his sonnets the 'most perfect of our age'. Modesty prevented him from publishing much.

From *The Lamentation of Ireland and Other Poems* (1823)

LISMORE

A meeting of bright streams and valleys green;
    Of heathy precipice; umbrageous glade;
    Dark, dimpling eddies, 'neath bird-haunted shade;
White torrents gushing, splintered rocks between;
With winding woodland roads; and, dimly seen
    Through the deep dell ere hazy sunset fade,
    Castle, and spire, and bridge, in gold arrayed;
While o'er the deepening mist of the ravine
The perspective of mountain looms afar.
    Such was our Raleigh's home[1] and here his eye
    Drank deep of Nature's wild variety,
Feeding on hopes and dreams! From the world's war
Retired, he dwelt: nor deemed how soon his star
    Should set, dishonoured, in a bloody sea!

From *A Song of Faith* (1842)

I. My Early Life

---

1 Lismore Castle was acquired by Sir Walter Raleigh, a favourite of Queen Elizabeth, in 1589. He was forced to sell it in 1602. He was imprisoned by James I in 1603, and after an ill-fated expedition to South America in 1617, he was excuted in 1618.

The morn of life to me was full of gloom
And dreariness, that never would depart;
   And melancholy clung around my heart;
Like willows, overshadowing a tomb.
Too oft, in lonely places, tears would start,
   And bodings, terrible in darkness, come:
   Dread shapes! which through our mental twilight loom,
Awful as Death with his uplifted dart!
O gentle Hope! breathe on me once again!
So shall I seek thee in the haunts of men,
   And Nature's solitude; and greet thy light
On the wave's bosom; down the leafy glen;
   O'er sunny hills; in the clear moon at night;
And glance of woman's eye, so exquisitely bright!

II. The Family Picture

With work in hand, perchance some fairy cap
   To deck the little stranger yet to come;
One rosy boy struggling to mount her lap,
The eldest studious, with a book or map;
   Her timid girl beside, with a faint bloom,
Conning some tale; while with no gentle tap
   Yon chubby urchin beats his mimic drum,
   Nor heeds the doubtful frown her eyes assume.
So sits the Mother! with her fondest smile
Regarding her sweet Little-ones the while:
   And he, the happy man! to whom belong
These treasures, feels their living charm beguile
   All mortal care; and eyes the prattling throng
With rapture-rising heart, and a thanksgiving tongue.

XVIII. From Petrarch

All day I weep; and through the live-long night,
   When miserable mortals find repose,
   I waste in tears, redoubling all my woes;
And thus I count the hours till morning's light.
O'erflowing sadness dims my aching sight,
   And grief consumes me: Heaven no creature knows
   Wretched like me! relentless passions close

Around; and Peace for ever takes her flight!
Ah me! that ceaseless thus, from day to day,
   And night to night, I run my weary course;
While this, which men call life, slow wastes away,
   But is as death indeed! Ah! cruel source
Of all my woe; more than these pangs I mourn,
That thou canst see me pine, unpitied, and forlorn!

XIX. Canzonet
in the Sonnet Form

The sun is risen o'er the trees;
   Light vapours drift along the plain;
The smoke curls upward on the breeze;
   Bold chanticleer crows out amain,
   While small birds pour a milder strain;
And every stirring sight one sees,
   And every sound that wakes again,
Comes fresh'ning with varieties.
The dew that fills the floweret's eye
   Is like the tear of tenderness;
And softer than a lover's sigh
   The light air lifts yon virgin's tress;
For now the milkmaid wanders by,
   Singing for very happiness.

MARGUERITE POWER, COUNTESS OF BLESSINGTON
(1789–1849)

Born in Knockbrit, Co. Tipperary, fourth of the seven children of Edmund Power, a small landowner from an old Waterford Catholic family, and Ellen Sheehy, from ancient Tipperary stock. In 1797 her father was appointed Magistrate in Waterford and Tipperary. He ruthlessly quenched the '98 Rising in his area, hunting down the insurgents, and shooting a young peasant, thus provoking hatred all round. A dissolute man, his foray into newspaper publishing was a disaster, as were his attempts to redeem his fortune in trade. A terror to his family, he became known locally as 'Shiver-the-Frills' and 'Beau Power' for his foppish dress. He forced Marguerite in 1804 to marry at 14 a violent officer, Captain Maurice Farmer, whom she left after three months, returning to her father's house in Clonmel; her husband died in 1817 from a drunken fall. Four months afterwards his widow married Charles John

Gardiner, second Viscount Mountjoy, and first Earl of Blessington. Seven years her senior, and a widower, he lavished every luxury upon his bride, who became a *belle* in the *beau monde* of London, where they lived until 1822, when they departed for a tour of the continent, which lasted seven years. They were accompanied by a large party, including Count Alfred D'Orsay. In Genoa they befriended Lord Byron, who became the subject of Marguerite's *Conversations of Lord Byron with the Countess of Blessington* (1834). The Earl of Blessington died from a stroke in Paris in 1829; upon his death all his honours became extinct. His widow returned to England, and set up a literary circle with the Count D'Orsay, her lover, who separated from her step-daughter. Lady Blessington supplemented her modest income by writing. For years she edited the *Keepsake* and *The Book of Beauty*, and she was a successful novelist and society gossip. In 1849 she went bankrupt, and moved to Paris with the Count, where she died the same year of a heart attack.

From *Sketches and Fragments*
(1822)

from JOURNAL OF A WEEK OF A LADY OF FASHION

Monday. – Awoke with a headache, the certain effect of being bored all the evening before by the never-dying strain at the Countess of Leyden's. Nothing ever was half so tiresome as musical parties: no one gives them except those who can exhibit themselves, and fancy they excel. If you speak, during the performance of one of their end-less pieces, they look cross and affronted: except that all the world of fashion are there, I never would go to another; for, positively, it is ten times more fatiguing than staying at home. To be compelled to look charmed, and to applaud when you are half-dead from suppressing yawns, and to see half-a-dozen very tolerable men, with whom one could have a very pleasant chat, except for the stupid music, is really too bad. Let me see, what have I done this day? Oh! I remember everything went wrong, as it always does when I have a headache. Flounce, more than usually stupid, tortured my hair; and I flushed my face by scolding her. I wish people could scold without getting red, for it disfigures one for the whole day; and the consciousness of this always makes me more angry, as I think it doubly provoking in Flounce to discompose me, when she must know it spoils my looks.

Dressing from twelve to three. Madame Tornure sent me a most unbecoming cap: mem. I shall leave her off when I have paid her bill. – Heigh-ho, when will that be? – Tormented by duns, jewellers, mercers, milliners: – I think they always fix on Mondays for dunning: I suppose it is because they know one is sure to be horribly vapoured after a Sunday-evening's party, and they like to increase one's miseries.

Just as I was stepping into my carriage, fancying that I had got over the *désagréments* of the day, a letter arrives to say that my mother is very ill and wants to see me: drove to Grosvenor Square in no very good humour for nursing, and, as I expected, found that Madame Ma Mère fancies herself much worse than she really is. Advised her to have dear Dr. Emulsion, who always tells people they are not in danger, and who never disturbs his patient's mind with the idea of death until the moment of its arrival: found my sister supporting mamma's head on her bosom, and heard that she had sat up all night with her: by-the by, she did not look half so fatigued and ennuied as I did. They seemed both a little surprised at me leaving them so soon; but really there is no standing a sick-room in May. My sister begged of me to come soon again, and cast a look of alarm (meant only for my eye) at my mother; I really think she helps to make her hyppish[1] for she is always fancying her in danger. Made two or three calls: drove in the Park: saw Belmont, who looked as if he expected to see me, and who asked if I was to be at the Duchess of Winterton's to-night. I promised to go – he seemed delighted. What would Lady Allendale say, if he saw the pleasure which the assurance of my going gave him?

I long to let her see my triumph. Dined *tête-à-tête* – my lord very sulky – abused my friend Lady Winstanley, purposely to pique me – he wished me not to go out; said it was shameful, and mamma so ill; just as if my staying at home would make her any better. Found a letter from Madame the governess, saying that the children want frocks and stockings: – they are always wanting: – I do really believe they wear out their things purposely to plague me. Dressed for the Duchess of Winterton's: wore my new Parisian robe of blonde lace, trimmed, in the most divine way, with lilies of the valley. Flounce said I looked myself, and I believe there was some truth in it; for the little discussion with my Caro had given an animation and lustre to my eyes. I gave Flounce my puce-coloured satin pelisse as a peace-offering for the morning scold. – The party literally full almost to suffocation. Belmont was hovering near the door of the ante-room, as if waiting my approach: he said I never looked so resplendent: – Lady Allendale appeared ready to die with envy – very few handsome women in the room – and still fewer well dressed. Looked in at Lady Calderwood's

---

1 *hyppish*: somewhat depressed.

and Mrs. Burnet's, Belmont followed me to each. Came home at half-past three o'clock, tired to death, and had my lovely dress torn past all chance of repair, by coming in contact with the button of one of the footmen in Mrs. B.'s hall. This is very provoking, for I dare say Madame Tornure will charge abominably high for it.

Tuesday. – Awoke in good spirits, having had delightful dreams: – sent to know how mamma felt, and heard she had a bad night: – must call there, if I can: wrote Madame a lecture, for letting the children wear out their clothes so fast: Flounce says, they wear out twice as many things as Lady Woodland's children. Read a few pages of 'Amelia Mansfield':[1] very affecting: put it by for fear of making my eyes red. Lady Mortimer came to see me, and told me a great deal of scandal chit-chat: she is very amusing. I did not get out until past five: too late then to go and see mamma. Drove in the Park and saw Lady Litchfield walking; got out and joined her: the people stared a good deal. Belmont left his horse and came to us: he admired my walking-dress very much. – Dined alone, and so escaped a lecture: – had not nerves sufficient to see the children – they make such a noise and spoil one's clothes. Went to the opera: wore my tissue turban, which has a good effect. Belmont came to my box, and sat every other visitor out. My lord came in, and looked, as usual, sulky. (Wanted me to go away without waiting for the dear delightful squeeze of the round-room.) My lord scolded the whole way home, and said I should have been by the sick-bed of my mother instead of being at the opera. I hummed a tune, which I find is the best mode of silencing him, and he muttered something about my being unfeeling and incorrigible.

Wednesday. – Did not rise till past one o'clock, and from three to five was occupied in trying on dresses and examining new trimmings. Determined on not calling to see mamma this day, because if I found her much worse, I might be prevented from going to Almack's,[2] which I have set my heart on: – drove out shopping, and bought some lovely things: – met Belmont, who gave me a note which he begged me to read at my leisure: – had half a mind to refuse taking it, but felt confused, and he went away before I recovered my self-possession: – almost determined on returning it without breaking the seal, and put it into my reticule with this intention; but somehow or other my

---

1 *Amelia Mansfield. Translated from the French of Madame* C[ottin] (1803), a romantic epistolary novel.
2 Almack's Assembley Rooms, King's Street, St James, London, where the London *ton* attended the Wednesday ball with supper during the social season.

curiosity prevailed, and I opened it. – Found it filled with hearts, and darts, and declarations: – felt very angry at first; for really it is very provoking that one can't have a comfortable little flirtation half-a-dozen times with a man, but that he fancies he may declare his passion, and so bring on a *dénouement*; for one must either cut the creature, which, if he is amusing, is disagreeable, or else he thinks himself privileged to repeat his love on every occasion. How very silly men are in acting thus; for if they continued their assiduities without a positive declaration, one might affect to misunderstand their attentions, however marked; but those decided declarations leave nothing to the imagination; and offended modesty, with all the guards of female propriety, are indispensably up in arms.

I remember reading in some book that 'A man had seldom an offer of kindness to make to a woman, that she had not a presentiment of it some moments before';[1] and I think it was in the same book that I read that a continuation of quiet attentions, leaving their meaning to the imagination, is the best mode of gaining a female heart. My own experience has proved the truth of this. – I wish Belmont had not written to me: – I don't know what to do: – how shocked my mother and sister would be if they knew it: – I have promised to dance with him at Almack's too: how disagreeable. I shall take the note and return it to him, and desire that he will not address me again in that style. I have read the note again, and I really believe he loves me very much: – poor fellow, I pity him: – how vexed Lady Winstanley would be if she knew it: – I must not be very angry with him: I'll look grave and dignified, and so awe him, but not to be too severe. I have looked over the billet again, and don't find it so presumptuous as I first thought it: – after all, there is nothing to be angry about, for fifty women of rank have had the same sort of thing happen to them without any mischief following it. Belmont says I am a great prude, and I believe I am; for I frequently find myself recurring to the sage maxims of mamma and my sister, and asking myself what would they think of so-and-so. Lady Winstanley laughs at them and calls them a couple of precise quizzes; but still I have remarked how much more lenient they are to a fault than she is. Heigh-ho, I am afraid they have been too lenient to mine: – but I must banish melancholy reflections, and dress for Almack's. Flounce told me, on finishing my toilette, that I was armed for conquest; and that I never looked so beautiful.

---

1 '*A man ... some moments before*': Laurence Sterne, *A Sentimental Journey through France and Italy*. 17. 'The Remise. Calais'.

Mamma would not much approve of Flounce's familiar mode of expressing her admiration; but, poor soul, she only says what she thinks. – I have observed that my lord dislikes Flounce very much; but so he does every one that I like.

Never was there such a delightful ball: – though I am fatigued beyond measure, I must note down this night's adventures: I found the rooms quite filled, and narrowly escaped being locked out (by the inexorable regulations of the Lady Patronesses, for it only wanted a quarter to twelve when I entered. By-the-by, I have often wondered why people submit to the haughty sway of those ladies; but I suppose it is that most persons dislike trouble, and so prefer yielding to their imperious dictates, to incurring a displeasure, which would be too warmly and too loudly expressed, not to alarm the generality of quiet people). There is a quackery in fashion, as in all other things, and any one who has courage enough (I was going to write impudence), rank enough, and wealth enough, may be a leader. But here am I moralizing on the requisites of a leader of fashion, when I should be noting down the delicious scene of this night in her favourite and favoured temple. I tried to look very grave at poor Belmont; but the lights, the music, and the gaiety of the scene around me, with the consciousness of my looking more than usually well, gave such an exhilaration to my spirits, that I could not contract my brows into anything like a frown; and without a frown, or something approaching it, it is impossible to look grave. Belmont took advantage of my good spirits to claim my hand, and pressed it very much.

I determined to postpone my lecture to him until the next good opportunity, for a ball-room is the worst place in the world to act the moral or sentimental. – *Apropos* of Belmont, what have I done with his note? – My God, what a scrape have I got into! – I left my reticule, into which I had put the note, on my sofa, and the note bears the evident marks of having been opened by some one who could not fold it again: it must have been Flounce. – I have often observed her curiosity – and now I am completely in her power. – What shall I do? – After serious consideration, I think it the wisest plan to appear not to suspect her, and part with her the first good opportunity. I feel all over in a tremor, and can write no more.

Thursday. – Could not close my eyes for three hours after I got to bed; and when I did, dreamt of nothing but detections, duels, and exposures: – awoke terrified: – I feel nervous and wretched: – Flounce looks more than usually important and familiar – or is it conscience that alarms me? Would to Heaven I had never received that horrid note – or that I had recollected to take it to Almack's, and give it back to him. I really feel quite ill. Madame requested an audience, and has told me she can no longer remain in my family, as she finds it impossible to do my children justice unassisted by me. I tried to persuade her to stay another quarter, but she firmly, but civilly, declined. This is very provoking, for the children are fond of, and obedient to Madame, and I have had no trouble since she has been with them; besides my mother recommended her, and will be annoyed at her going. I must write to Madame, and offer to double her salary; all governesses, at least all that I have tried, like money. I must lie down, I feel so fatigued and languid: – mamma is worse, and I really am unable to go to her; for I am so nervous that I could be of no use.

Friday. – I am summoned to my mother, and my lord says she is in the utmost danger. Madame, to add to my discomforts, has declined my offers: I feel a strong presentiment of evil, and dread I know not what....

Good Heavens! What a scene have I witnessed – my dear and excellent mother was insensible when I got to her, and died without seeing or blessing me. Oh! what would I not give to recall the past, or to bring back even the last fleeting week, that I might atone, in some degree, for my folly, my worse than folly – my selfish and cruel neglect of the best of mothers! Never shall I cease to abhor myself for it. – Never till I saw that sainted form for ever insensible did I feel my guilt. From day to day I have deceived myself with the idea that her illness was not dangerous, and silenced all the whispers of affection and duty, to pursue my selfish and heartless pleasures. How different are the resignation and fortitude of my sister, from my frantic grief! – she has nothing to accuse herself of, and knows that her care and attention soothed the bed of death. But how differently was I employed! – distraction is in the thought; I can write no more, for my tears efface the words.

Saturday. – My dear and estimable sister has been with me, and has spoken comfort to my afflicted soul. She conveyed to me a letter from my sainted parent, written a few hours before her death, which possibly this exertion accelerated. The veil which has so long shrouded my reason is for ever removed, and all my selfishness and misconduct are laid bare to my view. Oh! my mother – you whose pure counsel and bright example in life could not preserve your unworthy child, from the bed of death your last effort has been to save her. As a daughter, a wife, and a mother, how have I blighted your hopes and wounded your affections!

My sister says, that my mother blessed me with her last words, and expressed her hopes that her dying advice would snatch me from the paths of error. Those dying hopes, and that last blessing shall be my preservatives. I will from this hour devote myself to the performance of those duties that I have so shamefully, so cruelly neglected. My husband, my children, – with you I will retire from those scenes of dissipation and folly, so fatal to my repose and virtue; and in retirement commune with my own heart, correct its faults, and endeavour to emulate the excellencies of my lamented mother.

Oh! may my future conduct atone for the past, – but never, never let the remembrance of my errors be effaced from my mind.

GEORGE PETRIE (1789–1866)

Born in Dublin, the son of a portrait painter, he was educated at Samuel Whyte's school, which had been attended by Richard Brinsley Sheridan* and Thomas Moore*, and at the arts school of the Royal Dublin Society, developing an interest in the study of Irish antiquities. In 1808 he travelled through Wicklow, collecting material on Irish music, ecclesiastical architecture, and archaeological remains. A meticulous landscape painter, he exhibited regularly at the Royal Hibernian Academy, of which he became the librarian in 1830, and he contributed illustrations to various historical and travel books, including Thomas Cromwell's *Excursions in Ireland*, J. N. Brewer's *The Beauties of Ireland* and G. N. Wright's *Historical Guide To Dublin*, and *Guide to Wicklow and Killarney*. He joined the Royal Irish Academy in 1828, purchasing for its library the *Annals of the Four Masters*, and procuring for its museum such treasures as the Cross of Cong and the Tara Brooch. In 1833 he took charge of the topographical section of the Ordnance Survey of Ireland, working from his own home on a shoestring budget with a team of eminent scholars including John O'Donovan and Eugene O'Curry*, counting W. F. Wakeman and James Clarence Mangan* among his staff. The first 'Memoir' of the Ordnance Survey appeared in 1839, but the government ceased funding for this immense, ground-breaking enterprise. Petrie was awarded the RIA gold medals for his *An Inquiry into the Origin and Uses of the Round Towers of Ireland* (1833, published in 1845, with additions, as *The Ecclesiastical Architecture of Ireland*), and for a comprehensive *Essay on the Antiquities of Tara* (1837). In the former he proved that the towers were ecclesiastical buildings of refuge, refuting the many wayward theories of the use of the round towers, including Charles Vallancey's claim that they were Phœnician watch-towers (Mangan wrote with commendable irony that 'Vallancey / Proved us mere Irish to be

Orientals'). In 1832–33 he co-edited with Caesar Otway the *Dublin Penny Journal*, contributing many antiquarian essays, and in 1840 he founded the *Irish Penny Journal*, editing its 52 issues of nearly 'almost exclusively Irish' writings 'for the great body of people of this country'. Petrie made a significant contribution to the preservation of Irish music, publishing in 1855 *The Ancient Music of Ireland*, which contained 'The Pearl of the White Breast' and the song which became known as 'The Londonderry Air' ('Danny Boy'). He received a Civil List pension in 1849, and was elected president of the Royal Hibernian Academy in 1859. After his death appeared his *Christian Inscriptions in the Irish Language* (ed. Margaret Stokes, 1872) and the second volume of *The Ancient Music of Ireland* (1882).

The Pearl of the White Breast
péarla an bhrollaigh bháin – Anon.

There's a colleen fair as May,
For a year and for a day
I have sought by ev'ry way, – Her heart to gain.
There's no art of tongue or eye,
Fond youths with maidens try,
But I've tried with ceaseless sigh, – Yet tried in vain.
If to France or far-off Spain,
She'd cross the wat'ry main,
To see her face again, – The seas I'd brave.
And if 'tis heav'n's decree,
That mine she may not be,
May the Son of Mary me – In mercy save.

Oh, thou blooming milk-white dove,
To whom I've given true love,
Do not ever thus reprove – My constancy.
There are maidens would be mine,
With wealth in hand and kine,
If my heart would but incline – To turn from thee.
But a kiss, with welcome bland,
And touch of thy fair hand,
Are all that I'd demand, – Wouldst thou not spurn;
For if not mine, dear girl,
Oh, snowy-breasted Pearl!
May I never from the Fair – With life return!

Do You Remember That Night?
An Chuimhin Leat An Oiche 'ud? – Anon.

Do you remember that night
   That you were at the window,
   With neither hat, nor gloves,
   Nor coat to shelter you;
   I reached out my hand to you,
   And you ardently grasped it,
   And I remained to converse with you
   Until the lark began to sing?

Do you remember that night
   That you and I were
   At the foot of the rowan-tree,
   And the night drifting snow;
   Your head on my breast,
   And your pipe sweetly playing?
   I little thought that night
   Our ties of love would ever loosen.

O beloved of my inmost heart,
   Come some night, and soon,
   When my people are at rest,
   That we may walk together;
   My arms shall encircle you
   While I relate my sad tale
   That it is your pleasant soft converse
   That has deprived me of heaven.

The fire is unraked,
   The light unextinguished,
   The key under the door,
   And do you softly draw it.
   My mother is asleep,
   And I am quite awake;
   My fortune is in my hand,
   And I am ready to go with you.

George Petrie

From *The Ecclesiastical Architecture of Ireland*
(1845)

TO
THE VISCOUNT ADARE, M.P., M.R.I.A.,
AND
WILLIAM STOKES, M.D., M.R.I.A.,
REGIUS PROFESSOR OF PHYSIC IN THE UNIVERSITY OF DUBLIN

MY LORD, AND SIR,

You will remember that in one of the beautiful works of the great painter, Nicolo Poussin, he has depicted a group of shepherds at an ancient tomb, one of whom deciphers for the rest the simple inscription engraved upon it:

"ET EGO IN ARCADIA."[1]

And it was a natural and grateful desire of the Arcadian shepherd to be remembered in connexion with the beloved region in which he had found tranquillity and enjoyment.

In like manner, I would wish to be remembered hereafter, less for what I have attempted to do, than as one who, in the pure and warm hearts of the best and most intellectual of his local cotemporaries, had found, and enjoyed, a resting-place, – far superior to that of the Greek.

As two of the dearest of those friends, equally known, beloved, and honoured by all, as by me, – permit me, then, to inscribe your names on this humble monument; so that, if it should happily survive the wreck of time, it may be known as that of one who, though but a feeble and unskilled labourer in the fields of Art and Literature, was not deemed unworthy of the warmest regards of such as you, and who was not ungrateful for his happiness.

Believe, me, my Lord, and Sir,
With sentiments of the deepest Respect and Gratitude,
Your affectionate and faithful Servant,

GEORGE PETRIE

---

1 *ET EGO IN ARCADIA*: The inscription on a tomb in Poussin's pastoral painting reads 'Et in Arcadia ego' – 'Even in Arcadia I [Death] am found'. The inscription is also reproduced in paintings by Guercino and Reynolds.

An Inquiry into the Origin and Uses
of the Round Towers of Ireland

INTRODUCTION

HE question of the Origin and Uses of the Round Towers of Ireland has so frequently occupied the attention of distinguished modern antiquaries, without any decisive result, that it is now generally considered as beyond the reach of conclusive investigation; and any further attempt to remove the mystery connected with it may, perhaps, be looked upon as hopeless and presumptuous. If however, it be considered that most of those inquirers, however distinguished for general ability or learning, have been but imperfectly qualified for this undertaking, from the want of the peculiar attainments which the subject required—inasmuch as they possessed but little accurate skill in the science (if it may be so called) of architectural antiquities, but slight knowledge of our ancient annals and ecclesiastical records, and, above all, no extensive acquaintance with the architectural peculiarities observable in the Towers, and other ancient Irish buildings—it will not appear extraordinary that they should have failed in arriving at satisfactory conclusions, while, at the same time, the truth might be within the reach of discovery by a better directed course of inquiry and more diligent research.

Hitherto, indeed, we have had little on the subject but speculation, and that not unfrequently of a visionary kind, and growing out of a mistaken and unphilosophical zeal in support of the claims of our country to an early civilization; and even the truth – which most certainly has been partially seen by the more sober-minded investigators – having been advocated only hypothetically, has failed to be established, from the absence of that evidence which facts alone could supply.

Such at least appears to have been the conclusion at which the Royal Irish Academy arrived, when, in offering a valuable premium for any essay that would decide this long-disputed question, they prescribed, as one of the conditions, that the monuments to be treated of should be carefully examined, and their characteristic details described and delineated.

In the following inquiry, therefore, I have strictly adhered to the condition thus prescribed by the Academy. The Towers have been all subjected to a careful examination, and their peculiarities accurately noticed; while our ancient records, and every other probable source of information, have been searched for such facts or notices as might contribute to throw light upon their history. I have even gone further: I have examined, for the purpose of comparison with the Towers, not only all the vestiges of early Christian architecture remaining in Ireland, but also those of monuments of known or probable Pagan origin. The results, I trust, will be found satisfactory, and will suffice to establish, beyond all reasonable doubt, the following conclusions:

I. That the Towers are of Christian and ecclesiastical origin, and were erected at various periods between the fifth and thirteenth centuries.

II. That they were designed to answer, at least a twofold use, namely, to serve as belfries, and as keeps, or places of strength, in which the sacred utensils, books, relics, and other valuables were deposited, and into which the ecclesiastics, to whom they belonged, could retire for security in cases of sudden predatory attack.

III. That they were probably also used, when occasion required, as beacons, and watch-towers.

These conclusions, which have been already advocated *separately* by many distinguished antiquaries – among whom are Molyneux, Ledwich, Pinkerton, Sir Walter Scott, Montmorenci, Brewer, and Otway[1] – will be proved by the following evidences:

For the FIRST CONCLUSION, namely, that the Towers are of Christian origin:

1. The Towers are *never* found unconnected with ancient ecclesiastical foundations.
2. Their architectural styles exhibit no features or peculiarities not equally found in the *original* churches with which they are locally connected, when such remain.
3. On several of them Christian emblems are observable, and others display in the details a style of architecture universally acknowledged to be of Christian origin.
4. They possess, invariably, architectural features not found in any buildings in Ireland ascertained to be of Pagan times.

For the SECOND CONCLUSION, namely, that they were intended to serve the double purpose of belfries, and keeps, or castles, for the uses already specified:

1. Their architectural construction, as will appear, eminently favours this conclusion.
2. A variety of passages, extracted from our annals and other

---

1 Sir Thomas Molyneux (1661–1733), Edward Ledwich (1738–1823), John Pinkerton (1758–1826), Hervey de Montmorency–Morres (1767–1839) James Norris Brewer (fl. 1799–1829) and Caesar Otway (1780–1842).

authentic documents, will prove that they were constantly applied to both these purposes.

For the THIRD CONCLUSION, namely, that they may have also been occasionally used as beacons, and watch-towers:

1. There are some historical evidences which render such a hypothesis extremely probable.
2. The necessity which must have existed in early Christian times for such beacons, and watch-towers, and the perfect fitness of the Round Towers to answer such purposes, will strongly support this conclusion.

These conclusions – or, at least, such of them as presume the Towers to have had a Christian origin, and to have served the purpose of a belfry – will be further corroborated by the uniform and concurrent tradition of the country, and, above all, by authentic evidences, which shall be adduced, relative to the erection of several of the Towers, with the names and eras of their founders.

Previously, however, to entering on this investigation, it will be conformable with custom, and probably expected, that I should take a summary review of the various theories of received authority from which I find myself compelled to dissent, and of the evidences and arguments by which it has been attempted to support them. If each of these theories had not its class of adherents I would gladly avoid trespassing on the reader's time by such a formal examination; for the theory which I have proposed must destroy the value of all those from which it substantially differs, or be itself unsatisfactory. I shall endeavour, however, to be as concise as possible, noticing only those evidences, or arguments, that seem worthy of serious consideration, from the respectability of their advocates and the importance which has been attached to them.

These theories, which have had reference both to the origin and uses of the Towers, have been as follows:

FIRST, as respects their origin:

1. That they were erected by the Danes.
2. That they were of Phœnician origin.

SECONDLY, as respects their uses:

1. That they were fire-temples.
2. That they were used as places from which to proclaim the Druidical festivals.
3. That they were gnomons, or astronomical observatories.
4. That they were phallic emblems, or Buddhist temples.
5. That they were anchorite towers, or stylite columns.

6. That they were penitential prisons.
7. That they were belfries.
8. That they were keeps, or monastic castles.
9. That they were beacons and watch-towers.

It will be observed, that I dissent from the last three theories, only as far as regards the appropriation of the Towers exclusively to any one of the purposes thus assigned to them.

CHARLES WOLFE (1791–1823)

He was born at Blackhall, Co. Kildare, youngest of eleven children. His father died when he was eight, and he was educated at Bath, at the Abbey High School, Winchester, and at Trinity College, Dublin, where he graduated with a BA in 1814, refusing to pursue a Fellowship because he did not wish to commit himself to celibacy. He took orders in 1817, becoming a curate in Donoughmore, Co. Down. Suffering from consumption, he had to abandon his work in 1821. He died two years later in Cobh, Co. Cork. Wolfe's poetic output was scant; he left some fifteen poems, which were published, together with his sermons, in 1825, in a memorial volume edited by his friend, John Russell, archdeacon of Clogher. He is chiefly remembered for his elegy of the burial of Sir John Moore at Corunna during the Peninsular War (Wolfe had read Southey's account of the hero's death in the *Edinburgh Annual Register*). Published in the *Newry Telegraph* on 19 April 1817, it was forgotten until Byron praised it as 'such an ode as only Campbell could have written.'

The Burial of Sir John Moore after Corunna[1]

(c. 1815)

Not a drum was heard, not a funeral note,
    As his corse to the rampart we hurried;
Not a soldier discharged his farewell shot
    O'er the grave where our hero we buried.

We buried him darkly at dead of night,
    The sods with our bayonets turning;
By the struggling moonbeam's misty light,
    And the lanthorn dimly burning.

No useless coffin enclosed his breast,

---

1 Lt-General Sir John Moore (1761–1809) died of his wounds after the French had been repulsed in the Battle of La Coruña (16 January 1809). He was hastily buried the following day.

Not in sheet or in shroud we wound him;
But he lay like a warrior taking his rest,
With his martial cloak around him.

Few and short were the prayers we said,
And we spoke not a word of sorrow;
But we steadfastly gazed on the face that was dead,
And we bitterly thought of the morrow.

We thought, as we hollow'd his narrow bed,
And smooth'd down his lonely pillow,
That the foe and the stranger would tread o'er his head,
And we far away on the billow!

Lightly they'll talk of the spirit that's gone,
And o'er his cold ashes upbraid him, –
But little he'll reck, if they let him sleep on
In the grave where a Briton has laid him.

But half of our heavy task was done,
When the clock struck the hour for retiring;
And we heard the distant and random gun
That the foe was sullenly firing.

Slowly and sadly we laid him down,
From the field of his fame fresh and gory;
We carved not a line, and we raised not a stone –
But we left him alone with his glory!

JOHN MACHALE (1791–1881)

Archbishop of Tuam (1834–6), he was named by Daniel O'Connell 'the lion of the fold of Judah', an appellation popular enough to be alluded to by Mr Cunningham in Joyce's story 'Grace'. He was the chief opponent of Archbishop Paul Cullen in the Irish hierarchy. MacHale spoke out against the British authority over Ireland, and opposed the choice of Cardinal Newman, an Englishman, as Rector of the Catholic University. A native Irish speaker, MacHale's Irish translations include the *Pentateuch*, portions of the *Iliad*, and over eighty of Moore's Irish Melodies. His *Evidences and Doctrines of the Catholic Church* was published in 1827. His selected public letters, from 1820 to 1846, edited by himself, appeared in 1847.

John MacHale

Letter from the Place of His Birth

TOBARNAVIAN, July 4, 1834.

Graiorum cedant rivuli, cedant Romolidum fontes,
En ibi salubrior longe, scaturiens unda;
Quæ Uvam sanitate superans, nomen indidit agro
Ex quo eam hausere inclyti Fianorum Heroes.[1]

Air shriuf na Roimhe 'gus na n-Greug,
　　Bheir Tobar na bh-fian, sior bliar go h-eug;
Bhians de fhior-uisge 'g-coghnaid lánn,
　　'S tá map shú caora-fiona, slánn,
Do thug don bhaille anim 's cail
　　Od'ól as Fiani Innis Fail.[2]

Independently of the beautiful scenery by which it is encompassed, the spot from which I now write possesses for me those peculiar charms which are ever found associated with the place of our birth. It is, I think, St John Chrysostom remarks, contrasting the correct and truthful simplicity of youth with the false and fastidious refinement of after-life, that if you present to a child his mother and a queen, he hesitates not in his preference of the one, however homely her costume, to the other, though arrayed in the richest attire of royalty. It is a feeling akin to that filial reverence which the Almighty has planted in our breasts, towards our parents, that extends also to the place where we first drew our being, and hallows all its early associations. This religious feeling is the germ of true patriotism, radiating from the centre of home, and taking in gradually all that is around, until it embraces the entire of our country. It is this mysterious sentiment, common alike to the rude and the civilised, that gives his country the first place in each man's estimation, and makes him regard the most refined or the most prosperous, as only second to his own. I should not value the stoicism that would be indifferent to such a sentiment, and if it be a weakness, it is one that is as old as the times of the Patriarchs, and

---

1 'Let the brookes of the Greeks, let the springs of the Romans admit defeat! / Here bubbles forth far more salubrious water, / Which, surpassing the vine in health, gave its name to the land / Whence the famous Fenian heroes drew it.'
2 The Irish verse is a near–translation of the Latin: 'Surpassing the streams of Rome and Greece, / The Well of the Fenians produces perpetual water-cress, / Is always full of spring water / And also fresh grapes / Which gives to this town its name and fame / Since the Fenians of Ireland drank therefrom.'

which some of the best and wisest men in the Catholic Church have consecrated by their example.

To him who wishes to explore the ancient history of Ireland, its topography is singularly instructive. Many of its valuable records have been doomed to destruction; but there is a great deal of important information written on its soil. Unlike the topography of other countries, the names of places in Ireland, from its largest to its most minute denominations, are all significant, and expressive of some natural qualities or historical recollections. If the Irish language were to perish, as a living language, the topography of Ireland, if understood, would be a lasting monument of its significance, its copiousness, its flexibility, and its force. A vast number of its names is traceable to the influence of Christianity. Such are all those commencing with *cill,* of which the number is evidence how thickly its churches were scattered over the land. The same may be said of *teampul* and *tearmuin,* but, being derived from the Latin language, they are more rare than the word *cill,* a genuine Celtic word. The words commencing with *lios* and *rath* are supposed to ascend to the time of the incursions of the Danes; but, whatever be the period of their introduction, they and *dún* are expressive of military operations. Other denominations imply a territory, either integral or in parts, such as *tir, baille, leath, trian, ceathradh, cuigadh,* etc., and mean the country, the village, half, third, fourth, or fifth of such a district. It is from *cuigad,* or a fifth portion, our provinces were so called; and though now but four provinces are generally named, the corresponding word in Irish signifies a fifth, as *cuig cuighaide Eirean,* or the five provinces of Ireland. Hence, if a stone were not to be found to mark the ruins of the magnificence of Tara, the Irish name of a province will remain an enduring attestation of the ancient monarchy of Meath.

The name of *rus,* or Ros, so frequently characterizing some of our Irish townlands, always signifies a peninsula or promontory, or, for a similar reason, an inland spot, surrounded by moor or water. The words commencing with *magh,* or Moy, signify extensive plains, and assume the appellation of *cluan,* when comparatively retired. The highlands, from the mountain to the sloping knoll, are well known by *sliabh, chnoc, tullagh,* or Tully, and *learg,* while *glean, lág,* called in English Glyn and Lag, denominate the lowlands and the valleys. It is not to be supposed that the numberless lakes and streams that cover the plains or descend from its hills, had not a large influence in giving their names to a great portion of the country. Accordingly, we find *loch, tobar, abhain, seadán,* forming the commencement of the names of several townlands and villages. The qualities by which these several names are modified, are as various as the properties of the soil, and the traditional records of each locality.

Tobarnavian has, like other ancient names, employed and divided skilful etymologists and antiquaries. Some have derived the name from the excellent quality of its waters, not inferior to the juice of the grape, whilst others, with more strict regard to the just rules of etymology, as well as the truth of history, have traced it to the old legends of the Fenian Heroes. *Tobar an fhioin* would be its correct name, according to the first derivation, whereas *Tobar na b-fian* is its exact and grammatical appellation as connected with the historical and poetical legends of the followers of the great leader of the ancient Irish chivalry. Its situation, as well as the tales connected with the scenery by which it is surrounded, give additional force to this etymology. It is situated at the base of Nephin, the second among all the mountains of Connaught in elevation, and inferior but to few in Ireland. The south view is bounded by a portion of the Ox Mountains, stretching from the Atlantic, in the form of an amphitheatre. They are called the *Barna-na-gaoith* mountains from, a narrow and precipitous defile, where the storm rules supreme, and rendered famous by the passage of the French, in 1798, on their way to Castlebar.[1] Round the base of this circuitous range of hills is seen, as if to sleep, the peaceful surface of the beautiful Lake of Lavalla, bordering on the woods of Massbrook. Directly to the east, the large Lake of Con stretches from the Pontoon, to the northwest the lofty hill of *Chnoc Nania* intercepting the view of its surface, and again revealing to the eye, on the north side of the hill, another portion of the same sheet of waters. Beyond the extremity of the lake you can contemplate some of the most cultivated and picturesque portions of Tyrawley, stretching along in the distance as far as the hill of Lacken, of which the view is animated by a fanciful tower of modern construction.

Such is the view that presents itself from this elevated spot, forming the summit level of the district, from the sea to the Ox mountains. In this remote district, secluded by its encircling woods, hills, and lakes, the olden legends and traditions of the land were preserved with a fond and religious fidelity. When the other provinces of Ireland and a large portion of Connaught were overrun and parcelled out among strangers, the territories of Tyrawley were inherited by the descendants of the ancient septs until its fair fields were, at length,

---

1 As exciting events take a strong hold of the youthful mind, the age of seven years at the time – the interval between 1791 and 1798 – enables me vividly to recollect the distressing incidents of that period. [*MacHale's note.*]

invaded and violated by the ruthless followers of Cromwell. For its long immunity from the scourge of the despoiler it paid, at length, the forfeit in the increased oppression to which its inhabitants were doomed; and whilst the descendants of the ancient settlers were mingled in a community of blood and interest with those of the Celtic race in other parts of Ireland, the Catholics of Tyrawley, like those of Tipperary, were doomed to be treated, by those more recent taskmasters, as aliens in country, in language, and in creed.

The retired position of Glyn-Nephin afforded a secure asylum to the songs and traditions of the olden times and the indignities to which the inhabitants were subjected, by the Covenanters who were planted among them, served but to endear every relic of story or of minstrelsy, which time had transmitted. It was here Bunting[1] collected some of the most tender and pathetic of those ancient airs to which Moore has since associated his exquisite poetry. It was here, too, on the banks of Loch Con,[2] that Mr. Hardiman took down some of the sweetest specimens to be found in his collection of Irish minstrelsy. It was no wonder: the name of Carolan, who frequented the district, was yet familiar with the older natives of the valley of Nephin; and in no portion of Ireland did his soul-inspiriting airs find more tuneful voices than were there heard, artlessly pouring them forth, amidst the solitude of the listening mountains.

Of the legends of Ireland, both oral and written, the people were not less retentive than of the songs of their bards. I knew myself some who, though they could not at all read English, read compositions in the Irish language with great fluency; and even of those who were not instructed to read, many could recite the Ossianic poems with amazing accuracy. While Macpherson was exhausting his ingenuity in breaking up those ancient poems, and constructing an elaborate system of literary fraud out of their fragments, there were thousands in Ireland, and especially in Glyn-Nephin, who possessed those ancient Irish treasures of Ossian in all their genuine integrity, and whose depositions, could their depositions be heard, would have unveiled the huge imposture. There is scarcely a mountain, or rock, or river in Ireland that is not in some measure associated with the name of Fion and his followers. On the highest peak of Nephin, is still visible an immense cairne of large and loose stones called '*Leact Fionn*', or Fion's monument. Some fanciful etymologists are disposed to trace the name

---

1 See his *Ancient Music of Ireland*, Index. [*MacHale's note.*]
2 See Hardiman's *Irish Minstrelsy*, vol. I, page 341. [*MacHale's note.*]

of Nephin, or Nefin, to the chief of the Fiana, insisting that it means *Neamh-Fionn*, as Olympus was the seat of the pagan divinities. But though the monument just alluded to may give weight to this opinion, the authority of Duald Mac Firbis[1] is opposed to them, *Neamhthin* being, according to this learned antiquarian, its pure and primitive orthography. The circumstance of *Coll*, one of the most celebrated of those military champions belonging to this province, may well account for their intimate connection with our scenery; and as the Fiana were supposed to have been frequent and familiar visitors in those regions, it is no wonder that their superior quality would have drawn their attention to the waters of this fountain. The Latin and Irish lines with which I have prefaced this letter are inscribed on a stone slab – an appropriate and significant ornament of this ancient fountain, from which are continually gushing its classic or legendary waters.

From the disastrous period of the wars of Cromwell, few or none of the Bishops of Killala, to the time of my two immediate prede-cessors, had a permanent residence in the diocese. Doctor Waldron, my lamented predecessor of pious memory, and Doctor Bellew, filled up near the last half century of that dreary interval.[2] The notices of the lives of the bishops of the preceding portion are but scanty – nay, it would be difficult to supply some considerable chasms with their very names. This has been a misfortune not peculiar to the Diocese of Killala. The churches of Ireland shared in the same calamity. It is to be hoped, however, that, whilst the material edifices which they erect-ed have been destroyed or effaced, their names are written in the more valuable records of the Book of Life. Even of the bishops antecedent to that period the catalogue is imperfect. Duald Mac Firbis, whom I have already quoted, has preserved the names of seven bishops of the Mac Celes,[1] who flourished between the twelfth and thirteenth centuries. To such annalists as the Four Masters, and the authors of the Book of Lecan, &c., we are indebted for such frag-ments of ecclesiastical history as survived the wreck of violence and of time. I indulged a hope, when first I went to the Eternal City, to be able to trace back the unbroken stem of our episcopal succession, and, through it, many subordinate ecclesiastical branches. But even there the task became difficult, if not hopeless. It is some consolation that

---

1 Dubhaltach Mac Fhir Bhisigh (?1600–71), author of *Dúil Laithne* (1643), *Annals of Ireland* (1643), *Chronicon Scotorum* (c.1643), *Breatha Neimheadh Déidheanach*, and *Catalogue of Irish Bishops* (1665). His *Book of Genealogies* remained unfinished.

2 The names of their immediate predecessors were, Erwin, Skerret, Philips, Mac Donnell, of whom the last, or most remote in the series, is here still recollected by some of the old and patriarchal natives. [*MacHale's note.*]

this diocese has supplied some of those who have been most success-ful in illustrating the annals of Ireland. The Book of Lecan is prized by every scholar as one of the most valuable of our records, and the name of Mac Firbis ranks among those great benefactors who, in times of difficulty and darkness, cast a gleam of splendour over the declining literature of their country.

✠ John, Bishop of Killala.

WILLIAM HAMILTON MAXWELL (1792–1850)

Born in Newry, Co. Down, the son of a comfortably prosperous merchant, Maxwell was educated at Dr Henderson's Academy in Newry and at Trinity College, Dublin, graduating BA in 1812. He was ordained in 1813 and became a Church of Ireland curate at Clonallon, in the diocese of Dromore. In 1817 he married Mary Dobbin, a daughter of the MP for Armagh. After a naked ride through town on a Sunday morning he was moved to Mayo, becoming a canon of the diocese of Tuam, and relieved of most pastoral duties. He befriended the Marquis of Sligo and was given the use of Croy Lodge on the Erris Peninsula, where he wrote his novels. Maxwell had rooms in the officers' mess at Castlebar barracks, but he never served as a soldier. He did, however, 'father' the military novel, with *Stories of Waterloo* (1829) and *The Bivouac* (1837). *The Victories of the British Armies* (2 vols., 1839) and his *Life of Field Marshal His Grace the Duke of Wellington* (3 vols., 1839-1841) show his thorough knowledge of military matters. His *History of the Irish Rebellion in 1798* (1845), illustrated by George Cruikshank, is distinctive for its use of eye-witness accounts. His best-known book is *Wild Sports of the West of Ireland* (1832); it combines an account of a sportsman angler, a popular figure in fiction at the time, with a depiction of the customs in a part of Ireland which had escaped civilization. Maxwell shared the extravagance of the rollicking characters in his soldiering novels. He wrote twenty books but died in straitened circumstances.

From *Wild Sports of the West of Ireland*
(1832)
Chapter VII.

Symptoms of a coming Storm – A Sportsman's Dinner – Old John – Pattigo – Gale comes on – Shawn a tra buoy – Seals – The Blind Seal.

---

1 See the 'Hi–Fianna,' one of the last volumes published by the Archæological Society. The learned translator, Mr John O' Donovan, does great justice to the memory of Duald Mac Firbis, who earned the encomiums of O'Flagherty and Charles O'Conor.[*MacHale's note.*]

The morning had a sullen look; Slieve More retained his night-cap; the edge of the horizon, where the ocean met the sky, was tinged with a threatening glare of lurid sunshine; the wind was capricious as a woman's love, now swelling into gusts, now sinking to a calm, as the unsteady breeze shifted round to every point 'i' the shipman's card.' As evening approached, the clouds collected in denser masses, and the giant outline of Slieve More was lost in a sheet of vapour. The swell from the Atlantic broke louder on the bar, the piercing whistle of the curlew was heard more frequently, and the small hard-weather tern, which seldom leaves the Black Rock but to harbinger a coming tempest, was ominously busy, whirling aloft in rapid circles, or plunging its long and pointed wing into the broken surface of the billow; all portended a storm; the wind freshened momentarily, and at last blew steadily from the south-east.

I was at the door engaged in speculating upon the signs of the approaching gale, when old John, my kinsman's grey-headed butler, summoned me to dinner. Some say that a bachelor's repast has always a lonely and comfortless appearance – and it may be so; I grant that a sprinkling of the sexes adds to the social character of the table, but this apart, with the abatement of that best society, lovely woman, who shall dine more luxuriously than I? Two hours' rabbit-shooting in the sand-hills has given me a keen and wholesome appetite. That salmon at noon was disporting in the sea, and this kid was fatted among the heath-flowers of the mountain glen. Kitchener and Kelly[1] could take no exception to the cookery, and had these worthies still been inhabitants of this fair round globe, the Doctor would have found ample amusement for every man's master, the stomach, and honest Myke might have safely ventured to dinner without his *sauce piquante*.

In due time the cloth disappeared, a bundle of split bog-deal was laid upon the hearth, and speedily lighted into a cheerful blaze. Old John, with the privilege of an ancient retainer, conversed with us as he extracted a fresh cork for the evening's potation. 'Awful weather in July, Sir. Well, that *Shown a tra buoy*[2] is a wonderful beast; I knew a change of weather was at hand when he rose beside the shore last night, and showed his gray head and shoulders over the water.'

---

1 *Kitchener and Kelly*: Dr William Kitchiner (1775–1827), optician, telescope maker, gourmet and cook, was the author of *The Cook's Oracle* (1818) and *The Art of Invigorating and Prolonging Life, by Food, Clothes, Air, Wine, Sleep, &c. and Peptic Precepts ... to which is added, the pleasure of Making a Will* (1822); Michael Kelly (?1764–1826), British actor, singer and composer, friend of Mozart; he ran a unsuccessful wine-shop.
2 Jack of the yellow strand. [*Maxwell's note.*]

'Is the seal, John, a sure foreteller of an approaching storm?'

'A certain one, Sir; I remember him from I was a boy in the old master's kitchen, – the Lord be merciful to his soul! *Shown a tra buoy's* features are as familiar to me as my own; I would swear to him among a thousand.'

'You see him frequently?'

'Oh yes, Sir; when the salmon come in, he is every day upon the yellow strand opposite the lodge; there you will see him chase the fish into the shoal-water, catch them beside the boats, ay, or if that fails, take them from the nets and rob the fishermen. Year after year he has returned with the salmon, spending his summer on the 'tra buoy,' and his winter near Carrig-a-boddagh.'

'How has he escaped so long, John? has he not been often fired at?'

'A thousand times; the best marksmen in the country have tried him without success. People say that, like the master otter, he has a charmed life, and latterly nobody meddles with him.'

Old John's narrative was interrupted by the entrance of another personage; he was a stout burly-looking man, with indifferent good features, a figure of uncommon strength, and a complexion of the deepest bronze. He is the skipper of my cousin's hooker. After a career of perilous adventure in piloting the Flushing smugglers to the coast, he has abandoned his dangerous trade to pass an honester and safer life in future.

'Well, Pattigo,[1] what news?'

'The night looks dirty enough, sir; shall we run the hooker round to Tallaghon, and get the rowing-boats drawn up?' His master assented, and ordered him the customary glass of poteen. Pattigo received it graciously in the fingers of his right hand – for he has lost his thumb by the bursting of a blunderbuss in one of his skirmishes with the Revenue – made his ship-shape bow, clapped his sou-wester on, and vanished.

The storm came on apace; large and heavy drops struck heavily against the windows; the blast moaned round the house; I heard the boats' keels grate upon the gravel, as the fishermen launched them up the beach; I saw Pattigo slip his moorings, and, under the skirt of his main-sail, run for a safer anchorage. The rain now fell in torrents, the sea rose and broke upon the rocks in thunder; mine host directed the storm-shutters to be put up, ordered in candles, with a fresh supply of

---

1 A by-name. [*Maxwell's note.*]

billets for the fire, and we made final preparations to be comfortable for the night.

Were I required to name the most *recherché* of my kinsman's luxuries, I should specify his unrivalled canastre; an ample quantity of this precious *tabac* (brought from Holland by a smuggler), with excellent Dutch pipes, was produced by honest John, who rises hourly in my estimation. There was also an *addendum* in the shape of a foreign-looking bottle, which the ancient servitor averred to have been deposited in the cellar since the time of the master's father. If it were so, the thing is a marvel, for such liquor is rarely vouchsafed to mortals. Alas! while my aching head testifies a too devoted attachment to that mis-shapen flask, the unequalled flavour of the exquisite schiedam[1] it contained will ever haunt my memory.

'I remarked,' said my kinsman, as he struck the ashes from his meerschaum, 'that you appeared amused with old John's history of *Shown a tra buoy*. Although in its wild state the seal is always shy and sometimes dangerous, yet when taken young it is easily domesticated, and susceptible of strong attachment to its keepers.[2] There is a curious story told of one of these animals – I believe the leading incidents of the narrative to be perfectly authentic, and it is a memorable record of enduring attachment in the animal, and exquisite barbarity in the man. The tale runs thus: –

'About forty years ago a young seal was taken in Clew Bay, and domesticated in the kitchen of a gentleman whose house was situated on the sea-shore. It grew apace, became familiar with the servants, and attached to the house and family; its habits were innocent and gentle, it played with the children, came at its master's call, and. as the old man described him to me, was 'fond as a dog, and playful as a kitten.'

Daily the seal went out to fish, and after providing for his own wants, frequently brought in a salmon or turbot to his master. His delight in summer was to bask in the sun, and in winter to lie before the fire, or if permitted, creep into the large oven, which at that time formed the regular appendage of an Irish kitchen.

---

1 *schiedam:* Dutch gin named after the town where it was distilled.

2 In January, 1819, in the neighbourhood of Burntisland, a gentleman completely succeeded in taming a seal; its singularities attracted the curiosity of strangers daily. It appeared to possess all the sagacity of the dog, and lived in its master's house and ate from his hand. In his fishing excursions this gentleman generally took it with him, upon which occasion it afforded no small entertainment. When thrown into the water, it would follow for miles the track of the boat, and, although thrust back by the oars, it never relinquished its purpose; indeed, it struggled so hard to regain its seat, that one would imagine its fondness for its master had entirely overcome the natural predilection for its native element. [*Maxwell's note.*]

For four years the seal had been thus domesticated, when, unfortunately, a disease, called in this country 'the crippawn' – a kind of paralytic affection of the limbs which generally ends fatally – attacked some black cattle belonging to the master of the house; some died, others became infected, and the customary cure, produced by changing them to drier pasture, failed. A wise woman was consulted, and the hag assured the credulous owner that the mortality among his cows was occasioned by his retaining an unclean beast about his habitation – the harmless and amusing seal. It must be made away with directly, or the 'crippawn' would continue, and her charms be unequal to avert the malady. The superstitious wretch consented to the hag's proposal; and the seal was put on board a boat, carried out beyond Clare Island, and there committed to the deep, to manage for himself as he best could. The boat returned, the family retired to rest, and next morning a servant awakened her master to tell him that the seal was quietly sleeping in the oven. The poor animal over night came back to his beloved home, crept through an open window, and took possession of his favourite resting-place.

Next morning another cow was reported to be unwell – and the seal must now be finally removed. A Galway fishing-boat was leaving Westport on her return home, and the master undertook to carry off the seal, and not put him overboard until he had gone leagues beyond Innisboffin. It was done: a day and night passed; the second evening closed – the servant was raking the fire for the night – something scratched gently at the door – it was of course the house-dog – she opened it, and in came the seal! Wearied with his long and unusual voyage, he testified, by a peculiar cry expressive of pleasure, his delight to find himself at home, then, stretching himself before the glowing embers of the hearth, he fell into a deep sleep.

The master of the house was immediately apprised of this unexpected and unwelcome visit. In the exigency, the beldame was awakened and consulted; she averred that it was always unlucky to kill a seal, but suggested that the animal should be deprived of sight, and a third time carried out to sea. To this hellish proposition the besotted wretch who owned the house consented, and the affectionate and confiding creature was cruelly robbed of sight, on that hearth for which he had resigned his native element! Next morning, writhing in agony, the mutilated seal was embarked, taken outside Clare Island, and for the last time committed to the waves.

A week passed over, and things became worse instead of better; the cattle of the truculent wretch died fast, and the infernal hag gave him the pleasurable tidings that her arts were useless, and that the destructive visitation upon his cattle exceeded her skill and cure.

On the eighth night after the seal had been devoted to the Atlantic it blew tremendously. In the pauses of the storm a wailing noise at times was faintly heard at the door. The servants, who slept in the kitchen, concluded that the *Banshee* came to forewarn them of an approaching death, and buried their heads in the bed-coverings. When morning broke, the door was opened – and the seal was there lying dead upon the threshold!'

'Stop, Julius!' I exclaimed, 'give me a moment's time to curse all concerned in this barbarism.'

'Be patient, Frank,' said my cousin, 'the *finale* will probably save you that trouble. The skeleton of the once plump animal – for, poor beast, it perished from hunger, being incapacitated from blindness to procure its customary food – was buried in a sand-hill, and from that moment misfortunes followed the abettors and perpetrators of this inhuman deed. The detestable hag who had denounced the inoffensive seal, was, within a twelvemonth, hanged for murdering the illegitimate offspring of her own daughter. Everything about this devoted house melted away – sheep rotted, cattle died, and 'blighted was the corn.' Of several children, none reached maturity, and the savage proprietor survived everything he loved or cared for. He died blind and miserable.

There is not a stone of that accursed building standing upon another. The property has passed to a family of a different name, and the series of incessant calamity which pursued all concerned in this cruel deed is as romantic as true.'

It was midnight. I laid down my pipe, took a candle from the sideboard, wished my cousin a good night, and went to bed, full of pity for the gentle and affectionate seal.

ASENATH NICHOLSON (1792–1855)

Born in Chelsea, Vermont, the oldest child of Michael and Martha Hatch, Congregationalist Protestants, Asenath learnt from them her trust in charity and equality. She was trained as a teacher, and started teaching at sixteen. Her health deteriorated in her early thirties. Her physician suggested a change; never one to do things by half, Asenath went to New York, opened a school, married Norman Nicholson, and was converted to the temperance and vegetarian movement of

Sylvester Graham. In 1832, she opened a Temperance Boarding House. In the summer of 1844, a year after her husband's death, Nicholson sailed for Ireland, with evangelical purposes (she was not a proselyte – the practice is fiercely condemned in the *Annals*). She recorded her travels in *Ireland's Welcome to the Stranger; or, Excursions through Ireland, in 1844 & 1845, for the purpose of personally investigating the condition of the poor* (1847), which offers focused pictures of Ireland at the eve of the Famine. During the Famine she single-handedly brought relief to Dublin poor, in January 1847, moving to the west of Ireland in July. She herself lived frugally on two scant meals a day. Her account, *Annals of the Famine in Ireland* (1851) offers a clear and yet deeply-felt witness report. It formed part of *Lights and Shades of Ireland* (1850), a history of Ireland from the Milesians to Daniel O'Connell* (whose Repeal Association, she noted, did not bring any relief to the poor). Nicholson left Ireland in 1848. She died from typhoid in New Jersey.

From *Ireland's Welcome to the Stranger*
(1847)
Chapter XVI

When about leaving Cork for Killarney I intended taking the shortest and cheapest route; but Father Mathew[1] said, 'If you wish to seek out the poor, go to Bantry, there you will see misery in all and in every form.' I took his advice, went to Bantry, and there found a wild, dirty sea-port, with cabins built upon the rocks and hills, having the most antiquated and forlorn appearance of any town I had seen; the people going about not with sackcloth upon their heads, for this they could not purchase, but in rags and tatters such as no country but Ireland could hang out.

The night was dark and rainy when I reached the town, and a comfortable parlour and cheerful fire hid from my eyes the appalling desolation that brooded without. The morning opened my eyes, to look out upon sights which, as I write, flit before me like haggard spectres. I dressed, went forth, and made my way upon the rocks, found upon the sides of them some deplorable cabins, where smoke was issuing from the doors, and looking into one, the sight was appalling. Like an African kraal, the door was so low as to admit only a child of ten or twelve, and at the entrance a woman put out her head, with a dirty cloth about it; a stout pig was taking its breakfast within, and a lesser

---

1 Father Mathew: Theobald Mathew (1790–1856), leader of the Irish Temperance movement and Capuchin priest. He became a good friend of Asenath Nicholson.

one stood waiting at a distance. The woman crouched over the busy swine with her feet in mud, and asked what I wanted?

In truth, for a moment I wanted time to collect myself before I knew what I wanted; at last I told her my errand was to see how they do in Ireland, among the poor. 'An' faith, you see enough on'em here.' Looking in, I saw a pile of dirty broken straw, which served for a bed for both family and pigs, not a chair, table, or pane of glass, and no spot to sit except upon the straw in one corner, without sitting in mud and manure. On the whole, it was the most revolting picture my eyes ever beheld, and I prayed that they might never behold the like again. Leaving this abode, I ascended the rock a little higher, and entered a second. On the left hand of the door was a bank on which lay a young man upon straw; and upon a couple of stools sat the master and mistress, waiting the cooking of a pot of potatoes for breakfast. 'Is any one sick?' 'No, no, idle, idle,' answered the mother; 'nothin' to do, and so he lies in bed. The old man here has not airn'd but a shillin' since St. John's.' 'And how, do tell me, do you live?' 'We gets our potato when we can, ma'am; and that's all, ye see.' 'So you live, because you can't die.' 'Just so, lady; because the Almighty God don't see fit to take us away an' we must be content with what he sends us; but sure, may we ask, what brought ye here among these wild rocks?' 'To see the poor of Ireland; and I hope to go through the country and see them all.' 'And ye'll have a long purse when ye return.' Supposing she alluded to money, I told her, 'Not a pound perhaps.' 'But ye'll have the whole chart of Ireland, ma'am.'

I looked at this woman, and at the appurtenances that surrounded her. 'The whole chart of Ireland,' from lips that could neither read English nor Irish! She had a noble forehead, an intelligent eye, and a good share of common sense, she had breathed the air of this wild mountainous coast all her sad pilgrimage, and scarcely she said, had a 'dacent garment covered her, or a wholesome male of mate crassed her lips, save at Christmas, since the day she left the parents that raired her.' Telling them I wished some one to carry my carpet bag to Glengariff, the old man said he had a son as honest as any lad in Bantry, and he should take it for a shilling; the bargain was quickly concluded. A lofty well-finished poorhouse was back of these abodes of misery and the old lady leaving her potatoes, showed me up the slippery path-way to the gate. She had said there was no fire but in the kitchen and the school-mistress's room, I replied that this was not the case in any other poorhouse I had visited, and I should like to see it for myself. When we reached the gate it was closed, and no admittance; the keeper was not there, and not a person in it, and never had been, though all things had been ready for a year; the farmers stood out, and would not pay the taxes. The old lady was right respecting the farmers and their taxes, but was quite confused about the fires and fire-places. The poorhouse was certainly the most respectable looking of any building in Bantry; and it is much to be regretted, that the money laid out to build, and pay a keeper for sitting alone in the mansion, had not been expended in giving work to the starving poor, who might then have had no occasion for any house but a comfortable cottage.

I waded about the town an hour more to find, if possible, something more tolerable; but disheartened I returned to my lodgings, which were the only oasis in this woe-begone place. The next day found matters no better, and after again wading through a few streets, I returned disgusted at the nausea, which was sickening in the extreme. I left an Irish Testament where the man of the family could read Irish well, and where no Bible had ever been. The peasants in this part of the country are not so afraid of the scriptures if they speak Irish, because they attach a kind of sanctity to this language.

From *Annals of the Famine in Ireland*

(1851)

Chapter II

...The first starving person that I saw was a few days after the story of the woman and dog had been related. A servant in the house where I was stopping at Kingstown said that the milk woman wished me to see a man near by that was in a state of actual starvation; and he was going out to attempt to work on the Queen's highway. A little labour was beginning opposite the house, and fifteen-pence a day stimulated this poor man, who had seven to support, his rent to pay, and fuel to buy. He had been sick with fever; the clothes of his family that would fetch any price had been pawned or sold, and all were starving together. He staggered with his spade to the work; the overseer objected: but he entreated to be allowed to try. The servant went out and asked him to step into the kitchen; and, reader, if you have never seen a starving human being, *may you never!* In my childhood I had been frightened with the stories of ghosts, and had seen actual skeletons, but imagination had come short of the sight of this man. And here, to those who have never watched the progress of protracted hunger, it might be proper to say that persons will live for months, and pass through different stages, and life will struggle on to maintain her lawful hold, if occasional scanty supplies are given, till the walking skeleton is reduced to a state of inanity – he sees you not, he heeds you not, neither does he beg. The first stage is somewhat clamorous – will not easily be put off; the next is patient, passive stupidity; and the last is idiocy. In the second stage they will stand at a window for hours without asking charity, giving a vacant stare, and not until peremptorily driven away will they move. In the last stage the head bends forward and they walk with long strides and pass you unheedingly.

The man before mentioned was emaciated to the last degree; he was tall, his eyes prominent, his skin shrivelled, his manner cringing and childlike; and the impression *then* and *there* made never *has* nor never *can* be effaced; it was the *first*, and the beginning of these dreadful days yet in reserve. He had a breakfast, and was told to come in at four and get his dinner. The family were from home; the servant had an Irish heart, consequently my endeavours were all seconded. Often has she taken the loaf allowed for her board-wages (that is, so much allowed weekly for food), and sliced nearly the whole away – denying herself for the suffering around her. It must be mentioned that labourers for the public, on roads, seldom or never ate more than twice a day, at ten and four; their food was the potato and oatmeal stirabout, and buttermilk, the luxury which was seldom enjoyed. This man was fed on Indian meal, gruel, buttermilk or new milk and bread in the morning; stirabout, buttermilk and bread at four.

Workmen are not paid at night on the public works, they must wait a week; and if they commence labour in a state of hunger they often die before the week expires; many have been carried home to their wretched cabins, some dead and others dying, who had fallen down with the spade in their hands. The next day after this wretched man was fed, another, in like condition, at work in the same place, was called in and fed; he afterward died when the labour was finished, and he could get no more work. The first man gradually gained strength, and all for him was encouraging, when my purse became low – so many had been fed at the door that a pot was kept continually boiling from seven in the morning till seven at night. Indian meal was then dear, the Americans had not sent their supplies, and much did my heart shrink at the thought that my means must be exhausted.

Let me here speak of the virtues of Indian meal; though always having been accustomed to it, more or less, not till December 1846, in the Famine of Ireland did I know its value. It was made into gruel, boiled till it became a jelly; and once a day from twenty-five to thirty were fed – some who walked miles to get it, and every one who had this privilege recovered without tasting anything but that, once a day. They always took it till they wanted no more; and this too without bread. One old man daily walked three miles, on his staff for this and he grew cheerful, always most courteously thanking me, saying, 'It nourishes my old heart so that it keeps me warm all the night.'

I had told these two labourers that when they found the gate locked they must know that I had no more to give them and they must go home. The sad hour arrived; the overseer sent me word that he thanked me for feeding them so long; they must otherwise have died at their work. The gate was shut, and long and tedious were the next two days. One child of the poor man died, and he buried it in the morning before light because if he took an hour from labour he would be dismissed. When the poor creatures that had daily been fed with the gruel came and were told there was no more for them, I felt that I had sealed their doom. They turned away blessing me again and again, but 'we must die of the hunger. God be praised'.

I would not say that I actually murmured, but the question did arise: 'Why was I brought to see a famine, and be the humble instrument of saving some few alive, and then see these few die, because I had no more to give them?'

Two days and nights dragged on. News was constantly arriving of the fearful state of the people, and the spectres that had been before my eyes constantly haunted me. My bedroom overlooked the burying ground. I could fancy, as I often arose to look into it, that some haggard father was bringing a dead child lashed to his back, and laying him on some tombstone, as had been done, and leaving it to the mercy of whoever might find it a grave!

I was sitting in solitude, alone, at eleven o'clock, when the man of the house unexpectedly arrived. He had a parcel; in that parcel there was money from New York, and that money was for me!

No being, either Christian or pagan, if he never saw a famine, nor possesses a feeling heart, can understand what I then felt. I adored that watchful Hand that had so strangely led and upheld me in Ireland; and now, above all and over all, when my heart was sinking in the deepest despondency, when no way of escape appeared, this heavenly boon was sent! The night was spent in adoration and praise, longing for the day, when I might again hang over the 'blessed pot', as the Irish called it. I lay below on a sofa and saw no tombstones that night....

When the rumour of a famine had become authenticated in Dublin, Joseph Bewley, a Friend, possessing both a warm heart and full purse (which do not always go together), put in operation a soup-shop which fed many hundreds twice a day.[1] This soup was of the best quality, the best meat, peas, oatmeal, &c.; and when applications became so numerous that a greater supply was requisite and funds failing, mention was made to this benevolent man that the quantity of meat must be reduced, his answer was that not one iota should be taken off, but more added, if even it must be done entirely at his own expense. It shall, he added, be made rich and nourishing as well as palatable. The poor who could, were required to pay half-price for a ticket; and benevolent people purchased tickets by the quantity, and gave to the poor. The regulation of this soup establishment was a pattern worthy of imitation. The neatness and order of the shop; the comely attired Quaker matrons and their daughters, with their white sleeves drawn over their tidy-clad arms, their white aprons and caps, all moving in that quiet harmony so peculiar to that people; and there, too, at seven in the morning, and again at midday. All this beauty and finish contrasted with the woe-begone, emaciated, filthy, ragged beings that stood in their turn before them, was a sight at which angels if they could weep, might weep, and might rejoice too. Often have I stood, in painful admiration, to see the two extremes of degradation and elevation, comfort and misery, cleanliness and filth, in these two classes made alike in God's image, but thrown into different circumstances developing two such wide and strange opposites.

My task was a different one – operating individually. I took my own time and way – as woman is wont to do when at her own option: and before the supplies, which afterward came through the letters mentioned, I marked out a path which was pursued during that winter until July when I left for the North. A basket of good dimensions was provided, sufficient to contain three loaves of the largest made bread; this was cut in slices, and at eight o'clock I set off. The poor had watched the 'American lady' and were always on the spot, ready for an attack, when I went out; and the most efficient method of stopping their importunities was bread. No sooner well upon the street, than the army commenced rallying; and no one, perhaps, that winter, was so regularly guarded as was this basket and its owner. A slice was given to each till it was all exhausted; while in desperation, at times,

---

1 Joseph was a brother of Joshua Bewley, a tea merchant who founded what is now known as Bewley's café. Together with Jonathan Pim, a fellow Quaker, Joseph formed the Central Relief Committee in 1846.

lest I might be overpowered – not by violence, but by number – I hurried on, sometimes actually running to my place of destination, the hungry ones, men, women, and children who had not received the slice in pursuit till I rushed into some shop-door or house, for protection, till the troop should retire; sometimes the stay would be long and tedious, and ofttimes they must be driven back by force.

Cook street, a place devoted almost entirely to making coffins and well known by the name of Coffin street, was the field of my winter's labour. This was chosen for its extreme poverty, being the seat of misery refined; and here no lady of 'delicate foot' would like to venture; and beside, I saw that a little thrown over a wide surface was throwing all away, and no benefit that was lasting would ensue. Ten pounds divided among a hundred, would not keep one from starvation many days; but applied to twenty, economically, might save those twenty till more efficient means might be taken. So much a day was allowed to each family, according to their number – always cooking it myself in their cabins till they could and did do it prudently themselves. The turf was provided and the rent paid weekly, which must be done, or, in many cases, turning upon the street was the consequence. For it is no more than justice to observe that there are some kind slaveholders in the United States, and there are some kind landlords in Ireland, but in too many cases both are synonymous terms, so far as power may be equal.

One of these miserable families was that of a widow. I found her creeping upon the street one cold night, when snow was upon the ground. Her pitiful posture, bent over, leaning upon two sticks, with a little boy and girl behind her crying with the cold, induced me to inquire, and I found that she was actually lame, her legs much swollen, and her story proved to be a true one. She had been turned from the hospital as a hopeless case, and a poor, sick, starving friend had taken her in, and she had crawled out with a few boxes of matches to see if she could sell them, for she told me she could not yet bring herself to beg. She could work, and was willing to, could she get knitting or sewing. I inquired her number. 'I will not deny it again,' she replied. 'I did so to a lady, soon after I came out of the hospital, for I was ashamed to be found in such a dreadful place by a lady; but I have been so punished for that lie, that I will not do it again.' Giving her a few pence, and meaning to take her by surprise if I found her at all, an indirect promise was made to call at some future day. At ten the next morning my way was made into that fearful street, and still more fearful alley which led to the cheerless abode I entered.

The reader may be informed that in the wealthy, beautiful city of Dublin, which can boast some of the finest architecture on earth, there are in retired streets and dark alleys some of the most forbidding, most uncomfortable abodes that can be found in the wildest bogs of that wretched country. Finding my way through darkness and filth, a sight opened upon me, which, speaking moderately, was startling. When I had recovered a little, I saw on my right hand the miserable woman before-named, sitting in a dark corner on a little damp straw, which poorly defended her from the wet and muddy ground-floor she was occupying. The two ragged, hungry children were at her feet; on the other side of the empty grate (for there was not a spark of fire) sat the kind woman who had taken her in, on the same foundation of straw and mud, with her back against the wall. She was without a dress – she had pawned her last to pay her rent; her husband likewise had pawned his coat for the same purpose. He was lying upon the straw, with a fragment of a cotton shawl about him, for he had no shirt. They were all silent, and for a while I was a mute.

The woman first mentioned broke the pause, by saying, 'This, I believe, is the kind lady I met last night. You have found the way to our dark place, and I am sorry we cannot ask you to sit down.' There was not even a stool in the room. The young woman had been sick for weeks, and was now only able to sit up a little; but having neither food, fuel or covering, nothing but death stared them in the face; and the most affecting part of the whole to me was the simple statement of the widow who said, in the most resigned manner, 'We have been talking, Mary and I, this morning, and counting off our days; we could not expect any relief, for I could not go out again, and she could not, and the farthest that the good God will give us on earth cannot be more than fourteen days. The children, may be,' she added, 'God would let her take with her, for they must soon starve if left.' This had been a cool calculation made from the appearance of the present condition, and without the least murmuring they were bringing their minds to their circumstances. 'You are willing to live longer,' I said. 'If the good God wills it,' was the answer, 'but we cannot see how.'

They did live. Daily did I go and cook their food, or see it cooked, and daily did they improve; and in a few weeks many an apronful of shavings and blocks were brought to me from the coffin-shops by the young woman who was sitting almost naked on the straw. They both were good expert knitters and good seamstresses; and my garments, which were approaching to a sisterhood with many of the going-down genteel ones, were soon put in tidy repair by this young woman. Often, late in the evening, would I hear a soft footstep on the stairs, followed by a gentle tap, and the unassuming Mary would enter with her bountiful supply of fire-kindling; and when she was told that less would do very well, and she should keep more for herself, she replied, 'I can do with little, and you would not like to go to the shop for any.' She watched my wardrobe, kept everything in the best repair, and studied my comfort first, before she seemed to know that she needed any. I had saved her life, she said, and that was more than all she could do for me; and the day that I sailed from Dublin for England, as I was hurrying along the street, someone caught me by my dress, and turning about, Mary stood before me, whom I had not seen for months, having been absent in the mountains. She had a basket on her arm, was comfortably clad, said she was selling fruit and vegetables and doing well; the other was still with her, in ill health, but not suffering for food. 'Farewell, Mary, we shall meet no more on earth; may God fit us both for a better world!' 'Shall I never see you again? God be praised that he sent you to us!'

The man whom I found on the highway at Kingstown, having heard that I was going from Ireland, walked seven Irish miles that day to see and thank me, and leave his blessing. I was out and regretted much, for his sake as well as mine, that he was disappointed. These testimonials were more grateful to me than would have been a donation of plate from the government. They were God's testimonials – the offerings of the poor; and that heart is not to be envied that does not know their blessings....

Chapter IV

...The next day we were to visit Arranmore, a pretty sunny island, where peace and comfort had ever reigned. The peasantry here were about 1500 in number, occupying a green spot three miles in length, and had always maintained a good character for morality and industry. They kept cows, which supplied them with milk, sheep with wool, geese with beds, fowls with eggs; and grew oats, potatoes and barley; they wore shoes and stockings, which none of the female peasantry can do in the country places; they likewise spun and made their own wearing apparel, and as the difficulty of crossing the channel of the sea, which was three miles, was considerable, they seldom visited the mainland. When they knew the potato was gone, they ate their fowls, sheep and cows, and then began to cross the sea to Templecrone for relief. What could they find there? One man could do but little to stay the desolation. Hundreds had died before this, and though I knew that painful scenes were in waiting, yet, if possible, the half was not told me. Six men. beside Mr Griffith, crossed with me in an open boat, and we landed, not buoyantly, upon the once pretty island. The first that called my attention was the death-like stillness – nothing of life was seen or heard, excepting occasionally a dog. These looked so unlike all others I had seen among the poor I unwittingly said – 'How can the dogs look so fat and shining here, where there is no food for the people?'

'Shall I tell her?' said the pilot to Mr Griffith, not supposing that I heard him.

This was enough: if anything were wanting to make the horrors of a famine complete, this supplied the deficiency. Reader, I leave you to your thoughts, and only add that the sleek dogs of Arranmore were my horror, if not my *hatred*, and have stamped on my mind images which can never be effaced.

We made our first call at the door of the chapel. The fat surly-looking priest was standing there; and, saying to him, 'Your people, sir, are in a bad state'.

'Bad enough, they give *me* nothing.'

'Why should they? You cannot expect or *ask* anything of the poor, starving creatures.'

The curate withdrew, leaving the battle to be decided by the priest, pilot and myself, for he had known him before.

'Ah,' said the pilot, softly, 'he's a hard one; *there's* the Christian for you,' pointing to the curate, 'he's the man that has the pitiful heart – not a creature on the island but would lay down the life for him.'

This pilot was a Roman Catholic, but that characteristic impartiality peculiar to the Irish, where justice and mercy are concerned, belonged to him likewise. We went from cabin to cabin, till I begged the curate to show me no more. Not in a solitary instance did one beg. When we entered their dark, smoky, floorless abodes, made darker by the glaring of a bright sun which had been shining upon us, they stood up before us in a speechless, vacant, staring, stupid, yet most eloquent posture, mutely, *graphically* saying, 'Here we are, your bone and your flesh, made in God's image, like you. *Look at us!* What brought us here?'

May God forgive me, and I believe he will, or I would not say it. With Job, I said, 'Let darkness and the shadow of death stain that day when first the potato was planted in this green isle of the sea', to

301

oppress the poor labourer, and at last bring him to a valley of death – *deep, dark, intricate* – where slimy serpents, poison lizards and gnawing vultures creep and wind about his wasted limbs, and gnaw into the deepest recesses of his vitals.

In every cabin we visited, *some* were so weak that they could neither stand nor sit, and when we entered they saluted us, by crawling on all fours toward us, and trying to give some token of welcome. *Never, never*, was the ruling passion stronger in death. That *heartfelt* greeting which they give the stranger had not in the least died within them. It was not asking charity, for the curate answered my inquiries afterward, concerning the self-control, which was the wonder of all, that he had sent a man previously through the island to say that a stranger from across the sea was coming to visit them, but she had no money or food to give, and they must not trouble her. I gave a little boy a biscuit, and a thousand times since have I wished that it had been thrown into the sea. It could not save him: he took it between his bony hands, clasped it tight, and half-bent as he was, lifted them up, looked with his glaring eyes upon me, and gave a laughing grin that was truly horrible. The curate turned aside, and beckoned me away. 'Did you see that horrid attempt to laugh?'

'I cannot stay longer,' was my answer. We hurried away....

A famine burying-ground on the sea-coast has some peculiarities belonging to itself. First, it often lies on the borders of the sea without any wall, and the dead are put into the earth without a coffin, so many piles on piles that the top one often can be seen through the thin covering; loose stones are placed over, but the dogs can easily put these aside and tear away the loose dirt. This burial-place was on a cliff, whose sides were covered with rough stones, and the ascent in some parts very difficult. We ascended, sometimes keeping erect, and sometimes being obliged to stoop and use our hands. When we reached the top, the painful novelty repaid all our labour. It was an uneven surface of a few perches, with new-made graves and loose stones covering them. A straw-rope was lying near a fresh-dug grave, which the pilot said belonged to an old man who two days before he saw climbing the cliff, with a son of fifteen lashed to his back by that cord, bringing in his feeble hand a spade. 'I untied the cord, took the corpse from the father's back, and with the spade, as well as I could, made a grave and put in the boy,' adding, 'Here you see so many have been buried, that I could not cover him well.'

This was the burial-place of Arranmore, and here, at the foot, was the old roaring ocean, dashing its proud waves, embracing in its broad arms this trembling green gem, while the spray was continually sprinkling its salt tears upon its once fair cheek, as if weeping over a desolation that it could not repair. At a little distance was a smooth green field, rearing its pretty crop of young barley, whose heads were full and fast ripening for the sickle. 'This,' said Mr Griffith, 'is the growth of seed which was presented by William Bennett, last March; the poor creatures have sowed it, and if the hands that planted it live to reap the crop, they will have a little bread. Take a few heads of it, and send them to him as a specimen of its fine growth, and of their care in cultivating it. Had these industrious people,' he added, 'been supplied in the spring with seed of barley and turnips, they would not need charity from the public. The government sent a supply around the coast, the delighted people looked up with hope, when, to their sad disappointment, this expected gift was offered at a price considerably higher than the market one, and we saw the ship sailing away, without leaving its contents; for not one was able to purchase a pound. And we have since been told, that the "lazy dogs" were offered seed, but refused, not willing to take the trouble to sow it.'

JOHN D'ALTON (1792–1867)

Born at the ancestral mansion, Bessville, Co. Westmeath, he was educated at Summer Hill, Dublin; he passed the entrance examination to Trinity College, Dublin at the age of fourteen, graduating in 1811. He studied law at the Middle Temple, and the King's Inns, London, and was called to the Irish bar in 1813. A successful lawyer, renowned for his genealogical knowledge, he published a treatise on the 'Law of Tithes'. In 1827 he received the first prize and the Cunningham Gold Medal from the Royal Irish Academy for his essay on Irish civilization from the beginning of the Christian era to the twelfth century. In 1831 he won the Royal Irish Academy's prize for his account of the reign of Henry II in Ireland. His contributions to the *Irish Penny Journal* on druidical stones, raths, fortresses, castles, keeps and abbeys were illustrated by Samuel Lover*. A host of historical publications ensued; including a *History of the County of Dublin* (1838), *The History of Drogheda and its Environs* (1844), *Annals of Boyle* (1845) and *King James II's Irish Army List, 1689* (1855). His first poetry publication consisted of the twelve cantos of *Dermid, or Erin in the Days of Brian Boroimhe'* (1814), which was praised by Sir Walter Scott. He contributed translations to Hardiman's *Irish Minstrelsy* (1831).

Eileen A Roon[1]

from Hardiman's *Irish Minstrelsy or Bardic Remains of Ireland*

Blind to all else but thee,
        Eileen a Roon!
My eyes only ache to see
        Eileen a Roon!
My ears banquet on thy praise,
Pride and pleasure of my days!
Source of all my happiness!
        Eileen a Roon!
My dove of all the grove thou art,
Without thee sickness wastes my heart;
Who can alone the cure impart?
        Eileen a Roon!

Break not for king or throne,
        Eileen a Roon!
The vows that made thee mine alone;
        Eileen a Roon!
Venus of my ev'ry vow,
Brightest star on heaven's brow!
My Helen – without stain art thou,
        Eileen a Roon!
My rose – my lily – both confest, –
My treasure – all I wish possest; –
The hearted secret of my breast,
        Eileen a Roon!

With thee o'er seas I'd sport my way,
        Eileen a Roon!
Never – never from thee stray,
        Eileen a Roon!
I'd wander o'er thy honied lip,
With love-tales charm thee on the deep,
Then lull thee on my breast to sleep,
        Eileen a Roon!

---

1 *Eileen A Roon*: 'Dear Eileen'; cf. Thomas Furlong's translation (p. 313).

To vallies green I'd stray with thee
By murmuring rill and whispering tree –
The birds will our wild minstrels be,
                    Eileen a Roon!

Oh! Erin!

Oh! Erin! in thine hour of need
    Thy warriors wander o'er the earth;
For others' liberties they bleed,
    Nor guard the land that gave them birth:
In foreign fields, it is their doom
To seek – their fame, – to find – their tomb.

For them no friend of early days
    A tear of kindred grief shall shed:
Nor maiden's prayer, nor minstrel's lays,
    Shall hallow their neglected bed.
They sleep beneath the silent stone,
To country lost – to fame unknown.

Carroll O'Daly and Echo

Carroll.   Speak, playful echo, speak me well,
                    Thou knowest all our care;
            Thou sweet, responding sybil, tell
                    Who works this strange affair.
                            Echo – A fair.

A fair? No, no, I've felt the pain
    That, but from love can flow,
And never can my heart again
    That magic thraldom know.
            Echo – No?

Ah! then if envy's eye has ceased
    To mar my earthly bliss,
Speak consolation to my breast,
    If remedy there is.
            Echo – There is.

Gay, charming spirit of the air,
    If such relief be nigh,
At once the secret spell declare,
    To still my heavy sigh.
                Echo – To die.

To die? And if it be my lot,
    It comes in hour of need;
Death wears no terror but in thought,
    'Tis innocent in deed.
                Echo – Indeed?

Indeed, 'tis welcome to my woes,
    Thou airy voice of fate,
But ah, to none on earth disclose
    What you prognosticate!
         Echo (playfully) – To Kate.

To Kate! The devil's in your tongue
    To scare me with such thoughts.
To her, oh could I impute wrong,
    Who never knew her faults!
              Echo – Her false.

If thy Narcissus could awake
    Such doubts, he were an ass
If he did not prefer the lake
    To humouring such a lass.
                Echo – Alas!

A thousand sighs and sounds of woe
    Attend thee in the air,
What mighty grief can keep thee so,
    In such untired despair.
              Echo – Despair.

Despair! Not for Narcissus' sake,
    Who once was thy delight;
Another lover thou hast got,
    If our report is right.
             Echo – 'Tis right.

Sweet little sorceress, farewell,
 I feel thou'st told me true,
But since thou'st many a tale to tell,
 I bid thee now adieu.
　　　　Echo – Adieu!

WILLIAM MAGINN (1793–1842)

B orn at Marlboro's Fort, Cork, the son of a private schoolmaster, he was educated at Trinity College, Dublin, graduating with a BA in 1811. He returned to
Cork, assisting his father in his school, and running it after the latter's death in
1813. In 1819 he received his LL.D. from Trinity, and began contributing, unpaid,
to the *Literary Gazette* and *Blackwood's Magazine*. He visited his publisher William
Blackwood in 1821, and was introduced to the Edinburgh Tory literati. Adopting
the pseudonym of Morgan O'Doherty he wrote Hibernian mock epics, parodying
Thomas Moore*, Wordsworth and Coleridge, amongst others, and 'exposing'
Byron's indebtedness to Miss Lee's *Canterbury Tales*. O'Doherty's *Maxims* parody
de la Rochefoucauld. He contributed the motto and racy dialogues to the *Noctes
Ambrosianæ* (1822–28). In 1823 he relinquished his school, and moved to London.
John Murray considered entrusting him with writing Byron's biography, but enlist-
ed him instead on the staff of a journal, *The Representative*. He was dispatched to
Paris as foreign correspondent, where he began a novel, which he never finished.
He was brought back as he was gaining a reputation as a drunkard, and was made
editor of the paper's lighter fare, subsequently becoming joint editor of *The
Evening Standard*. In 1827 he published *Whitehall, or the Days of George IV*, a
witty extravaganza. *The City of Demons*, written for *The Literary Souvenir* the following year, showed him capable of writing serious fiction. He broke with the
Standard and with *Blackwood's* in 1828, and in 1830 founded *Fraser's Magazine*,
filling its first four numbers but never acting as editor. Carlyle and Thackeray were
among its contributors. Maginn's 'Gallery of Literary Characters', popular parodies
(of, among others, Disraeli and Carlyle) were complemented by Daniel Maclise's
caricatures. In 1834, Maginn returned to *Blackwood's* where 'The Story without a
Tail' appeared – an account of an intemperate night in the London Temple – as well
as his comic masterpiece, 'Bob Burke's Duel with Ensign Brady'. His vituperative
attack on Grantley Berkeley's novel *Berkeley Castle*, written in a drunken hour, led
to a duel (three rounds of shots were exchanged but neither party was injured). He
wrote a Rabelaisian mock review of Southey's *The Doctor*, and three essays on
Shakespeare's learning. His 'Homeric Ballads', which appeared in *Fraser's* from
1838, episodes from the *Odyssey* in verse, received praise from Matthew Arnold.
In 1839 he produced comic versions of Lucian's Dialogues in blank verse. The
death of Letitia E. Landon affected him gravely. Dissipation took its toll: he land-

ed in a debtor's prison, from which he emerged consumptive and broken-hearted. He retired to Walton-on-Thames. *John Manesty, the Liverpool Merchant*, a novel set in eighteenth-century Liverpool, was published by his widow (under her name) two years after his death. Thackeray depicted him as 'Captain Shandon' in *Pendennis*, while Mangan* offers him as a frightening example of dissipation in 'The Nameless One'.

From *The Odoherty Papers*

(1855)

If a Lover, Sweet Creature, Should Foolishly Seek

If a lover, sweet creature, should foolishly seek
  On thy face for the bloom of the rose,
Oh tell him, although it has died on thy cheek,
  He will find it at least on thy *nose*.

Sweet emblem of virtue! rely upon this,
  Should thy bosom be wantonly prest,
That if the rude ravisher gets but a kiss,
  He'll be ready to *fancy the rest!*

Confusion Seize Your Lowsy Sowl, Ye Nasty Dirty Varment

'Confusion seize your lowsy sowl, ye nasty dirty varment,
Ye goes your ways, and leaves me here without the least preferment;
When you've drunk my gin, and robbed my till, and stolen all my pelf, ye
Sail away, and think no more on your wife at Philadelphy.'

from *Moore-ish Melodies*

'Tis the Last Glass of Claret[1]

'Tis the last glass of Claret,
  Left sparkling alone,
All its rosy companions
  Are *clean'd out* and gone.
No wine of her kindred,

---

1 A parody of Thomas Moore's ''Tis the Last Rose of Summer'*.

No Red Port is nigh,
To reflect back her blushes,
　And gladden my eye.

I'll not leave thee, thou lone one,
　This desert to crown:
As the bowls are all empty,
　Thou too shalt float down.
Thus kindly I drink up
　Each drop of pure red,
And fling the bright goblet
　Clean over my head.

So soon may dame Fortune
　Fling me o'er her head,
When I quit brimming glasses,
　And bundle to bed.
When Champaigne is exhausted,
　And Burgundy's gone,
Who would leave even Claret,
　To perish alone.

THOMAS FURLONG (1794–1827)

Born in Scarawalsh, Co. Wexford, the son of a small farmer, Furlong was apprenticed to a Dublin grocer at the age of 14. An elegy which he wrote on the death of his employer brought him to the attention of John Jameson, the distiller, who gave him a job in the counting house of the distillery, and encouraged his writing. His first book, *The Misanthrope and Other Poems* (1819; 1821), attracted the attention of Thomas Moore* and Lady Morgan*. *The Plagues of Ireland* (1824), a political satire, brought him the friendship of Daniel O'Connell*, whose confidant he became. Furlong described his own work as 'a little sketch and hasty picturing' of the wrongs in his 'harassed land'. He contributed to the *New Monthly Magazine* and various other Dublin journals, and in 1821 he co-founded *The New Irish Magazine*. At the suggestion of Thomas Hardiman*, he undertook the translation of the Gaelic verse of Carolan* and others. Furlong's *The Doom of Derenzie* (1829), a poem in blank verse on the superstitions of the Wexford peasantry, was published posthumously.

From Hardiman's *Irish Minstrelsy or Bardic Remains of Ireland*

Volume I

(1831)

Gracey Nugent[1]

Oh joy to the blossom of white-bosom'd maids,
    To the girl whose young glance is endearing,
Whose smile, like enchantment, each circle pervades,
    She who makes even loneliness cheering.
Oh! he that beholds thee by night or day,
    He who sees thee in beauty before him,
Tho' stricken and spell-bound may smile and say,
    That he blesses the charm that's o'er him

Her neck is like snow – rich and curling her hair,
    Her looks like the sun when declining
Oh happy is he who may gaze on the fair,
    While her white arms round him are twining
Her words are all joyous – and mildly the while
    Her soft blue eyes seem glancing;
And her varying blush and dimpled smile,
    With those eyes and tones are entrancing.

Then joy to young Gracey, the gentle dame,
    'Tis bliss on one's pathway to meet her;
Where! where's the proud spirit her voice cannot tame?
    Oh! where is the sound can be sweeter?
'Tis soothing the song of the birds to hear –
    But her tones are yet more thrilling;
But where's the bowl ? – let the bowl be near,
    And I'll finish the theme while filling.

Cashel of Munster, or the 'Clar Bog Deal'[2]

I would wed thee my dear girl without herds or land,
Let me claim as a portion but thy own white hand;

---

1 Translation from Carolan.
2 *Clar Bog Deal*: 'soft deal board'.

On each soft dewy morn shall I bless thy charms,
And clasp thee all fondly in my anxious arms.

It grieves me, my fairest, still here to stay,
To the south, to the south love! let us haste away;
There plainly, but fondly, shall thy couch be spread,
And this breast be as a pillow to support thy head.

Bethink thee my sweet maid of old *Slieve-na-mon,*
And the vales where I sported in the days long gone;
Tho' my locks now look grey, and my blood runs chill,
The fond heart that then lov'd thee can love thee still.

Oh! turn not upon me that cold glance of scorn,
Nor deem me as a mean one, or one basely born;
Nay, take me to thy arms love! and thou shalt see,
That the gentlest of the gentle I can prove to thee.

Not from wealth closely hoarded can I claim delight,
Not with herds or fair flocks can I tempt thy sight;
Nay! these gifts of frail fortune midst the crowd may fall,
But the soul fraught with fondness is beyond them all.

On thy young brow my sweet one, a cold gloom appears,
And thy glance of mild brightness seems dim'd with tears;
The world, dear, may slight thee, but when friends are gone,
This heart ever constant shall thro' life love on.

Molly A Store[1]

Oh! Mary dear! bright peerless flower,
    Pride of the plains of Nair,
Behold me droop through each dull hour,
    In soul-consuming care.
In friends – in wine – where joy was found –
    No joy I now can see;
But still while pleasure reigns around,
    I sigh – and think of thee.

---

1 *Molly a store*: 'Molly, my dear'.

The cuckoo's notes I love to hear,
    When summer warms the skies;
When fresh the banks and brakes appear,
    And flowers around us rise:
That blithe bird sings her song so clear,
    And she sings where the sun-beams shine –
Her voice is sweet – but Mary dear,
    Not half so sweet as thine.

From town to town I've idly stray'd,
    I've wander'd many a mile;
I've met with many a blooming maid,
    And own'd her charms the while:
I've gaz'd on some that then seem'd fair,
    But when thy looks I see,
I find there's none that can compare,
    My Mary, dear, with thee!

Roisin Dubh[1]

Oh! my sweet little rose, cease to pine for the past,
For the friends that come eastward shall see thee at last;
They bring blessings – they bring favors which the past never knew,
To pour forth in gladness on my Roisin Dubh.

Long, long with my dearest, thro' strange scenes I've gone,
O'er mountains and broad valleys I have still toil'd on;
O'er the Erne I have sail'd as the rough gales blew,
While the harp pour'd its music for my Roisin Dubh.

Tho' wearied oh! my fair one! do not slight my song,
For my heart dearly loves thee, and hath lov'd thee long;
In sadness and in sorrow I shall still be true,
And cling with wild fondness round my Roisin Dubh.

There's no flower that e'er bloom'd can my rose excel,
There's no tongue that e'er moved half my love can tell;

---

1 *Roisin Dubh*: 'the little black rose,' a personification of Ireland. Hardiiman notes that the original is 'an allegorical ballad in which strong political feelings are conveyed from a lover to his fair one.' Ferguson* and Mangan* (in 'Dark Rosaleen') have given powerful translations of this *aisling*.

Had I strength, had I skill the wide world to subdue,
Oh! the queen of that wide world should be Roisin Dubh.

Had I power, oh! my lov'd one, but to plead thy right,
I should speak out in boldness for my heart's delight;
I would tell to all around me how my fondness grew,
And bid them bless the beauty of my Roisin Dubh.

The mountains, high and misty, thro' the moors must go,
The rivers shall run backward, and the lakes overflow;
And the wild waves of old ocean wear a crimson hue,
Ere the world sees the ruin of my Roisin Dubh.

Eileen A Roon[1]

I'll love thee evermore,
        Eileen a Roon!
I'll bless thee o'er and o'er,
        Eileen a Roon!
Oh! for thy sake I'll tread,
Where the plains of Mayo spread;
By hope still fondly led,
        Eileen a Roon!

Oh! how may I gain thee?
        Eileen a Roon!
Shall feasting entertain thee
        Eileen a Roon!
I would range the world wide,
With love alone to guide,
To win thee for my bride,
        Eileen a Roon

Then wilt thou come away?
        Eileen a Roon!
Oh! wilt thou come or stay?
        Eileen a Roon!
Oh yes! oh yes! with thee
I will wander far and free,
And thy only love shall be,
        Eileen a Roon!

---

1 Eileen A Roon: 'Dear Eileen'; cf. John D'Alton's translation (p. 304).

A hundred thousand welcomes,
                    Eileen a Roon!
A hundred thousand welcomes,
                    Eileen a Roon!
Oh! welcome evermore,
With welcomes yet in store,
Till love and life are o'er,

Eileen a Roon!

In This Calm Sheltered Villa

In this calm shelter'd villa my fair one remains,
The flower of all flow'rets, the pride of the plains;
She's my heart's hoarded treasure, my soul's sole delight,
In winter she's my summer, and my sunshine at night.

Oh! love, cruel love, thou hast led me astray,
My heart sinks within me, and my strength wastes away;
Speak, speak, dearest maiden, to my passion reply,
Or breathe all I dread, and then leave me to die.

Oh ! thou my soul's darling! most lovely, most dear,
There's nought can bring pleasure if thou art not near;
Our trust through the future in kind heaven shall be,
I'll long not for wealth love! if bless'd but with thee.

Then smile my beloved – let this coldness depart,
Oh! come till I press thee in bliss to this heart;
Nay! nay – then I'm doom'd for thy loss to repine,
I die, dearest maiden, and the blame shall be thine.

Nay, call me not senseless – nay, deem me not vain,
Nor think that of pangs all unfelt I complain;
Tho' lowly my kindred, and scanty my store,
Oh! why wilt thou tell me to love thee no more.

WILLIAM CARLETON (1794–1869)

In 1830, the *Dublin Monthly Magazine* hailed Carleton's *First Series of Traits and Stories* as 'so true to life … that in reading them we had the scenes of our youth … often brought in a panorama with our view'. This accuracy frequently attributed to Carleton's depiction of the Irish peasantry earned him the title of social historian, recording, from memory, the life of his own people – a trademark he fully exploited. He was born on a small farm in the Clogher Valley of Co. Tyrone, and heard the legends, tales, traditions, customs and superstitions from his father, who was a noted story-teller. His mother only spoke Irish. Carleton was bilingual, and this enabled him, he claimed, to capture the flavour of peasant speech. He pointed out that his father was a yeoman, not a peasant, and that his own ambitions were to escape from the rural background which he fictionally embraces. He was educated in a hedge-school, and was destined for the priesthood, but renounced Catholicism once settled in Dublin, where he contributed to Caesar Otway's proselytizing *Christian Examiner* before adopting a conciliatory stance. His unfinished *Autobiography*, published posthumously, stops where Carleton's transformation into a writer – and thus his break with the past – had been achieved. When he switched from telling stories to writing novels, some eleven years after settling in Dublin, he relied on written records to furnish him with material to authenticate the crucial episodes of his fictional plots. *Fardarougha the Miser*, which was first serialized in the *Dublin University Magazine* (1837–38), deals with the agrarian violence of Ribbonmen (a subject which Carleton had vividly explored in 'Wildgoose Lodge'); *Valentine M'Clutchy* (1841) presents the dire effects of absenteeism and exposes the oppressive regime of the Orange Order and the Established Church in the person of the land agent and his attorney – the scene of an eviction on Christmas Eve proved popular with the Land League. *The Black Prophet* (1847), his most successful novel, gives a harrowing picture of the Famine of 1817.

From *Traits and Stories of the Irish Peasantry*
(2nd edn. 1832)

from THE PARTY FIGHT AND FUNERAL

We ought, perhaps, to inform our readers that the connection between a party fight and funeral is sufficiently strong to justify the author in classing them under the title which is prefixed to this story. The one, being usually the natural result of the other, is made to proceed from it, as is the custom in real life among the Irish. Such is the preface with which we deem it necessary to introduce the following sketch to those who shall honour us with a perusal.

It has long been laid down as a universal principle that self-preservation is the first law of nature. An Irishman, however, has nothing to do with this; he disposes of it as he does of the other laws, and washes his hands out of it altogether. But commend him to a fair, dance, funeral, or wedding, or to any other sport where there is a likelihood of getting his head or his bones broken, and if he survives he will remember you, with a kindness peculiar to himself, to the last day of his life; will drub you from head to heel if he finds that any misfortune has kept you out of a row beyond the usual period of three months; will render the same service to any of your friends that stand in need of it; or, in short, will go to the world's end, or fifty miles farther, as he himself would say, to serve you, provided you can procure him a bit of decent fighting. Now, in truth and soberness, it is difficult to account for this propensity, especially when the task of ascertaining it is assigned to those of another country, or even to those Irishmen whose rank in life places them too far from the customs, prejudices, and domestic opinions of their native peasantry – none of which can be properly known without mingling with them. To my own knowledge, however, it proceeds from *education*. And here I would beg leave to point out an omission of which the several boards of education have been guilty, and which, I believe, no one but myself has yet been sufficiently acute and philosophical to ascertain, as forming a *sine quâ non* in the international instruction of the lower orders of Irishmen.

The cream of the matter is this. A species of ambition prevails in the Green Isle not known in any other country. It is an ambition of about three miles by four in extent; or, in other words, is bounded by the limits of the parish in which the subject of it may reside. It puts itself forth early in the character, and a hardy perennial it is. In my own case, its first development was noticed in the hedge-school which I attended. I had not been long there till I was forced to declare myself either for the Caseys or the Murphys, two tiny factions that had split the school between them. The day on which the declaration of my ceremony took place was a solemn one. After school, we all went to the bottom of a deep valley, a short distance from the school-house. Up to the moment of our assembling there, I had not taken my stand under either banner: that of the Caseys was a sod of turf stuck on the end of a broken fishing-rod – the eagle of the Murphys was a cork-

---

1 Cudgel Player. [*Carleton's note.*]
2 Paddy Riot [*Carleton's note.*]

red potato, hoisted in the same manner. The turf was borne by an urchin who afterwards distinguished himself at fair and markets as a *builla batthah*[1] of the first grade, and from this circumstance he was nicknamed *Parrah Rackhan*.[2] The potato was borne by little Mickle M'Phaudeen Murphy, who afterwards took away Katty Bane Sheridan, without asking her own consent or her father's. They were all then boys, it is true, but they gave a tolerable promise of that eminence which they subsequently attained.

When we arrived at the bottom of the glen, the Murphys and the Caseys, including their respective followers, ranged themselves on either side of a long line which was drawn between the belligerent powers with the butt-end of one of the standards. Exactly on this line was I placed. The word was then put to me in full form – 'Whether will you side with the dacent Caseys or the blackguard Murphys?' 'Whether will you side with the dacent Murphys or the blackguard Caseys?' 'The potato for ever!' said I, throwing up my caubeen, and running over to the Murphy standard. In the twinkling of an eye we were at it; and in a short time the deuce an eye some of us had to twinkle. A battle royal succeeded that lasted near half an hour, and it would probably have lasted about double the time were it not for the appearance of the 'master,' who was seen by a little shrivelled *vidette*, who wanted an arm, and could take no part in the engagement. This was enough; we instantly radiated in all possible directions, so that by the time he had descended through the intricacies of the glen to the field of battle, neither victor nor vanquished was visible, except, perhaps, a straggler or two as they topped the brow of the declivity, looking back over their shoulders to put themselves out of doubt as to their visibility by the master. They seldom looked in vain, however; for there he usually stood, shaking up his rod, silently prophetic of its application on the following day. This threat, for the most part, ended in smoke; for except he horsed about forty or fifty of us, the infliction of impartial justice was utterly out of his power.

* * *

For my part, I was early trained to cudgelling, and before I reached my fourteenth year, could pronounce as sage and accurate an opinion upon the merits of a *shillelagh*, as it is called, or cudgel, as a veterinary surgeon of sixty could upon a dead ass at first sight. Our plan of preparing is this: – we sallied out to any place where there was an underwood of blackthorn or oak, and, having surveyed the premises with the eye of a connoisseur, we selected the straightest root-growing

317

piece which we could find: for if not root-growing, we did not consider it worth cutting, knowing from experience that a branch, how
straight and fair soever it might look, would snap in the twist and tug
of war. Having cut it as close to the root as possible, we then lopped
off the branches, and put it up in the chimney to season. When sea-
soned, we took it down, and wrapping it in brown paper, well steeped
in hog's lard or oil, we buried it in a horse-dunghill, paying it a daily
visit for the purpose of making it straight by doubling back the bends
or angles across the knee, in a direction contrary to their natural tendency. Having daily repeated this until we had made it straight, and
renewed the oiled wrapping paper until the staff was perfectly saturat-
ed, we then rubbed it well with a woollen cloth, containing a little
black-lead and grease, to give it a polish. This was the last process,
except that if we thought it too light at the top, we used to bore a hole
in the lower end with a red-hot iron spindle, into which we poured
melted lead, for the purpose of giving it the knock-down weight.

*   *   *

The boy who was the handiest and the most daring with the cudgel at Paddy Mulligan's school was Denis Kelly, the son of a wealthy
farmer in the neighbourhood. He was a rash, hot-tempered, good-
natured lad, possessing a more than common share of this blackthorn
ambition; on which account he was cherished by his relations as a boy
that was likely at a future period to be able to walk over the course of
the parish, in fair, market, or patron. He certainly grew up a stout,
able young fellow; and before he reached nineteen years, was unrivalled at the popular exercises of the peasantry. Shortly after that time
he made his *début* in a party-quarrel, which took place in one of the
Christmas *Margamores*,[1] and fully sustained the anticipations which
were formed of him by his relations. For a year or two afterwards no
quarrel was fought without him; and his prowess rose until he had
gained the very pinnacle of that ambition which he had determined to
reach. About this time I was separated from him, having found it necessary, in order to accomplish my objects in life, to reside with a relation in another part of the country.

The period of my absence, I believe, was about fourteen years, during which space I heard no account of him whatsoever. At length,
however, that inextinguishable attachment which turns the affections

---

1 Big Markets. [*Carleton's note.*]

and memory to the friends of our early days – to those scenes which we traversed when the heart was light and the spirits buoyant – determined me to make a visit to my native place, that I might witness the progress of time and care upon those faces that were once so familiar to me; that I might once more look upon the meadows and valleys, and groves, and mountains where I had so often played, and to which I still found myself bound by a tie that a more enlightened view of life and nature only made stronger and more enduring. I accordingly set off, and arrived, late in the evening of December, at a little town within a few miles of my native home. On alighting from the coach and dining, I determined to walk home, as it was a fine frosty night....

I left the inn at seven o'clock, and as I had only five miles to walk, I would just arrive about nine, allowing myself to saunter on at the rate of two miles and a half per hour. My sensations, indeed, as I went along, were singular; and as I took a solitary road across the mountains, the loneliness of the walk, the deep gloom of the valleys, the towering height of the dark hills, and the pale silvery light of a sleeping lake, shining dimly in the distance below, gave me such a distinct notion of the sublime and beautiful as I have seldom since experienced. I recommend every man who has been fourteen years absent from his native fields to return by moonlight....

There was perfect silence and solitude around me; and as I stood alone in the dark chamber of the mountains, I felt the impressiveness of the situation gradually supersede my terrors. A sublime sense of religious awe descended on me; my soul kindled into a glow of solemn and elevated devotion, which gave me a more intense perception of the presence of God than I had ever before experienced....

I then proceeded further into the valley, completely freed from the influence of old and superstitious associations. A few perches below me a small river crossed the road, over which was thrown a little stone bridge of rude workmanship. This bridge was the spot on which the apparition was said to appear; and as I approached it I felt the folly of those terrors which had only a few minutes before beset me so strongly. I found my moral energies recruited, and the dark phantasms of my imagination dispelled by the light of religion, which had refreshed me with a deep sense of the Almighty presence. I accordingly walked forward, scarcely bestowing a thought upon the history of the place, and had got within a few yards of the bridge, when, on resting my eye accidentally upon the little elevation formed by its rude arch, I perceived a black coffin placed at the edge of the road, exactly upon the bridge!

It may be evident to the reader that, however satisfactory the force of philosophical reasoning might have been upon the subject of the solitude, I was too much the creature of sensation for an hour before to look on such a startling object with firm nerves. For the first two or three minutes, therefore, I exhibited as finished a specimen of the dastardly as could be imagined. My hair absolutely raised my cap some inches off my head; my mouth opened to an extent which I did not conceive it could possibly reach; I thought my eyes shot out from their sockets; and my fingers spread out and became stiff, though powerless. The *obstupui*[1] was perfectly realised in me, for, with the exception of a single groan which I gave on first seeing the object, I found that if one word would save my life, or transport me to my own fireside, I could not utter it. I was also rooted to the earth as if by magic; and although instant tergiversation[2] and flight had my most hearty concurrence, I could not move a limb, nor even raise my eye off the sepulchral-looking object which lay before me. I now felt the perspiration fall from my face in torrents, and the strokes of my heart fell audibly on my ear. I even attempted to say 'God preserve me,' but my tongue was dumb and powerless, and could not move. My eye was still upon the coffin, when I perceived that, from being motionless, it instantly began to swing, first in a lateral, then in a longitudinal direction, although it was perfectly evident that no human hand was nearer it than my own. At length I raised my eyes off it, for my vision was strained to an aching intensity which I thought must have occasioned my eye-strings to crack. I looked instinctively about me for assistance – but all was dismal, silent, and solitary: even the moon had disappeared among a few clouds that I had not noticed in the sky.

As I stood in this state of indescribable horror I saw the light gradually fade away from the tops of the mountains, giving the scene around me a dim and spectral ghastliness, which, to those who were never in such a situation, is altogether inconceivable.

At length I thought I heard a noise as it were of a rushing tempest sweeping from the hills down into the valley; but on looking up I could perceive nothing but the dusky desolation that brooded over the place. Still the noise continued: again I saw the coffin move; I then felt the motion communicated to myself, and found my body borne and swung backwards and forwards, precisely according to the motion of the coffin. I again attempted to utter a cry for assistance, but could not: the motion of my body still continued, as did the

---

1 *obstupui*: 'I stood silent'.
2 *tergiversation*: 'The action of "turning one's back on", *i.e.* forsaking, something' (O.E.D.).

approaching noise in the hills. I looked up a second time in the direction in which the valley wound off between them, but judge of what I must have suffered when I beheld one of the mountains moving, as it were, from its base, and tumbling down towards the spot on which I stood. In the twinkling of an eye the whole scene, hills and all, began to tremble, to vibrate and to fly round me, with a rapid, delirious motion; the stars shot back into the depths of heaven, and disappeared; the ground on which I stood began to pass from beneath my feet; a noise like the breaking of a thousand gigantic billows again burst from every direction, and I found myself instantly overwhelmed by some deadly weight, which prostrated me on the earth, and deprived me of sense and motion.

I know not how long I continued in this state; but I remember that, on opening my eyes, the first object that presented itself to me was the sky, glowing as before with ten thousand stars, and the moon walking in her unclouded brightness through the heavens. The whole circumstance then rushed back upon my mind, but with a sense of horror very much diminished; I arose, and, on looking towards the spot, perceived the coffin in the same place. I then stood, and endeavouring to collect myself, viewed it as calmly as possible; it was, however, as motionless and distinct as when I first saw it. I now began to reason upon the matter, and to consider that it was pusillanimous in me to give way to such boyish terrors. The confidence, also, which my heart, only a short time before this, had experienced in the presence and protection of the Almighty, again returned, and, along with it, a degree of religious fortitude which invigorated my whole system. 'Well,' thought I, 'in the name of God, I shall ascertain what you are, let the consequence be what it may.' I then advanced until I stood exactly over it, and raising my foot, gave it a slight kick. 'Now,' said I, 'nothing remains but to ascertain whether it contains a dead body, or not,' but, on raising the end of it, I perceived by its lightness that it was empty. To investigate the cause of its being left in this solitary spot was, however, not within the compass of my philosophy, so I gave that up. On looking at it more closely I noticed a plate marked with the name and age of the person for whom it was intended, and on bringing my eye near the letters, I was able between fingering and reading to make out the name of my old cudgel-fighting school-fellow, Denis Kelly.

This discovery threw a partial light upon the business; but I now remembered to have heard of individuals who had seen black, unearthly coffins, inscribed with the names of certain living persons;

and that these were considered as ominous of the death of those persons. I accordingly determined to be certain that this was a real coffin; and as Denis's house was not more than a mile before me, I decided on carrying it that far. 'If he be dead,' thought I, 'it will be all right, and if not, we will see more about it.' My mind, in fact, was diseased with terror. I instantly raised the coffin, and as I found a rope lying on the ground under it, I strapped it about my shoulders and proceeded: nor could I help smiling when I reflected upon the singular transition which the man of sentiment and sensation so strangely underwent: – from the sublime contemplation of the silent mountain solitude and the spangled heavens to the task of carrying a coffin! It was an adventure, however, and I was resolved to see how it would terminate.

* * *

I had given my friends no notice of this visit; my reception was consequently the warmer, as I was not expected. That evening was a happy one, which I shall long remember, At supper I alluded to Kelly, and received from my brother a full account, as given in the following narrative, of the circumstances which caused his death.

* * *

'Well, Lachlin,' said my brother, 'if you didn't see it, I did. I happened to be looking out of John Carson's upper window – for it wasn't altogether safe to contemplate it within reach of the missiles. It was certainly a dreadful and a barbarous sight. You have often observed the calm, gloomy silence that precedes a thunderstorm; and had you been there that day you might have seen it illustrated in a scene much more awful. The thick living mass of people extended from the corner-house, nearly a quarter of a mile, at this end of the town, up to the parsonage on the other side. During the early part of the day, every kind of business was carried on in a hurry and an impatience which denoted the little chance they knew there would be for transacting it in the evening.

'Up to the hour of four o'clock the fair was unusually quiet, and, on the whole, presented nothing in any way remarkable; but after that hour you might observe the busy stir and hum of the mass settling down into a deep, brooding, portentous silence, that was absolutely fearful. The females, with dismay and terror pictured in their faces, hurried home; and in various instances you might see mothers, and wives, and sisters clinging about the sons, husbands and brothers, attempting to drag them by main force from the danger which they knew impended over them. In this they seldom succeeded; for the person so urged was usually compelled to tear himself from them by superior strength.

'The pedlars, and basket-women, and such as had tables and standings erected in the streets, commenced removing them with all possible haste. The shopkeepers, and other inhabitants of the town, put up their shutters, in order to secure their windows from being shattered. Strangers, who were compelled to stop in town that night, took shelter in the inns and other houses of entertainment where they lodged; so that about five o'clock the street was completely clear and free for action.

*   *   *

'Both parties arranged themselves against each other, forming something like two lines of battle, and these extended along the town nearly from one end to the other. I was curious to remark the difference in the persons and appearances of the combatants. In the Orange line the men were taller and of more powerful frames; but the Ribbonmen were more hardy, active and courageous. Man to man, notwithstanding their superior bodily strength, the Orangemen could never fight the others; the former depend too much upon their fire and side-arms, but they are by no means so well trained to the use of the cudgel as their enemies. In the district where the scene of this fight is laid, the Catholics generally inhabit the mountainous part of the country, to which, when the civil feuds of worse times prevailed, they had been driven at the point of the bayonet; the Protestants and Presbyterians, on the other hand, who came in upon their possessions, occupy the richer and more fertile tracts of the land, living, of course, more wealthily, with less labour, and on better food. The characteristic features produced by these causes are such as might be expected – the Catholic being, like his soil, hardy, thin, and capable of bearing all weathers; and the Protestants, larger, softer, and more inactive.

'Their advance to the first onset was far different from a faction fight. There existed a silence here that powerfully evinced the inextinguishable animosity with which they encountered. For some time they fought in two compact bodies, that remained unbroken so long as the chances of victory were doubtful. Men went down, and were up, and went down in all directions with uncommon rapidity; and as the weighty phalanx of Orangemen stood out against the nimble line of their mountain adversaries, the intrepid spirit of the latter, and their surprising skill and activity, soon gave symptoms of a gradual superiority in the conflict. In the course of about half an hour the Orange party began to give way in the northern end of the town; and, as their opponents pressed them warmly and with unsparing hand, the heavy mass formed by their numbers began to break, and this decomposition ran up their line, until in a short time they were thrown into utter confusion. They now fought in detached parties; but these subordinate conflicts, though shorter in duration than the shock of the general battle, were much more inhuman and destructive; for whenever any particular gang succeeded in putting their adversaries to flight, they usually ran to the assistance of their friends in the nearest fight – by which means they often fought three to one. In these instances the persons inferior in number suffered such barbarities as it would be painful to detail.

... I have no doubt but the Orangemen would have been ultimately beaten and deprived of their weapons, were it not that many of them, who had got their pistols out of Sherlock's, discharged them among their enemies, and wounded several. The Catholics could not stand this; but, wishing to retaliate as effectually as possible, lifted stones wherever they could find them, and kept up the fight at a distance as they retreated. On both sides, wherever a solitary foe was caught straggling from the rest, he was instantly punished with a most cruel and bloodthirsty spirit.

'It was just about this time that I saw Kelly engaged with two men, whom he kept at bay with great ease – retrograding, however, as he fought, towards his own party. Grimes, who had some time before this recovered and joined the fight once more, was returning, after having pursued several of the Ribbonmen past the market-house, where he spied Kelly thus engaged. With a volunteer gun in his hand, and furious with the degradation of his former defeat, he ran over and struck him with the butt-end of it upon the temple, and Denis fell. When the stroke was given an involuntary cry of 'Murder – foul, foul!' burst from those who looked on from the windows; and long John Steele, Grimes's father-in-law, in indignation raised his cudgel to knock him down for this treacherous and malignant blow; but a person out of Neil Cassidy's back-yard hurled a round stone, about six pounds in weight, at Grimes's head, that felled him to the earth, leaving him as insensible, and nearly in as dangerous a state as Kelly – for his jaw was broken.

'By this time the Catholics had retreated out of the town, and Denis might probably have received more punishment had those who were returning from the pursuit recognised him; but James Wilson, seeing the dangerous situation in which he lay, came out, and, with the assistance of his servant-man, brought him into his own house. When the Orangemen had driven their adversaries off the field, they commenced the most hideous yellings through the streets – got music and played party tunes – offered any money for the face of a Papist; and any of that religion who were so unfortunate as to make their appearance were beaten in the most relentless manner. It was precisely the same thing on the part of the Ribbonmen; if a Protestant, but above all an Orangeman, came in their way, he was sure to be treated with barbarity: for the retaliation on either side was dreadfully unjust – the innocent suffering as well as the guilty. Leaving the window, I found Kelly in a bad state below stairs.

"What's to be done?" said I to Wilson.

"I know not," replied he, "except I put him between us on my jaunting car and drive him home."

'This appeared decidedly the best plan we could adopt; so, after putting to the horse, we placed him on the car, sitting one on each side of him, and in this manner left him at his own house.

'Did you run no risk,' said I, 'in going among Kelly's friends, whilst they were under the influence of party feeling and exasperated passion?'

'No,' said he; 'we had rendered many of them acts of kindness, and had never exhibited any spirit but a *friendly* one towards them; and such individuals, but only such, *might walk through a crowd of enraged Catholics or Protestants quite unmolested.*'

'The next morning Kelly's landlord, Sir W. R——, and two magistrates, were at his house, but he lay like a log, without sense or motion. Whilst they were there, Surgeon S——e arrived, and, after examining his head, declared that the skull was fractured. During that and the following day the house was surrounded by crowds, anxious to know his state; and nothing might be heard amongst most of them but loud and undisguised expressions of the most ample revenge. The wife was frantic; and, on seeing me, hid her face in her hands, exclaiming:

"Ah, sir, I knew it would come to this; and you, too, tould him the same thing. *My* curse and *God's* curse on it for quarrelling! Will it never stop in the counthry, till they rise some time, and murdher one another out of the face!"

'As soon as the swelling in his head was reduced, Surgeon S———e performed the operation of trepanning, and thereby saved his life; but his strength and intellect were gone – and he just lingered for four months, a feeble, drivelling simpleton, until, in consequence of a cold, which produced inflammation in the brain, he died, as hundreds have died, the victim of party spirit.'

Such was the account which I heard of my old schoolfellow, Denis Kelly; and, indeed, when I reflected upon the nature of the education he received, I could not but admit that the consequences were such as might naturally be expected to result from it.

from THE HEDGE SCHOOL

There never was a more unfounded calumny, than that which would impute to the Irish peasantry an indifference to education. I may, on the contrary, fearlessly assert, that the lower orders of no country ever manifested such a positive inclination for literary acquirements, and that, too, under circumstances strongly calculated to produce care-lessness and apathy on this particular subject. Nay, I do maintain that he who is intimately acquainted with the character of our country-men, must acknowledge, that their zeal for book learning, not only is strong and ardent, when opportunities of scholastic education occur, but that it increases in proportion as these opportunities are rare and unattainable. The very name and nature of hedge schools are proof of this: for what stronger point could be made out, in illustration of my position, than the fact that, despite of obstacles, whose very idea would crush ordinary enterprise – when not even a shed could be obtained in which to assemble the children of an Irish village, the worthy pedagogue selected the first green spot on the sunny side of a quickset-hedge, which he conceived adapted for his purpose, and there, under the scorching rays of a summer sun, and in defiance of spies and statutes, carried on the work of instruction. From this cir-cumstance the name of hedge school originated; and, however it may be associated with the ludicrous, I maintain that it is highly creditable to the character of the people, and an encouragement to those who wish to see them receive pure and correct educational knowledge. A hedge school, however, in its original sense, was but a temporary establishment, being only adopted until such a school-house could be erected, as was in those days deemed sufficient to hold such a num-ber of children as were expected, at all hazards, to attend it.

The opinion, I know, which has been long entertained of hedge schoolmasters, was, and still is, unfavourable; but the character of these worthy and eccentric persons has been misunderstood, for the stigma attached to their want of knowledge should have rather been applied to their want of morals, because on this latter point only were they indefensible. The fact is that hedge schoolmasters were a class of men from whom morality was not expected by the peasantry; for, strange to say, one of their strongest recommendations to the good opinion of the people, as far as their literary talents and qualifications were concerned, was an inordinate love of whiskey, and if to this could be added a slight touch of derangement, the character was complete—

On once asking an Irish peasant why he sent his children to a schoolmaster who was notoriously addicted to spiritous liquors, rather than to a man of sober habits who taught in the same neighbourhood—

'Why do I sind them to Mat Meegan, is it?' he replied; 'and do you think, Sir,' said he, 'that I'd sind them to that dry-headed dunce, Mr. Frazher, wid his black coat upon him and his caroline hat, and him wouldn't taste a glass of poteen wanst in seven years? Mat, Sir, likes it, and teaches the boys ten times betther whin he's dhrunk nor whin he's sober; and you'll never find a good tacher, Sir, but's fond of it. As for Mat, when he's *half gone*, I'd turn him agin the county for deepness in larnin; for it's thin he rhimes it out of him, that it would do one good to hear him.'

'So,' said I, 'you think that a love of drinking poteen is a sign of talent in a schoolmaster.'

'Ay, or in any man else, Sir,' he replied. 'Look at tradesmen, and 'tis always the cleverest that you'll find fond iv the dhrink! If you had hard Mat and Frazher the other evening at it – what a hare Mat mad iv 'im; but he was jist in proper tune for it, being, at the time, purty well I thank you, and did not lave him a leg to stand upon. He took him in Euclid's Ailments and Logicals, and proved, in Frazher's teeth, that the candlestick before them was the church-steeple, and Frazher himself the parson; and so sign was on it, the other couldn't disprove it, but had to give in.'

'Mat, then,' I observed, 'is the most learned man on this walk.'

'Why, thin, I doubt that same, Sir,' replied he, 'for all he's so great in the books; for, you see, while they were ding dust at it, who comes in but mad Delany, and he attacked Mat, and, in less than no time rubbed the consate out of *him*, as clane as *he* did out of Frazher.'

'Who is Delany?' I enquired.

'He was the makins of a priest, Sir, and was in Maynooth a couple of years, but he took in the knowledge so fast, that, bedad, he got *cracked wid larnin'* – for a *dunce,* you see, never cracks wid it, in regard of the thickness of the skull; no doubt but he's too many for Mat, and can go far beyant him in the books, but then, like that, he's still brightest whin he has a sup in his head.'

These are prejudices which the Irish peasantry have long entertained concerning the character of hedge schoolmasters; but, granting them to be unfounded, as they generally are, yet it is an indisputable fact that hedge schoolmasters were as superior in literary knowledge and acquirements to the class of men who are now engaged in the general education of the people as they were beneath them in moral and religious character. The former part of this assertion will, I am aware, appear rather startling to many: but it is true; and one great cause why the character of the Society teachers is undervalued, in many instances, by the people, proceeds from a conviction on their parts that they are, and must be, incapable, from the slender portion of learning they have received, of giving their children a sound and practical education.

But that we may put this subject in a clearer light, we will give a sketch of the course of instruction which was deemed necessary for a hedge schoolmaster, and let it be contrasted with that which falls to the lot of those engaged in the conducting of schools patronised by the Education Societies of the present day.

When a poor man, about twenty or thirty years ago, understood from the schoolmaster who educated his sons that any of them was particularly 'cute at his larnin',' the ambition of the parent usually directed itself to one of three objects – he would either make him a priest, a clerk, or a schoolmaster. The determination once fixed, the boy was set apart from every kind of labour, that he might be at liberty to bestow his undivided time and talents to the objects set before him. His parents strained every nerve to furnish him with the necessary books, and always took care that his appearance and dress should be more decent than those of any other member of the family. If the Church was in prospect, he was distinguished, after he had been two or three years at his Latin, by the appellation of 'the young priest,' an epithet to him of the greatest pride and honour; but if destined only to wield the ferula, his importance in the family, and the narrow circle of his friends, was by no means so great. If, however, the goal of his future ambition as a schoolmaster was humbler, that of his literary career was considerably extended. He usually remained at the next school in the vicinity until he supposed that he had completely drained the master of all his knowledge. This circumstance was generally discovered in the following manner: – As soon as he judged himself a match for his teacher, and possessed sufficient confidence in his own powers, he penned him a formal challenge to meet him in literary contest, either in his own school, before competent witnesses, or at the chapel green, on the Sabbath day, before the arrival of the priest, or probably after it – for the priest himself was generally the moderator and judge upon these occasions. This challenge was generally couched in rhyme, and either sent by the hands of a common friend, or posted upon the chapel door.

These contests, as the reader perceives, were always public, and were witnessed by the peasantry with intense interest. If the master sustained a defeat, it was not so much attributed to his want of learning, as to the overwhelming talent of his opponent; nor was the success of the pupil generally followed by the expulsion of the master – for this was but the first of a series of challenges which the former proposed to undertake, ere he eventually settled himself in the exercise of his profession.

I remember being present at one of them, and a ludicrous exhibition it was. The parish priest, a red-faced, jocular little man, was president, and his curate, a scholar of six feet two inches in height, and a schoolmaster from the next parish were judges. I will only touch upon two circumstances in their conduct which evinced a close instinctive knowledge of human nature in the combatants. The master would not condescend to argue off his throne – a piece of policy to which, in my opinion, he owed his victory (for he won): whereas the pupil insisted that he should meet him on equal ground, face to face, in the lower end of the room. It was evident that the latter could not divest himself of his boyish terrors as long as the other sat, as it were, in the plenitude of his former authority, contracting his brows with habitual sternness, thundering out his arguments, with a most menacing and stentorian voice; while he thumped his desk with his shut fist, or struck it with his great rule at the close of each argument, in a manner that made the youngster put his hands behind him several times, to be certain that that portion of his dress which is *unmentionable* to 'ears polite' was tight upon him.

If in these encounters the young candidate for the honours of the literary sceptre was not victorious, he again resumed his studies under his old preceptor with renewed vigour and becoming humility; but if he put the schoolmaster down, his next object was to seek out some other teacher whose celebrity was unclouded within his own range. With him he had a fresh encounter, and its result was similar to what I have already related. If victorious, he sought out another and more learned opponent; and if defeated, he became the pupil of his conqueror – going night about, during his sojourn at the school, with the neighbouring farmers' sons, whom he assisted in their studies, as a compensation for his support. He was called, during these peregrinations, the *Poor Scholar,* a character which secured him the esteem and hospitable attention of the peasantry, who never fail in respect to any one characterised by a zeal for learning and knowledge.

In this manner he proceeded, a literary knight-errant, filled with a chivalrous love of letters which would have done honour to the most learned peripatetic of them all; enlarging his own powers, and making fresh acquisitions of knowledge as he went along. His contests, his defeats, and his triumphs, of course, were frequent; and his habits of thinking and reasoning must have been considerably improved, his acquaintance with classical and mathematical authors rendered more intimate, and his powers of illustration and comparison more clear and happy. After three or four years spent in this manner, he usually returned to his native place, sent another challenge to the schoolmaster, in the capacity of a candidate for his situation, and, if successful, drove him out of the district, and established himself in his situation. The vanquished master sought a new district, sent a new challenge, in his turn, to some other teacher, and usually put him to flight in the same manner. The terms of defeat or victory, according to their application, were called *sacking* and *bogging*.

'There was a great argument entirely, Sir,' said a peasant once, when speaking of these contests,' ''twas at the chapel on Sunday week, betune young Tom Brady, that was a poor scholar in Munsther, and Mr. Hartigan, the schoolmasther.'

'And who was victorious?' I enquired.

'Why, Sir, and may be 'twas young Brady that didn't *sack* him clane, before the priest an' all; and went nigh to *bog* the priest himself in Greek. His Reverence was only two words beyant him; but he sacked the masther, any how, an' showed him in the Grammatical and the Dixonary where he was wrong.'

'And what is Brady's object in life?' I asked. 'What does he intend to do?'

'Intend to do, is it? I'm tould nothin' less nor goin' into Thrinity College in Dublin, an' expects to bate them all there, out an' out: he's first to make something they call a seizure[1]; and afther makin' that good, he's to be a Counsellor. So, Sir, you see what it is to resave good schoolin', and to have the larnin'; but, indeed, 'tis Brady that's the great headpiece entirely.'

Unquestionably, many who received instruction in this manner have distinguished themselves in the Dublin University; and I have no hesitation in saying, that young men educated in Irish hedge schools, as they were called, have proved themselves to be better classical scholars and mathematicians, generally speaking, than any proportionate number of those educated in our first-rate academies. The Munster masters have long been, and still are, particularly celebrated for making excellent classical and mathematical scholars.

That a great deal of ludicrous pedantry generally accompanied this knowledge is not at all surprising, when we consider the rank these worthy teachers held in life, and the stretch of inflation at which their pride was kept by the profound reverence excited by their learning among the people. 'Tis equally true that each of them had a stock of *crambos* ready for accidental encounter which would have puzzled Euclid or Sir Isaac Newton himself; but even these trained their minds to habits of acuteness and investigation. When a schoolmaster of this class had established himself as a good mathematician, the predominant enjoyment of his heart and life was to write the epithet *Philomath* after his name; and this, whatever document he subscribed, was never omitted. If he witnessed a will, it was Timothy Fagan, Philomath; if he put his name to a promissory note, it was Tim. Fagan, Philomath; if be addressed a love-letter to his sweetheart, it was still Timothy Fagan – or whatever the name might be – Philomath; and this was always written in legible and distinct copy-hand, sufficiently large to attract the observation of the reader.

It was also usual for a man who had been a pre-eminent and extraordinary scholar, to have the epithet GREAT prefixed to his name. I remember one of this description, who was called the *Great O'Brien, par excellence.* In the latter years of his life he gave up teaching, and led a circulating life, going round from school to school, and remaining a week or a month alternately among his brethren. His visits were considered an honour, and raised considerably the literary character of those with whom he resided; for he spoke of dunces with the most dignified contempt, and the general impression was that he would scorn even to avail himself of their hospitality. Like most of his

---

1 Sizar. [*Carleton's note.*]

brethren, he could not live without the *poteen*; and his custom was to drink a pint of it in its native purity before he entered into any literary contest, or made any display of his learning at wakes or other Irish festivities; and most certainly, however blameable the practice, and injurious to health and morals, it threw out his talents and his powers in a most surprising manner.

It was highly amusing to observe the peculiarity which the consciousness of superior knowledge impressed upon the conversation and personal appearance of this decaying race. Whatever might have been the original conformation of their physical structure, it was sure, by the force of acquired habit, to transform itself into a stiff, erect, consequential, and unbending manner, ludicrously characteristic of an inflated sense of their extraordinary knowledge, and a proud and commiserating contempt of the dark ignorance by which, in despite of their own light, they were surrounded. Their conversation, like their own *crambos,* was dark and difficult to be understood; their words, truly sesquipedalian; their voice, loud and commanding in its tones; their deportment, grave and dictatorial, but completely indescribable, and certainly original to the last degree, in those instances where the ready, blundering but genuine humour of their country maintained an unyielding rivalry in the disposition against the natural solemnity which was considered necessary to keep up the due dignity of their character.

In many of these persons, where the original humour and gaiety of the disposition were known, all efforts at the grave and dignified were complete failures, and these were enjoyed by the peasantry and their own pupils, nearly with the sensations which the enactment of Hamlet by Liston would necessarily produce. At all events, their education, allowing for the usual exceptions, was by no means superficial; and the reader has already received a sketch of the trials which they had to undergo before they considered themselves qualified to enter upon the duties of their calling. Their life was, in fact, a state of literary warfare; and they felt that a mere elementary knowledge of their business would have been insufficient to carry them, with suitable credit, through the attacks to which they were exposed from travelling teachers, whose mode of establishing themselves in schools, was, as I have said, by driving away the less qualified, and usurping their places. This, according to the law of opinion and the custom which prevailed, was very easily effected, for the peasantry uniformly encouraged those whom they supposed to be the most competent; as to moral or religious instruction, neither was expected from them, so that the indifference of the moral character was no bar to their success....

GEORGE DARLEY (1795–1846)

B orn in Dublin, he entered Trinity College, Dublin, in 1815, and took his B.A. degree in 1820. His father seems to have been opposed to his literary leanings. Darley went to London in 1821; the following year he published *The Errors of Ecstasie*, a dialogue in blank verse between a Mystic and his Muse. In London he met John Clare, Hazzlitt, Lamb and Beddoes, who printed Darley's praise for his *Brides' Tragedy* in an afterword to the play. In his drama criticism for the *London Magazine* and the *Athenæum*, Darley criticized the contemporary playwrights' preference for the poetic over the rhetorical – his own lyrical drama, *Sylvia, or the May Queen* (1827), admired by Coleridge and Elizabeth Barrett Browning, showed that he did not practice what he preached. Among the 'dramaticules' (verses and stories that he wrote for the *London Magazine*) 'Lilian of the Vale', contained the song, 'I've been Roaming', the only work of his that attained popularity. Lack of success, and an embarrassing stammer contributed to his depression and isolation. Darley turned to mathematics, and wrote for Taylor's series a number of popular treatises – *A System of Popular Geometry, A System of Popular Algebra, A System of Popular Trigonometry*, and *The Geometrical Companion* – which were praised by Thomas Carlyle. A self-styled neo-Elizabethan, for Darley verbal exuberance was beauty, as attested in *Nepenthe* (1835), his long and most striking poem, which was privately printed on coarse discoloured paper in broken type. From the intoxication of over-joy in Canto I to the abyss of depression in Canto II (the third canto was never published), it is the English embodiment of German *Sturm und Drang*.

On the Death of A Recluse

Love droop'd when Beauty fled the bow'r,
 And languid closed the day,
Wept ev'ry little flow'r,
 And turn'd its head away.

The wind spoke with a fallen tongue,
 The green reed sigh'd amain,
And sable forests swung
 Rude melody again.

Wild caves rang deep, and rocks grew cold,
 Whilst rivers wept by them,
All nature's death-bells toll'd
 A requiem! a requiem!

Mid roaring brooks and dark moss-vales
   Where speechless Thought abides,
Still her sweet spirit dwells,
   That knew no world besides.

Her form, the woodland still retains –
   Wound but a creeping flow'r,
Her very life-blood stains
   Thee, in a falling show'r.

Touch but the stream, drink but the air,
   Her cheek, her breath is known –
Ravish that red rose there,
   And she is all thy own.

Robin's Cross

A little cross,
To tell my loss;
A little bed
To rest my head;
A little tear is all I crave
Upon my very little grave.

I strew thy bed
Who loved thy lays;
The tear I shed,
The cross I raise,
With nothing more upon it than –
Here lies the little friend of Man!

From *Nepenthe*[1]

(1835)

from CANTO I

O blest unfabled Incense Tree,
That burns in glorious Araby,
With red scent chalicing the air,

---

1 *Nepenthe*: a sorrow-lulling drink from the ashes of the Phoenix.

Till earth-life grow Elysian there!

Half buried to her flaming breast
In this bright tree, she makes her nest,
Hundred-sunned Phoenix! when she must
Crumble at length to hoary dust!

Her gorgeous death-bed! her rich pyre
Burnt up with aromatic fire!
Her urn, sight high from spoiler men!
Her birthplace when self-born again!

The mountainless green wilds among,
Here ends she her unechoing song!
With amber tears and odorous sighs
Mourned by the desert where she dies!

  Laid like the young fawn mossily
In sun-green vales of Araby,
I woke, hard by the Phoenix tree
That with shadeless boughs flamed over me,
And upward called by a dumb cry
With moonbroad orbs of wonder, I
Beheld the immortal Bird on high
Glassing the great sun in her eye.
Steadfast she gazed upon his fire,
Still her destroyer and her sire!
As if to his her soul of flame
Had flown already, whence it came;
Like those that sit and glare so still,
Intense with their death struggle, till
We touch, and curdle at their chill! –
But breathing yet while she doth burn
  The deathless Daughter of the sun!
Slowly to crimson embers turn
  The beauties of the brightsome one.
O'er the broad nest her silver wings
Shook down their wasteful glitterings;
Her brinded neck high-arched in air
Like a small rainbow faded there;
But brighter glowed her plumy crown

Mouldering to golden ashes down;
With fume of sweet woods, to the skies,
Pure as a Saint's adoring sighs,
Warm as a prayer in Paradise,
Her life-breath rose in sacrifice!
The while with shrill triumphant tone
Sounding aloud, aloft, alone,
Ceaseless her joyful deathwail she
Sang to departing Araby!

      *   *   *

Here on the mountain's sunburnt side
Trip we round our steepy slide,
With tinsel moss, dry-woven pall,
Minist'ring many a frolic fall;
Now, sweet Nymphs, with ankle trim
Foot we around this fountain brim,
Where even the delicate lilies show
Trangressing bosoms in bright row
(More lustrous-sweet than yours, I trow!)
Above their deep green bodices.
Shall you be charier still than these?
Garments are only good to inspire
Warmer, wantoner desire;
For those beauties make more riot
In our hearts, themselves at quiet
Under veils and vapoury lawns
Thro' which their moon-cold lustre dawns,
And might perchance if full revealed
Seem less wondrous than concealed,
Greater defeat of Virtue made
When Love shoots from an ambuscade,
Than with naked front and fair.
Who the loose Grace in flowing hair
Hath ever sought with so much care,
As the crape-enshrouded nun
Scarce warmed by touches of the sun?
Nathless, whatsoe'er your tire,
Hurry me, sweet Nymphs, higher, higher!
Till the broad seas shrink to streams,
Or, beneath my lofty eye,

Ocean a broken mirror seems,
Whose fragments 'tween the lands do lie,
Glancing me from its hollow sky
Till my cheated vision deems
My place in heaven twice as high!

Ho! Evoe! I have found
True Nepenthe, balm of pain,
Sought by sagest wits profound,
Mystic Panacée! in vain.
Virtuous Elixir, this
Sure the supreme sense of bliss!
Feeling my impetuous soul
Ravish me swifter than Earth's roll
Tow'rds bright day's Eoan goal;
Or if West I chose to run,
Would sweep me thither before the sun,
Raising me on ethereal wing
Lighter than the lark can spring
When drunk with delight which the Morn
Pours from her translucent horn
To steep his sweet throat in the corn.
Still, O still my step sublime
Footless air would higher climb,
Like the Chaldee Hunter bold,
Builder of towery Babel old!
O what sweeter, finer pleasure
Than this wild, unruly measure,
Reeling hither, thither, so
Higher to the heavens we go!
Nymph and swain, with rosy hand,
Wreathed together in a band,
Like embracing vines that loop
Browner elms with tendril hoop,
Let us, liker still to these
In rich autumn's purple weather,
Mix, as the vineyard in the breeze,
Our wine-dropping brows together!

   * * *

In the caves of the deep – lost Youth! lost Youth! –

O'er and o'er, fleeting billows! fleeting billows! –
Rung to his restless everlasting sleep
By the heavy death-bells of the deep,
Under the slimy-dropping sea-green willows,
   Poor Youth! lost Youth!
  Laying his dolorous head, forsooth,
  On Carian reefs uncouth –
    Poor Youth! –
On the wild sand's ever-shifting pillows!

In the foam's cold shroud – lost Youth! lost Youth! –
And the lithe waterweed swathing round him! –
Mocked by the surges roaring o'er him loud,
'Will the sun-seeker freeze in his shroud,
Aye, where the deep-wheeling eddy has wound him?'
   Lost Youth! poor Youth!
  Vail him his Dædalian wings, in truth?
  Stretched there without all ruth –
    Poor Youth! –
Weeping fresh torrents into those that drowned him!

List no more the ominous din,
Let us plunge deep Helle in!
Thracia hollos! – what to us
Sky-dejected Icarus?
Shall we less than those wild kine
That swam this shallow salt confine,
Venture to shew how mere a span
Keeps continental man from man?
Welcome, gray Europe, native clime
Of clouds, and cliffs yet more sublime!
Gray Europe, on whose Alpine head
The Northwind makes his snowy bed,
And fostered in that savage form
Lies down a blast and wakes a storm!
Up! up! to shrouded Rhodope
That seems in the white waste to be
An icerock in a foaming sea!

  ....

George Darley

from CANTO II

Across the desert's shrivelled scroll
I past, myself almost to sands
Crumbling, to make another knoll
Amidst the numberless of those lands.
Welcome! Before my bloodshot eyes,
Steed of the East, a camel stands,
Mourning his fallen lord that dies.
Now, as forth his spirit flies,
Ship of the Desert! bear me on,
O'er this wavy-bosomed lea,
That solid seemed and staid anon,
But now looks surging like a sea. –
On she bore me, as the blast
Whirling a leaf, to where in calm
A little fount poured dropping-fast
On dying Nature's heart its balm.
Deep we sucked the spongy moss,
And cropt for dates the sheltering palm,
Then with fleetest amble cross
Like desert, fed upon like alm.
That most vital beverage still,
Tho' near exhaust, preserved me till
Now the broad Barbaric shore
Spread its havens to my view,
And mine ear rung with ocean's roar,
And mine eye glistened with its blue!
Till I found me once again
By the ever-murmuring main,
Listening across the distant foam
My native church bells ring me home.
Alas! why leave I not this toil
Thro' stranger lands, for mine own soil?
Far from ambition's worthless coil,
From all this wide world's wearying moil, –
Why leave I not this busy broil,
For mine own clime, for mine own soil,
My calm, dear, humble, native soil!
There to lay me down at peace
In my own first nothingness?

From *Syren Songs*

(1837)

The Sea Ritual

Prayer unsaid and mass unsung,
Deadman's dirge must still be rung:
  Dingle-dong, the dead-bells sound;
  Mermen chant his dirge around.

Wash him bloodless, smoothe him fair,
Stretch his limbs and sleek his hair:
  Dingle-dong, the dead-bells go;
  Mermen swing them to and fro!

In the wormless sands shall he
Feast for no foul gluttons be:
  Dingle-dong, the dead-bells toll;
  Mermen ring his requiem-knoll!

We must with a tombstone brave
Shut the shark out of his grave:
  Dingle-dong, the dead-bells chime;
  Mermen keep the tune and time!

Such a slab will we lay o'er him,
All the dead shall rise before him:
  Dingle-dong, the dead-bells boom;
  Mermen lay him in his tomb!

JAMES (JEREMIAH) J. CALLANAN (1795–1829)

Born in Ballinhassig, Co. Cork, of a medical family, he was brought up locally, where he learnt Irish. At the wish of his parents, he studied for the priesthood at Maynooth, but left without taking orders, and became a pensioner in Trinity College, Dublin, leaving after two years, then enlisted in the Royal Irish Regiment, from which he was bought out by his friends. He returned to Cork, where he joined the literary circle of Thomas Crofton Croker*, and taught in the school of William Maginn, father of the man of letters who got Callanan's poetry published in *Blackwood's Magazine*. He left teaching, and devoted himself to 'rescuing from oblivion all that [he] could find of the songs and traditions of the south-west of Munster'. In 1828

Blackwood's published his 'Outlaw of Logh Lene', an adaptation of an Irish love song. Much of Callanan's own poetry was never published, and indeed never entrusted to writing. His health failing, he took up a tutoring post in Lisbon, where he died of consumption.

Dirge of O'Sullivan Bear[1]

The sun upon Ivera
  No longer shines brightly;
The voice of her music
  No longer is sprightly;
No more to her maidens
  The light dance is dear,
Since the death of our darling,
  O'Sullivan Bear.

Scully! thou false one,
  You basely betray'd him;
In his strong hour of need
  When thy right hand should aid him;
He fed thee; – he clad thee; –

---

1 In 17—, one of the O'Sullivans of Bearhaven who went by name of Morty Oge, fell under the vengeance of the Law. He had long been a turbulent character in the wild district which he inhabited, and was particularly obnoxious to the local authorities, who had good reason to suspect him of enlisting men for the Irish Brigade in the French service, in which it was said he held a Captain's Commission.

Information of his raising these 'wild geese,' (the name by which such recruits were known) was given by a Mr. Puxley, on whom in consequence O'Sullivan vowed revenge, which he executed by shooting him on Sunday, while on his way to church. This called for the interposition of the higher powers, and accordingly a party of military were sent round from Cork to attack O'Sullivan's house. He was daring and well armed, and the house was fortified, so that he made an obstinate defence. At last a confidential servant of his, named Scully, was bribed to wet the powder in the guns and pistols prepared for his defence, which rendered him powerless. He attempted to escape; but while springing over a high wall in the rere of his house, he received a mortal wound in the back. They tied his body to a boat and dragged it in that manner through the sea, from Bearhaven to Cork, where his head was cut off and fixed on the county jail, where it remained for several years.

Such is the story current among the lower orders about Bearhaven. In the version given of it in the rude chronicle of the local occurrences of Cork, there is no mention made of Scully's perfidy, and perhaps that circumstance might have been added by those by whom O'Sullivan was deemed a hero, in order to save his credit as much as possible. The dirge was composed by his nurse, who has made no sparing use of the energy of cursing, which the Irish language is by all allowed to possess.

(In the following song, Morty, in Irish, Muiertach, or Muircheartach, is a name very common among the old families of Ireland. It signifies expert at sea; Og, or Oge is young— Where a whole district is peopled in a great measure by a sept of one name, such distinguishing titles are necessary, and in some cases even supersede the original appellation. I-vera or Aoi-vera is the original name of Bearhaven; Aoi, or I, signifying an island, or territory). [*Callanan's note.*]

You had all could delight thee;
You left him; – you sold him; –
  May Heaven requite thee!

Scully! may all kinds
  Of evil attend thee;
On thy dark road of life
  May no kind one befriend thee;
May fevers long burn thee,
  And agues long freeze thee;
May the strong hand of God
  In his red anger seize thee.

Had he died calmly,
  I would not deplore him,
Or if the wild strife
  Of the sea-war closed o'er him;
But with ropes round his white limbs,
  Through ocean to trail him,
Like a fish after slaughter! –
  'Tis therefore I wail him.

Long may the curse
  Of his people pursue them;
Scully that sold him,
  And soldier that slew him,
One glimpse of Heaven's light
  May they see never;
May the hearth-stone of hell
  Be their best bed for ever!

In the hole which the vile hands
  Of soldier's had made thee,
Unhonoured, unshrouded,
  And headless they laid thee;
No sigh to regret thee,
  No eye to rain o'er thee,
No dirge to lament thee,
  No friend to deplore thee.

Dear head of my darling,

Jeremiah J. Callanan

How gory and pale,
These aged eyes saw thee
    High spiked on their gaol;
That cheek in the summer sun
    Ne'er shall grow warm,
Nor that eye e'er catch light,
    But the flash of the storm.

A curse, blessed ocean,
    Is on thy green water,
From the haven of Cork
    To Ivera of slaughter,
Since the billows were dyed
    With the red wounds of fear,
Of Muiertach Oge,
    Our O'Sullivan Bear.

The Girl I Love[1]

Súd i síos an caóin ban álain óg.

The girl I love is comely, straight and tall,
Down her white neck her auburn tresses fall,
Her dress is neat, her carriage light and free –
Here's a health to that charming maid whoe'er she be!

---

1 A large proportion of the songs I have met with are love songs. Somehow or other, truly or untruly, the Irish have obtained a character for gallantry, and the peasantry beyond doubt do not belie the 'soft impeachment.' Their modes of courtship, are sometimes amusing. The *'malo me Galatea petit'* of Virgil would still find a counterpart among them — except that the missile of love (which I am afraid is not so poetical as the apple of the pastoral, being neither more or less than a potato), comes first from the gentleman. He flings it with aim designedly erring at his sweetheart, and if she returns the fire a warmer advance concludes the preliminaries and establishes the suitor. Courtships, however, are sometimes carried on among them with a delicacy worthy of a more refined stage of society, and unchastity is very rare. This perhaps is in a great degree occasioned by their extremely early marriages, the advantage or disadvantage of which I give to be discussed by Mr. Malthus and his antagonists.

At their dances (of which they are very fond), whether a-field, or in ale-house, a piece of gallantry frequently occurs which is alluded to in the following song. A young man, smitten suddenly by the charms of a *danseuse,* belonging to a company to which he is a stranger, rises, and with his best bow offers her his glass and requests her to drink to him. After due refusal it is usually accepted, and is looked on as a good omen of successful wooing. Goldsmith alludes to this custom of his country in the Deserted Village:—

The! coy maid, half willing to be prest,
Shall kiss the cup, and pass it to the rest.

The parties may be totally unacquainted, and perhaps never meet again, under which circumstances it would appear that this song was written. [*Callanan's note.*]

The rose's blush but fades beside her cheek,
Her eyes are blue, her forehead pale and meek,
Her lips like cherries on a summer tree –

Here's a health to the charming maid whoe'er she be!
When I go to the field no youth can lighter bound,
And I freely pay when the cheerful jug goes round;
The barrel is full, but its heart we soon shall see –
Come, here's to that charming maid whoe'er she be!

Had I the wealth that props the Saxon's reign,
Or the diamond crown that decks the King of Spain,
I'd yield them all if she kindly smiled on me –
Here's a health to the maid I love whoe'er she be!

Five pounds of gold for each lock of her hair I'd pay,
And five times five, for my love one hour each day;
Her voice is more sweet than the thrush on its own green tree –
Then my dear may I drink a fond deep health to thee!

The Convict of Clonmel[1]

ιs ουbᴀᴄ ἐ mo ᴄᴀ́s.

How hard is my fortune
And vain my repining;
The strong rope of fate

---

1 Who the hero of this song is, I know not, but convicts, from obvious reasons, have been peculiar objects of sympathy in Ireland. Hurling, which is mentioned in one of the verses, is the principal national diversion, and is played with intense zeal by parish against parish, barony against barony, county against county, or even province against province. It is played not only by the peasant, but by the patrician students of the University, where it is an established pastime. Twiss, the most sweeping calumniator of Ireland, calls it, if I mistake not, the cricket of barbarians, but though fully prepared to pay every tribute to the elegance of the English game, I own that I think the Irish sport fully as civilized, and much better calculated for the display of vigour and activity. Perhaps I shall offend Scottish nationality if I prefer either to golf, which is, I think, but trifling compared with them. In the room belonging to the Golf Club on the Links of Leith, there hangs a picture of an old lord (Rosslyn) which I never could look at without being struck with the disproportion between the gaunt figure of the peer and the petty instrument in his hand. Strutt, in 'Sports and Pastimes,' (page 78) eulogises the activity of some Irishmen, who played the game about twenty-five years before the publication of his work (1801), at the back of the British Museum, and deduces it from the Roman harpastum. It was played in Cornwall formerly, he adds: but neither the Romans nor the Cornishmen used a bat, or, as we call it in Ireland, a hurly. The description Strutt quotes from old Carew is quite graphic. The late Dr. Gregory, I am told, used to be loud in panegyric on the superiority of this game when played by the Irish students, over that adopted by his young countrymen north and south of the Tweed, particularly over golf, which he called 'fiddling wi' a pick;' but enough of this—[*Callanan's note.*]

For this young neck is twining!
My strength is departed,
    My cheeks sunk and sallow,
While I languish in chains
    In the gaol of Clonmala.[1]

No boy of the village
    Was ever yet milder;
I'd play with a child
    And my sport would be wilder;
I'd dance without tiring
    From morning 'til even,
And the goal-ball I'd strike
    To the light'ning of Heaven.

At my bed foot decaying
    My hurl-bat is lying;
Through the boys of the village
    My goal-ball is flying;
My horse 'mong the neighbours
    Neglected may fallow,
While I pine in my chains
    In the gaol of Clonmala.

Next Sunday the patron[2]
    At home will be keeping,
And the young active hurlers
    The field will be sweeping;
With the dance of fair maidens
    The evening they'll hallow,
While this heart once so gay
    Shall be cold in Clonmalla.

1 Clonmala, *i.e.*, the solitude of deceit, the Irish name of Clonmel. [*Callanan's note.*]
2 Patron, – Irish *Patruin*,—a festive gathering of the people on tented ground. [*Callanan's note.*]

O Say, My Brown Drimin[1]
Ꭺ Ꮐꭱimin ꭰóꭷꭧ ꭰiꮮis no sioꭰꭥ[2] nꭥ mbo.

O say, my brown Drimin, thou silk of the kine,
Where, where are thy strong ones, last hope of thy line?
Too deep and too long is the slumber they take,
At the loud call of freedom why don't they awake?

My strong ones have fallen – from the bright eye of day
All darkly they sleep in their dwelling of clay;
The cold turf is o'er them; – they hear not my cries,
And since Louis no aid gives I cannot arise.

O! where art thou, Louis, our eyes are on thee?
Are thy lofty ships walking in strength o'er the sea?
In freedom's last strife if you linger or quail,
No morn e'er shall break on the night of the Gael.

But should the King's son, now bereft of his right,
Come, proud in his strength, for his country to fight,
Like leaves on the trees will new people arise,
And deep from their mountains shout back to my cries.

When the Prince, now an exile, shall come for his own,
The isles of his father, his rights and his throne,
My people in battle the Saxon will meet,
And kick them before, like old shoes from their feet.

O'er mountains and valleys they'll press on their rout,
The five ends of Erin shall ring to their shout;
My sons all united shall bless the glad day
When the flint-hearted Saxon they've chased far away.

The Outlaw of Loch Lene

O many a day have I made good ale in the glen,
That came not of stream, or malt, like the brewing of men.

1 *Drimin* is the favourite name of a cow, by which Ireland is here allegorically denoted. The five ends of Erin are the five kingdoms; – Munster, Leinster, Ulster, Connaught, and Meath, into which the island was divided under the Milesian dynasty. [*Callanan's note.*]
2 *Silk of the Cows*—an idiomatic expression for the most beautiful of cattle, which I have

My bed was the ground, my roof, the greenwood above,
And the wealth that I sought – one far kind glance from my love.

Alas! on that night when the horses I drove from the field,
That I was not near from terror my angel to shield.
She stretched forth her arms, – her mantle she flung to the wind,
And swam o'er Loch Lene, her outlawed lover to find
O would that a freezing sleet-winged tempest did sweep,
And I and my love were alone far off on the deep!
I'd ask not a ship, or a bark, or pinnace to save, –
With her hand round my waist, I'd fear not the wind or the wave.

'Tis down by the lake where the wild tree fringes its sides,
The maid of my heart, the fair one of Heaven resides –
I think as at eve she wanders its mazes along,
The birds go to sleep by the sweet wild twist of her song.

JAMES TIGHE (1795–1869)

Born at Dove Hill, near Carrickmacross, Co. Monaghan, he ran a bookshop in Great Britain Street, Dublin, and contributed poems to the Almanacs. Mangan*, whose first rebus had spelt out Tighe's name, befriended him (Tighe would later admit that some of the poems written under his signature were actually by Mangan). He became a writer of temperance tracts, and he also contributed poetry to the *Comet*, the *Irish Penny Journal* and *The Irishman*, where 'The Boreen Side' appeared in 1849.

The Boreen Side

A stripling, the last of his race, lies dead
In a nook by the Boreen side;
The rivulet runs by his board and his bed,
Where he ate the green cresses and died.

The Lord of the plains where that stream wanders on, –
Oh! he loved not the Celtic race –
By a law of the land cast out fellow man,
And he feeds the fat ox in his place.

The hamlet he levelled, and issued commands,
Preventing all human relief,
And out by the ditches, the serfs of his lands,
Soon perished of hunger and grief.

He knew they should die – as he ate and he drank
Of the nourishing food and wine;
He heard of the death cries of the famish'd and lank
And fed were his dogs and his swine.

That Lord is a Christian! and prays the prayer,
'Our Father' – the Father of all –
And he reads in the Book of wonderful care,
That marks when a sparrow may fall.

And there lies that youth on his damp cold bed,
And the cattle have stall and straw;
No kindred assemble to wail the lone dead –
They perished by landlord law.

He lies by the path where his forefathers trod –
The race of the generous deeds,
That sheltered the Poor for the honor of God,
And fed them with bread – not weeds.

Unshrouded he lies by the trackless path,
And he died as his kindred died –
And vengeance Divine points the red bolt of wrath,
For that death by the Boreen side.

EUGENE O'CURRY (1796–1862)

B orn in Dunaha, near Carrigaholt, Co. Clare, where his father, a story-teller and manuscript-collector, taught him reading and writing, and Irish. He worked for some twenty years in a mental asylum in Limerick. He was a well-known collector of Irish manuscripts, some of which were purchased by the Royal Irish Academy.

He was invited to Dublin, and in 1835 joined the Topographical Section of the Ordnance Survey, working from George Petrie's* home, with his brother-in-law John O'Donovan, and with James Clarence Mangan*. This section of the Ordnance Survey was closed down in 1842, and O'Curry was employed by the Royal Irish Academy, and by Trinity College, Dublin, in transcribing and cataloguing their Irish manuscripts.

In 1854, on the establishment of the Catholic University in Dublin, he was appointed to the chair of Irish history and archæology. In 1861 Cardinal Newman arranged for publication of his *Lectures on the Manuscript Materials of Ancient Irish History* (1861). These formed a valuable source for Matthew Arnold's *On the Study of Celtic Literature* – Arnold claimed O'Curry 'belonged to the race of the giants in literary research and industry, a race now almost extinct.' O'Curry's *On the Manners and Customs of the Ancient Irish* was published posthumously, under the editorship of W. K. Sullivan.

From *On the Manners and Customs of the Ancient Irish* (1873)

from Introduction

IMPORTANCE OF IRISH HISTORY AND ARCHÆOLOGY, AND CHARACTER OF EXISTING SOURCES.

Somewhat more than a century ago a new field of scientific research was opened up. Men yearned to know something of the past of the globe we inhabit, and of the beginnings of the early nations who have lived upon its surface. In the course of the last half century this new scientific territory has been well occupied, and the domain of the human intellect pushed far into the shadowy regions of the past. The great stone book, in which are written the annals of the globe, every page of which unfolds to us manifold forms of life, which, like the dynasties of ancient kingdoms, have passed away for ever, has been carefully examined; and from those annals science has enabled us to construct the geography of our globe at the dawn of its time, to people its waters with fish, to clothe its land with vegetation, and people it with birds and beasts. We may, as it were, walk by the shores of its ancient sea, follow the tracks of the marine animals that crawled upon its sands, or of the land animals that came down to its shore, count the ripples left by its receding tide, nay, even note the impressions left upon the dried sand by the rain-drops of the passing summer shower. The vastness and beauty of those annals of the globe diverted attention for a long time from the last though perhaps most important pages, in which are visible the first vestiges of man. Within the last few years, however the superficial gravel heaps, the alluvions of rivers and lake bottoms, the caverns in the hill side, have been ransacked, and such numbers of the works of man, of his bones, and of those of his contemporary animals, have been brought to light, that already attempts are made to rehabilitate primeval man.

Simultaneously with these researches of the geologist, the archaeologist has been busy in excavating the sites of ancient cities and removing the earth of centuries. Adopting the spirit and method of physical science, the sounds of dead languages of which scarce an echo had reached our ears, have been reawakened; we can rebuild the fallen cities, people them anew with their ancient inhabitants, assign to them their various duties, and partake in imagination of their daily life.

As a chip of flint, a fragment of pottery, an inscribed stone, a spear, or a ruined building, helps to realize the physical past of mankind, so a fragment of an ancient poem, a legend, or a myth, helps us to resuscitate the intellectual past.

Just as now, man migrated in ancient times from one region to another, and carried with him his arms, his tools, and his mode of building houses. The comparison of the tools and weapons and ancient buildings found in various countries, like the gravel and boulders of the geologist, enables us to trace the stream of migration, and its probable starting point. But there are also intellectual boulders: stray words of languages, fragments of myths, even nursery rhymes, have become important helps in tracing out the early history of peoples....

According as antique weapons, tools, and implements are collected, classified, and compared, ancient ruins examined, inscriptions read, languages comparatively studied, myths traced back to their source, legends analysed and their meaning determined, annals sifted, corrected, and synchronized, the primitive history of man becomes a reality. At the same time a profound change is taking place in our notions of the scope and objects of history. We are no longer content that it should be a rehearsal of the drama of a national life, in which the principal performers alone should appear on the stage in conventional dress, and play their game of political chess. We are only satisfied with the full opera, in which the chorus of the Plebs is heard as well as the solos of the Kings and Nobles; in which the labours, joys, and sufferings of the peasant and artizan receive their meed of attention equally with the heroic deeds, the pageants, the pleasures, and misfortunes of kings; in which the creations of art and the discoveries of science, the conquests of man over nature, receive their share of glory, as well as the victories of man over man.

It is now a recognized fact in science that from the Indus to the Atlantic ocean, and thence across the American continent to the shores of the Pacific, the descendants of one primitive, blue-eyed, fair-haired race, divided into several branches and speaking dialects of what was once a common language, hold sway. To determine the common elements in the languages, mythologies, legends, laws, and customs of the several branches of this great Aryan race, and thence inductively rehabilitate, as it were, the primitive parent race whence they issued, is one of the most interesting, as undoubtedly it is one of the most important, problems of historical science. The solution of this problem requires the union of every possible streamlet of knowledge bearing upon the subject. No tribe of the race can be so obscure, or land so insignificant, that its history may not contribute materials for the purpose. Though it were true, therefore, that in ancient times Ireland was an isolated corner of the earth, whose inhabitants were no better than savages, still the study of the ancient language of the people, and such historical traditions and legends of them as may have survived, would be valuable. But the ancient language, laws, and traditions of Ireland are, in truth, among the most valuable, nay, indispensable materials for the solution of the problem above stated. The Romans, Celts, and Germans have so commingled with each other on the continent of Europe and in Great Britain, that it is almost impossible to say what is peculiar to each and what borrowed. The fully-developed judicial, fiscal, and administrative system of the Romans, as well as their otherwise high physical culture, have, as might have been expected, deeply modified the political and social organization of the Gauls, Britons, and Germans. The only branch of the Celtic race not directly in contact with this highly-developed political organization was the Irish. That Ireland was not unaffected by Roman civilization, and even by the earlier civilization of other Mediterranean nations in pre-Christian times, is undoubtedly true. But that influence was not such as could deeply modify the laws or customs of the people, and hence in them we ought to find a precious mine of information regarding the political and social organization of Europe before the rise of the Roman power. Fortunately, we possess in the remains of the Irish language, poetry, laws, etc., such a mine, and in greater fulness too than is to be found in the other branches of the Aryan race, except the Sanskrit, Greek, and Latin.

The early history of Ireland possesses value from another point of view, which, if more limited in its scope, is of more immediate interest and of far greater importance than the prehistoric history of the greatest of the human races, namely in connection with the rise of the laws and institutions of France, Germany, and especially of England. All French institutions, in the opinion of many, are supposed to have a Roman origin, and to have been subsequently somewhat modified by German influence. That the Gauls had political institutions which survived the Roman and Frankish conquests, and in reality formed the basis of the various custumals out of which the later institutions were evolved by a natural process of growth, has only occurred vaguely to a few. That the great principles of English law are the gift of the Anglo-Saxons, who not only borrowed nothing from their predecessors the Britons, but actually exterminated them, has so much the force of an axiom among English writers, that no one, so far as I know, has ever doubted the first part of the statement, and but few the latter part. And yet it may be maintained, that the organization of society in Gaul and in Britain before the dawn of the Christian era, was substantially the same as in Germany; that all the fundamental principles of Anglo-Saxon law existed among the Britons and Irish; and that the Saxons of Hengist and Horsa found on their arrival what we call Saxon laws and customs, and only effected territorial changes. This is precisely the conclusion to which a study of ancient Irish history in the broad sense of that word inevitably leads.

The sources of ancient Irish history are two-fold:—one, the brief and often very vague notices of Greek and Roman writers; the other, the prose and poetic tales and legendary histories, and reliques of the laws of the Irish themselves. With the exception of the geographical notices of Strabo and Ptolemy, which are of some use, the materials afforded by the first source are worthless. They consist of mere hearsay reports, without any sure foundation, and in many cases not in harmony with the results of modern linguistic and archaeological investigations. The fuller and more trustworthy accounts of the customs and institutions of Gaul and Germany, left us by Caesar and Tacitus, are no doubt indirectly of use because they relate to peoples closely allied to the ancient Irish.

I have already said that we do not lack the second category of historic materials, at least as far as quantity is concerned; but the quality requires careful and critical examination. The Irish historical and legal materials which we possess in our vellum manuscripts are in the first place necessarily fragmentary and incomplete. No early writer in the fifth or sixth century attempted to weave into a connected narrative the legendary history of the country, still fresh and full in the memories of the bards. And it was long after before any attempt was made to establish a chronology of Irish historical events, and synchronize them with those of other nations. In the second place, our materials of ancient Irish history, such as they are, have not come down to us in the language which was spoken at the period at which the poems and tales are assumed to have been written. Our oldest historical manuscripts belong to the first half of the twelfth century; while some of the most valuable fragments of our ancient laws are contained in manuscripts written at the end of the fourteenth or even the beginning of the sixteenth century. It is true, the age of a manuscript does not necessarily fix that of its contents; but before we give them a higher antiquity, we should weigh well the grounds upon which we do so. In some cases the evidence of this higher antiquity is conclusive, because the language of some tracts is so obsolete that it required to be glossed in more modern language when they were being copied into the manuscript. In other cases, too, we find the grammatical endings fuller and more archaic than a number of pieces admittedly contemporary with, or only little anterior in date to, the writing of the manuscript itself.

But even such evidences of antiquity only help us to carry further back the age of a tale or poem or law a few centuries at most than that of the manuscript in which it is contained, and leave us still in face of the difficulty, that all the tales and poems referring to pagan times, or perhaps we might say to the first two centuries after the arrival of Saint Patrick, are written in the language of much later times; and this, too, in cases where we are distinctly told in the manuscript itself that it was compiled from another manuscript written at a certain much earlier period.

*   *   *

... in a country divided into numerous petty states, subject to internal dissensions and foreign intrusive elements affecting the phonetic system of its language, and where, although many writers would flourish, no great ones could arise whose authority would fix for a time its orthography, the written language would always coincide with the spoken, and, consequently, change almost equally with it. In this case, we should have the example of what may be considered a language living rapidly. In reality, however, it would be merely the want of what may be called a classical period which would have crystallized its phonetic system for some time, leaving the under-current of spoken language to go on developing. In the former case the literature would, as it were, float down the stream of popular language.

The last paragraph describes accurately the Irish language and literature: there is no fixed standard of orthography, no classic type. Every bard, as he copied a poem or story, wrote it, not according to the orthography of the text before him, but spelled as it should sound to the ears of the time. Sometimes a piece was literally copied, and then had to be glossed. Now, the pieces thus written are in general not such as would be recited by a bard at a feast or fair, and therefore did not require to have the orthography adapted to existing pronunciation.

But there is another reason why ancient bardic poems and tales should not appear in manuscripts of the twelfth century in the archaic language in which they were first composed. Those poems and tales were learned by heart by the bards, and recited by them for the princes, at fairs and assemblies. As the language lost its inflections, and some of its words and expressions became obsolete, and new ones were taken up, the bards naturally adapted more or less those tales to the language of their hearers. There can be no doubt that many copies of tales in our existing manuscripts were not taken directly from old books, but written down from memory. This accounts for the different versions of the same tale which may be found in manuscripts of almost the same date — one version being often in very archaic language, retaining considerable relics of the case endings and fuller forms of the personal endings of verbs.

If we had no other means of determining the age of the materials of pre-Christian history we possess, than the language in which they are written, we could not go back farther than, at most, the middle of the ninth century. But many of the pieces bear internal evidence of their real antiquity. The heroic period of Irish history has left as indelible an impression upon the popular mind as that of Grecian history upon the Greeks. The tales relating to the pre-Christian period have in some form or other floated down the stream of tradition, preserving in the midst of a richly developed Christian mythos much of their original pagan character. Of course they did not all preserve this character with equal fidelity. While some have all the characteristics of the legends of a primitive people — unaffected simplicity, truthful description, confiding faith in the marvellous as the result of supernatural agency, and not introduced merely as part of the plot of the tale, — others, on the other hand, show unmistakable evidence of having been recast by bards. In the pieces thus recast, instead of descriptions which, though often highly coloured by the fancy of the poet, retain always the outlines of reality, we have generally a string of almost synonymous epithets which convey no accurate image to the mind, while they abound in the marvellous, often introduced merely to heighten the effect of the tale. This is the character of the greater part of the bardic literature of the twelfth, thirteenth, and later centuries....

Druids and Druidism

Lecture IX.

[delivered 25th June, 1857]

...Let us begin with the earliest mention of Druids as preserved in our annals and historical traditions.

The origin of Druids in Erinn is carried back by our ancient writings, (and I am convinced with great probability), to the earliest colonizers of the country, who were all, it is to be remembered, referred to the race of Japhet; and whether there was or was not in the more ancient times anything more than traditional authority for this belief, it is, I think, sufficient to show that the ancient Gaedhils never assumed the origin of the Druidic system themselves, nor acknowledged to have received it, any more than any other part of their social system, from any neighbouring country.

Parthalon is by our most ancient authorities recorded to have come into Erinn about three hundred years after the deluge. He is said to have come from '*Migdonia*', or Middle Greece, with a small company; but among these we are told that there were three Druids, — whose names are given: *Fios*, *Eolus*, and *Fochmarc*; that is, if we seek the etymological meaning of the words, Intelligence, Knowledge, and Inquiry. We have no record of any performance of these Druids of *Parthalon*.

The next colony, led by *Nemid* and his sons, is said to have come from 'Scythia', about three hundred and thirty years after the coming of *Parthalon*. *Nemid*'s sons were: *Starn*, *Iarbonel* 'the Prophet', *Fergus* 'the Half-Red', and *Aininn*. And this colony soon, according to our oldest records, came in contact with the power of hostile Druidism, to which they opposed their own. *Nemid*, it appears, had not remained long in peace in the country, before he was disturbed by the incursions of the sea rovers, who are known in our old writings under the name of the Fomorians. These adventurers, under a valiant leader named *Conaing*, son of *Faebhar*, took possession of Tory Island (on the north-west of the coast of Donegal), which they fortified, and converted into a sort of citadel or depot, and by this means made themselves most formidable and oppressive to the Nemidians on the main land. The Nemidians, driven to despair at last, assembled all their forces, men and women, from all parts of the country, on the shore opposite Tory Island; which the Fomorians perceiving, sent their Druids and Druidesses, we are told, to confound them by their

Druidic spells; but these were met by the Nemidian Druids and Druidesses, under the leadership of *Reilbeó*, 'daughter of the king of Greece', *Nemid*'s wife, and chief of the Druidesses. A fierce contest of spells as well as of blows ensued between them, in which the Fomorian party were defeated. A general battle ensued then, which resulted in the utter rout of the Fomorians, whose tower or fortress on Tory Island was demolished, and their chief leader, *Conaing*, and his sons, were killed.

The Nemidians did not long enjoy the peace and freedom which this victory brought them; for *Morc* the son of *Dela*, another famous rover or Fomorian chief, came, with sixty ships, took possession again of Tory Island, and renewed the oppressions practised by his predecessor upon the Nemidians. This led to another great battle, in which the destruction of the parties was mutual; *Morc* and a few of his followers, only, escaping to the island, and but one ship of the Nemidians, with only thirty warriors and three leaders on board, escaping to the land. These three leaders were: *Beothach*, the son of *Iarbonel* 'the Prophet', son of *Nemid*; *Simeon Breac* (or 'the speckled'), son of *Starn*, son of *Nemid*; and *Britan Mael* (or 'the bald',) son of *Fergus* the Half-Red, son of *Nemid*. And it is to these three cousins that the races of the *Tuatha Dé Danann*, the *Firbolgs*, and the Britons, are traced by our early genealogists, from whom we learn that the three soon afterwards left Erinn, and proceeded to seek a better fortune elsewhere. *Beothach*, we are told, with his clann, went to the northern parts of Europe, where they made themselves perfect in all the arts of Divination, Druidism, and Philosophy, and returned, after some generations, to Erinn, under the name of the *Tuatha Dé Danann*. *Simeon Breac* with his clann wandered southward into Greece; and in many generations after, returned to Erinn under the name of the *Firbolgs*. And we learn that *Britan Mael*, with his father *Fergus*, and his clann, went to *Moinn* or *Mainn Chonaing*, the present Island of Mona (or Anglesey); 'from which', says the Book of Ballymote (folio 15), 'their children filled the great Island of Britain, which they inhabited until the coming in of the Saxons, who drove the descendants of Brutus to the one border of the country, and the descendants of *Britan Mael* back to *Moinn Chonaing* [or Anglesey], on the other border'....

Now going back to the ancient legendary history of the Gaedhils, it is to be remembered that on the flight of *Nemid*'s three grandsons from Erinn, one of them, *Simeon Breac*, the son of *Starn*, is said to have gone with his clann into Thrace, that is into Greece. There, we are told, they remained and multiplied during more than two hundred years; when at last they fled from the oppression which, it seems, held them there in a state of slavery, and after many wanderings returned to Erinn again, and with little trouble made themselves masters of the country. These were the *Firbolgs*. These again, in their turn were soon after invaded by the *Tuatha Dé Danann*, the descendants of *Iobath*, the third grandson or great-grandson of *Nemid*; and their power and rule were overthrown in the great battle of *Magh Tuireadh*....

The *Tuatha Dé Danann*, or *Dadanann* tribes, as we have already seen, during the long period of their exile from Erinn, devoted themselves much to the cultivation of Divination, Druidism, and the Philosophy of the northern and eastern parts of Europe; so that they appear to have returned perfectly accomplished in all the secrets and mysteries of the occult sciences of those times. They had a druidical chief or demigod, the great *Daghda*, as he was called, who was also their military leader. They had, besides him, three chief Druids: *Brian*, *Iuchar*, and *Iucharba*; and two chief professional Druidesses: *Becuill* and *Danann*; — besides a great number of private Druids and Druidesses, mentioned by name in the early accounts of the coming of this race.

On the first arrival of the *Tuatha Dé Danann*, they took up their position in the fastnessess of Middle Connacht, but soon discovered that the country was inhabited by the Firbolgs; they then moved farther south and west, to the plain called *Magh Tuireadh*, near Cong, in the present county of Galway.... The ancient tales record that while they were making this important movement three of their noble non-professional Druidesses, namely, *Bodhbh*, *Macha*, and *Mór Rigan*, went to Tara, where the Firbolg hosts were assembled in a council of war; and that there, by their Druidical arts, they caused clouds of impenetrable darkness and mist to envelope the assembled multitudes, and showers of fire and blood to pour down upon them from the heavens, so that for three days all business was suspended; that at last the spell was broken by the Firbolg Druids, *Cesarn*, *Gnathach*, and *Ingnathach*; but that during this time, the *Tuatha Dé Danann* had already established themselves without opposition in a new defensive position at a safer distance from their enemies. This may serve as one instance of the ancient tradition of the practical use of Druidical magic at a very early period in Erinn.

Again we are told, in the oldest accounts, that previous to the invasion of the *Tuatha Dé Danann*, the king of the Firbolgs, *Eochaidh Mac Erc*, had an unusual dream, which he submitted for interpretation to his chief Druid, *Cesarn*. The Druid is said to have had recourse to the secret agencies of his art, and to have discovered from a vision the approach of a powerful enemy; and this he is said to have communicated to the king in a series of short simple sentences, of which a few are preserved in the account of the great battle of *Magh Tuireadh*.... The great battle came at last; and it is stated that the men of science and 'knowledge' of both parties took up their positions on rocks and stages on the battle-field, practising their druidic arts in favour of their friends and against their foes respectively; until at last the *Tuatha Dé Danann* prevailed, and the Firbolgs were defeated....

So much for what is found in the few records we possess of our very early colonists.

We now come to the Milesian Colony. According to our ancient traditions, these people, who were also Japhetians, passed in their migrations back from Scythia into Greece, out of which they had previously come; then into Egypt; then into Spain; and so, from Spain into Erinn, which they reached about two hundred years after the conquest of the *Tuatha Dé Danann*; that is, in the year of the world 3,500, or above 1,530 years before Christ, according to the chronology of the Annals of the Four Masters.

In the entire course of the migrations of this people, the Druids hold a conspicuous place. Among the most remarkable was *Caicher*, who is said to have foretold to them, on their way to Spain, that Erinn was their ultimate destination.

The chief Druids of the Milesians, on their arrival in Erinn, were *Uar* and *Eithear* (who were both killed in the battle of *Slibh Mis*, in Kerry), and *Amergin*, one of the Milesian brothers, who was the Poet and Judge of the expedition, and a famous Druid, though not by profession.

A remarkable instance of Druidism is stated to have happened even on the very occasion of the landing of the first Milesian colony. Having landed in Kerry, they marched direct to the seat of sovereignty, now called Tara, a place which at the time we are speaking of was called *Cathair Crofinn*, or *Crofinn*'s Court, from a *Tuatha Dé Danann* lady of that name, who had previously resided there.[1] On arriving at Tara, the Milesians demanded the sovereignty of the country from the three joint kings of the *Tuatha Dé Danann*, the brothers *MacCuill*,

1 The Hill of Tara had five names. The first was *Druim Descain*, or the Conspicuous Hill; the second was *Liath Druim*, or *Liath's* Hill, from a Firbolg chief of that name who was the first to clear it of wood; the third was *Druim Cain*, or the beautiful Hill; the fourth was *Cathair Crofinn*, as shown above; and the fifth name was *Teamair* (now Anglicised Tara, from the genitive case *Teamhrach* of the word), a name which it got from being the burial place of Téa, the wife of *Eremon*, the son of Milesius [*O'Curry's note.*]

MacCecht, and *MacGreiné*. These complained of their having been taken by surprise, alleging that if they had had notice of the coming invasion they would have prevented it, and offering to leave it with *Amergin* to give judgment between them. To this proposition the Milesians are said to have consented; and *Amergin* is recorded to have made the very singular decision that himself and his friends should reënter their ships, and should move to the distance of 'nine waves', (as the authorities agree in stating), out from the land; and then that if they were able to land despite of the *Dé Danann*, the sovereignty of Erinn should be surrendered to them.

This decision, according to this most ancient tradition, was accepted by both parties; and the Milesians reëntered their ships, and went out the prescribed distance upon the sea. No sooner, however, had they done so, than the *Dé Danann* Druids raised such a tempest as drove the fleet out to sea, and dispersed them. One part of the fleet was driven to the south, — and so round the island, to the north-east again, — under *Eremon*, son of Milesius. The other part was suffering dreadfully from the tempest, when it occurred to them that the storm was raised by Druidical agency. *Donn*, the eldest of the Milesian brothers, then sent a man to the topmast of his ship to discover if the power of the wind extended as high as that point. The man ascended, and announced that it was quite calm at that elevation; upon hearing which, *Donn* cried out: 'It is treachery in our men of science not to allay this wind'. [By this expression, 'men of science', the Druids are referred to here, as well as in many other places]. 'It is not treachery', said his brother *Amergin*; and he arose and pronounced a Druidical oration, — of the ancient gloss on which the following is a literal translation, taken from the Book of Invasions of the O'Clerys, in the Royal Irish Academy:

'I pray that they reach the land of Erinn, those who are riding upon the great, productive, vast sea.

'That they be distributed upon her plains, her mountains, and her valleys; upon her forests that shed showers of nuts and all other fruits; upon her rivers and her cataracts; upon her lakes and her great waters; upon her abounding springs, [or, upon her spring-abounding hills].

'That we may hold our fairs and equestrian sports upon her territories.

'That there may be a king from us in Tara; and that it (Tara) be the territory of our many kings'.[1]

'That the sons of Milesius be manifestly seen upon her territories.

---

1 The Hill had not at this time received the name of *Teamair* or Tara; but *Amergin* is made to speak of it by the name by which it was subsequently known. [*O'Curry's note.*]

'That noble Erinn be the home of the ships and boats of the sons of Milesius.

'Erinn which is now in darkness, it is for her that this oration is pronounced.

'Let the learned wives of *Breas* and *Buaigné* pray that we may reach the noble woman, great *Erinn*.

'Let *Eremon* pray, and let *Ir* and *Eber* implore that we may reach Erinn'.

At the conclusion of this oration the tempest ceased, according to our authority, and the survivors landed again. And then *Amergin*, upon putting his foot on dry land, pronounced another propitiatory oration (couched in the same obscure and general language), on the land, and on the waters, to render them more prolific.

In this example we have a curious instance of the very form of words in which it was anciently believed that, in still more remote ages, the Druids framed their incantations. We cannot, however, perceive anything of druidic or magical power, or character, in this oration — nothing, in short, to distinguish it from the prayer of any Christian of the present day, so far as the expression of the speaker's wants and desire. It does not clearly appear to whom the prayer was addressed, or that any ceremony or rite accompanied the delivery of it. I do not, of course, quote it as the certainly genuine prayer of *Amergin*; but it is, without any doubt, a very ancient piece of composition, and it must, I am persuaded, have been written either by some ancient Druid, or by some person conversant with the style of Druidic practices, and probably at a time long before Druidism became extinct in this country. And as regards the intrinsic innocence of the words used, it is curious enough that the Irish people to this day have an old tradition, that in the most profane and forbidden performances of sorcery and witchcraft, harmless and blessed words have been always used. The common proverb still is: 'Blessed words and cursed deeds'.

All that I have set down here is taken directly from our most ancient manuscripts, or those compiled from them; and they show clearly as the historical tradition of the country that each of the older colonies in Ireland was accompanied by its Druids; so that the suggestion, of modern British writers that Druidism came first from Britain, or from Anglesey, into Erinn, is totally unfounded. I now proceed to select from the long list of Druidic references found in our old books, such as may serve to characterize the profession, so far, at least, as the limits of these lectures will allow....

...The ancient tract called *Dinnseanchas* (on the Etymology of the names of several remarkable places in Erinn) gives the following singular legendary account of the origin of the names of *Midhe* (now Meath), and of *Uisnech*, in Meath.

Midhe the son of *Brath*, son of *Detha* (says this legend), was the first that lighted a fire for the sons of the Milesians in Erinn, on the Hill of *Uisnech* in Westmeath; and it continued to burn for seven years; and it was from this fire that every chief fire in Erinn used to be lighted. And his successor was entitled to a sack of corn and a pig from every house in Erinn, every year. The Druids of Erinn, however, said that it was an insult to them to have this fire ignited in the country; and all the Druids of Erinn came into one house to take council; but *Midhe* had all their tongues cut out, and he buried the tongues in the earth of *Uisnech* and then sat over them; upon which his mother exclaimed: 'It is *Uaisnech* [i.e. proudly] you sit up there this night'; — and hence the names of *Uisnech*, and of *Midhe* (or Meath).

This, I believe, is the first reference to a Druidical fire to be found in our old books.

The next remarkable allusion to this subject that is to be found is the account of King *Eochaidh Airemh*.

It was a century before the Incarnation that *Eochaidh Airemh* was monarch of Erinn; and his queen was the celebrated *Edain*, a lady remarkable not only for her beauty, but for her learning and accomplishments. One day that *Eochaidh* was in his palace at *Teamair*, according to this ancient story, a stranger of remarkable appearance presented himself before him. 'Who is this man who is not known to us, and what is his business?' said the king. 'He is not a man of any distinction, but he has come to play a game at chess with you', said the stranger. 'Are you a good chess player?' said the king. 'A trial will tell', said the stranger. 'Our chess-board is in the queen's apartment, and we cannot disturb her at present', said the king. 'It matters not, for I have a chess-board of no inferior kind here with me', said the stranger. 'What do we play for?' said the king. 'Whatever the winner demands', said the stranger. [They played then a game which was won by the stranger.] 'What is your demand now?' said the king. '*Edain*, your queen', said the stranger, 'but I will not demand her till the end of a year'. The king was astonished and confounded; and the stranger, without more words, speedily disappeared.

On that night twelvemonths, the story goes on to tell us, the king held a great feast at *Teamair*, surrounding himself and his queen with the great nobles and choicest warriors of his realm, and placing around his palace on the outside a line of experienced and vigilant guards, with strict orders to let no stranger pass them in. And thus secured, as he thought, he awaited with anxiety the coming night, while revelry reigned all round. As the middle of the night advanced, however, the king was horrified to see the former stranger standing in the middle of the floor, apparently unperceived by any one else. Soon he advanced to the queen, and addressed her by the name of *Bé Finn*, (Fair Woman), in a poem of seven stanzas, of which the following is a literal translation:

> 'O *Befinn*! will you come with me
>> To a wonderful country which is mine,
>> Where the people's hair is of golden hue,
>> And their bodies the colour of virgin snow?
> 'There no grief or care is known;
>> White are their teeth, black their eyelashes;
>> Delight of the eye is the rank of our hosts,
>> With the hue of the fox-glove on every cheek.
> 'Crimson are the flowers of every mead,
>> Gracefully speckled as the blackbird's egg;
>> Though beautiful to see be the plains of *Inisfail*,
>> They are but commons compared to our great plains.
> 'Though intoxicating to you be the aledrink of *Inisfail*,
>> More intoxicating the ales of the great country;
>> The only land to praise is the land of which I speak,
>> Where no one ever dies of decrepit age.
> 'Soft sweet streams traverse the land;
>> The choicest of mead and of wine;
>> Beautiful people without any blemish;
>> Love without sin, without wickedness.
> 'We can see the people upon all sides,
>> But by no one can we be seen;
>> The cloud of Adam's transgression it is,
>> That prevents them from seeing us.
> 'O woman! should you come to my brave land,
>> It is golden hair that will be on your head;
>> Fresh pork, beer, new milk, and ale,
>> You there with me shall have, O *Béfinn*!'

At the conclusion of this poem, the stranger put his arm around the queen's body, raised her from her royal chair, and walked out with her, unobserved by any one but the king, who felt so overcome by some supernatural influence, that he was unable to offer any opposition, or even to apprise the company of what was going on. When the monarch recovered himself, he knew at once that it was some one of the invisible beings who inhabited the hills and lakes of Erinn that played one of their accustomed tricks upon him. When daylight came, accordingly, he ordered his chief Druid, *Dallan*, to his presence, and he commanded him to go forth immediately, and never to return until he had discovered the fate of the queen.

The Druid set out, and traversed the country for a whole year, without any success, notwithstanding that he had drawn upon all the ordinary resources of his art. Vexed and disappointed at the close of the year he reached the mountain (on the borders of the present counties of Meath and Longford) subsequently named after him *Sliabh Dallain*. Here he cut four wands of yew, and wrote or cut an *Ogam* in them; and it was revealed to him, 'through his keys of science and his *ogam*', that the queen *Edain* was concealed in the palace of the fairy chief, *Midir*, in the hill of *Bri Leith*, (a hill lying to the west of Ardagh, in the present county of Longford). The Druid joyfully returned to Tara with the intelligence; and the monarch *Eochaidh* mustered a large force, marched to the fairy mansion of *Bri Leith*, and had the hill dug up until the diggers approached the sacred precincts of the subterranean dwelling; whereupon the wily fairy sent out to the hill side fifty beautiful women, all of the same age, same size, same appearance in form, face, and dress, and all of them so closely resembling the abducted lady *Edain*, that the monarch *Eochaidh* himself, her husband, failed to identify her among them, until at length she made herself known to him by unmistakable tokens, — upon which he returned with her to Tara.

This tale exhibits two curious and characteristic features of Irish Druidism; the first, that the Irish Druid's wand of divination was formed from the yew, and not from the oak, as in the other countries; the second, that the Irish Druid called in the aid of actual characters, letters, or symbols, — those, namely, the forms of which have come down to our own times cut in the imperishable monuments of stone, so well known as *Ogam* stones, (many of which may be seen in the National Museum of the Royal Irish Academy.)

The antiquity of this story of *Eochaidh Airemh* is unquestionable. There is a fragment of it in *Leabhar na-h-Uidhré*, in the Royal Irish Academy, a manuscript which was actually written before the year 1106; and it is there quoted from the Book of *Dromsnechta*, which was undoubtedly written before or about the year 430. There is a better copy, but still not perfect nor so old, in the collection formerly in the possession of the late Mr. William Monk Mason, in England....

SAMUEL LOVER (1797–1868)

Maginn* described Lover as 'at once a musician, a painter, a novelist, and a poet'. He was born in Dublin, the eldest son of a stockbroker, and was educated privately, showing precocious musical and artistic talents. He joined his father's office, but found the work uncongenial, and left acrimoniously. He soon made a name for himself as a portraitist and miniaturist, and in 1828 was elected to the Royal Hibernian Academy, becoming its secretary two years later. He also earned a reputation as a song-writer and reciter; his eulogy at a banquet for Thomas Moore* earned him the poet's friendship. In 1826 he wrote 'Rory O'More', his most popular ballad; its stage-Irish protagonist became the eponymous hero of a novel and a play which he wrote in 1837. In 1831 he published the first volume of his *Legends and Stories of Ireland*, illustrated by himself, which was an instant success. It consisted of tales loosely based on urban and country folklore which he had contributed to Dublin magazines, and it was followed in 1834 by a second instalment, and in 1839 by his *Songs and Ballads*. In 1833 he co-founded the *Dublin University Magazine*. He moved to London in 1835, where he enjoyed considerable success as a society painter. He counted Lady Blessington* among his acquaintances, and with Dickens he founded *Bentley's Miscellany*, in which his novel *Handy Andy: A Tale of Irish Life* (1842) was first serialized. Lover wrote several dramas and musicals, including *The Greek Boy* (1840), and a burlesque opera, *Paddy Whack in Italia*, which was produced by Balfe at the English Opera House. He abandoned miniature painting in 1844 because of failing eyesight, and devised his 'Irish Evenings', one-man-shows with songs, recitations and stories. With these he toured Canada and the United States from 1846 to 1848. These tours offered him material for a new entertainment called *Paddy's Portfolio* (1848). He produced two libretti for Balfe, and, after his second marriage in 1852, devoted himself fully to song writing. He returned to Ireland some years before his death.

From *Handy Andy*
(1842)

PREFACE

I have been accused, in certain quarters, of giving flattering portraits of my countrymen. Against this charge I may plead that, being a portrait-painter by profession, the habit of taking the best view of my subject, so long prevalent in my eye, has gone deeper, and influenced my mind, – and if to paint one's country in its gracious aspect has been a weakness, at least, to use the word of an illustrious compatriot,

'The failing leans to virtue's side.'[1]

I am disinclined, however, to believe myself an offender in this particular. That I love my country dearly I acknowledge, and I am sure every Englishman will respect me the more for loving *mine*, when he is with justice, proud of *his* – but I repeat my disbelief that I overrate my own.

The present volume, I hope, will disarm any cavil from old quarters on the score of national prejudice. The hero is a blundering fellow whom no English or other gentleman would like to have in his service; but still he has some redeeming natural traits: he is not made either a brute or a villain; yet his 'twelve months' character,' given in the successive numbers of this volume, would not get him a place upon advertisement either in the *Times* or the *Chronicle*. So far am I clear of the charge of national prejudice as regards the hero of the following pages.

In the subordinate personages, the reader will see two 'Squires' of different types – good and bad; there are such in all countries. And, as a tale cannot get on without villains, I have given some touches of villainy, quite sufficient to prove my belief in Irish villains, though I do not wish it to be believed that the Irish are *all villains*.

I confess I have attempted a slight sketch, in one of the persons represented, of a gentleman and a patriot; and I conceive there is a strong relationship between the two. He loves the land that bore him – and so did most of the great spirits recorded in history. His own mental cultivation, while it yields him personal enjoyment, teaches him not to treat with contumely inferior men. Though he has courage to protect his honour, he is not deficient in conscience to feel for the consequences; and when opportunity offers the means of *amende*, it is embraced. In a word, I wish it to be believed that, while there are knaves, and fools, and villains in Ireland, – as in other parts of the world, — honest, intelligent, and noble spirits are there also....

---

1 *The failing ... side*: Oliver Goldsmith, 'The Deserted Village', 21. 2: 'Even his failings leaned to virtue's side'.

from Chapter XLVI

...Andy was once more in service in the Egan family; for the Squire, on finding him still more closely linked by his marriage with the desperate party whose influence over Andy was to be dreaded, took advantage of Andy's disgust against the woman who had entrapped him, and offered to take him off to London instead of enlisting; and as Andy believed he would be there sufficiently out of the way of the false Bridget, he came off at once to Dublin with Dick, who was the pioneer of the party to London.

Dick gave Andy the necessary directions for icing the champagne, which he set apart and pointed out most particularly to our hero, lest he should make a mistake and perchance ice the port instead.

After Edward and Dick had gone, Andy commenced operations according to orders. He brought a large tub up-stairs containing rough ice, which excited Andy's wonder, for he never had known till now that ice was preserved for and applied to such a use, for an ice-house did not happen to be attached to any establishment in which he had served.

'Well, this is the quarest thing I ever heerd of,' said Andy. 'Musha! What outlandish inventions the quolity has among them! They're not contint with wine, but they must have ice along with it – and in a tub, too! – just like pigs! – throth, it's a dirty thrick, I think. Well, here goes! said he; and Andy opened a bottle of champagne, and poured it into the tub with the ice. 'How it fizzes!' said Andy. 'Faix, it's almost as lively as the soda-wather that bothered me long ago. Well, I know more about things now; sure it's wondherful how a man improves with practice!' and another bottle of champagne was emptied into the tub as he spoke. Thus, with several other complacent comments upon his own proficiency, Andy poured half-a-dozen of champagne into the tub of ice, and remarked, when he had finished his work, that he thought it would be 'mighty cowld on their stomachs.'

*   *   *

from CHAPTER XLVII

Edward, on returning to his hotel, found Gusty there before him, in great delight at having seen a 'splendid' horse, as he said, which had been brought for Edward's inspection, he having written a note on his arrival in town to a dealer stating his want of a first-rate hunter.

'He's in the stable now,' said Gusty; 'for I desired the man to wait knowing you would be here soon.'

'I cannot see him now, Gusty,' said Edward: 'will you have the kindness to tell the groom I can look at the horse in his own stables when I wish to purchase?'

Gusty departed to do the message, somewhat in wonder, for Edward loved a fine horse. But the truth was, Edward's disposable money, which he had intended for the purchase of a hunter, had a serious inroad made upon it by the debts he had discharged for other men, and he was forced to forego the pleasure he had proposed to himself in the next hunting season; and he did not like to consume any one's time, or raise false expectations, by affecting to look at disposable property with the eye of a purchaser, when he knew it was beyond his reach; and the flimsy common-places of 'I'll think of it,' or 'If I don't see something better,' or any other of the twenty hackneyed excuses which idle people make, after consuming busy men's time, Edward held to be unworthy. He could ride a hack and deny himself hunting for a whole season, but he would not unnecessarily consume the useful time of any man for ten minutes.

This may be sneered at by the idle and thoughtless; nevertheless, it is a part of the minor morality which is ever present in the conduct of a true gentleman.

Edward had promised to join Dick's dinner-party on an *impromptu* invitation, and the clock striking the appointed hour warned Edward it was time to be off; so, jumping up on a jaunting car, he rattled off to Dick's lodgings, where a jolly party was assembled ripe for fun.

Amongst the guests was a rather remarkable man, a Colonel Crammer, who had seen a monstrous deal of service – one of Tom Durfy's friends whom he had asked leave to bring with him to dinner. Of course Dick's card and a note of invitation for the gallant colonel were immediately despatched; and he had but just arrived before Edward, who found a bustling sensation in the room as the colonel was presented to those already assembled, and Tom Durfy giving whispers, aside, to each person touching his friend; such as –'Very remarkable man' – 'Seen great service' – 'A little odd or so' – 'A fund of most extraordinary anecdote,' etc., etc.

Now this Colonel was no other than Tom Loftus, whose acquaintance Dick wished to make, and who had been invited to dinner after a preliminary visit; but Tom sent an excuse in his own name, and preferred being present under a fictitious one – this being one of the odd ways in which his humour broke out, desirous of giving people a 'touch of his quality' before they knew him. He was in the habit of assuming various characters; a Methodist missionary – the patentee of some unnheard-of invention – the director of some new joint-stock company – in short, anything which would give him an opportunity of telling tremendous bouncers was equally good for Tom. His reason for assuming a military guise on this occasion was to bother Moriarty, whom he knew he should meet, and held a special reason for tormenting; and he knew he could achieve this by throwing all the stories Moriarty was fond of telling about his own service into the shade by extravagant inventions of 'hair-breadth 'scapes' and feats by 'flood and field.' Indeed, the dinner would not be worth mentioning but for the extraordinary capers Tom cut on the occasion, and the unheard-of lies he squandered.

Dinner was announced by Andy, and with good appetite soup and fish were soon despatched; sherry followed as a matter of necessity. The second course appeared, and was not long under discussion, when Dick called for the 'champagne.'

Andy began to drag the tub towards the table, and Dick, impatient of delay, again called 'champagne.'

'I'm bringin' it to you, sir,' said Andy, tugging at the tub.

'Hand it round the table,' said Dick.

Andy tried to lift the tub, 'to hand it round the table;' but, finding he could not manage it, he whispered to Dick, 'I can't get it up, sir.'

Dick fancying Andy meant he had got a flask not in a sufficient state of effervescence to expel its own cork, whispered in return, 'Draw it, then.'

'I was dhrawin' it to you, sir, when you stopped me.'

'Well, make haste with it,' said Dick.

'Mister Dawson, I'll trouble you for a small slice of the turkey,' said the colonel.

'With pleasure, colonel; but first do me the honour to take champagne. Andy – champagne!'

'Here it is, sir!' said Andy, who had drawn the tub close to Dick's chair.

'Where's the wine, sir?' said Dick, looking first at the tub and then at Andy.

'There, sir,' said Andy, pointing down to the ice. 'I put the wine into it, as you told me.'

Dick looked again at the tub, and said, 'There is not a single bottle there – what do you mean, you stupid rascal?'

'To be sure, there's no bottle there, sir. The bottles is all on the sideboard, but every dhrop o' the wine is in the ice, as you towld me, sir; if you put your hand down into it, you'll feel it, sir.'

The conversation between master and man, growing louder as it proceeded, attracted the attention of the whole company, and those near the head of the table became acquainted as soon as Dick with the mistake Andy had made, and could not resist laughter; and as the cause of their merriment was told from man to man, and passed round the board, a roar of laughter uprose, not a little increased by Dick's look of vexation, which at length was forced to yield to the infectious merriment around him, and he laughed with the rest, and making a joke of the disappointment, which is the very best way of passing one off, he said that he had the honour of originating at his table a magnificent scale of hospitality; for, though he had heard of company being entertained with a whole hogshead of claret, he was not aware of champagne being ever served in a tub before. The company were too determined to be merry to have their pleasantry put out of tune by so trifling a mishap, and it was generally voted that the joke was worth twice as much as the wine. Nevertheless, Dick could not help casting a reproachful look now and then at Andy, who had to run the gauntlet of many a joke cut at his expense, while he waited upon the wags at dinner, and caught a lowly muttered anathema whenever he passed near Dick's chair. In short, master and man were both glad when the cloth was drawn, and the party could be left to themselves.

From *Songs and Ballads*

(1858)

Rory O'More; Or, Good Omens

Young Rory O'More courted Kathleen Bawn,
He was bold as a hawk, – she as soft as the dawn;
He wished in his heart pretty Kathleen to please,
And he thought the best way to do *that* was to *teaze*.
'Now, Rory, be aisy,' sweet Kathleen would cry,
(Reproof on her lip, but a smile in her eye,)
'With your tricks I don't know, in troth, what I'm about,
Faith you've teazed till I've put on my cloak inside out.'
'Oh! jewel,' says Rory, 'that same is the way

You've thrated my heart for this many a day;
And 'tis plaz'd that I am, and why not to be sure?
For 'tis all for good luck,' says bold Rory O'More.

'Indeed, then,' says Kathleen, 'don't think of the like,
For I half gave a promise to *soothering* Mike,
The ground that I walk on he loves, I'll be bound,'
'Faith,' says Rory, 'I'd rather love *you* than the ground.'
'Now Rory, I'll cry if you don't let me go;
Sure I dhrame ev'ry night that I'm hating you so!'
'Oh,' says Rory, 'that same I'm delighted to hear,
For *dhrames* always go by *conthrairies*, my dear;
Oh! jewel, keep dhraming that same till you die,
And bright morning will give dirty night the black lie!
And 'tis plazed that I am, and why not to be sure?
Since 'tis all for good luck,' says bold Rory O'More.

'Arrah, Kathleen, my darlint, you've teazed me enough,
Sure I've thrash'd for your sake Dinny Grimes and Jim Duff;
And I've made myself, drinking your health, quite *a baste*,
So I think, after that, I may *talk to the priest*.'[1]
Then Rory, the rogue, stole his arm round her neck,
So soft and so white, without freckle or speck,
And he look'd in her eyes that were beaming with light,
And he kiss'd her sweet lips; – don't you think he was right?
'Now Rory, leave off, sir; you'll hug me no more,
That's eight times to-day you have kissed me before.'
'Then here goes another,' says he, 'to make sure,
For there's luck in odd numbers,' says Rory O'More.

St. Kevin: A Legend of Glendalough

At Glendalough lived a young saint,
    In odor of sanctity dwelling,
An old-fashion'd odor, which now
    We seldom or never are smelling;
A book or a hook were to him
    The utmost extent of his wishes;
Now, a snatch at the 'lives of the saints;'

---

1 Paddy's mode of asking a girl to name the day. [*Lover's note*]

Then, a catch at the lives of the fishes.

There was a young woman one day,
   Stravagin[1] along by the lake, sir;
She looked hard at St. Kevin, they say,
   But St. Kevin no notice did take, sir.
When she found looking hard wouldn't do,
   She look'd soft – in the old sheep's eye fashion;
But, with all her sheep's eyes, she could not
   In St. Kevin see signs of soft passion.

'You're a great hand at fishing,' says Kate;
   ''Tis yourself that knows how, faith, to hook them;
But, when you have caught them, *agra*,
   Don't you want a young woman to cook them?'
Says the saint, 'I am *'sayrious inclined*,'
   I intend taking orders for life, dear.'
'Only marry,' says Kate, 'and you'll find
   You'll get orders enough from your wife, dear.'

'You shall never be flesh of my flesh,'
   Says the saint, with an anchorite groan, sir;
'I see that myself,' answer'd Kate,
   'I can only be "bone of your bone," sir.
And even your bones are so scarce,'
   Said Miss Kate, at her answers so glib, sir;
'That I think you would not be the worse
   Of a little additional rib, sir.'

The saint in a rage, seized the lass,
   He gave her one twirl round his head, sir,
And, before Doctor Arnott's invention,[2]
   Flung her on a watery bed, sir.
Oh! – cruel St. Kevin! – for shame!
   When a lady her heart came to barter,
You should not have been Knight of the Bath
   But have bowed to the order of Garter.

---

1 *stravaging*: 'sauntering'. [*Lover's note*]
2 *Doctor Arnott's invention*: Dr Neil Arnott (1788–1874) invented a chair-bed for preventing
sea-sickness.

JOHN BANIM (1798–1842)

B orn in Kilkenny, the second son of a small farmer and shopkeeper, he attended Kilkenny College before receiving training as an artist at the Academy of the Royal Dublin Society. After two years, he returned to his home town, taught drawing, and fell in love with one of his pupils. Her father removed the girl from Kilkenny; soon after she died. Banim, heartbroken, returned to Dublin and embarked on a literary career. His long mythological poem, *The Celt's Paradise* (1821) received considerable acclaim. It was followed by a number of plays, one of which, *Damon and Pythias*, was a literary success: it was produced in 1821 at Covent Garden. With his older brother Michael he turned to fiction. Under the pseudonyms of Abel and Barnes O'Hara they collaborated on the 24 volumes of the *Tales by the O'Hara Family*. The first chapter of *The Nowlans* was based on an account of Michael's travels through the Slieve Bloom mountains. It relates the conclusion of the novel, which details the struggles of its main protagonist, John Nowlan, with his religious vows.

From *The Nowlans*

(1826)

Volume One
Chapter 1
From Mr. Abel O'Hara to Mr. Barnes O'Hara.

MY DEAR BARNES,

While following, in furtherance of our Boyne Water, the steps of the immortal Sarsfield[1] during his route to *Lacken na Choppel*,[2] some circumstances distinct from the business of my pilgrimage came under my notice, which I have since put together in the manuscript herewith sent as my humble contribution to our second series of Tales. But, before it encounters your severe eye, please to make yourself acquainted with the manner in which the facts happened to be conveyed to me.

Upon the first evening of my peregrinations among the Llieuve Illeum hills,[3] I directed my steps, guided by a little peasant boy, to the house of a small farmer, where, I had been told, rest, refreshment, and

1 *the immortal Sarsfield*: Patrick Sarsfield, 1st Earl of Lucan (c. 1655–93), Jacobite commander, raided the Williamite artillery at Ballyneety, Co. Limerick in August 1690; he attempted to defend Limerick against the forces of Ginkel in 1691, before agreeing to the latter's terms in October of that year.
2 Leacán na gCappall: 'The Hillside of the Horses'; cf the anglicised 'Lacken-na-chapel' (p. 386).
3. *Llieuve Illeum hills*: Slieve Bloom mountains.

a bed for the night, would readily be afforded to me; as to an inn, or common public house, no such thing should be calculated upon at the place and time that were to end my daily wanderings among the crowd of black mountains I had the courage to explore. In some few instances, indeed, a 'sod' of turf, standing upright in the thatch of a cabin, was interpreted by my bare-legged guide to denote (and he spat out to clear his passage in case I was generous enough to take his hint) 'that a bottle wid something inside iv id was behint the noggin on the dhresser' – the turf being figuratively meant 'as a token among the hill boys to larn 'em where to find a good dhrop that 'ud warm the sowl in a body;' but these mysterious places of refreshment had altogether such a chilly, wretched appearance, as the mountain dew to be obtained within them, taken ever so liberally, could, I concluded, scarcely dispel.

About half-past six, in August, after walking many miles along the steep side of a barren ridge, we came in sight of the dwelling of Mr. Daniel Nowlan. My guide, pointing it out to me, said with evident satisfaction, that he could now return home; and when I paid a shining half-crown into his little horny hand, the urchin, after many acknowledgments and many prayers for my happy extrication from the bleak mazes around Keeper-hill, bounded off like a deer, rejoicing in the probability of being yet able to gain his 'mammy's cabin dour,' before the shades of night should heighten the real perils of his path, and the supernatural influence of the scenery by which it was on every side overhung.

I then descended the hill, at the bottom of which the farmer's house was situated. It seemed a comfortable dwelling: its back turned to the hill; its face into a yard planted in front with fir, elm, and ash, amongst which the ornamental berries of the mountain ash also occasionally peeped out. I found 'the woman of the house' seated in the middle of the kitchen floor, employed in spinning worsted. Her salutation at my entrance was mute and, I then thought, very cold for an Irish farmer's wife. I enquired for Mr. Nowlan: coolly enough still, she informed me he was not at home. I said, I had been recommended to him as an intelligent person who would direct me on my way: she enquired by whom; I named my passing friend of the morning, but she did not know him. I then asked if she could procure me a guide to some place where I might sleep for the night: – this was impossible; all her men were in the meadow at some distance; and, besides, it would be too far to travel at such an hour, in such a country; and I was welcome to whatever accommodation her house at present afforded.

While she spoke, I could not help thinking that her hospitality was rather unwillingly granted; but she had scarcely finished, when a stifled groan sounded from an inner room, and the old woman started up with such woebegone energy of manner, and with such a deep cloud of sorrow on her brow, as quickly informed me that some all-engrossing misfortune was at her heart, and had abstracted her feelings from the ordinary show of attention and kindness to a stranger. In another second she entered the inner apartment, taking no further notice of me, and I was left alone in the kitchen.

The groan I had heard was succeeded by others, all announcing the struggles of a man in bodily agony. I listened to them for some time. The door through which the old woman had disappeared soon re-opened, and I was approached by a young girl, whose eyes were red with weeping, and whose soft voice, as she spoke to me, was low and quivering. She bade me welcome, however, with a faint smile, invited me to sit, and regretted that, on 'account of there being sickness and sorrow in the house,' my stay might not be as pleasant as all in the house would wish to make it. Not venturing to enquire into the privacy of her grief, I apologized, in my turn, for the inconvenience my visit might occasion, by my ignorance of the extent of the journey I had undertaken, which left me, on this evening, only half-way on my road, when I thought to have been at the end of it; and I hinted, that if a guide could be obtained, I was most anxious to relieve the embarrassment which, under the circumstances, my presence must naturally cause.

Calmly, and, without polish, politely, the young girl gave me to understand, that any little trouble I might occasion was too much a matter of course to be thought of; that her father and mother, and not only they, but the poor people of the meanest cabin in the glen, regarded it as one of the duties of their situation to bid every stranger welcome; that every stranger had a right to walk into every house in her country, and ask his night's rest and refreshment; and again, she could only regret that my comforts might not, at present, be such as it was her father's and mother's wish to afford. I know not how it was, Barnes, but I felt the mild unaffected manners of this young woman inspire me with a respect and esteem that brilliant affectation, or the show of ostentatious politeness, would, perhaps, have failed to excite. I felt, too, that she was sincere; that I was indeed welcome; that I was at home; that, notwithstanding the family affliction, any further apology would be ungracious, and any further offer to seek another roof, something like an offence: in a word, I sat down, as I had been invited to do; and in two minutes conversed with Peggy Nowlan like an old friend.

The door of the sick chamber again opened, and Mrs. Nowlan re-appeared, somewhat more composed than when she had left me, and, apparently, more awake to the duties of hospitality. 'He's quieter now, ma graw baun,'[1] she said to Peggy, 'an' maybe there is God's mercy for us yet.' Peggy's eyes streamed afresh, and we were all silent. But the old woman soon asked me if I would take any thing before my meal was ready: when I mentioned a draught of milk, she quickly present-ed it; and she and her daughter then went about their household occupations, assisted by a serving-wench, as intently as if I had not been present.

A sister of Peggy shortly after made her appearance; younger, but not quite so pretty as my first acquaintance; dressed with somewhat more care and style, however: for instance, she had a frill about her neck, whereas Peggy had only a plain silk handkerchief folded mod-estly across her bosom; and she wore white stockings too, while Peggy's whiter ankles glanced above the substantial shoes that served her for tramping to milk the cows every evening. Both young women showed nearly the same quiet and mild propriety of manner and speech, that pleased, and, indeed, surprised me; yet Peggy was still my favourite. I saw her moving about the kitchen with a light though active step, which, as she approached the chamber of the invalid, ever grew lighter. Among other things, I saw her put down a small kettle-full of potatoes; and when they were boiled, she spread a clean cloth on a clean white table, and, along with the staple Irish food, cold meat, milk, eggs, and butter, were offered for my repast. By this time the mother had again visited the sick person in the inner room; and now, out of a recollected sense of consideration to me, as I thought, the door remained open, so that the old woman might at once seem in some degree present during my meal, and sit on the sufferer's bed, holding his hand, and whispering comfort. I caught a glimpse of the hand she held, and it appeared that of a young man wasted with suf-fering; but it was also fairer and more delicate than the hand of a young person engaged in even occasional bodily exertion could be; and how any other description of person happened to claim the domestic solicitude of this humble family surprised me. I not only asked no questions, however, but, after my first involuntary glance, when Peggy's eye, full of tears, met mine, I forbore further scrutiny.

---

1 *ma graw baun*: 'my white or fair darling'. [*Banim's note.*]

The young girl sat down with me, and pressed me to eat; but I saw the struggle between politeness to her guest, and her watchful glances towards the sick bed. I could only taste the food, and Peggy understood me. The mother came out to the table, leaving her younger daughter in the inner chamber, and I tried to speak a few words of comfort to both: they heard me with little appearance of lively hope, and still avoided any direct allusions to their misfortune; yet I perceived they were thankful for the kindness of my manner.

My repast was over, my table cleared, and again I was alone with Peggy. She now employed herself in making whey, and in preparing supper for the workmen who were expected from the fields. I followed her with a pleased eye, and saw that, so far as her domestic griefs permitted, she was not free from that little vanity which, when not too far insisted upon, in the fair sex, is not only excusable, but I think graceful. She sent me back, now and then, a smile, sobered by sadness, and that never could have been unregulated by modesty; and I certainly felt towards her all the kindliness that virtue and discretion, not without a considerable share of beauty, are apt to engender in the breast of a poor fellow, not yet wholly deserted (notwithstanding the green glasses) by the warmth of youth; and this, I can assure you, Barnes, – this can be felt apart from any selfish association of ideas. Occasionally she sat down with me, and I found her conversation as engaging as that of many young females I have met: it had not, indeed, the graces of the boarding-school: nor its emptiness and affectation either.

Towards the dusk of the evening, the old man of the house came home; and, after a visit to the sick chamber, he seemed rejoiced to find a stranger under his roof. He talked to me of O'Connell, and of the wars to be expected in Ireland in the year 25, 'according to the prophecy.'[1] I regarded him as a man of great simplicity of heart and manner, and of good natural strong sense, but with his ideas bounded by the Slieve-Bloom mountains. And I was not a little surprised to find, from his discourse, that the local particulars of the expected struggle in 1825, which I thought had applied exclusively to my part of the country, were claimed with equal precision for certain spots among these isolated hills: – for instance, that the boy with the two thumbs, who, I had heard it confidently stated, lived at Knock-Killen-

---

1 *according to the prophecy*: Pastorini (Charles Walmesley) (1722–97) predicted, on the basis of the Book of Revelation, that the plague of Protestantism would last 300 years. Popular Catholic Irish opinion forcast that 1825 was to be the year of the total annihilation of the Protestant churches.

all, near Inismore, and who was to hold the horses of the Duke of York and four of his generals, during the battle, also lived somewhere in the vicinity of Keeper Mountain.

In discussing these momentous affairs, I perceived that while he gave a half-credit to the truth of 'the prophecy,' the old man hoped from the bottom of his heart it might never come to pass: for himself, he said, he only wanted 'rest an' pace from his neighbours, far and near, in the Black North, and in England itself; and even if the Duke of York did come over to Ireland, head all the Orangemen, and un-head all the poor Catholics,[1] he laid such misfortunes as a judgment from God upon the latter, on account of the doings of some of them, lately, in his country, and the next to it again – doings which could not but be punished here or hereafter. I observed that he talked garru-lously; and Peggy told me in a whisper, while her eyes rested watch-fully upon his, that the poor man was glad to have a stranger to speak to, as a kind of charm against grief; for, when not so engaged, his old spirit failed and flagged, thinking of his heavy trials.

While she was yet whispering me, in a very confidential manner, a young and handsome man stept to the threshold of the kitchen door, but started ere he entered among us, and, glancing from Peggy to me, seemed surprised, at least, if not offended; while she, endeavouring to assume an easy smile of best welcome, blushed in spite of herself, and sat upright and demurely in her chair.

'Won't you come in and discourse the strange gentleman has just walked this way through the hills, Davy,' Peggy then said, addressing the young man, whose brow speedily cleared up, as he no longer hesitated to join us; and after he had greeted the man of the house, and bowed, not very clumsily, at me, I caught, with the tail of my eye, certain mute communings between him and Peggy, that explained, I thought, why he should have wondered to see us whispering cheek by jowl together.

'And how is poor father John, this evening?' enquired the new-comer, after all this was over; but he had scarce pronounced the words, in a very low tone, when old Mr. Nowlan shifted himself on his seat, and, still with a sly glance, I saw Peggy raise her finger to her lip, and look and nod towards me.

Now the workmen came in from the fields, and the scene changed into one of general bustle. About twenty of them sat round a large

---

1 *the Duke of York ... unhead all the poor Catholics*: Frederick Augustus, Duke of York & Albany (1763–1827) joined the Orange Order in 1813, and became its Grand Master of Great Britain in February 1821. At the time he was heir to the throne.

table, half covered with a heap of smoking potatoes, flanked by ample noggins of milk; and it was surprising to witness the dispatch with which they demolished a pile that might serve three city families, even Irish ones, for a week. Their silence too, considering the spirits in which Irish peasants ever sit down to the humblest meal, was nearly as remarkable as their industry; if, indeed, I did not recollect that 'sickness and sorrow were in the house,' and that their nearness to the sick chamber evidently curbed their usual chat and glee.

Only a few words spoken by them, almost in a whisper, reached me; and even these, although in allusion to some person whose vagaries diverted the men, were gravely uttered. Some of them wondered what could have come over 'rakin' Peery Conolly,' and why he did not accompany them home to supper; for, big an *omadhaun* as he was, all his life long, not to talk of his behaviour in a field, at a day's work, 'no one 'ud wish him in bed with an empty belly.' At this, Peggy, in evident interest, commenced enquiries about the individual in question; but the men answered that, barring he got into the sulks, for the last 'hoising' and flogging they gave him, in regard of his 'slobbering' work, the day long, and his fits and starts that would let nobody else work clean, – (and it was not a likely thing that Peery Conolly would be the man to sulk at such a turn, either,) – why, barring this, or that he staid in a corner of the field to dance 'cover-the-buckle' for his own private amusement, or had gone after Cauth Flannigan, that was gone after the cows, or something or other of the kind, any how, – barring all those casualties, no one could conjecture why he was not then eating his good supper.

But, while they spoke, a young peasant, rather low in stature, clumsily made about the body, light in the limbs, and his clothes hanging off and on, in folds and shreds, came towards the open door of the kitchen, at a hop-step-and-jump, and, holding his head down, as he flourished a short stick round it, there continued a few seconds shuffling his feet, in a cautious modification of the step most esteemed as an accompaniment to the 'jig polthoge:' – and, from the smiles, nods, and whispers of the workmen, I could not doubt that I beheld the eccentric person of whom they were speaking. As, in some admiration, I watched his movements, Peery Conolly suddenly raised his head, fixed his eyes on mine, started back into an attitude, gave his stick another flourish, and then darted on me with an appearance of hostile intent that made me rise from my seat; but a whisper from Peggy – 'Don't mind him, Sir – 'tis only the poor boy's humour – he's as harmless as the infant,' – reassured me; and, as she spoke, Peery

changed his symptoms of headlong attack into a caper round me and
the chair by which I stood, still flourishing his cudgel, as in a very low
and cautious key he sung,

> My name it is Conolly the rake,
> > I don't care a sthraw for any man;
> I dhrinks good whishkey an' ale,
> > An' I'd bate out the brains iv a Connought-man –
> > > > Whew!

'Be asy, there, wid your behaviour, Peery,' said one of the men; and
instantly he fixed his eyes on the speaker, as he had done on me, and
darted towards him with the same death-promising but harmless
motions of his shillelagh.

'Quiet, Peery, quiet,' said Peggy, 'and remember who's in the next
room.'

'Oh, yeah, yes, Miss Peggy, a cuishla; yis, yis; we'd mind id whin
you spake the word, if we never minded id afore.' Tho' it was evident, indeed, that nothing but a recollection of his proximity to the
sick chamber had previously subdued his capers and his song into the
caution I have mentioned; 'and,' Peery continued – 'sure it's the
dance – the dance, a-vourneen, that puts it into our head, at-all-at-
all;' – and, so saying, he jumped towards the supper-table, deposited
himself on a form between two men who had been sitting closely
together, chucked his stick under his left arm, and jirking his head
from side to side, and tapping the floor with his feet, commenced a
serious attack on the diminished pile of potatoes and noggins of
skimmed-milk.

'And where did the dance send you, of late, Peery?' inquired one
of his neighbours, winking around; as, his head and feet still in
motion, he ravenously persevered in his meal.

'Up the hills, an' over the hills, an' down the hills,' replied Peery,
'widout the moon, and wid the moon; an' to Limerick's oun town,
the last fair mornin', an' home to the Foil Dhuiv,[1] afore the next
mornin', where there wasn't as much starlight as 'ud make me know
one foot from anodher, while I done the step. *You* know the Foil-
Dhuiv, Miss Peggy-baun?'

I was surprised to see the young woman smile and turn pale at this
random question, while she remained perfectly silent.

---

1 *Foil Dhuiv*: Black-valley. [*Banim's note.*]

'An' Father John knows it, too,' Peery continued: 'how is id wid him, this evenin'?'

'Hould your whisht, you scatther-brain o' the divil,' said Mrs. Nowlan.

'Yis, Peery, do,' pursued a workman, 'an' jist tell us who put the dance on you first?'

'Who bud the saint that had id on himself? him, an' th' auld rip iv an aunt I have – who else put id on me?'

'An' for what, or for why, Peery?'

'For what, or for why? To keep me from the work, to be sure, an' sometimes from the mass idself, an' to send me here an' there, over-an hether, an' to make me love an' like the dhrop o' liquor, an' to make a May-boy o' me, an' a rakin' fellow, – a tatther'n, tear'n fellow – hurroo! –

> My name it is Conolly the rake,
>   I don't care a sthraw for any man;
> I dhrinks good whishkey an' ale,
>   An' I'd bate out the brains iv a Connought-man –

And up he bounced and jumped off through the kitchen-door, flourishing his stick, as usual.

When he had disappeared, I gathered from Peggy's answers to my questions, that some youthful troubles, aided by a 'draught,' received at the hands of an old female relative, who meant it should serve him, had turned Peery's brain, and produced, occasionally, the singular conduct I had just witnessed; that his misfortunes alone made him an object of interest to the family, though he scarce ever did any work otherwise to claim their assistance; but that a great service, of a peculiar kind, (and here the young girl sighed deeply, as she glanced at the door of the inner room) which he had lately rendered to them all, gave poor Peery a right, for life, to their kindness and protection. She added, that when he was once brought to a country physician, for an opinion on his case, the sage practitioner declared him to be afflicted with St. Vitus's dance; that Peery, getting this notion very vaguely into his head, never since gave it up, but was anxious to attribute to 'the dance,' as he called it, all his vagaries, all his inability or disinclination to work, and all his visits to the ale-house; – while some thought that his real fits of aberration were not so frequent as he wished to have inferred; that there was, occasionally, as much cunning as folly in his extravagance; that, if he liked, he might now and then work, and be as wise a man as his neighbours; that, more than once, he had been known to possess the power of showing an extraordinary change of character; and, indeed, Peggy herself had witnessed, on a late occasion, just such a change.

The workmen now rose from their table, knelt down, one by one, to their prayers, and quietly retired to the out-house appointed for their repose. Soon after, Peggy's handsome male visitor bade us good night; Peggy seeing him to the door, and, indeed, a few steps beyond it, where there was only an instant's pause, yet one long enough for any little civility the fair reader may please to imagine; when she returned, looking as simple as an infant, her father shook me by the hand, and went to seek his bed, praying his good God, that, after all, there might be no truth in the prophecy; and then the younger girl joined Peggy and me, from the invalid's chamber, to arrange about my disposition for the night.

After a few words of consultation, they informed me that, although there was a spare bed in the sick-room, they could not think of putting me to sleep there, as, besides the inconvenience I should find from the presence of the 'sick gentleman' – (this phrase struck me as singular) – they would have to pass in and out, during the night; but they hoped still to make me comfortable; and the two girls forthwith proceeded to make up a couch for me on the huge kitchen table: where, when they for a time retired to allow me to avail myself of it, I found a good feather-bed, clean white sheets, a patch-work quilt, and, as they had promised, every thing indeed comfortable.

As soon as I had been afforded time enough to fall asleep, they returned, accompanied by their mother, and stealthily sat down by the kitchen fire. Although I could not close my eyes, I thought it most delicate to permit them to think I was sunk in repose; and taking this fact for granted, the good woman and her daughters, – one or other of them occasionally stealing into the inner room, – conversed in earnest whispers for some time. Their whole theme related to the illness and probable fate of the young man, about whom all were so deeply interested; and, without my feeling any satisfaction at being thus an involuntary listener, some allusions to his past life also escaped them, that, joined with the previous mystery under which their sorrow seemed to have been indulged, much interested me. My interest was not diminished, when I became aware that he was indeed (as from some former inquiries I had suspected) a clergyman, and the only son and brother of the family; that he had been once their hope and pride; afterwards their shame and affliction; once good and innocent; afterwards, through scenes of retributive misery and trial, a misguided sinner; and now, in complicated suffering, bodily and mental, in humiliation and penitence, their only hope, once again.

All I heard did not serve to give me, however, any thing like a clear notion of the real history of the young clergyman; and the mother and her second daughter retired, about midnight, to repose, leaving my feelings, I will not say merely my curiosity, in a more anxious state than they were before I lay down. Owing to this rather excited mood, as well, perhaps, as to the novelty of my situation, I still lay awake, while Peggy, all along my favourite, remained up to tend the couch of her sick brother. When, afterwards, I fell into a light slumber, I could, during its breaks, see her moving noiselessly about, in the dying glimmer of the turf-blaze, stealing, on tip-toe, into the sick chamber, or warming a draught for the sufferer's parched lips; or, at times, sitting upon a low stool, before the embers, her elbow on her raised knee, and her cheek rested on her hand, as she gazed at the flickering fire, and sighed profoundly. Ay, woman, thought I, from the highest to the lowest rank, you are, to man, the 'ministering angel,' indeed; his consoler in misery, the soother of his sick pillow; and, without you, joy were indeed joyless, and misfortune not to he borne. All very trite and common-place sentiment, you will say, Barnes, as I lay on my kitchen table, between my nice white sheets, and pretty Peggy Nowlan so near to me, in the dead of the night; but I couldn't help it: and no other sentiments prevailed. As the morning peeped into the windows of my rather unusual bed-chamber, Peggy was still upon her watch: I gave signs of preparations to rise; she withdrew in silence; I dressed myself; she returned, and her mild 'good morrow' sounded on my ear. As I braced on my back the Bramah portfolio you were good enough to send me from London, she hoped I did not intend to go away without my breakfast; when I expressed my intention of starting immediately, she went, with a face of concern, to communicate my purpose to her father; and the old man quickly returned by her side, to join his hospitable requests to those of his daughter. But neither could prevail; and then he shook my hand, and wished me safe and happy to my journey's end; and I, too, took Peggy's little hand in mine, and after a few words, expressive, I believe, of my esteem and respect for her conduct, manners, and person, set out, with something like a way-

ward and smothered sigh, accompanied by a man to direct me 'a bit'
on my mountain path.

But fortune willed that Peggy and I should not so soon part. Ere,
with my guide, I had mastered the top of the first steep and weary
ascent on our road, black clouds gathered over our heads, lightning
quivered, thunder crashed and bellowed above and around us, and a
torrent of rain rushed down, that, in a trice, drenched us to the skin.
To proceed four or five miles further during such a storm, or, even
supposing it should pass off, in such a trim, was a madness against
which my guide warmly remonstrated, and to which I had almost
equal objection; so, at his instance, we once more turned our faces
to Mr. Nowlan's house, and, the road being now a steep descent, and
therefore most favourable to our speed, retraced our steps in a good
race.

All the family stood at the threshold to receive me; exclamations
of condolence came from every tongue; and, almost by main force,
the old woman, her daughters, and the robust maid-servant, forced
me off to a bedchamber, where I was commanded to doff every tack
upon me, and cover myself up in a neat little bed, until every tack
should be well dried. In vain I remonstrated: Mrs. Nowlan and her
handmaid whisked off my coat and vest, even while I spoke; the latter, squatting herself on her haunches, then attacked my shoes and
stockings; Peggy appropriated my cravat; and I began to entertain
some real alarm as to the eventual result of their proceedings, when
away they went in a body, each laden with a spoil, and all renewing
their commands that I should instantly peel off my Russia-ducks and
my inner garment, drop them at the bedside, and then retiring
between the sheets, call out to have them removed.

I did even as I was bid; and when properly disposed to give the
appointed signal, Cauth Flannigan, the maid of all-work, speedily
attended to it, re-entering with something on her arm, from which
her eye occasionally wandered to my half-seen face, in a struggle, as
I thought, and I believe I was not wrong in my reading, between
most provoking merriment, and a decent composure of countenance; The misthess sent this shirt, Sir – only it isn't a shirt, entirely, bud one belongin' to the misthess, becase it's the washin week,
an' the sickness in the place, an' all, an' the misthess couldn't make
off a betther at a pinch' – and, laying it on the edge of the bed,
Cauth strove to hide her giggle and her blushes by stooping to take
up the last of my drenched garments. When she had again retired
with them, I examined the nicely-folded article she had left with me,

and, truly, it was *not* 'a shirt entirely' – but what shall I call it, Barnes? – a female shirt, haply; the personal property, as Cauth would have it, of Mrs. Nowlan; yet, from the earnestness with which that zealous Abigail strove to impress the fact upon me, as also from the hasty erasure of an initial, near its upper edge, I had my own doubts, while I put it on, concerning the identity of its owner.

And so, while the storm vented its fury among the black hills, thus I lay, safe and comfortable, in (I am sure it was, from the visions of bonnets, &c. I caught at every side) the sleeping chamber of the young ladies of the mansion. In a short time Peggy returned with my breakfast; three eggs, just laid, home-made bread, sweet butter, tea not to be much faulted, and cream, such as you have never seen since you went to live in Gray's Inn, 'any how;' the sugar was my only dread, for it looked as brown as gingerbread, and as coarse as a handful of pebbles. But Peggy's smile, when she put down my provisions, was sweeter than any sugar; and as soon as she a second time disappeared, I can assure you I managed to make a good breakfast.

My clothes were restored, as dry as chips; my Bramah was again buckled across my shoulders, and again I put on a resolute face of departure; but the storm was more resolute than I: the sky frowned back my challenge; the old man and woman and his daughters told me that, although the thunder might soon cease, there would not be a dry half-hour that day among the mountains; and, in fact, I remained where I was; not really regretting, perhaps, though I persuaded myself I did, the stern necessity that interposed to prevent a manful and conscientious fulfilment of my duties.

I sat down at the kitchen hearth with the young women, and, while they employed their needles, we conversed freely together. I have before given you to understand that they were neither uninformed nor unintelligent; and now I got new proofs of the fact. Both had been pupils at the convent of Thurles; but, perhaps, the younger, Anty, from having remained there longer than her sister, and returned home later, had acquired, or retained more of the ideas and accomplishments usually taught in an Irish nunnery; or, perhaps, Peggy, after coming back to the duties of her life and situation, and continuing for six or seven years chiefly occupied by them, had forgotten part of her former proficiency in books and graces. Good sense and useful information they possessed in common; I should not, indeed, insist that their tastes were equally cultivated: they knew little of poetry; less of plays; they had never been but once to see a play; then it was their fate to see Othello performed in a village barn; and the hearty indignation they jointly expressed, as we talked the matter over, towards the *man* who acted Iago, (not towards the character, merely,) gave me a lively, and almost envious idea of the incipiency of their theatrical criticism, and the simplicity and goodness of their hearts.

I described good acting, and a great theatre to them, and they listened with evident interest. I hinted at novels; they knew nothing of that branch of literature; and, indeed, the vehement manner of their disavowal rather caused me (for certain reasons) to draw in my horns, and pass to another topic. Moore's songs they could play, if they had an instrument; and Peggy knew most of the figures of country dances, and Anty whispered something about quadrilles. I opened my Bramah, and showed them some bad sketches of fine scenery; they were loud in their applause; I read some other sketches from my note book, and they thought me *'l'huitième merveille du monde:'* and, to crown all, I pulled out a *New Monthly*, before we finished our sitting; as we were about to part, for some time, handed it to them to peruse; and after dinner, when we again put our heads together, the young women expressed, and, I am sure, really felt much thanks for my trifling attentions.

Meantime they had been in and out of their brother's chamber, or alternately engaged in some household duty. I asked as seldom as possible how the brother went on; yet now they spoke of him to me with less restraint; called him by the appellation that before they would have dropt in my presence, namely, 'Father John;' and answered all my enquiries by an assurance that he was much better. In fact I saw that, merely by acting a kind, and, at the same time, a considerate part, I had induced the solitary young girls to think well of me; while my manifold accomplishments added (none of your horse-laughs, Barnes,) some interest and respect to their esteem.

However it happened, I was not this night 'laid out,' corpse-like, on the kitchen table; and when, next morning, I again began to gird myself for travel, Peggy and Anty heard their father, with evident pleasure, predict that, for many days the mist and rain which had succeeded to the storm, would not clear away. But why should I garrulously lengthen out this introduction to a true tale? Let me hasten to inform you that, after a week's residence in the house, the poor girls told me the story of their brother's misfortune, together with certain occurrences of Peggy's own life, that were involved in his; – that, after a visit from his bishop, the invalid grew so much better, as to allow of my appearance at his bed-side, for which his sisters had prepared and given him an anxiety; that I was then afforded an opportunity of studying his character, and, at last, of receiving from his own lips, explanations of his feelings and motives during his trials, which otherwise I could not have been able to supply; and, lastly, that out of the whole information thus collected, the following tale is compiled.

For the immediate conclusion of it, after the period of my first journey among the Slieve-bloom hills, I am indebted chiefly to you, Barnes, I thank you; for when you sent me over your commands to go back all the ways to Lacken-na-chapel, and assure myself of one certain point (and only one) upon which I had left you doubtful, it was but natural that I should pay a second visit to the kind and hospitable Nowlans; and again, it was but natural for me to enquire into what had happened during the nine months I had been away from them.

'A. O'H.'

Index of First Lines

General Index

Cork City Library
WITHDRAWN
FROM STOCK